COMMUNITY POLICING
CLASSICAL READINGS

WILLARD M. OLIVER
GLENVILLE STATE COLLEGE

Prentice Hall
Upper Saddle River, NJ 07458

Library of Congress Cataloging-in-Publication Data

Community policing : classical readings / [edited by] Willard M.
   Oliver.
       p.   cm.
    Includes bibliographical references.
    ISBN 0-13-080075-9 (pbk.)
       1. Community policing—United States.   I. Oliver, Willard M.
    HV7936.C83C664   2000
    363.2'3—dc21   99-26033
                                                                CIP

Senior acquisitions editor: *Kim Davies*
Production editor: *Gail Gavin*
Production liaison: *Barbara Marttine Cappuccio*
Director of manufacturing and production: *Bruce Johnson*
Managing editor: *Mary Carnis*
Manufacturing buyer: *Ed O'Dougherty*
Creative director: *Marianne Frasco*
Editorial assistant: *Brian Hyland*
Formatting/page make-up: *Clarinda Company*
Printer/Binders: *R.R. Donnelley & Sons*
Cover design: *Bruce Kenselaar*
Cover photo: *This was Virginia 1900–1927: As Shown by the Glass Negatives of
   J. Harry Shannon, The Rambler.* Reprinted with permission from
   Constance Pendleton Stuntz and Mayo S. Stuntz © 1998.

Editor's note: These readings have been reprinted in their original state,
   and many of the readings predominately use the masculine
   pronoun. We have not edited these readings in order to ensure
   consistency of style.

Printed in the United States of America

10 9 8 7 6 5 4 3 2 1

ISBN 0-13-080075-9

Prentice-Hall International (UK) Limited, *London*
Prentice-Hall of Australia Pty. Limited, *Sydney*
Prentice-Hall Canada Inc., *Toronto*
Prentice-Hall Hispanoamericana, S.A., *Mexico*
Prentice-Hall of India Private Limited, *New Delhi*
Prentice-Hall of Japan, Inc., *Tokyo*
Pearson Education Asia Pte. Ltd., *Singapore*
Editora Prentice-Hall do Brasil, Ltda., *Rio de Janeiro*

CONTENTS

FOREWORD

The 1980s, the era during which most of the readings in this volume were published, was an extraordinary period in American policing. Police entered the 1980s almost literally defeated. The 1960s riots highlighted their estranged relationship with the African-American community—police may not have caused the conditions that gave rise to riots, but they were the triggers that set them off. Also, during the 1960s, the Supreme Court moved to end torture as a means of conducting criminal investigations—a well-known practice, but one that police administrators either could not or would not cope with. Moreover, during the 1970s, research into the core competencies of American police, i.e., preventive patrol and rapid response to calls for service, failed to find them effective. And, finally, crime was inexorably rising. Nothing seemed to work. In retrospect, at the beginning of the 1980s, policing was an occupation in search of a strategy.

Police came out of the 1980s with a viable new strategy called community or problem-oriented policing. After decades of "law enforcement," police rediscovered "policing." Whatever resistance to change still remained, few police practitioners or academics doubted that policing had gone through a major paradigmatic shift during the 1980s. Community, or problem-oriented, policing integrated at least four strands of thought and experiences into a new police strategy that was internally coherent and externally viable and popular. First, policing came to understand the significance of team policing: it was not, as largely thought at the time, a tactic that could fit into the reform paradigm (1920s to 1960s). Instead, it was a competing strategy and, not surprisingly, during the 1970s, unsustainable in police organizations as then configured and administered. But, like community relations efforts, team policing gave many neighborhoods and police undeniable and powerful joint experiences. It is not surprising that some of our most capable police leaders—William Bratton (Boston and New York), Paul Evans (Boston), William Finney (St. Paul), Dennis Nowicki (Charlotte), Jerry Sanders

(San Diego), Norm Stamper (Seattle), and many others—cut their teeth on experiments in team policing and community relations. Among the lessons they learned and later applied were that policing in a democracy must ultimately be a partnership with citizens and other public and private sectors.

Second and third, two articles, both included in this volume, were published around the turn of the decade (1980) that framed then-current police practices and pointed to future directions of policing. Herman Goldstein's 1979 article, "Improving Policing: A Problem-Oriented Approach," laid the groundwork for the development of problem-solving as a mainstream police tactic. Moreover, the adoption of problem-solving as a major substantive thrust of the Police Executive Research Forum (PERF) by the late Gary Hayes and his successor Daryl Stephens, gave impetus and body to Goldstein's ideas and launched PERF into center stage as a leading police professional organization. The other article, published in 1982 by James Q. Wilson and this author, and known popularly as "Broken Windows," raised the issue of minor offenses and their link to fear of crime, serious crime, and urban decay. Although this article remains controversial, especially in light of New York City's 1990s crime decline, it nevertheless convinced policy makers and police that citizen concerns for problems ranging from graffiti to aggressive panhandling to street prostitution had to be taken seriously. They had to be taken seriously both to improve the quality of neighborhood life and to improve the quality of the relationship between citizens and police, especially in poor and minority communities.

Finally, foot patrol experiments in both Flint, Michigan, and Newark, New Jersey, demonstrated that police tactics that laid open citizens and police to each other, in addition to reducing fear of crime, substantially changed their attitudes towards each other. In each study, citizens came to appreciate police and police, citizens. And, this occurred despite race: many of the neighborhoods studied were comprised of African Americans and most of the officers were white.

Most of the readings that Professor Oliver has put together in this volume—more than half of them products of Harvard's Executive Session on Community Policing—are 1980s attempts to try to figure out where policing had been, where it was, why it remained that way, where it had to go, and what police leadership had to do if policing was to get where it was going. Those of us embroiled in the police business during the 1960s and 1970s, whether as practitioners, policy makers, or academics, remember that the period around the turn of the decade (1980) was a terribly confusing and disturbing time. Team policing seemed to have some benefit, but it just couldn't stick in departments. Foot patrol seemed to have an impact on fear, but certainly police had to do better than that. For a time, regarding criminal investigation, cases either appeared to solve themselves or be solved randomly.

Slowly, however, the new community paradigm emerged during the 1980s. There is neither the need nor space to describe it here—this is the purpose of collecting the readings. The Harvard Executive Sessions, consisting of police, scholars, policy makers, and political leaders, produced a series of "think pieces," most authored jointly by police and academics. Many of them are republished here. Clearly, many people who should have been at the Session "table" and also drafting papers were not. Not because they were not qualified, but simply because of lack of "seats." Researchers John Eck, Stephen Mastrofski, Lawrence Sherman, William Spelman, and Samuel Walker—whose works are included in this volume—come to mind. They, and others, would have contributed enormously to the process. Including them in this volume enriches our understandings of the intellectual and professional ferment of the decade. Numerous police leaders, policy makers, and politicians who properly should have been involved in the Session come to mind as well.

It is clear, however, that long before the concept of government "reinventing" itself became popular, American policing was reinventing itself. Arguably, in the process of doing so, it more than just "led the way" in the public sector; rather, policing pulled first municipal and later criminal justice agencies with it into new relationships with the community—responding to local priorities, decentralizing, forming partnerships, and solving problems. Many of the papers in this volume both "caught the winds" of change in policing and helped to define and communicate them.

GEORGE L. KELLING
Boston, Massachusetts

PREFACE

There can be little doubt that in the field of law enforcement, community policing has become a household name. Beginning in the early 1980s, in the wake of the police–community relations movement, team policing, and the Law Enforcement Assistance Administration (LEAA), community policing was seen as the new way of policing. In a sense, it developed out of these earlier movements and was the chance to truly professionalize and learn from past mistakes. Combined with the concepts of problem-oriented policing, community policing fast became the newest innovation to experience a grass-roots diffusion by the middle to late 1980s. Although the federal government provided a vast array of grant funds to assist these endeavors, it is clear that the movement truly was an innovation by progressive police chiefs, sheriffs, and academicians. By the 1990s, the movement had created a "bandwagon effect" and the majority of agencies throughout the United States were beginning to jump on. If they had not done so by 1994, with the passage of the crime bill (The Violent Crime Control and Law Enforcement Act of 1994), the federal government began to provide the incentive for agencies *to* jump on the wagon. And as we enter the twenty-first century, it is clear that community policing has become the practice of choice for the majority of agencies across the country, regardless of their reasons for making this move.

Academic literature on the subject of community policing has also seen a relatively parallel development. Most discussions revolving around how police police, or how they should police, centered on the police-community relations movement, team policing, and the LEAA during the 1970s and early 1980s. By the early 1980s, there was an extensive amount of thoughtful discussion that was largely prescriptive in nature. It would take the initiative of forward-thinking chiefs to begin implementing the concepts of community policing and problem-solving policing before any analysis could be conducted to determine the effectiveness of these new ideas. It was not until the late 1980s that much of the writing and research findings on community policing began to enter the academic setting. Since then the amount of published material on community policing has increased exponentially each year.

Although there has been an enormous amount written about community policing in the 1990s, which Lee P. Brown accurately predicted would be the "decade of community policing," most of the material that is emphasized comes not from the early period of the 1980s but from what has been written in the 1990s. Although two key seminal articles, "Broken Windows" (Wilson and Kelling 1982) and "Improving Policing" (Goldstein 1979), are almost always cited and reprinted, many of the earlier works are cited but see little in the way of reprinting. And although these two articles are crucial to understanding the origins of community policing and problem-oriented policing, there are a number of other articles that are critical to understanding the historical background and framework of the movement. This situation was the impetus for this collection of "classical" readings on community policing.

The articles in this collection were selected for a number of reasons. First and foremost, they were selected for the simple fact that they are "classical" readings in providing content on the early development of community policing. Second, they have been selected because of the fact that they are heavily cited in the academic literature and because several of them have seen numerous reprintings in other collections focusing on the topic of policing. And finally, a number of them come from the federal document collection on community policing, which had a significant impact on police chiefs and sheriffs in the 1980s who were actively moving their agencies toward community policing. In 1985, the program in Criminal Justice Policy and Management at the John F. Kennedy School of Government at Harvard University, through funding by the National Institute of Justice and private sources (such as the Charles Stewart Mott and Guggenheim Foundations), pooled thirty-one high-level practitioners and scholars together to discuss the status of policing in the United States. It was a chance to create a dialogue between practitioners and scholars, in which the practitioners, not the scholars, would have majority representation. They began meeting in 1985 and met periodically for several years, nearly ten times, for three-day meetings. The insights, discussion, and debates were then brought forward into a collection of articles published by the U.S. Department of Justice, National Institute of Justice, under the title *Perspectives on Policing.* This series made an important contribution to the community policing literature and, in a sense, set the stage for the increase in academic literature on the subject from not only those that participated in the sessions but also from a number of academics who have turned their time and research agenda toward community policing.

Once the collection was prepared and the articles were selected for this reader, it was apparent that it would be the first collection of articles that consisted entirely of reprinted articles on community policing. That was until Geoffrey P. Alpert and Alex Piquero published *Community Policing: Contemporary Readings* (Waveland Press 1998). Their collection consisted of a number of reprinted articles on community policing, mixed with some original articles, that presented a contemporary perspective on the subject. What was interesting was the fact that I had selected only one article they had: "Making Neighborhoods Safe" by James Q. Wilson and George L. Kelling. I therefore decided to drop that article from this collection and juxtapose my title to theirs: *Classical Readings*. Hence, I would like to acknowledge Geoffrey P. Alpert and Alex Piquero for that little assistance and for their publishing an excellent reader on community policing.

This collection is divided into six parts and consists of twenty-one articles on community policing. The first two articles present the origins of community policing: "Broken Windows: The Police and Neighborhood Safety" by James Q. Wilson and George L. Kelling and "Improving Policing: A Problem-Oriented Approach" by Herman Goldstein. These two articles are perhaps most deserving of the title "classical" and have contributed greatly to the community policing (and problem-oriented policing) movement. The second section details the philosophy of community policing, which is driven not by some form of management style or through the application of an "effective" program but by values that should be instilled throughout the police department to guide its every action. The third section looks at the "systemic approach" to policing, which I refer to in the textbook *Community-Oriented Policing: A Systemic Approach to Policing* (Prentice Hall 1998). The systemic approach is the realization that community policing is not an add-on program but rather a complete change in every facet of policing, which includes, rather than a specific program, a collection of various types of programs that must be adapted to the needs of the community. In continuing the concept of a systemic change, the fourth section describes the changes that must occur within the police organization and in how police leaders manage their line officers. The fifth section describes the role of the actors under community policing, specifically the police and the community. The final section presents two early articles that raised some issues with the many assumptions underlying the concept of community policing. All told, this collection of articles should provide the reader with a historical framework for community policing and a background to how this grass-roots movement began.

ACKNOWLEDGMENTS

Having written a textbook on community policing, I thought that serving as editor on a collection of previously published articles would be a simple feat. How wrong I was. I also thought that in the end, I would not really need to acknowledge that many people. Again, how wrong I was. Taking on a project such as this makes you realize that even when you *think* you did something all by yourself, you really were helped by a number of people, either directly or indirectly. In light of that fact, I must first thank my wife, Judy Ilaria Oliver, for all the love and support she has given me during the creation of this publication. It is not so much the feedback or the help in typing (although those were helpful) but also the time. And with that same thought, I must thank my sons—Paul Thomas, for letting Daddy work on the "'puter," and James Patrick, who was born during the preparation of this book and who always has a special smile when I come home.

I would also like to thank all of the people at Prentice Hall who have supported me over the past several years, especially Neil Marquardt, who has been very agreeable to work with; Bryce Dodson, who has provided assistance in getting this work off the ground; Kim Davies, who has recently come on board with Prentice Hall; Jean Auman, who always sends what I need; and the production staff, which seems to do a lion's share of the work behind the scenes and often doesn't get the credit it deserves.

I would like to thank several people at Glenville State College, but especially James Hilgenberg, who was my "once and future chair," who stayed in there and fought the good fight. But more importantly than being my chair, he has been a very good mentor and friend. I would also like to thank Debi Jenkins for assisting me in this project; she has demonstrated once again that Glenville State College hires some of the best secretaries and friendliest people. I would also like to thank Amie Starcher and Crystal Affolter, who improved their typing skills tenfold. And finally, I thank all of the Glenville State College students who have had to endure my community-oriented policing class—you have provided the feedback that was well needed.

I would also like to thank a number of people who have been there along the way in my academic career. From my past at Radford University: Dr. Paul Lang, Dr. Jack E. Call, and Dr. James Gilbert. And from my present at West Virginia University: Dr. Kevin Leyden, Dr. John Kilwein, Dr. Jeffrey Worsham, Dr. Robert DiClerico, and Dr. David Williams. In addition, I would like to thank Dr. Hammock for his support.

Also, I must thank many other members of my family, including my mother, Carol Oliver; my father, Charles J. Oliver; and my other parents, Donald and Ilaria Fellers. I especially thank Don, who was the first family member to read the textbook; and finally, Gene and Julia Oliver for always being there.

A special thank you goes to Mrs. Connie Pendleton Stuntz and Mr. Mayo Sturdevant Stuntz for their kind permission to reprint the photograph used on the front cover. I discovered this photo in the Stuntzes' fine publication, *This Was Virginia 1900–1927: As Shown by the Glass Negatives of J. Harry Shannon, The Rambler* (Hallmark Publishing, 1998). I was so enamored with the photograph of the Harrisonburg, Virginia, Police Chief that I knew it was the right picture for my front cover. Mr. and Mrs. Stuntz were gracious enough to allow me to reproduce the photograph.

Finally, I would like to give a special thanks to George L. Kelling for agreeing to write the foreword to this book. His insights and writings have paved the way for this book to be possible. This is also true of James Q. Wilson and Herman Goldstein, who have been instrumental in the community policing movement. And I would like to thank a number of publishers who were very gracious in their assistance: the International Association of Chiefs of Police, Sage Publications, and the Academy of Criminal Justice Sciences.

WILLARD M. OLIVER
Glenville, West Virginia

ABOUT THE EDITOR

Willard M. Oliver is an assistant professor of criminal justice at Glenville State College, where he also serves as program coordinator. He is the author of *Community-Oriented Policing: A Systemic Approach to Policing* (Prentice Hall 1998) and a co-author of *The Politics of Crime in America* (Prentice Hall, forthcoming 2001). He has written extensively on community policing and has published in a variety of journals, including *Policing: An International Journal of Police Strategies and Management, Journal of Criminal Justice Education, West Virginia Criminal Justice Journal, West Virginia Public Affairs Reporter, Police Disciplinary Bulletin,* and *Community Links.* He is a member of the West Virginia Regional Community Policing Institute's executive board and serves as the research and evaluation coordinator. He is also a former police officer and military police officer. Finally, and most importantly, he is a husband and the father of two boys.

PART 1

THE ORIGINS
OF COMMUNITY POLICING

Community policing has become what many have called a paradigm shift in the way policing is being performed in the United States and among various countries around the world, such as Canada and Britain. As we move into the twenty-first century with two decades of community policing behind us, there seems little doubt that this paradigm will drive policing in the years to come. It is important, however, that community policing in the twenty-first century retain its philosophical roots and historical perspective. This is why the first section of this book includes two key seminal and classical articles that form the basis for the community policing movement.

The first article, which was actually published after the second, is by James Q. Wilson and George L. Kelling. Wilson, a political scientist, gained much credibility in the criminal justice field by grounding his research in the political science discipline but looking at topics that related to the academic discipline of criminal justice. It was in such publications as *Varieties of Police Behavior* and *Thinking about Crime* that Wilson made his earlier contributions. George L. Kelling's earliest and most significant contribution to the criminal justice discipline came when he worked with the Police Foundation and was the lead researcher in the *Kansas City Preventive Patrol Experiment*. In the case of both authors, these earlier works set the stage for their collaboration in the article describing the "broken windows" theory, first published in *The Atlantic Monthly* in 1982. This theoretical essay became the basis for the police and community movement toward developing partnerships and the establishment of various strategic- and neighborhood-oriented policing methods.

The second selection, which was actually published before the "Broken Windows" article, is by Herman Goldstein. The Evjue-Bascom Professor of Law at the University of Wisconsin Law School, Goldstein made his earlier contributions on the President's Commission on Law Enforcement and Administration of Justice and in his book, *Policing a Free Society*. These contributions would lead Goldstein to begin thinking

1

about not only what did not work in policing but what did. Subsequently, he applied basic problem-solving methods of decision making to the police, because he felt these methods would prove far more successful than the confrontational, win-lose style of decision making the police most often employed. As a result of these methods proving to be highly successful and a necessary component of community policing, Goldstein contributed significantly to the community policing movement and is often referred to as the father of problem-oriented policing.

ARTICLE 1

BROKEN WINDOWS: THE POLICE AND NEIGHBORHOOD SAFETY

James Q. Wilson and George L. Kelling

In the mid-1970s, the state of New Jersey announced a "Safe and Clean Neighborhoods Program," designed to improve the quality of community life in twenty-eight cities. As part of that program, the state provided money to help cities take police officers out of their patrol cars and assign them to walking beats. The governor and other state officials were enthusiastic about using foot patrol as a way of cutting crime, but many police chiefs were skeptical. Foot patrol, in their eyes, had been pretty much discredited. It reduced the mobility of the police, who thus had difficulty responding to citizen calls for service, and weakened headquarters control over patrol officers.

Many police officers also disliked foot patrol, but for different reasons: it was hard work; it kept them outside on cold, rainy nights; and it reduced their chances for making a "good pinch." In some departments, assigning officers to foot patrol had been used as a form of punishment. And academic experts on policing doubted that foot patrol would have any impact on crime rates; it was, in the opinion of most, little more than a sop to public opinion. But since the state was paying for it, local authorities were willing to go along.

Five years after the program started, The Police Foundation, in Washington, D.C., published an evaluation of the foot-patrol project. Based on its analysis of a carefully controlled experiment carried out chiefly in Newark, the foundation concluded, to the surprise of hardly anyone, that foot patrol had not reduced crime rates. But residents of the foot-patrolled neighborhoods seemed to feel more secure than persons in other areas, tended to believe that crime had been reduced, and seemed to take fewer steps to protect themselves from crime (staying home with the doors locked, for example). Moreover, citizens in the foot-patrol areas had a more favorable opinion of the police than did those living elsewhere. And officers walking beats had higher morale, greater job satisfaction, and a more favorable attitude toward citizens in their neighborhoods than did officers assigned to patrol cars.

These findings may be taken as evidence that the skeptics were right—foot patrol has no effect on crime; it merely fools the citizens into thinking that they are safer. But in our view, and in the view of the authors of the Police Foundation study (of whom Kelling was one), the citizens of Newark were not fooled at all. They knew what the foot-patrol officers were doing, they knew it was different from what motorized officers do, and they knew that having officers walk beats did in fact make their neighborhoods safer.

But how can a neighborhood be "safer" when the crime rate has not gone down—in fact, may have gone up? Finding the answers requires first that we understand what most often frightens people in public places. Many citizens, of course, are primarily frightened by crime, especially crime involving a sudden, violent attack by a stranger. This risk is very real in Newark as in many large cities. But we tend to overlook or forget another source of fear—the fear of being bothered by disorderly people. Not violent people, nor necessarily criminals, but disreputable or obstreperous or unpredictable people: panhandlers, drunks, addicts, rowdy teenagers, prostitutes, loiterers, the mentally disturbed.

What foot-patrol officers did was to elevate, to the extent they could, the level of public order in these neighborhoods. Though the neighborhoods were predominately black and the foot patrolmen were mostly white, this "order-maintenance" function of the police was performed to the general satisfaction of both parties.

One of us (Kelling) spent many hours walking with Newark foot-patrol officers to see how they defined "order" and what they did to maintain it. One beat was typical: a busy but dilapidated area in the heart of Newark, with many abandoned buildings, marginal shops (several of which prominently displayed knives and straight-edged razors in their windows), one large department store, and, most important, a train station and several major bus stops. Though the area was run-down, its streets were filled with people because it was a major transportation center. The good order of this area was important not only to those who lived and worked there but also to many others, who had to move through it on their way home, to supermarkets, or to factories.

The people on the street were primarily black; the officer who walked the street was white. The people were made [up] of "regulars" and "strangers." Regulars included both "decent folk" and some drunks and derelicts who were always there but who "knew their place." Strangers were, well, strangers, and viewed suspiciously, sometimes apprehensively. The officer—call him Kelly—knew who the regulars were, and they knew him. As he saw his job, he was to keep an eye on strangers and make certain that the disreputable regulars observed some informal but widely understood rules. Drunks and addicts could sit on the stoops but could not lie down. People could drink on side streets, but not at the main intersection. Bottles had to be in paper bags. Talking to, bothering, or begging from people waiting at the bus stop was strictly forbidden. If a dispute erupted between a businessman and a customer, the businessman was assumed to be right, especially if the customer was a stranger. If a stranger loitered, Kelly would ask him if he had any means of support and what his business was; if he gave unsatisfactory answers, he was sent on his way. Persons who broke the informal rules, especially those who bothered people at bus stops, were arrested for vagrancy. Noisy teenagers were told to keep quiet.

These rules were defined and enforced in collaboration with the "regulars" on the street. Another neighborhood might have different rules, but these, everybody understood, were the rules for *this* neighborhood. If someone violated them, the regulars not only turned to Kelly for help but also ridiculed the violator. Sometimes what Kelly did could be described as "enforcing the law," but just as often it involved taking informal or extralegal steps to help protect what the neighborhood had decided was the appropriate level of public order. Some of the things he did probably would not withstand a legal challenge.

A determined skeptic might acknowledge that a skilled foot-patrol officer can maintain order but still insist that this sort of "order" has little to do with the real sources of community fear—that is, violent crime. To a degree, that is true. But two things must be borne in mind. First, outside observers should not assume that they know how much of the anxiety now endemic in many big-city neighborhoods stems from a fear of "real" crime and how much from a sense that the street is disorderly, a source of distasteful, worrisome encounters. The people of Newark, to judge from their behavior and their remarks to interviewers, apparently assign a high value to public order and feel relieved and reassured when the police help them maintain that order.

Second, at the community level, disorder and crime are usually inextricably linked, in a kind of developmental sequence. Social psychologists and police officers tend to agree that if a window in a building is broken *and is left unrepaired,* all the rest of the windows will soon be broken. This is as true in nice neighborhoods as in run-down ones. Window-breaking does not necessarily occur on a large scale because some areas are inhabited by determined window-breakers whereas others are populated by window-lovers; rather, one unrepaired broken window is a signal that no one cares, and so breaking more windows costs nothing. (It has always been fun.)

Philip Zimbardo, a Stanford psychologist, reported in 1969 on some experiments testing the broken-window theory. He arranged to have an automobile without license plates parked with its hood up on a street in the Bronx and a comparable automobile on a street in Palo Alto, California. The car in the Bronx was attacked by "vandals" within ten minutes of its "abandonment." The first to arrive were a family—father, mother, and young son—who removed the radiator and battery. Within twenty-four hours, virtually everything of value had been removed. Then random destruction began—windows were smashed, parts torn off, upholstery ripped. Children began to use the car as a playground. Most of the adult "vandals" were well-dressed, apparently clean-cut whites. The car in Palo Alto sat untouched for more than a week. Then Zimbardo smashed part of it with a sledgehammer. Soon, passersby were joining in. Within a few hours, the car had been turned upside down and utterly destroyed. Again, the "vandals" appeared to be primarily respectable whites.

Untended property becomes fair game for people out for fun or plunder, and even for people who ordinarily would not dream of doing such things and who probably consider themselves law-abiding. Because of the nature of community life in the Bronx—its anonymity, the frequency with which cars are abandoned and things are stolen or broken, the past experience of "no one caring"—vandalism begins much more quickly than it does in Palo Alto, where people have come to believe that private possessions are cared for and that mischievous behavior is costly. But vandalism can occur anywhere once communal boundaries—the sense of mutual regard and the obligations of civility—are lowered by actions that seem to signal that "no one cares."

We suggest that "untended" behavior also leads to the breakdown of community controls. A stable neighborhood of families who care for their homes, mind each other's children, and confidently frown on unwanted intruders can change, in a few years or even a few months, to an inhospitable and frightening jungle. A piece of property is abandoned, weeds grow up, a window is smashed. Adults stop scolding rowdy children; the children, emboldened, become more rowdy. Families move out, unattached adults move in. Teenagers gather in front of the corner store. The merchant asks them to move; they refuse. Fights occur. Litter accumulates. People start drinking in front of the grocery; in time, an inebriate slumps to the sidewalk and is allowed to sleep it off. Pedestrians are approached by panhandlers.

At this point it is not inevitable that serious crime will flourish or violent attacks on strangers will occur. But many residents will think that crime, especially violent crime, is on the rise, and they will modify their behavior accordingly. They will use the streets less often, and when on the streets will stay apart from their fellows, moving with averted eyes, silent lips, and hurried steps. "Don't get involved." For some residents, this growing atomization will matter little, because the neighborhood is not their "home" but "the place where they live." Their interests are elsewhere; they are cosmopolitans. But it will matter greatly to other people, whose lives derive meaning and satisfaction from local attachments rather than worldly involvement; for them, the neighborhood will cease to exist except for a few reliable friends whom they arrange to meet.

Such an area is vulnerable to criminal invasion. Though it is not inevitable, it is more likely that here, rather than in places where people are confident they can regulate public behavior by informal controls, drugs will change hands, prostitutes will solicit, and cars will be stripped. [It is more likely] that the drunks will be robbed by boys who do it as a lark, [that] the prostitute's customers will be robbed by men who do it purposefully and perhaps violently, [and] that muggings will occur.

Among those who find it difficult to move away from this are the elderly. Surveys of citizens suggest that the elderly are much less likely to be the victims of crime than younger persons, and some have inferred from this that the well-known fear of crime voiced by the elderly is an exaggeration; perhaps we ought to design special programs to protect persons; perhaps we should even try to talk them out of their mistaken fears. This argument misses the point. The panhandler can be as fear-inducing for defenseless persons as the prospect of meeting an actual robber; indeed, to a defenseless person, the two kinds of confrontation are often indistinguishable. Moreover, the lower rate at which the elderly are victimized is a measure of the steps they have already taken— chiefly, staying behind locked doors—to minimize the risks they face. Young men are more frequently attacked than older women, not because they are easier or more lucrative targets but because they are on the streets more.

Nor is the connection between disorderliness and fear made only by the elderly. Susan Estrich, of the Harvard Law School, has recently gathered together a number of surveys on the sources of public fear. One, done in Portland, Oregon, indicated that three-fourths of the adults interviewed cross to the other side of the street when they see a gang of teenagers; another survey, in Baltimore, discovered that nearly half would cross the street to avoid even a single strange youth. When an interviewer asked people in a housing project where the most dangerous spot was, they mentioned a place where young persons gathered to drink and play music, despite the fact that not a single crime had occurred there. In Boston public housing projects, the greatest fear was expressed by persons living in the buildings where disorderliness and incivility, not crime, were the greatest. Knowing this helps one understand the significance of such otherwise harmless displays as subway graffiti. As Nathan Glazer has written, the proliferation of graffiti, even when not obscene, confronts the subway rider with the "inescapable knowledge that the environment he must endure for an hour or more a day is uncontrolled and uncontrollable, and that anyone can invade it to do whatever damage and mischief the mind suggests."

In response to fear, people avoid one another, weakening controls. Sometimes they call the police. Patrol cars arrive, an occasional arrest occurs, but crime continues and disorder is not abated. Citizens complain to the police chief, but he explains that his department is low on personnel and that the courts do not punish petty or first-time offenders. To the residents, the police who arrive in squad cars are either ineffective or uncaring; to the police, the residents are animals who deserve each other. The citizens may soon stop calling the police, because "they can't do anything."

The process we call urban decay has occurred for centuries in every city. But what is happening today is different in at least two important respects. First, in the period before, say, World War II, city dwellers— because of money costs, transportation difficulties, familial and church connections—could rarely move away from the neighborhood problems. When movement did occur, it tended to be along public-transit routes.

Now mobility has become exceptionally easy for all but the poorest or those who are blocked by racial prejudice. Earlier crime waves had a kind of built-in self-correcting mechanism: the determination of a neighborhood or community to reassert control over its turf. Areas in Chicago, New York, and Boston would experience crime and gang wars, and then normalcy would return, as the families for whom no alternative residences were possible reclaimed their authority over the streets.

Second, the police in this earlier period assisted in that reassertion of authority by acting, sometimes violently, on behalf of the community. Young toughs were roughed up, people were arrested "on suspicion" or for vagrancy, and prostitutes and petty thieves were routed. "Rights" were something enjoyed by decent folk, and perhaps also by the serious professional criminal, who avoided violence and could afford a lawyer.

This pattern of policing was not an aberration or the result of occasional excess. From the earliest days of the nation, the police function was seen primarily as that of a night watchman: to maintain order against the chief threats to order—fire, wild animals, and disreputable behavior. Solving crimes was viewed not as a police responsibility but as a private one. In the March 1969 [issue of] *Atlantic* [*The Atlantic Monthly*], one of us (Wilson) wrote a brief account of how the police role had slowly changed from maintaining order to fighting crimes. The change began with the creation of private detectives (often ex-criminals), who worked on a contingency-fee basis for individuals who had suffered losses. In time, the detectives were absorbed into municipal agencies and paid a regular salary; simultaneously, the responsibility for prosecuting thieves was shifted from the aggrieved private citizen to the professional prosecutor. This process was not complete in most places until the twentieth century.

In the 1960s, when urban riots were a major problem, social scientists began to explore carefully the order-maintenance function of the police and to suggest ways of improving it—not to make streets safer (its original function) but to reduce the incidence of mass violence. Order maintenance became, to a degree, coterminous with "community relations." But, as the crime wave that began in the early 1960s continued without abatement throughout the decade and into the 1970s, attention shifted to the role of the police as crime-fighters. Studies of police behavior ceased, by and large, to be accounts of the order-maintenance function and became, instead, efforts to propose and test ways whereby the police could solve more crimes, make more arrests, and gather better evidence. If these things could be done, social scientists assumed, citizens would be less fearful.

A great deal was accomplished during this transition, as both police chiefs and outside experts emphasized the crime-fighting function in their plans, in the allocation of resources, and in deployment of personnel. The police may well have become better crime-fighters as a result. And doubtless they remained aware of their responsibility for order. But the link between order maintenance and crime prevention, so obvious to earlier generations, was forgotten.

That link is similar to the process whereby one broken window becomes many. The citizen who fears the ill-smelling drunk, the rowdy teenager, or the importuning beggar is not merely expressing his distaste for unseemly behavior; he is also giving voice to a bit of folk wisdom that happens to be a correct generalization—namely, that serious street crime flourishes in areas in which disorderly behavior goes unchecked. The unchecked panhandler is, in effect, the first broken window. Muggers and robbers, whether opportunistic or professional, believe they reduce their chances of being caught or even identified if they operate on streets where potential victims are already intimidated by prevailing conditions. If the neighborhood cannot keep a bothersome panhandler from annoying passersby, the thief may reason, it is even less likely to call the police to identify a potential mugger or to interfere if the mugging actually takes place.

Some police administrators concede that this process occurs, but argue that motorized-patrol officers can deal with it as effectively as foot-patrol officers. We are not so sure. In theory, an officer in a squad car can observe as much as an officer on foot; in theory, the former can talk to as many people as the latter. But the reality of police–citizen encounters is powerfully altered by the automobile. An officer on foot cannot separate himself from the street people; if he is approached, only his uniform and his personality can help him manage whatever is about to happen. And he can never be certain what that will be—a request for directions, a plea for help, an angry denunciation, a teasing remark, a confused babble, a threatening gesture.

In a car, an officer is more likely to deal with street people by rolling down the window and looking at them. The door and the window exclude the approaching citizen; they are a barrier. Some officers take advantage of this barrier, perhaps unconsciously, by acting differently in the car than they would on foot. We have seen this countless times. The police car pulls up to a corner where teenagers are gathered. The window is rolled down. The officer stares at the youths. They stare back. The officer says to one, "C'mere." He saunters over, conveying to his friends by his elaborately casual style the idea he is not intimidated by authority. "What's your name?" "Chuck." "Chuck who?" "Chuck Jones." "What'ya doing, Chuck?" "Nothin." "Got a P.O. [parole officer]?" "Nah." "Sure?" "Yeah." "Stay out of trouble, Chuckie." Meanwhile, the other boys laugh and exchange comments among themselves, probably at the officer's expense. The officer stares harder. He cannot be certain what is being said, nor can he join in and, by displaying his own skill at street banter, prove that he cannot be "put down." In the process, the officer has learned almost nothing, and the boys have decided the officer is an alien force who can be safely disregarded, even mocked.

Our experience is that most citizens like to talk to a police officer. Such exchanges give them a sense of importance, provide them with the basis for gossip, and allow them to explain to the authorities what is worrying them (whereby they gain a modest but significant sense of having "done something" about the problem). You approach a person on foot more easily, and talk to him more readily, than you do a person in a car. Moreover, you can more easily retain some anonymity if you draw an officer aside for a private chat. Suppose you want to pass on a tip about who is stealing handbags, or who offered to sell you a stolen TV. In the inner city, the culprit, in all likelihood, lives nearby. To walk up to a marked patrol car and lean in the window is to convey a visible signal that you are a "fink."

The essence of the police role in maintaining order is to reinforce the informal control mechanisms of the community itself. The police cannot, without committing extraordinary resources, provide a substitute for that informal control. On the other hand, to reinforce those natural forces, the police must accommodate them. And therein lies the problem.

Should police activity on the street be shaped, in important ways, by the standards of the neighborhood rather than by the rules of the state? Over the past two decades, the shift of police [focus] from order maintenance to law enforcement has brought them increasingly under the influence of legal restrictions, provoked by media complaints and enforced by court decisions and departmental orders. As a consequence, the order-maintenance functions of the police are now governed by rules developed to control police relations with suspected criminals. This is, we think, an entirely new development. For centuries, the role of the police as watchmen was judged primarily not in terms of its compliance with appropriate procedures but rather in terms of its attaining a desired objective. The objective was order, an inherently ambiguous term but a condition that people in a given community recognized when they saw it. The means were the same as those the community itself would employ if its members were sufficiently determined, courageous, and authoritative. Detecting and apprehending criminals, by contrast, was [a] means to an end, not an end in itself; a judicial determination of guilt or innocence was the hoped-for result of the law-enforcement mode. From the first, the police were expected to follow rules defining that process, though states differed in how stringent the rules should be. The criminal-apprehension process was always understood to involve individual rights, the violation of which was unacceptable because it meant that the violating officers would be acting as a judge and jury—and that was not his job. Guilt or innocence was to be determined by universal standards under special procedures.

Ordinarily, no judge or jury ever sees the person caught up in a dispute over the appropriate level of neighborhood order. That is true not only because most cases are handled informally on the street but also because no universal standards are available to settle arguments over disorder, and thus a judge may [not] be any wiser or more effective than a police officer. Until quite recently in many states, and even today in some places, the police make arrests on such charges as "suspicious person" or "vagrancy" or "public drunkenness"—charges with scarcely any legal meaning. These charges exist not because society wants judges to punish vagrants or drunks but because it wants an officer to have the legal tools to remove undesirable persons from a neighborhood when informal efforts to preserve order in the streets have failed.

Once we begin to think of all aspects of police work as involving the application of universal rules under special procedures, we inevitably ask what constitutes an "undesirable person" and why we should "criminalize" vagrancy or drunkenness. A strong and commendable desire to see that people are treated fairly makes us worry about allowing the police to rout persons who are undesirable by some vague or parochial standard. A growing and not-so-commendable utilitarianism leads us to doubt that any behavior that does not "hurt" another person should be made illegal. And thus many of us who watch over the police are reluctant to allow them to perform, in the only way they can, a function that every neighborhood desperately wants them to perform.

This wish to "decriminalize" disreputable behavior that "harms no one"—and thus remove the ultimate sanction the police can employ to maintain neighborhood order—is, we think, a mistake. Arresting a single drunk or a single vagrant who has harmed no identifiable person seems unjust, and in a sense, it is. But failing to do anything about a score of drunks or a hundred vagrants may destroy an entire community. A particular rule that seems to make sense in the individual case makes no sense when it is made a universal rule and applied to all cases. It makes no sense because it fails to take into account the connection between one broken window left untended and a thousand broken windows. Of course, agencies other than the police could attend to the problems posed by drunks or the mentally ill, but in most communities—especially where the "deinstitutionalization" movement has been strong—they do not.

The concern about equity is more serious. We might agree that certain behavior makes one person more undesirable than another, but how do we ensure that age or skin color or national origin or harmless mannerism will not also become the basis for distinguishing the undesirable from the desirable? How do we ensure, in short, that the police do not become the agents of neighborhood bigotry?

We can offer no wholly satisfactory answer to this important question. We are not confident that there *is* a satisfactory answer, except to hope that by their selection, training, and supervision, the police will be inculcated with a clear sense of the outer limit of their discretionary authority. That limit, roughly, is this—the police exist to help regulate behavior, not to maintain the racial or ethnic purity of a neighborhood.

Consider the case of the Robert Taylor Homes in Chicago, one of the largest public-housing projects in the country. It is home for nearly 20,000 people, all black, and extends over ninety-two acres along South State Street. It was named after a distinguished black who had been, during the 1940s, chairman of the Chicago Housing Authority. Not long after it opened, in 1962, relations between project residents and the police deteriorated badly. The citizens felt that the police were insensitive or brutal; the police, in turn, complained of unprovoked attacks on them. Some Chicago officers tell of times they were afraid to enter the Homes. Crime rates soared.

Today, the atmosphere has changed. Police–citizen relations have improved—apparently, both sides learned something from the earlier experience. Recently, a boy stole a purse and ran off. Several young persons who saw the theft voluntarily passed along to the police information on the identity and residence of the thief, and they did this publicly, with friends and neighbors looking on. But problems persist, chief among them the presence of youth gangs that terrorize residents and recruit members in the project. The people expect the police to "do something" about this, and the police are determined to do just that.

But do what? Though the police can obviously make arrests whenever a gang member breaks the law, a gang can form, recruit, and congregate without breaking the law. And only a tiny fraction of gang-related crimes can be solved by an arrest; thus, if an arrest is the only recourse for the police, the residents' fear will go unassuaged. The police will soon feel helpless, and the residents will again believe that the police "do nothing." What the police in fact do is to chase known gang members out of the project. In the words of one officer, "We kick ass." Project residents both know and approve of this. The tacit police–citizen alliance in the project is reinforced by the police view that the cops and the gangs are the two rival sources of power in the area and that the gangs are not going to win.

None of this is easily reconciled with any conception of due process or fair treatment. Since both residents and gang members are black, race is not a factor. But it could be. Suppose [residents of] a white project confronted a black gang, or vice versa. We would be apprehensive about the police taking sides. But the substantive problem remains the same: how can the police strengthen the informal social-control mechanisms of natural communities in order to minimize fear in public places? Law enforcement, per se, is no answer. A gang can weaken or destroy a community by standing about in a menacing fashion and speaking rudely to passersby without breaking the law.

We have difficulty thinking about such matters, not simply because the ethical and legal issues are so complex but because we have become accustomed to thinking of the law in essentially individualistic terms. The law defines *my* rights, punishes *his* behavior, and is applied by *that* officer because of *this* harm. We assume, in thinking this way, that what is good for the individual is good for the community, and what doesn't matter when it happens to one person won't matter if it happens to many. Ordinarily, those are plausible assumptions. But in cases where behavior that is tolerable to one person is intolerable to many others, the reaction of others—fear, withdrawal, flight—may ultimately make matters worse for everyone, including the individual who first professed his indifference.

It may be their greater sensitivity to communal as opposed to individual needs that helps explain why the residents of small communities are more satisfied with their police than are the residents of similar neighborhoods in big cities. Elinor Ostrom and her co-workers at Indiana University compared the perception of police services in two poor, all-black Illinois towns—Phoenix and East Chicago Heights—with those of three comparable all-black neighborhoods in Chicago. The level of criminal victimization and the quality of police–community relations appeared to be about the same in the towns and the Chicago neighborhoods. But the citizens living in their own villages were much more likely than those in Chicago neighborhoods to say that they do not stay at home for fear of crime, to agree that the local police have "the right to take any action necessary" to deal with problems, and to agree that the police "look out for the needs of the average citizen." It is possible that the residents of the small town saw themselves as engaged in a collaborative effort to maintain a certain standard of communal life, whereas those of the big city felt themselves to be simply requesting and supplying particular services on an individual basis.

If this is true, how should a wise police chief deploy his meager forces? The first answer is that nobody knows for certain, and the most prudent course of action would be to try further variations on the Newark experiment, to see more precisely what works in what kinds of neighborhoods. The second answer is also a hedge—many aspects of order maintenance in neighborhoods can probably best be handled in ways that involve the police minimally, if at all. A busy, bustling shopping center and a quiet, well-tended suburb may need almost no visible police presence. In both cases, the ration of respectable to disreputable people is ordinarily so high as to make informal social control effective.

Even in areas that are in jeopardy from disorderly elements, citizen action without substantial police involvement may be sufficient. Meetings between teenagers who like to hang out on a particular corner and adults who want to use that corner might well lead to an amicable agreement on a set of rules about how many people can be allowed to congregate, where, and when.

Where no understanding is possible—or if possible, not observed—citizen patrols may be a sufficient response. There are two traditions of communal involvement in maintaining order. One, that of the "community watchmen," is as old as the first settlement of the New World. Until well into the nineteenth century, volunteer watchmen, not policemen, patrolled their communities to keep order. They did so, by and large, without taking the law into their own hands—without, that is, punishing persons or using force. Their presence deterred disorder or alerted the community to disorder that could not be deterred. There are hundreds of such efforts today in communities all across the nation. Perhaps the best known is that of the Guardian Angels, a group of unarmed young persons who first came to public attention when they began patrolling New York City subways but who claim now to have chapters in more than thirty American cities. Unfortunately, we have little information about the effect of these groups on crime. It is possible, however, that whatever their effect on crime, citizens find their presence reassuring, and they thus contribute to maintaining a sense of order and civility.

The second tradition is that of the "vigilante." Rarely a feature of the settled communities of the East, it was primarily to be found in those frontier towns that grew up in advance of the reach of government. More than 350 vigilante groups are known to have existed; their distinctive feature was that their members did take the law into their own hands, by acting as judge, jury, and often executioner as well as policeman. Today, the vigilante movement is conspicuous by its rarity, despite the great fear expressed by citizens that the older cities are becoming "urban frontiers." But some community-watchmen groups have skirted the line, and others may cross it in the future. An ambiguous case, reported in *The*

Wall Street Journal, involved a citizens' patrol in the Silver Lake area of Belleville, New Jersey. A leader told the reporter, "We look for outsiders." If a few teenagers from outside the neighborhood enter it, "we ask them their business," he said. "If they say they're going down the street to see Mrs. Jones, fine, we let them pass. But then we follow them down the block to make sure they're really going to see Mrs. Jones."

Though citizens can do a great deal, the police are plainly the key to order maintenance. For one thing, many communities, such as the Robert Taylor Homes, cannot do the job by themselves. For another, no citizen in a neighborhood, even an organized one, is likely to feel the sense of responsibility that wearing a badge confers. Psychologists have done many studies on why people fail to go to the aid of persons being attacked or seeking help, and they have learned that the cause is not "apathy" or "selfishness" but the absence of some plausible grounds for feeling that one must personally accept responsibility. Ironically, avoiding responsibility is easier when a lot of people are standing about. On streets and in public places, where order is important, many people are likely to be "around," a fact that reduces the chance of any one person acting as the agent of the community. The police officer's uniform singles him out as a person who must accept responsibility if asked. In addition, officers, more easily than their fellow citizens, can be expected to distinguish between what is necessary to protect the safety of the street and what merely protects its ethnic purity.

But the police forces of America are losing, not gaining, members. Some cities have suffered substantial cuts in the number of officers available for duty. These cuts are not likely to be reversed in the near future. Therefore, each department must assign its existing officers with great care. Some neighborhoods are so demoralized and crime-ridden as to make foot patrol useless; the best the police can do with limited resources is respond to the enormous number of calls for service. Other neighborhoods are so stable and serene as to make foot patrol unnecessary. The key is to identify neighborhoods at the tipping point—where the public order is deteriorating but not unreclaimable, where the streets are used frequently but by apprehensive people, where a window is likely to be broken at any time and must quickly be fixed if all are not to be shattered.

Most police departments do not have ways of systematically identifying such areas and assigning officers to them. Officers are assigned on the basis of crime rates (meaning that marginally threatened areas are often stripped so that police can investigate crimes in areas where the situation is hopeless) or on the basis of calls for service (despite the fact that most citizens do not call the police when they are merely frightened or annoyed). To allocate patrol wisely, the department must look at the neighborhoods and decide, from first-hand evidence, where an additional officer may make the greatest difference in promoting a sense of safety.

One way to stretch limited police resources is being tried in some public-housing projects. Tenant organizations hire off-duty police officers for patrol work in their buildings. The costs are not high (at least

Broken Windows: The Police and Neighborhood Safety

not per resident), the officer likes the additional income, and the residents feel safer. Such arrangements are probably more successful than hiring night watchmen, and the Newark experiment helps us to understand why. A private security guard may deter crime or misconduct by his presence, and he may go to the aid of persons needing help, but he may well not intervene—that is, control or drive away—someone challenging community standards. Being a sworn officer—a "real cop"—seems to give one the confidence, the sense of duty, and the aura of authority necessary to perform this difficult task.

Patrol officers might be encouraged to go to and from duty stations on public transportation and, while on the bus or subway car, enforce rules about smoking, drinking, disorderly conduct, and the like. The enforcement need involve nothing more than ejecting the offender (the offense, after all, is not one with which a booking officer or a judge wishes to be bothered). Perhaps the random but relentless maintenance of standards on buses would lead to conditions on buses that approximate the level of civility we now take for granted on airplanes.

But the most important requirement is to think that to maintain order in precarious situations is a vital job. The police know this is one of their functions, and they also believe, correctly, that it cannot be done to the exclusion of criminal investigation and responding to calls. We may have encouraged them to suppose, however, on the basis of our oft-repeated concerns about serious, violent crime, that they will be judged exclusively on their capacity as crime-fighters. To the extent that this is the case, police administrators will continue to concentrate police personnel in the highest-crime areas (though not necessarily in the areas most vulnerable to criminal invasion), emphasize their training in the law and criminal apprehension (and not their training in managing street life), and join too quickly in campaigns to decriminalize "harmless" behavior (though public drunkenness, street prostitution, and pornographic displays can destroy a community more quickly than any team of professional burglars).

Above all, we must return to our long-abandoned view that the police ought to protect communities as well as individuals. Our crime statistics and victimization surveys measure individual losses, but they do not measure communal losses. Just as physicians now recognize the importance of fostering health rather than simply treating illness, so the police—and the rest of us—ought to recognize the importance of maintaining, intact, communities without broken windows.

Article 2

Improving Policing:
A Problem-Oriented Approach

Herman Goldstein

The police have been particularly susceptible to the "means over ends" syndrome, placing more emphasis on their improvement efforts in organization and operating methods than on the substantive outcomes of their work. This condition has been fed by the professional movement within the police field, with its concentration on the staffing, management, and organization of police agencies. More and more persons are questioning the widely held assumption that improvements in the internal management of police departments will enable the police to deal more effectively with the problems they are called upon to handle. If the police are to realize a greater return on the investment made in improving their operations, and if they are to mature as a profession, they must concern themselves more directly with the end product of their efforts.

Meeting this need requires that the police develop a more systematic process for examining and addressing the problems that the public expects them to handle. It requires identifying these problems in more precise terms, researching each problem, documenting the nature of the current police response, assessing its adequacy and the adequacy of existing authority and resources, engaging in a broad exploration of alternatives to present responses, weighing the merits of these alternatives, and choosing from among them.

Improvements in staffing, organization, and management remain important, but they should be achieved—and may, in fact, be more achievable—within the context of a more direct concern with the outcome of policing.

Complaints from passengers wishing to use the Bagnall to Green-fields bus service that "the drivers were speeding past queues of up to thirty people with a smile and a wave of a hand" have been met by a statement pointing out that "it is impossible for the drivers to keep their timetables if they have to stop for passengers."[1]

All bureaucracies risk becoming so preoccupied with running their organizations and getting so involved in their methods of operating that they lose sight of the primary purposes for which they were created. The police seem unusually susceptible to this phenomenon.

One of the most popular new developments in policing is the use of officers as decoys to apprehend offenders in high-crime areas. A speaker at a recent conference for police administrators, when asked to summarize new developments in the field, reported on a sixteen-week experiment in his agency with the use of decoys, aimed at reducing street robberies.

One major value of the project, the speaker claimed, was its contribution to the police department's public image. Apparently, the public was intrigued by the clever, seductive character of the project, especially by the widely publicized demonstrations of the makeup artists' ability to disguise burly officers. The speaker also claimed that the project greatly increased the morale of the personnel working in the unit. The officers found the assignment exciting and challenging, a welcome change from the tedious routine that characterizes so much of regular police work, and they developed a high esprit de corps.

The effects on robberies, however, was much less clear. The methodology used and the problems in measuring crime apparently prevented the project staff from reaching any firm conclusions. But it was reported that, of the 216 persons arrested by the unit for robbery during the experiment, more than half would not have committed a robbery, in the judgment of the unit members, if they had not been tempted by the situation presented by the police decoys. Thus, while the total impact of the project remains unclear, it can be said with certainty that the experiment actually increased the number of robberies by over 100 in the sixteen weeks of the experiment.

The account of this particular decoy project (others have claimed greater success) is an especially poignant reminder to just how serious an imbalance there is within the police field between the interest in organizational and procedural matters and the concern for the substance of policing. The assumption, of course, is that the two are related, that improvements in internal management will eventually increase the capacity of the police to meet the objectives for which police agencies are created. But the relationship is not clear and direct and is increasingly being questioned.

Perhaps the best example of such questioning relates to response time. Tremendous resources were invested during the past decade in

---

1. Newspaper report from the Midlands of England, cited in Patrick Ryan, "Get Rid of the People, and the System Runs Fine," *Smithsonian* 1977, p. 140.

personnel, vehicles, communications equipment, and new procedures in order to increase the speed with which the police respond to calls for assistance. Much less attention was given in this same period to what the officer does in handling the variety of problems he confronts on arriving, albeit fast, where he is summoned. Now, ironically, even the value of a quick response is being questioned.[2]

This article summarizes the nature of the "means over ends" syndrome in policing and explores ways of focusing greater attention on the results of policing—on the effect that police efforts have on the problems that the police are expected to handle.

THE "MEANS OVER ENDS" SYNDROME

Until the late 1960s, efforts to improve policing in this country concentrated almost exclusively on internal management: streamlining the organization, upgrading personnel, modernizing equipment, and establishing more businesslike operating procedures. All of the major commentators on the police since the beginning of the century—Leonhard F. Fuld (1909), Raymond B. Fosdick (1915), August Vollmer (1936), Bruce Smith (1940), and O. W. Wilson (1950)—stressed the need to improve the organization and management of police agencies. Indeed, the emphasis on internal management was so strong that professional policing was defined primarily as the application of modern management concepts to the running of a police department.

The sharp increase in the demands made on the police in the late 1960s (increased crime, civil rights demonstrations, and political protest) led to several national assessments of the state of policing.[3] The published findings contained some criticism of the professional model of police organization, primarily because of its impersonal character and failure to respond to legitimate pressures from within the community.[4]

---

2. The recent study in Kansas City found that the effect of response time on the capacity of the police to deal with crime was negligible, primarily because delays by citizens in reporting crimes make the minutes saved by the police insignificant. See Kansas City, Missouri, Police Department, *Response Time Analysis*, Executive Summary (Kansas City, 1977).
3. See President's Commission on Law Enforcement and Administration of Justice, *The Challenge of Crime in a Free Society* (Washington, D.C.: Govt. Printing Office, 1967); National Advisory Commission on Civil Disorders, *Report to the National Advisory Commission on Civil Disorders* (Washington, D.C.: Govt. Printing Office, 1968); National Commission on the Causes and Prevention of Violence, *To Establish Justice, to Insure Domestic Tranquility*, Final Report (Washington, D.C.: Govt. Printing Office, 1969); President's Commission on Campus Unrest, *Report of the President's Commission on Campus Unrest* (Washington, D.C.: Govt. Printing Office, 1970); and National Advisory Commission on Criminal Justice Standards and Goals, *Police* (Washington, D.C.: Govt. Printing Office, 1973).
4. See, for example, National Advisory Commission on Civil Disorders, *Report*, p. 155.

Many recommendations were made for introducing a greater concern for the human factors in policing, but the vast majority of the recommendations that emerged from the reassessments demonstrated a continuing belief that the way to improve the police was to improve the organization. Higher recruitment standards, college education for police personnel, reassignment and reallocation of personnel, additional training, and greater mobility were proposed. Thus the management-dominated concept of police reform spread and gained greater stature.

The emphasis on secondary goals—on improving the organization—continues to this day, reflected in the prevailing interests of police administrators, in the factors considered in the selection of police chiefs and the promotion of subordinates, in the subject matter of police periodicals and texts, in the content of recently developed educational programs for the police, and even in the focus of major research projects.

At one time this emphasis was appropriate. When Vollmer, Smith, and Wilson formulated their prescription for improved policing, the state of the vast majority of police agencies was chaotic: personnel were disorganized, poorly equipped, poorly trained, inefficient, lacking accountability, and often corrupt. The first priority was putting the police house in order. Otherwise, the endless crises that are produced by an organization out of control would be totally consuming. Without a minimum level of order and accountability, an agency cannot be redirected—however committed its administrators may be to addressing more substantive matters.

What is troubling is that administrators of those agencies that have succeeded in developing a high level of operating efficiency have not gone on to concern themselves with the end results of their efforts—with the actual impact that their streamlined organizations have on the problems the police are called upon to handle.

The police seem to have reached a plateau at which the highest objective to which they aspire is administrative competence. And, with some scattered exceptions, they seem reluctant to move beyond this plateau—toward creating a more systematic concern for the end product of their efforts. But strong pressures generated by several new developments may now force them to do so.

1. The Financial Crisis

The growing cost of police services and the financial plight of most city governments, especially those under threat of Proposition 13 movements, are making municipal officials increasingly reluctant to appropriate still more money for police services without greater assurance that their investments will have an impact on the problems that the police are expected to handle. Those cities that are already reducing their budgets are being forced to make some of the hard choices that must be made in weighing the impact of such cuts on the nature of the service rendered to the public.

2. Research Findings

Recently completed research questions the value of two major aspects of police operations—preventive patrol and investigations conducted by detectives.[5] Some police administrators have challenged the findings[6]; others are awaiting the results of replications.[7] But those who concur with the results have begun to search for alternatives, aware of the need to measure the effectiveness of a new response before making a substantial investment in it.

3. Growth of a Consumer Orientation

Policing has not yet felt the full impact of consumer advocacy. As citizens press for improvements in police service, improvements will increasingly be measured in terms of results. Those concerned about battered wives, for example, could not care less whether the police who respond to such calls operate with one or two officers in a car, whether the officers are short or tall, or whether they have a college education. Their attention is on what the police do for the battered wife.

4. Questioning the Effectiveness of the Best-Managed Agencies

A number of police departments have carried out most, if not all, of the numerous recommendations for strengthening a police organization and enjoy a national reputation for their efficiency, their high standards of personnel selection and training, and their application of modern technology to their operations. Nevertheless, their communities apparently

---

5. George L. Kelling et al., *The Kansas City Preventive Patrol Experiment: A Summary Report* (Washington, D.C.: Police Foundation, 1974); and Peter W. Greenwood et al., *The Criminal Investigation Process,* 3 vols. (Santa Monica, Calif.: Rand Corporation, 1976).
6. For questioning by a police administrator of the findings of the Kansas City Preventive Patrol Project, see Edward M. Davis and Lyle Knowles, "A Critique of the Report: An Evaluation of the Kansas City Preventive Patrol Experiment," *Police Chief,* June 1975, pp. 22–27. For a review of the Rand study on detectives, see Daryl F. Gates and Lyle Knowles, "An Evaluation of the Rand Corporation's Analysis of the Criminal Investigation Process," *Police Chief,* July 1976, p. 20. Each of the two papers is followed by a response from the authors of the original studies. In addition, for the position of the International Association of Chiefs of Police on the results of the Kansas City Project, see "IACP Position Paper on the Kansas City Preventive Patrol Experiment," *Police Chief,* September 1975, p. 16.
7. The National Institute of Law Enforcement and Criminal Justice is sponsoring a replication of the Kansas City Preventive Patrol Experiment and is supporting further exploration of the criminal investigation process. See National Institute of Law Enforcement and Criminal Justice, *Program Plan, Fiscal Year 1978* (Washington, D.C.: Govt. Printing Office, 1977), p. 12.

continue to have the same problems as do others with less advanced police agencies.[8]

5. Increased Resistance to Organizational Change

Intended improvements that are primarily in the form of organizational change, such as team policing, almost invariably run into resistance from rank-and-file personnel. Stronger and more militant unions have engaged some police administrators in bitter and prolonged fights over such changes.[9] Because the costs in terms of disruption and discontent are so great, police administrators initiating change will be under increasing pressure to demonstrate in advance that the results of their efforts will make the struggle worthwhile.

Against this background, the exceptions to the dominant concern with the police organization and its personnel take on greater significance. Although scattered and quite modest, a number of projects and training programs carried out in recent years have focused on a single problem that the public expects the police to handle, such as child abuse, sexual assault, arson, or the drunk driver.[10] These projects and programs, by their very nature, subordinate the customary priorities of police reform, such as staffing, management, and equipment, to a concern about a specific problem and the police response to it.

Some of the earliest support for this type of effort was reflected in the crime-specific projects funded by the Law Enforcement Assistance Administration [LEAA].[11] Communities—not just police—were encouraged to direct their attention to a specific type of crime and to make those changes in existing operations that were deemed necessary to reduce its incidence. The widespread move to fashion a more effective police response to domestic disturbances is probably the best example of a major reform that has, as its principal objective, improvement in the quality of service delivered and that calls for changes in organization,

---

8. Admittedly, precise appraisals and comparisons are difficult. For a recent example of an examination by the press of one department that has enjoyed a reputation for good management, see "The LAPD: How Good Is It?" *Los Angeles Times,* Dec. 15, 1977.
9. Examples of cities in which police unions recently have fought vigorously to oppose innovations introduced by police administrators are Boston, Massachusetts, and Troy, New York.
10. These programs are reflected in the training opportunities routinely listed in such publications as *Police Chief, Criminal Law Reporter, Law Enforcement News,* and *Crime Control Digest* and by the abstracting service of the National Criminal Justice Reference Center.
11. See, for example, National Institute of Law Enforcement and Criminal Justice, Law Enforcement Assistance Administration, "Planning Guidelines and Program[s] to Reduce Crime," mimeographed (Washington, D.C., 1972), pp. vi–xiii. For a discussion of the concept, see Paul K. Wormeli and Steve E. Kolodney, "The Crime-Specific Model: A New Criminal Justice Perspective," *Journal of Research in Crime and Delinquency,* January 1972, pp. 54–65.

staffing, and training only as these are necessary to achieve a primary goal.

Are these scattered efforts a harbinger of things to come? Are they a natural development in the steadily evolving search for ways to improve police operations? Or are they, like the programs dealing with sexual assault and child abuse, simply the result of the sudden availability of funds because of intensified citizen concern about a specific problem? Whatever their origin, those projects that do subordinate administrative considerations to the task of improving police effectiveness in dealing with a specific problem have a refreshing quality to them.

WHAT IS THE END PRODUCT OF POLICING?

To urge a more direct focus on the primary objectives of a police agency requires spelling out these objectives more clearly. But this is no easy task, given the conglomeration of unrelated, ill-defined, and often inseparable jobs that the police are expected to handle.

The task is complicated further because so many people believe that the job of the police is, first and foremost, to enforce the laws: to regulate conduct by applying the criminal law of the jurisdiction. One commentator on the police recently claimed: "We do not say to the police: 'Here is the problem. Deal with it.' We say: 'Here is a detailed code. Enforce it.'"[12] In reality, the police job is perhaps most accurately described as dealing with problems.[13] Moreover, enforcing the criminal code is itself only a means to an end—one of several that the police employ in getting their job done.[14] The emphasis on law enforcement, therefore, is nothing more than a continuing preoccupation with means.

Considerable effort has been invested in recent years in attempting to define the police function: inventorying the wide range of police responsibilities, categorizing various aspects of policing, and identifying some of the characteristics common to all police tasks.[15] This work will be of great value in refocusing attention on the end product of policing, but the fact that it is still going on is not cause to delay giving greater attention to substantive matters. It is sufficient, for our purposes here, sim-

12. Ronald J. Allen, "The Police and Substantive Rulemaking: Reconciling Principle and Expediency," *University of Pennsylvania Law Review,* November 1976, p. 97.

13. Egon Bittner comes close to this point of view when he describes police functioning as applying immediate solutions to an endless array of problems. See Egon Bittner, "Florence Nightingale in Pursuit of Willie Sutton," in *The Potential for Reform of Criminal Justice,* Herbert Jacob, ed. (Beverly Hills, Calif.: Sage, 1974), p. 30. James Q. Wilson does also when he describes policing as handling situations. See James Q. Wilson, *Varieties of Police Behavior: The Management of Law and Order in Eight Communities* (Cambridge, Mass.: Harvard University Press, 1968), p. 31.

14. I develop this point in an earlier work. See Herman Goldstein, *Policing a Free Society* (Cambridge, Mass.: Ballinger, 1977), pp. 30, 34–35.

15. In the 1977 book I presented a brief summary of these studies. *Ibid,* pp. 26–28.

ply to acknowledge that the police job requires that they deal with a wide range of behavioral and social problems that arise in a community—that the end product of policing consists of dealing with these *problems.*

By problems, I mean the incredibly broad range of troublesome situations that prompt citizens to turn to the police, such as street robberies, residential burglaries, battered wives, vandalism, speeding cars, runaway children, accidents, acts of terrorism, even fear. These and other similar problems are the essence of police work. They are the reason for having a police agency.

Problems of this nature are to be distinguished from those that frequently occupy police administrators, such as lack of manpower, inadequate supervision, inadequate training, or strained relations with police unions. They differ from those most often identified by operating personnel, such as lack of adequate equipment, frustrations in the prosecution of criminal cases, or inequities in working conditions. And they differ, too, from the problems that have occupied those advocating police reform, such as the multiplicity of police agencies, the lack of lateral entry, and the absence of effective controls over police conduct.

Many of the problems coming to the attention of the police become their responsibility because no other means has been found to solve them. They are the residual problems of society. It follows that expecting the police to solve or eliminate them is expecting too much. It is more realistic to aim at reducing their volume, preventing repetition, alleviating suffering, and minimizing the other adverse effects they produce.

DEVELOPING THE OVERALL PROCESS

To address the substantive problems of the police requires developing a commitment to a more systematic process for inquiring into these problems. Initially, this calls for identifying in precise terms the problems that citizens look to the police to handle. Once identified, each problem must be explored in greater detail. What do we know about the problem? Has it been researched? If so, with what results? What more should we know? Is it a proper concern of government? What authority and resources are available for dealing with it? What is the current police response? In the broadest-ranging search for solutions, what would constitute the most intelligent response? What factors should be considered in choosing from among alternatives? If a new response is adopted, how does one go about evaluating its effectiveness? And finally, what changes, if any, does implementation of a more effective response require in the police organization?

This type of inquiry is not foreign to the police. Many departments conduct rigorous studies of administrative and operational problems. A police agency may undertake a detailed study of the relative merits of adopting one of several different types of uniforms. And it may regularly develop military-like plans for handling special events that require the assignment of large numbers of personnel.[16] However, systematic analysis and planning have rarely been applied to the specific behavioral and social problems that constitute the agency's routine business. The situation is somewhat like that of a private industry that studies the speed of its assembly line, the productivity of its employees, and the nature of its public relations program, but does not examine the quality of its product.

Perhaps the closest police agencies have come to developing a system for addressing substantive problems has been their work in crime analysis. Police routinely analyze information on reported crimes to identify patterns of criminal conduct, with the goal of enabling operating personnel to apprehend specific offenders or develop strategies to prevent similar offenses from occurring. Some police departments have, through the use of computers, developed sophisticated programs to analyze reported crimes.[17] Unfortunately, these analyses are almost always put to very limited use—to apprehend a professional car thief or to deter a well-known cat burglar—rather than serving as a basis for rethinking the overall police response to the problem of car theft or cat burglaries. Nevertheless, the practice of planning operational responses based on an analysis of hard data, now a familiar concept to the police, is a helpful point of reference in advocating developments of more broadly based research and planning.

The most significant effort to use a problem[-solving] orientation for improving police responses was embodied in the crime-specific concept initiated in California in 1971 and later promoted with LEAA funds throughout the country.[18] The concept was made an integral part of the anticrime program launched in eight cities in January 1972 aimed at bringing about reductions in five crime categories: murder, rape, assault, robbery, and burglary.[19] This would have provided an excellent opportunity to develop and test the concept, were it not for the commitment that this politically motivated program carried to achieving fast and dramatic results: a 5 percent reduction in each category in two years and a 20 percent reduction in five years. These rather naive, unrealistic goals and the emphasis on quantifying results placed a heavy shadow over the program from the outset. With the eventual abandonment of the projects, the crime-specific concept seems to have lost ground as well. However, the national evaluation of the program made it clear that progress was

---

16. For an up-to-date description of the concept of planning and research as it has evolved in police agencies, see O. W. Wilson and Roy C. McLaren, *Police Administration,* fourth ed. (New York: McGraw-Hill, 1977), pp. 157–181.

17. For examples, see National Institute of Law Enforcement and Criminal Justice, *Police Crime Analysis Unit Handbook* (Washington, D.C.: Govt. Printing Office, 1973), pp. 90–92, 113–121.

18. For a brief description, see Joanne W. Rockwell, "Crime Specific . . . An Answer?" *Police Chief,* September 1972, p. 38.

19. The program is described in Eleanor Chelimsky, High Impact Anti-Crime Program, Final Report, vol. 2 (Washington, D.C.: Govt. Printing Office, 1976), pp. 19–38.

made, despite the various pressures, in planning a community's approach to the five general crime categories. The "crime-oriented planning, implementation, and evaluation" process employed in all eight cities had many of the elements one would want to include in a problem-oriented approach to improving police service.[20]

DEFINING PROBLEMS WITH GREATER SPECIFICITY

The importance of defining problems more precisely becomes apparent when one reflects on the long-standing practice of using overly broad categories to describe police business. Attacking police problems under a categorical heading— "crime" or "disorder," "delinquency," or even "violence"—is bound to be futile. While police business is often further subdivided by means of the labels tied to the criminal code, such as robbery, burglary, and theft, these are not adequate, for several reasons.

First, they [the labels] frequently mask diverse forms of behavior. Thus, for example, incidents classified under "arson" might include fires set by teenagers as a form of vandalism, fires set by persons suffering severe psychological problems, fires set for the purpose of destroying evidence of a crime, fires set by persons (or their hired agents) to collect insurance, and fires set by organized criminal interests to intimidate. Each type of incident poses a radically different problem for the police.

Second, if police depend heavily on categories of criminal offenses to define problems of concern to them, others may be misled to believe that, if a given form of behavior is not criminal, it is of no concern to the police. This is perhaps best reflected in the proposals for decriminalizing prostitution, gambling, narcotics use, vagrancy, and public intoxication. The argument, made over and over again, is that removing the criminal label will reduce the magnitude and complexity of the police function, freeing personnel to work on more serious matters and ridding the police of some of the negative side effects, such as corruption, that these problems produce. But decriminalization does not relieve the police of responsibility. The public expects drunks to be picked up only because they find their presence on the street annoying or because they feel that the government has an obligation to care for persons who cannot care for themselves. The public expects prostitutes who solicit openly on the streets to be stopped because such conduct is offensive to innocent passersby, blocks pedestrian or motor traffic, and contributes to the deterioration of a neighborhood. The problem is a problem for the police whether or not it is defined as a criminal offense.

Finally, use of offense categories as descriptive of police problems implies that the police role is restricted to arresting and prosecuting offenders. In fact, the police job is much broader, extending, in the case of burglary, to encouraging citizens to lock their premises more securely, to

---

20. *Ibid.,* pp. 145–50, 418–21.

eliminating some of the conditions that might attract potential burglars, to counseling burglary victims on ways they can avoid similar attacks in the future, and to recovering and returning burglarized property.

Until recently, the police role in regard to the crime of rape was perceived primarily as responding quickly when a report of a rape was received, determining whether a rape had really occurred (given current legal definitions), and then attempting to identify and apprehend the perpetrator. Today, the police role has been radically redefined to include teaching women how to avoid attack, organizing transit programs to provide safe movement in areas where there is a high risk of attack, dealing with the full range of sexual assaults not previously covered by the narrowly drawn rape statutes, and—perhaps most important—providing needed care and support to the rape victim to minimize the physical and mental damage resulting from such an attack. Police are now concerned with sexual assault not simply because they have a direct role in the arrest and prosecution of violators, but also because sexual assault is a community problem which the police and others can affect in a variety of ways.

It seems desirable, at least initially in the development of a problem-solving approach to improved policing, to press for as detailed a breakdown of problems as possible. In addition to distinguishing different forms of behavior and the apparent motivation, as in the case of incidents commonly grouped under the heading of "arson," it is helpful to be much more precise regarding locale and time of day, the type of people involved, and the type of people victimized. Different combinations of these variables may present different problems, posing different policy questions and calling for radically different solutions.[21]

For example, most police agencies already separate the problem of purse snatching in which force is used from the various other forms of conduct commonly grouped under robbery. But an agency is likely to find it much more helpful to go further—to pinpoint, for example, the problem of teenagers snatching the purses of elderly women waiting for buses in the downtown section of the city during the hours of early darkness. Likewise, a police agency might find it helpful to isolate the robberies of grocery stores that are open all night and are typically staffed by a lone attendant; or the theft of vehicles by a highly organized group engaged in the business of transporting them for sale in another jurisdiction; or the problem posed by teenagers who gather around hamburger stands each evening to the annoyance of neighbors, customers, and management. Eventually, similar problems calling for similar re-

---

21. For an excellent example of what is needed, see the typology of vandalism developed by the British sociologist Stanley Cohen, quoted in Albert M. Williams, Jr., "Vandalism," *Management Information Service Report* (Washington, D.C.: International City Management Association, May 1976), pp. 1–2. Another excellent example of an effort to break down a problem of concern to the police—in this case, heroin—is found in Mark Harrison Moore, *Buy and Bust: The Effective Regulation of an Illicit Market in Heroin* (Lexington, Mass.: Lexington Books, 1977), p. 83.

sponses may be grouped together, but one cannot be certain that they are similar until they have been analyzed. Each calls for a different response.

In the analysis of a given problem, one may find, for example, that the concern of the citizenry is primarily fear of attack, but the fear is not warranted, given the pattern of actual offenses. Where the situation becomes apparent, the police have two quite different problems: to deal more effectively with the actual incidents where they occur and to respond to the groundless fears.

The importance of subdividing problems was dramatically illustrated by the recent experience of the New York City Police Department in its effort to deal more constructively with domestic disturbances. An experimental program, in which police were trained to use mediation techniques, was undertaken with obvious public support. But, in applying the techniques, the department apparently failed to distinguish sufficiently those cases in which wives were repeatedly subject[ed] to physical abuse. The aggravated nature of the latter cases resulted in a suit against the department in which the plaintiffs argued that the police are mandated to enforce the law when *any* violation comes to their attention. In the settlement, the department agreed that its personnel would not attempt to reconcile the parties or to mediate when a felony was committed.[22] However, the net effect of the suit is likely to be more far-reaching. The vulnerability of the department to criticism for not having dealt more aggressively with the aggravated cases has dampened support—in New York and elsewhere—for the use of alternatives to arrest in less serious cases, even though alternatives still appear to represent the more intelligent response.

One of the major values in subdividing police business is that it gives visibility to some problems which have traditionally been given short shrift, but which warrant more careful attention. The seemingly minor problem of noise, for example, is typically buried in the mass of police business lumped together under such headings as "complaints," "miscellaneous," "noncriminal incidents," or "disturbances." Both police officers and unaffected citizens would most likely be inclined to rank it at the bottom in any list of problems. Yet the number of complaints about noise is high in many communities—in fact, noise is probably

---

22. See *Bruno v. Codd,* 90 Misc. 2d 1047, 396 N.Y.S.2d 974 (1977), finding a cause of action against the New York City Police Department for failing to protect battered wives. On June 26, 1978, the city agreed to a settlement with the plaintiffs in which it committed the police to arrest in all cases in which "there is reasonable cause to believe that a husband has committed a felony against his wife and/or has violated an Order of Protection or Temporary Order of Protection." See consent decree, Bruno against McGuire, New York State Supreme Court, index #21946/76. (Recognizing the consent decree, the New York Appellate Court, First Department, in July of 1978 [#3020] dismissed an appeal in the case as moot in so far as it involved the police department. From a reading of the court's reversal as to the other parts of the case, however, it appears that it would also have reversed the decision of the lower court in sustaining the action against the police department if there had not been a consent decree.)

among the most common problems brought by the public to the police.[23] While some of those complaining may be petty or unreasonable, many are seriously aggrieved and justified in their appeal for relief: sleep is lost, schedules are disrupted, mental and emotional problems are aggravated. Apartments may become uninhabitable. The elderly woman living alone, whose life has been made miserable by inconsiderable neighbors, is not easily convinced that the daily intrusion into her life of their noise is any less serious than other forms of intrusion. For this person, and for many like her, improved policing would mean a more effective response to the problem of the noise created by her neighbors.

RESEARCHING THE PROBLEM

Without a tradition for viewing in sufficiently discrete terms the various problems making up the police job, gathering even the most basic information about a specific problem—such as complaints about noise—can be extremely difficult.

First, the magnitude of the problem and the various forms in which it surfaces must be established. One is inclined to turn initially to police reports for such information. But over-generalization in categorizing incidents, the impossibility of separating some problems, variations in the reporting practices of the community, and inadequacies in report writing seriously limit their value for purposes of obtaining a full picture of the problem. However, if used cautiously, some of the information in police files may be helpful. Police agencies routinely collect and store large amounts of data, even though they may not use them to evaluate the effectiveness of their responses. Moreover, if needed information is not available, often it can be collected expeditiously in a well-managed department, owing to the high degree of centralized control of field operations.

How does one discover the nature of the current police response? Administrators and their immediate subordinates are not a good source. Quite naturally, they have a desire to provide an answer that reflects well on the agency, is consistent with legal requirements, and meets the formal expectations of both the public and other agencies that might have a responsibility relating to the problem. But even if these concerns did not color their answers, top administrators are often so far removed from street operations, in both distance and time, that they would have great difficulty describing current responses accurately.

Inquiry, then, must focus on the operating level. But mere questioning of line officers is not likely to be any more productive. We know

---

23. It was reported that, on a recent three-day holiday weekend in Madison, Wisconsin, police handled slightly more than 1,000 calls, of which 118 were for loud parties and other types of noise disturbances. See "Over 1,000 Calls Made to Police on Weekend," *Wisconsin State Journal* (Madison, Wisc.: June 1, 1978).

from the various efforts to document police activity in the field that there is often tremendous variation in the way in which different officers respond to the same type of incident.[24] Yet the high value placed on uniformity and on adhering to formal requirements and the pressures from peers inhibit officers from candidly discussing the manner in which they respond to the multitude of problems they handle—especially if the inquiry comes from outside the agency. But one cannot afford to give up at this point, for the individualized practices of police officers and the vast amount of knowledge they acquire about the situations they handle, taken together, are an extremely rich resource that is too often overlooked by those concerned about improving the quality of police services. Serious research into the problems police handle requires observing police officers over a period of time. This means accompanying them as they perform their regular assignments and cultivating the kind of relationship that enables them to talk candidly about the way in which they handle specific aspects of their job.

The differences in the way in which police respond, even in dealing with relatively simple matters, may be significant. When a runaway child is reported, one officer may limit himself to obtaining the basic facts. Another officer, sensing as much of a responsibility for dealing with the parents' fears as for finding the child and looking out for the child's interests, may endeavor to relieve the parents' anxiety by providing information about the runaway problem and about what they might expect. From the standpoint of the consumers—in this case, the parents —the response of the second officer is vastly superior to that of the first.

In handling more complicated matters, the need to improve has prompted some officers to develop what appear to be unusually effective ways of dealing with specific problems. Many officers develop a unique understanding of problems that frequently come to their attention, learning to make important distinctions among different forms of the same problem and becoming familiar with the many complicating factors that are often present. And they develop a feel for what, under the circumstances, constitutes the most effective response. After careful evaluation, these types of responses might profitably be adopted as standard for an entire police agency. If the knowledge of officers at the operating level were more readily available, it might be useful to those responsible for drafting crime-related legislation. Many of the difficulties in implementing recent changes in statutes relating to sexual assault,

---

24. See, for example, the detailed accounts of police functioning in Minneapolis, in Joseph M. Livermore, "Policing," *Minnesota Law Review,* March 1971, pp. 649–729. Among the works describing the police officers' varying styles in responding to similar situations are [James Q.] Wilson, *Varieties of Police Behavior;* Albert J. Reis, Jr., *The Police and the Public* (New Haven, Conn.: Yale University Press, 1971); Jerome H. Skolnick, *Justice without Trial: Law Enforcement in Democratic Society* (New York: John Wiley, 1966); and Egon Bittner, *The Functions of the Police in Modern Society: A Review of Background Factors, Current Practices, and Possible Role Models* (Washington, D.C.: Govt. Printing Office, 1970).

public drunkenness, drunk driving, and child abuse could have been avoided had police expertise been tapped.

By way of example, if a police agency were to decide to explore the problem of noise, the following questions might be asked: What is the magnitude of the problem as reflected by the number of complaints received? What is the source of the complaints: industry, traffic, groups of people gathered outdoors, or neighbors? How do noise complaints from residents break down between private dwellings and apartment houses? How often are the police summoned to the same location? How often are other forms of misconduct, such as fights, attributable to conflicts over noise? What is the responsibility of a landlord or an apartment house manager regarding noise complaints? What do the police now do in responding to such complaints? How much of the police procedure has been thought through and formalized? What is the authority of the police in such situations? Is it directly applicable or must they lean on somewhat nebulous authority, such as threatening to arrest for disorderly conduct or for failure to obey a lawful order, if the parties fail to quiet down? What works in police practice and what does not work? Are specific officers recognized as more capable of handling such complaints? If so, what makes them more effective? Do factors outside the control of a police agency influence the frequency with which complaints are received? Are noise complaints from apartment dwellers related to the manner in which the buildings are constructed? And what influence, if any, does the relative effectiveness of the police in handling noise complaints have on the complaining citizen's willingness to cooperate with the police in dealing with other problems, including criminal conduct traditionally defined as much more serious?

Considerable knowledge about some of the problems with which the police struggle has been generated outside police agencies by criminologists, sociologists, psychologists, and psychiatrists. But as has been pointed out frequently, relatively few of these findings have influenced the formal policies and operating decisions of practitioners.[25] Admittedly, the quality of many such studies is poor. Often the practitioners find it difficult to draw out from the research its significance for [their] operations. But most important, the police have not needed to employ these studies because they have not been expected to address specific problems in a systematic manner. If the police were pressured to examine in great detail the problems they are expected to handle, a review of the literature would become routine. If convinced that research findings had practical value, police administrators would develop into more sophisticated users of such research; their responsible criticism could, in

---

25. See, for example, the comments of Marvin Wolfgang in a congressionally sponsored discussion of federal support for criminal justice research, reported in the U.S. House, Committee on the Judiciary, Subcommittee on Crime, *New Directions for Federal Involvement in Crime Control* (Washington, D.C.: Govt. Printing Office, 1977). Wolfgang claims that research in criminology and criminal justice has had little impact on the administration of justice or on major decision makers.

turn, contribute to upgrading the quality and usefulness of future research efforts.

EXPLORING ALTERNATIVES

After the information assembled about a specific problem is analyzed, a fresh, uninhibited search should be made for alternative responses that might be an improvement over what is currently being done. The nature of such a search will differ from past efforts in that, presumably, the problem itself will be better defined and understood, the commitment to past approaches (such as focusing primarily on the identification and prosecution of offenders) will be shelved temporarily, and the search will be much broader, extending well beyond the present or future potential of just the police.

But caution is in order. Those intent on improving the operations of the criminal justice system (by divesting it of some of its current burdens) and those who are principally occupied with improving the operating efficiency of police agencies frequently recommend that the problem simply be shifted to some other agency of government or to the private sector. Such recommendations often glibly imply that a health department or social work agency, for example, is better equipped to handle the problem. Experience over the past decade, however, shows that this is rarely the case.[26] Merely shifting responsibility for the problem, without some assurance that more adequate provisions have been made for dealing with it, achieves nothing.

Police in many jurisdictions, in a commendable effort to employ alternatives to the criminal justice system, have arranged to make referrals to various social, health, and legal agencies. By tying into the services provided by the whole range of other helping agencies in the community, the police in these cities have taken a giant step toward improving the quality of their response. But there is a great danger that referral will come to be an end in itself, that the police and others advocating the use of such a system will not concern themselves adequately with the consequences of referral. If referral does not lead to reducing the citizens' problem, nothing will have been gained by this change. It may even cause harm: expectations that are raised and not fulfilled may lead to further frustration; the original problem may, as a consequence, be compounded; and the resulting bitterness about government services may feed the tensions that develop in urban areas.

The search for alternatives obviously need not start from scratch. There is much to build on. Crime prevention efforts of some police agencies and experiments with developing alternatives to the criminal justice system and with diverting cases from the system should be reassessed

---

26. For further discussion of this point, see American Bar Association, *The Urban Police Function*, approved draft (Chicago: American Bar Association, 1978), pp. 41–42.

for their impact on specific problems; those that appear to have the greatest potential should be developed and promoted.[27] Several alternatives should be explored for each problem.

1. Physical and Technical Changes

Can the problem be reduced or eliminated through physical or technical changes? Some refer to this as part of a program of "reducing opportunities" or "target hardening." Extensive effort has already gone into reducing, through urban design, factors that contribute to behavior requiring police attention.[28] Improved locks on homes and cars, the requirement of exact fares on buses,[29] and the provision for mailing social security checks directly to the recipients' banks exemplify recent efforts to control crime through this alternative.

What additional physical or technical changes might be made that would have an effect on the problem? Should such changes be mandatory, or can they be voluntary? What incentives might be offered to encourage their implementation?

2. Changes in the Provision of Government Services

Can the problem be alleviated by changes in other government services? Some of the most petty but annoying problems the police must handle originate in the policies, operating practices, and inadequacies of other public agencies: the scattering of garbage because of delays in collection, poor housing conditions because of lax code enforcement, the interference with traffic by children playing because they have not been provided adequate playground facilities, the uncapping of hydrants on hot summer nights because available pools are closed. Most police agencies long ago developed procedures for relaying reports on such conditions to the appropriate government service. But relatively few police agencies see their role as pressing for changes in policies and operations that would eliminate the recurrence of the same problems. Yet the police are the only people who see and who must be-

---

27. Many of these programs are summarized in David E. Aaronson et al., *The New Justice: Alternatives to Conventional Criminal Adjudication* (Washington, D.C.: Govt. Printing Office, 1977); and David E. Aaronson et al., *Alternatives to Conventional Criminal Adjudication: Guidebook for Planners and Practitioners,* Caroline S. Cooper, ed. (Washington, D.C.: Govt. Printing Office, 1977).
28. The leading work on the subject is Oscar Newman, *Defensible Space: Crime Prevention through Urban Design* (New York: Macmillan, 1972). See also Westinghouse National Issues Center, *Crime Prevention through Environmental Design—A Special Report* (Washington, D.C.: National League of Cities, 1977).
29. For a summary of a survey designed to assess the effect of this change, see Russell Grindle and Thomas Aceituno, "Innovations in Robbery Control," in *The Prevention and Control of Robbery,* vol. 1, Floyd Feeney and Adrianne Weir, eds. (Davis, California: [University of California], 1973), pp. 315–20.

come responsible for the collective negative consequences of current policies.

3. Conveying Reliable Information

What many people want, when they turn to the police with their problems, is simply reliable information.[30] The tenant who is locked out by his landlord for failure to pay the rent wants to know his rights to his property. The car owner whose license plates are lost or stolen wants to know what reporting obligations he has, how he goes about replacing the plates, and whether he can drive his car in the meantime. The person who suspects his neighbors of abusing their child wants to know whether he is warranted in reporting the matter to the police. And the person who receives a series of obscene telephone calls wants to know what can be done about them. Even if citizens do not ask specific questions, the best response the police can make to many requests for help is to provide accurate, concise information.

4. Developing New Skills among Police Officers

The greatest potential for improvement in the handling of some problems is in providing police officers with new forms of specialized training. This is illustrated by several recent developments. For example, the major component in the family-crisis intervention projects launched all over the country is instruction of police officers in the peculiar skills required to de-escalate highly emotional family quarrels. First aid training for police is being expanded, consistent with the current trend toward greater use of paramedics. One unpleasant task faced by the police, seldom noted by outsiders, is notifying families of the death of a family member. Often, this problem is handled poorly. In 1976, a film was made specifically to demonstrate how police should carry out this responsibility.[31] Against this background of recent developments, one should ask whether specialized training can bring about needed improvement in the handling of each specific problem.

5. New Forms of Authority

Do the police need a specific, limited form of authority [that] they do not now have? If the most intelligent response to a problem, such as a person causing a disturbance in a bar, is to order the person to leave, should

---

30. In one of the most recent of a growing number of studies of how police spend their time, it was reported that, of the 18,012 calls made to the police serving a community of 24,000 people in a four-month period, 59.98 percent were requests for information. Police responded to 65 percent of the calls they received by providing information by telephone. See Robert Lilly, "What Are the Police Now Doing?" *Journal of Police Science and Administration,* January 1978, p. 56.
31. *Death Notification* (New York: Harper & Row, 1976).

the police be authorized to issue such an order, or should they be compelled to arrest the individual in order to stop the disturbance? The same question can be asked about the estranged husband who has returned to his wife's apartment or about the group of teenagers annoying passersby at a street corner. Police are called upon to resolve these common problems, but the authority is questionable unless the behavior constitutes a criminal offense. And even then, it may not be desirable to prosecute the offender. Another type of problem is presented by the intoxicated person who is not sufficiently incapacitated to warrant being taken into protective custody, but who apparently intends to drive his car. Should a police officer have the authority to prevent the person from driving by temporarily confiscating the car keys or, as a last resort, by taking him into protective custody? Or must the officer wait for the individual to get behind the wheel and actually attempt to drive and then make the arrest? Limited specific authority may enable the police to deal more directly and intelligently with a number of comparable situations.

6. Developing New Community Resources

Analysis of a problem may lead to the conclusion that assistance is needed from another government agency. But often the problem is not clearly within the province of an existing agency, or the agency may be unaware of the problem or, if aware, without the resources to do anything about it. In such cases, since the problem is likely to be of little concern to the community as a whole, it will probably remain the responsibility of the police, unless they themselves take the initiative, as a sort of community ombudsman, in getting others to address it.

A substantial percentage of all police business involves dealing with persons suffering from mental illness. In most acute cases, where the individual may cause immediate harm to himself or others, the police are usually authorized to initiate an emergency commitment. Many other cases that do not warrant hospitalization nevertheless require some form of attention: the number of these situations has increased dramatically as the mental health system has begun treating more and more of its patients in the community. If the conduct of these persons, who are being taught to cope with the world around them, creates problems for others or exceeds community tolerance, should they be referred back to a mental health agency? Or, because they are being encouraged to adjust to the reality of the community, should they be arrested if their behavior constitutes a criminal offense? How are the police to distinguish between those who have never received any assistance, and who should therefore be referred to a mental health agency, and those who are in community treatment? Should a community agency establish services for these persons comparable to the crisis-intervention services now offered by specially organized units operating in some communities?

Such crisis-intervention units are among a number of new resources that have been established in the past few years for dealing with several long-neglected problems: detoxification centers for those incapacitated by alcohol, shelters and counseling for runaways, shelters for battered wives, and support services for the victims of sexual assault. Programs are now being designed to provide a better response to citizen disputes and grievances, another long-neglected problem. Variously labeled, these programs set up quasi-judicial forums that are intended to be inexpensive, easily accessible, and geared to the specific needs of their neighborhoods. LEAA has recently funded three such experimental programs, which they call Neighborhood Justice Centers.[32] These centers will receive many of their cases from the police.

Thus, the pattern of creating new services that bear a relationship [to] police operations is now well established, and one would expect that problem-oriented policing will lead to more services in greater variety.

7. Increased Regulation

Can the problem be handled through a tightening of regulatory codes? Where easy access to private premises is a factor, should city building codes be amended to require improved lock systems? To reduce the noise problem, should more soundproofing be required in construction? The incidence of shoplifting is determined, in part, by the number of salespeople employed, the manner in which merchandise is displayed, and the use made of various anti-shoplifting devices. Should the police be expected to combat shoplifting without regard to the merchandising practices by a given merchant, or should merchants be required by a "merchandising code" to meet some minimum standards before they can turn to the police for assistance?

8. Increased Use of City Ordinances

Does the problem call for some community sanction less drastic than a criminal sanction? Many small communities process through their local courts, as ordinance violations, as many cases of minor misconduct as possible. Of course, this requires that the community have written ordinances, usually patterned after the state statutes, that define such misconduct. Several factors make this form of processing desirable for certain offenses: it is less formal than criminal action; physical detention is not necessary; cases may be disposed of without a court appearance; the judge may select from a wide range of alternative penalties; and the offender is spared the burden of a criminal record. Some jurisdictions now use a system of civil forfeitures in proceeding against persons found to be in possession of marijuana, though the legal status of the procedure is

---

32. The concept is described in Daniel McGillis and Joan Mullen, *Neighborhood Justice Centers: An Analysis of Potential Models* (Washington, D.C.: Govt. Printing Office, 1977). See also R. F. Conner and R. Suretta, *The Citizen Dispute Settlement Program: Resolving Disputes Outside the Courts—Orlando, Florida* (Washington, D.C.: American Bar Association, 1977).

unclear in those states whose statutes define possession as criminal and call for a more severe fine or for imprisonment.

9. Use of Zoning

Much policing involves resolving disputes between those who have competing interests in the use made of a given sidewalk, street, park, or neighborhood. Bigger and more basic conflicts in land use were resolved long ago by zoning, a concept that is now firmly established. Recently, zoning has been used by a number of cities to limit the pornography stores and adult movie houses in a given area. And at least one city has experimented with the opposite approach, creating an adult entertainment zone with the hope of curtailing the spread of such establishments and simplifying the management of attendant problems. Much more experimentation is needed before any judgment can be made as to the value of zoning in such situations.

IMPLEMENTING THE PROCESS

A fully developed process for systematically addressing the problems that make up police business would call for more than the three steps just explored—defining the problem, researching it, and exploring alternatives. I have focused on these three because describing them may be the most effective way of communicating the nature of a problem-oriented approach to improving police service. A number of intervening steps are required to fill out the processes: methods for evaluating the effectiveness of current responses, procedures for choosing from among available alternatives, means of involving the community in the decision making, procedures for obtaining the approval of the municipal officials to whom the police are formally accountable, methods for obtaining any additional funding that may be necessary, adjustments in the organization and staffing of the agency that may be required to implement an agreed-upon change, and methods for evaluating the effectiveness of the change.

How does a police agency make the shift to problem-oriented policing? Ideally, the initiative will come from police administration. What is needed is not a single decision implementing a specific program or a single memorandum announcing a unique way of running the organization. The concept represents a new way of looking at the process of improving police functioning. It is a way of thinking about the police and their function that, carried out over an extended period, would be reflected in all that the administrator does: in the relationship with personnel, in the priorities he sets in his own work schedule, in what he focuses on in addressing community groups, in the choice of training curriculums, and in the questions raised with local and state legislators. Once introduced, this orientation would affect subordinates, gradually filter through the rest of the organization, and reach other administrators and agencies as well.

An administrator's success will depend heavily, in particular, on the use made of planning staff, for systematic analysis of substantive problems requires developing a capacity within the organization to collect and analyze data and to conduct evaluations of the effectiveness of police operations. Police planners (now employed in significant numbers) will have to move beyond their traditional concern with operating procedures into what might best be characterized as "product research."

The police administrator who focuses on the substance of policing should be able to count on support from others in key positions in the police field. Colleges with programs especially designed for police personnel may exert considerable leadership through their choice of offerings and through the subject matter of individual courses. In an occupation in which so much deference is paid to the value of a college education, if college instructors reinforce the impression that purely administrative matters are the most important issues in policing, police personnel understandably will not develop their interests beyond this concern.

Likewise, the LEAA, its state and local offspring, and other grant-making organizations have a unique opportunity to draw the attention of operating personnel to the importance of addressing substantive problems. The manner in which these organizations invest their funds sends a strong message to the police about what is thought to be worthwhile.

EFFECT OF THE ORGANIZATION

In the context of this reordering of police priorities, efforts to improve the staffing, management, and procedures of police agencies must continue.

Those who have been strongly committed to improving policing through better administration and organization may be disturbed by any move to subordinate their interests to a broader concern with the end product of policing. However, a problem-oriented approach to police improvements may actually contribute in several important ways to achieving their objectives.

The approach calls for the police to take greater initiatives in attempting to deal with problems rather than resign themselves to living with them. It calls for tapping police expertise. It calls for the police to be more aggressive partners with other public agencies. These changes, which would place the police in a much more positive light in the community, would also contribute significantly to improving the working environment within a police agency—an environment that suffers much from the tendency of the police to assume responsibility for problems [that] are unsolvable or ignored by others. And an improved working environment increases, in turn, the potential for recruiting and keeping qualified personnel and for bringing about needed organizational change.

Focusing on problems, because it is a practical and concrete approach, is attractive to both citizens and the police. By contrast, some of the most frequent proposals for improving police operations, because they do not produce immediate and specifically identifiable results, have no such attraction. A problem-oriented approach, with its greater appeal, has the potential for becoming a vehicle through which long-sought organizational change might be more effectively and more rapidly achieved.

Administrative rule making, for example, has gained considerable support from policy makers and some police administrators as a way of structuring police discretion, with the expectations that applying the concept would improve the quality of the decisions made by the police in the field. Yet many police administrators regard administrative rule making as an idea without practical significance. By contrast, police administrators are usually enthusiastic if invited to explore the problem of car theft or vandalism. And within such exploration, there is the opportunity to demonstrate the value of structuring police discretion in responding to reports of vandalism and car theft. Approached from this practical point of view, the concept of administrative rule making is more likely to be implemented.

Long-advanced changes in the structure and operations of police agencies have been achieved because of a concentrated concern with a given problem: the focus on the domestic disturbance, originally in New York and now elsewhere, introduced the generalist-specialist concept that has enabled many police agencies to make more effective use of their personnel; the problem in controlling narcotics and the high mobility of drug sellers motivated police agencies in many metropolitan areas to pool their resources in special investigative units, thereby achieving in a limited way one of the objectives of those who have urged consolidation of police agencies; and the recent interest in the crime of rape has resulted in widespread backing for the establishment of victim-support programs. Probably the support for any of these changes could not have been generated without the problem-oriented context in which they have been advocated.

An important factor contributing to these successes is that a problem-oriented approach to improvement is less likely to be seen as a direct challenge to the police establishment and the prevailing police value system. As a consequence, rank-and-file personnel do not resist and subvert the resulting changes. Traditional programs to improve the police—labeled as efforts to "change," "upgrade," or "reform" the police or to "achieve minimum standards"—require that police officers openly acknowledge their own deficiencies. Rank-and-file officers are much more likely to support an innovation that is cast in the form of a new response to an old problem—a problem with which they have struggled for many years and which they would like to see handled more effectively. It may be that addressing the quality of the police product will turn out to be the most effective way of achieving the objectives that have for so long been the goal of police reform.

PART 2

THE COMMUNITY
POLICING PHILOSOPHY

Community policing is first and foremost a philosophy. It has been argued for more than two decades that police departments must realize that, for the concept of community policing to work, it must be understood as a change in the way we think about policing rather than as a change in policies, procedures, or programs a department employs. If there is to be any change in these specific areas, and there is little doubt that there will be, it must be driven by the philosophy of community policing. The articles selected for this section are primarily essays articulating the philosophical underpinnings of community policing.

The first selection is by Mark H. Moore, Robert C. Trojanowicz, and George L. Kelling, who are all key proponents of the community policing philosophy. In this essay, they describe the basics of crime and policing in the twentieth century and explain the precipitating causes of serious crime. They then articulate how society has attempted to control serious crime in the twentieth century, primarily with an independent police force, and how this has failed to capitalize on a number of opportunities that could improve the quality of life of communities across the country and reduce levels of crime, fear, and disorder. Their proposal is rooted in the philosophical underpinnings of community policing.

The second selection is by George L. Kelling. In this essay, he explains that the philosophical movement of community policing is in reality a grassroots movement based on a new philosophy, one that describes the police and community working in partnership to deal with crime, fear, and disorder. He addresses why there is optimism for this new philosophy and answers those that find fault with it from a philosophical perspective.

The final selection in this section is by Herman Goldstein. It was adapted from his address at a national conference sponsored by the National Institute of Justice entitled *"Community Policing for Safe Neighborhoods:*

Partnership for the 21st Century." In this essay, he explores the philosophical roots of change found in the community policing movement and details why this change has been highly successful and why we must capitalize on its momentum. Although it is a later article (1993) than most of the articles in this reader and is based on a speech, it has truly become a classic and often-cited essay on community policing.

Article 3

CRIME AND POLICING

Mark H. Moore, Robert C. Trojanowicz,
and George L. Kelling

The core mission of the police is to control crime. No one disputes this. Indeed, professional crime fighting enjoys wide public support as the basic strategy of policing precisely because it embodies a deep commitment to this objective. In contrast, other proposed strategies, such as problem-solving or community policing, appear on the surface to blur this focus.[1] If these strategies were to leave the community more vulnerable to criminal victimization, they would be undesirable alternatives. In judging the value of alternative police strategies in controlling crime, however, one should not be misled by rhetoric or mere expressed commitment to the goal; one must keep one's eye on demonstrated effectiveness in achieving the goal.

Professional crime fighting now relies predominately on three tactics: (1) motorized patrol; (2) rapid response to calls for service; and (3) retrospective investigation of crimes.[2] Over the past few decades, police responsiveness has been enhanced by connecting police to citizens by telephones, radios, and cars and by matching police officer schedules and locations to anticipated calls for service.[3] The police focus on serious crime has also been sharpened by screening calls for service, targeting patrol, and developing forensic technology (e.g., automated fingerprint systems, computerized criminal record files, etc.).[4]

Although these tactics have scored their successes, they have been criticized within and outside policing for being reactive rather than proactive. They have also been criticized for failing to prevent crime.[5]

Reprinted from Mark H. Moore, Robert C. Trojanowicz, and George L. Kelling, "Crime and Policing," *Perspectives on Policing,* no. 2 (Washington, D.C.: National Institute of Justice, U.S. Department of Justice, and the Program in Criminal Justice Policy and Management, John F. Kennedy School of Government, Harvard University, June 1988).

Reactive tactics have some virtues, of course. The police go where crimes have occurred and when citizens have summoned them; otherwise, they do not intrude. The police keep their distance from the community and thereby retain their impartiality. They do not develop the sorts of relationships with citizens that could bias their responses to crime incidents. These are virtues insofar as they protect citizens from an overly intrusive, too familiar police.

Moreover, the reactive tactics do have preventive effects—at least in theory. The prospect of the police arriving at a crime in progress as a result of a call or a chance observation is thought to deter crimes.[6] The successful prosecution of offenders (made possible by retrospective investigation) is also thought to deter offenders.[7] And even if it does not deter, a successfully prosecuted investigation incapacitates criminals who might otherwise go on to commit other crimes.[8]

Finally, many police forces have developed proactive tactics to deal with crime problems that could not be handled through conventional reactive methods. In drug dealing, organized crime, and vice enforcement, for example, where no immediate victims exist to mobilize the police, the police have developed specialized units, which rely on informants, covert surveillance, and undercover investigations rather than responses to calls for service.[9] In the area of juvenile offenses, where society's stake in preventing crime seems particularly great, the police have created athletic leagues, formed partnerships with schools to deal with drug abuse and truancy, and so on.[10] It is not strictly accurate, then, to characterize modern policing as entirely reactive.

Still, the criticism of the police as being too reactive has some force. It is possible that the police could do more to control serious crime than they now achieve. Perhaps research will yield technological breakthroughs that will dramatically improve the productivity of police investigation. For now, however, the greatest potential for improved crime control may not lie in the continued enhancement of response times, patrol tactics, and investigative techniques. Rather, improved crime control can be achieved by (1) diagnosing and managing problems in the community that produce serious crimes; (2) fostering closer relationships with the community to facilitate crime solving; and (3) building self-defense capabilities with the community itself. Among the results may be increased apprehension of criminals. To the extent that problem-solving or community strategies of policing direct attention to and prepare the police to exploit local knowledge and capacity to control crime, they will be useful to the future of policing. To explore these possibilities, this paper examines what is known about serious crime: what it is, where and how it occurs, and natural points of intervention. Current and proposed police tactics are then examined in light of what is known about their effectiveness in fighting serious crime.

SERIOUS CRIME

To individual citizens, a serious crime is an offense that happened to *them*. That is why police departments throughout the country are burdened with calls requesting responses to offenses that the police regard as minor. While there are reasons to take such calls seriously, there is also the social and administrative necessity to weigh the relative gravity of the offenses. Otherwise, there is no principle for apportioning society's indignation and determination to punish; nor is there any basis for rationing police responses. The concept of serious crime, then, is necessarily a *social* judgment—not an individual one. Moreover, it is a value judgment—not simply a technical issue. The question of what constitutes serious crime is resolved formally by the criminal code. But the criminal code often fails to give precise guidance to police administrators who must decide which crimes to emphasize. They need some concept that distinguishes the offenses that properly outrage the citizenry and require extended police attention from the many lesser offenses that pose less urgent threats to society.

Like many things that require social value judgments, the issue of what constitutes serious crime is badly neglected.[11] Rather than face a confusing public debate, society relies on convention, or administrative expertise, or some combination of the two, to set standards. Yet, if we are to assess and improve police practice in dealing with serious crime, it is necessary to devote some thought to the question of what constitutes serious crime.

Defining Serious Crime

The usual view of serious crime emphasizes three characteristics of offenses. The most important is physical violence or violation. Death, bloody wounds, crippling injuries, even cuts and bruises increase the severity of a crime.[12] Sexual violation also has a special urgency.[13] Crime victims often suffer property losses as well as pain and violation. Economic losses count in reckoning the seriousness of an offense. Still, society generally considers physical attacks—sexual and nonsexual—as far more serious than attacks on property.[14]

A second feature of serious crime concerns the size of the victim's losses. A robbery resulting in a murder or a permanent, disfiguring injury is considered worse than one that produces only cuts, bruises, and fears. An armored car heist netting millions is considered more serious than a purse-snatching yielding the price of a junkie's fix.

Third, the perceived seriousness of an offense is influenced by the relationship between offenders and victims. Commonly, crimes against strangers are viewed as more serious than crimes committed in the context of ongoing relationships.[15] The reason is partly that the threat to society from indiscriminate predators is more far-reaching than the threat from offenders who limit their targets to spouses, lovers, and friends. Moreover, society judges the evil intent of the offender to be more evident in crimes against strangers. In these crimes, there are no chronic grievances or provocations in the background to raise the issue of who attacked whom first and in what way. The crime is an out-and-out attack, not a mere dispute.[16]

These characteristics—violence, significant losses to victims, predatory strangers—capture much of what is important to societal and police images of serious crime. The intuitive appeal of these criteria is reflected

in the categories of the FBI's Uniform Crime Reports. Murder, rape, robbery, burglary, aggravated assault, and auto theft (most presumably committed by strangers) are prominently reported as Part I offenses. This key
national account of crime not only reflects but anchors society's view of
serious crime as predatory street crime.

While this notion has the sanction of intuitive appeal, convention,
and measurement, it also contains subtle biases [that], once pointed out,
might cause society and the police to adjust their traditional views. First,
the accepted image of crime seems to downplay the importance of crime
committed in the context of ongoing relationships. From the perspective
of the general citizenry, such offenses seem less important because they
do not pose a *general* threat to society. From the perspective of the police
(and other criminal justice officials), such crimes are less clear-cut because the existence of the prior relationship muddies the distinction between offender and victim and increases the likelihood that a case will
be dropped when the antagonists resolve the dispute that produced the
offense.

From the victim's point of view, however, the fact of a relationship to
the offender dramatically intensifies the seriousness of the offense. A
special terror arises when one is locked into an abusive relationship
with a spouse or lover. A date that turns into a rape poisons a victim's
psyche much more than an attack by a stranger. And, as Boston Police
Commissioner Mickey Roache found when he was heading a unit dealing with interracial violence in Boston, serious interracial intimidation
and violence did not appear in crime reports as robberies or burglaries.
Rather, the serious crimes appeared as vandalism. What made the vandalism terrifying was that it was directed at the same address night after
night.

Second, the view of serious crime as predatory violence tends to obscure the importance of fear as a separate, pernicious aspect of the crime
problem. To a degree, the issue of fear is incorporated in the conventional view of serious crime. Indeed, fear is what elevates predatory
street crimes above crimes that occur within personal relationships.
What the conventional view misses, however, is the empirical fact that
minor offenses and incivilities trigger citizens' fears more than actual
crime victimization. Rowdy youths, abandoned cars, and graffiti frighten
people, force them to restrict their movements, and motivate them to buy
guns, locks, and dogs. To the extent that the conventional view of serious crime deflects attention from fear and the offenses that stimulate fear,
it may obscure an important opportunity for the police to contribute to
the solution of the serious crime problem.

Third, defining serious crime in terms of the absolute magnitude of
material losses to victims (without reference to the victim's capacity to
absorb the loss or the implications of the losses for people other than the
victim) introduces the potential for injustice and ineffectiveness in targeting police attention. In the conventional view, a jewel theft at a
swank hotel attracts more attention than the mugging of an elderly
woman for her Social Security check. Yet it is clear that the stolen Social
Security check represents a larger portion of the elderly woman's wealth

than the losses to the hotel's well-insured customers. The robbery of a federally insured bank would attract more attention than the robbery of an inner-city convenience store. But the robbery of the ghetto store could end the entrepreneurial career of the owner, drive the store from the area, and, with the store's departure, deprive the neighborhood of one of its few social underpinnings.

Fourth, to the extent that the conventional view of crime emphasizes the reality of individual criminal victimization, it underplays crimes that have symbolic significance. The current emphasis on child sexual abuse, for example, is important in part because it sustains a broad social commitment to the general care and protection of children. The current emphasis on domestic assault, among other things, helps to sustain a normative movement that is changing the status of women in marriages. The interest in white-collar economic crimes and political corruption can be explained by the desire to set higher standards for the conduct of those in powerful positions. The social response to these offenses is important because it strengthens, or redefines, broad social norms.

In sum, the view of crime as predatory, economically significant violence stresses the substantial losses associated with street offenses. It obscures the losses to society that result from offenses that poison relationships, transform neighborhoods into isolated camps, and undermine important social institutions. It misses the terror of the abused spouse or molested child, the wide social consequences of driving merchants out of business, the rot that drug dealing brings to an urban community, and the polarizing effect of fear. An alternative view of serious crime would be one that acknowledged violence as a key component of serious crime but added the issue of safety within relationships, the importance of fear, and the extent to which offenses collapse individual lives and social institutions as well as inflict individual losses. This enlarged conception rests on the assumption that the police can and should defend more social terrain than the streets. Their challenge is to preserve justice and order within the institutions of the community.

Levels, Trends, and Social Location of Serious Crime

It is no simple matter to represent the current levels, recent trends, and social location of serious crime. Still, several important observations can be made.

First, in any year, a noticeable fraction of American households is touched by serious crime. In 1986, five percent of American households experienced the violence associated with a rape, robbery, or assault. Almost eight percent of households were touched by at least one serious crime: rape, robbery, aggravated assault, or burglary.[17] When considering the likelihood that a household will be victimized sometime in the next five years, these figures increase dramatically, for a household faces these risks *each year.* Thus, most American households have firsthand or secondhand experience with serious crime.

Second, from the mid-1960s to the mid-1970s, the United States experienced a dramatic increase in the level of serious crime. In fact, the level of serious crime reached historic highs. Since the mid-70s, the level of serious crime has remained approximately constant, or declined slightly.[18]

Third, criminal victimization is disproportionately concentrated among minority and poor populations in the United States. Homicide is the leading cause of death for young minority males living in metropolitan areas.[19] Black households are victimized by violence crimes, such as robbery, rape, and aggravated assault at one and a half times the frequency of white families. The poor are victimized at one and a half times the rate of the wealthy.[20] These numbers probably underestimate the real differences in the losses—material and psychological—experienced by rich and poor victims, since those who are black and poor have fewer resources to deal with the losses associated with victimization.

Precipitating Causes of Serious Crime

In searching for ways to prevent or control serious crime, the police look for precipitating causes. While it may be useful to examine what some call the root causes of crime (e.g., social injustice, unequal economic opportunity, poor schooling, weak family structures, or mental illness), such things are relatively unimportant from a police perspective since the police exercise little influence over them.[21] The police operate on the surface of social life. They must handle incidents, situations, and people as they are now—not societies or people as they might have been. For these reasons, the immediately precipitating causes of serious crime are far more important to the police than are the broader questions about the root causes of crime. Four precipitating causes of crime seem relevant to policing: (1) dangerous people; (2) criminogenic situations; (3) alcohol and drug use; and (4) frustrating relationships.

One way the police view serious crime is to see the precipitating cause in the character of the offender. A crime occurs when a predatory offender finds a victim. One could reduce such events by teaching potential victims to avoid situations and behaviors that make them vulnerable. And, to some degree, the police do this. But the far more common and attractive path for controlling predatory crime is to identify and apprehend the predators. Thus, dangerous offenders can be seen as a precipitating cause of serious crime and an important focus of police attention.[22]

Recent research on criminal careers provides a firm empirical basis for this view.[23] Interviews with convicted criminals conducted by the Rand Corporation indicate that some criminal offenders committed crime very frequently and sustained this activity over a long career.[24] Moreover, these violent predators accounted for a substantial amount of the serious crime.[25] Now, an investigation of the root causes of such patterns of offending might disclose strong influences of social disadvantage and psychological maltreatment in shaping personalities of such offenders. Moreover, the influence of these factors might reasonably mitigate their guilt. One might also hold out some hope for their future rehabilitation (through the natural process of aging, if nothing else). So, the criminal proclivities of violent predators need not be viewed as either inevitable or unchangeable. From the vantage point of the police, however, the presence of such offenders in the community can reasonably be viewed as an important precipitating cause of crime. Controlling such offenders through incapacitation or close surveillance thus becomes an important crime control strategy.

Having noted the role of dangerous offenders in producing serious crime, it is worth emphasizing that such offenders account for only a portion of the total amount of serious crimes—far more than their share, but still only about half of all serious crime.[26] The necessary conclusion is that a significant portion of the serious crime problem cannot be attributed to determined attacks by career criminals or to predatory offenders. These crimes arise from quite different causes.

Some of these crimes might be produced by situational effects. Darkness and congestion around a subway exit may create an attractive location for muggings. An after-hours bar may host more than its share of fights. A rock house from which crack is being sold may become a magnet for violence. Closing time in a popular disco may produce fights among teenagers leaving the scene. In sum, there are some places, times, and activities that bring people together in ways that increase the likelihood of serious crime.

The fact that this occurs is knowable to police. By analyzing calls for service, they can observe that there are repeated calls made from certain places and at certain times.[27] These "hot spots" become important targets of police attention.[28] For example, patrol units might be dispatched just to sit and observe at the appropriate times. There may also be other solutions, including permanent changes in the criminogenic situations. For example, the subway area could be lighted; the attention of a neighborhood watch group could be directed to the trouble spot; the after-hours bar could be put out of business; aggressive street-level enforcement could be directed against the rock house; or transportation could be arranged for the kids leaving the disco so the crowd thins out more quickly.[29]

Crimes are also significantly related to alcohol or drug abuse.[30] It is now quite clear that (1) a surprisingly high percentage of those arrested for serious crimes are drug or alcohol users;[31] (2) many offenders have drunk alcohol or taken drugs prior to committing crimes;[32] and (3) victims as well as offenders are often intoxicated or under the influence of drugs.[33] What is unclear is exactly how alcohol and drugs produce their criminogenic effect. Four hypotheses have been advanced to explain this phenomenon.[34]

The first is that physiological effects [of drugs] stimulate or license the person to commit crimes. The theory of stimulation may be appropriate to methamphetamines or PCP, which sometimes seem to produce violent reactions among consumers. The theory of licensing or disinhibition seems more appropriate in the case of alcohol, where the release of inhibitions is arguably the mechanism that permits offenses to occur.[35]

Second, dependence or addiction forces users to spend more money on purchasing drugs, and they turn to crime in a desperate effort to maintain their habits. This is a powerful theory in the case of heroin (under conditions of prohibition) and perhaps for cocaine. It is far less powerful for alcohol or marijuana.

Third, drug use gradually demoralizes people by putting them on the wrong side of the law, bringing them into contact with criminals, and gradually weakening their commitment to the obligations of a civil society. Again, this seems more appropriate for those who become deeply involved with drugs and alcohol over a long period of time, and therefore relies more on the dependence-producing attributes of drugs rather than on the immediate intoxicating effects.

Fourth, intoxicated people make particularly good victims. In some cases, intoxication makes people vulnerable to victimization.[36] In other cases, it causes victims to provoke their attackers.[37] In either case, a serious crime can result.

Whichever theory, or theories, is correct, the close association among drugs, alcohol, and serious crime suggests that the amount of serious crime might be decreased by reducing levels of alcohol and drug use or by identifying those offenders who use drugs intensively and reducing their consumption.[38]

Finally, the fact that many serious offenses occur in the context of ongoing relationships suggests that some relationships may be criminogenic. Relationships can cause crime because they create expectations. If the expectations are not met, the resulting disappointment produces anger. Anger may lead to vengeance and retaliation. In such cycles, the question of who caused the ultimate crime becomes confused. Usually, the offender is the one least damaged after the fight. A court may conclude that the crime stemmed from the evil intentions of the person identified as the offender. But this may not be the best way to view the problem from the vantage point of crime control or crime prevention.

It might be more suitable to see the crimes as emerging from a set of relationships that are frustrating and provocative. The proper response might be to work on the relationship through mediation, restructuring, or dissolution. Indeed, this is often the challenge confronting the police when they encounter spouse abuse, child abuse, and other sorts of intrafamily violence. In such situations, arrests may be appropriate and effective in deterring future crime and in restructuring the relationship.[39] There are many other crimes [that] emerge from less obvious relationships: the personal relationships of neighbors and friends; the economic relations of landlord and tenant or employer and employee; or transient relations that last just long enough to provoke a quarrel or seed a grudge. Seen this way, many serious crimes—including murders, robberies, rapes, and burglaries—are disputes and grievances among people rather than criminal attacks.

CONTROLLING SERIOUS CRIME

Currently the police fight serious crime by developing a capacity to intercept it—to be in the right place at the right time so that the crime is thwarted, or to arrive so quickly after the fact that the offender is caught.

Reactive crime fighting is intuitively appealing to both the police and those to whom the police are accountable. It is unclear, however, whether the reactive response really works. Over the last two decades, confidence in the reactive approach has been eroded by the accumulation of empirical evidence suggesting that the approach fails to control crime. (It would be foolish to imagine that levels of serious crime would stay the same if police patrols and investigations were halted.) Rather, the limits of the reactive strategy are now becoming apparent. Further gains in police effectiveness in dealing with serious crime must come from different approaches. Key research findings suggesting the limitation of the reactive approach are these.

First, the Kansas City Preventive Patrol Study found that levels of serious crime were not significantly influenced by doubling the number of cars patrolling the streets.[40] This cast doubt on the potential for reducing serious crime simply by increasing the level of preventive patrol.

Second, a study of the effectiveness of rapid response to calls for service (also in Kansas City) found that the probability of making an arrest for most serious crimes was unaffected by the speed with which the police responded. The crucial factor was not the speed of the police response, but the speed with which citizens raised the alarm. If citizens did not notice the crime or did not call the police quickly, no amount of speed in the police response helped much.[41]

Third, studies of the investigative process revealed that the key factor in determining whether a crime was solved was the quality of the information contributed to the investigation by victims and witnesses about the identity of the offender.[42] If they could not be helpful, forensic wizardry generally was not up to solving the crime.

It is important to understand that these weaknesses appeared in precisely those areas of crime control where the reactive strategy should have been particularly strong, i.e., in dealing with crimes such as murder, rape, robbery, assault, and burglary. These crimes could be expected to produce alarms; they also were interceptable and solvable by a vigilant police force waiting to be mobilized by outraged citizens.

There are, of course, many other kinds of serious crimes for which the reactive police strategy is much more obviously inappropriate.[43] It cannot, for example, deal with consensual crimes such as drug dealing behind closed doors. Nor can it deal with crimes such as extortion and loan sharking where the victims are too afraid to report the crimes. A reactive strategy cannot deal with sophisticated white-collar crimes or political corruption where the losses associated with the crimes are so widely distributed that people do not notice that they have been victimized. Finally, a reactive strategy cannot deal even with traditional street crimes in those parts of cities where confidence in the police has eroded to such a degree that the citizens no longer call when they are victimized.

Although these findings and intrinsic limitations of the reactive strategy have not unseated the intuitive appeal of and wide experience with the reactive crime-fighting strategy, they have added to a growing sense of frustration within police departments. Confronted by high levels of crime and limited budgets, the police felt a growing need for initiatives and thoughtfulness in tackling serious crime. Working within the logic of their current approaches but reaching for additional degrees of effectiveness, during the 1970s the police developed new proactive tactics.

Developments in Proactive Crime Fighting

To deal with serious street crime, the police developed the tactic of directed patrol. Sometimes these patrols were aimed at locations that seemed particularly vulnerable to crimes, such as branch banks, convenience stores, and crowded bars. Other times, the patrols were focused on individuals who, on the basis of past records or recent information, were thought to be particularly active offenders.[44]

The police sought to attack street robberies and muggings through anticrime squads that sent decoys into the streets to prompt active muggers into committing a crime in the full view of the police. The police also sought to control home robberies and burglaries through sting operations involving undercover officers who operate as fences to identify and gather evidence against the offenders.

Finally, the police sought to enhance the effective impact of their enforcement efforts by increasing the quality of the cases they made. Quality Investigation Programs[45] and Integrated Criminal Apprehension Programs[46] were adopted by many departments to increase the likelihood that arrests would be followed by convictions and long prison sentences.

For the most part, each of these innovations produced its successes. The perpetrator-oriented patrols, sting operations, and quality investigation efforts were a little more successful than the location-oriented directed patrols and the undercover operations directed against street robbery. Nonetheless, the police did demonstrate that concentrated efforts could increase arrests, clearances, and convictions. These efforts did not show that these programs alone—without the support of courts and corrections and the involvement of the community—could reduce aggregate levels of serious crime in the cities in which they were tried.

Moreover, insofar as each program took a more aggressive and proactive approach to crime, it also troubled those who were concerned that the police not become too intrusive. Perpetrator-oriented patrols, for example, raised the question of whether it was appropriate to target offenders rather than offenses, and if so, on what evidentiary basis.[47] The use of undercover tactics to deal with both robbery and burglary raised important questions about entrapment.[48] And the emphasis on producing convictions from arrests prompted worries that the police might be motivated to manufacture as well as simply record and preserve evidence. Arguably, these civil liberties concerns were inappropriate at a time when the police seemed unable to deal with high crime rates. The fact that these concerns arose, however, indicated that the police were, in fact, using their authority more intensively than they had when they were relying principally on reactive strategies. Such concerns must be reckoned a cost of the new efforts.

The police also made substantial investments in their ability to deal with those crimes that could not be handled through routine patrol or investigative operations, either because the crimes were too complicated to handle with ordinary arrest and investigative methods or because the routine operations would not disclose the crime. In terms of dealing with especially demanding crimes, like hostage takings or well-armed offenders, the police developed Special Weapons and Arrest Teams. They also enhanced their capacities to deal with riots and demonstrations. And at the other end of the spectrum, the police developed special procedures for dealing with deranged and disordered offenders who often looked violent (and sometimes were) but mostly were simply mentally disturbed.

To deal with crimes that were not always revealed through the ordinary procedures of complaints by victims and witnesses, the police developed special units skilled in investigating the sensitive areas of child sexual abuse, rape, and domestic assault. They also created special investigative units to deal with high-level drug dealing, organized crime, arson, and sophisticated frauds. These units often relied on special intelligence files as well as special investigative procedures, such as the recruitment of informants, electronic wiretaps, and sustained undercover investigations. These programs also scored their successes and enhanced the ability of the police to deal with serious crime.

Missed Opportunities in Crime Fighting?

These innovations demonstrated the resourcefulness and creativity of the police as they faced the challenge of high crime rates with limited financial resources, diminished authority, and constrained managerial prerogatives. With the benefit of hindsight, however, some crucial oversights are apparent.

First, there was little appreciation of the crucial role that better information from the community could play in strengthening police performance.[49] It was not that the police were unaware of their dependency on citizens for information. Long before it was demonstrated that the success of rapid response to crime calls and retrospective investigation depended on the willingness of victims and witnesses to report crimes and aid in their solution, the police had mounted campaigns mobilizing citizens to support their local police.

The real problem was that the police did not adequately consider what was needed to attract that support. They thought that their interests and ready availability would be sufficient. They did not understand that citizens felt vulnerable to retaliation by offenders in the community and needed a closer connection with the police if they were going to help them solve the crime. Nor did the police understand that a partnership with the community could be constructed only from the material of daily encounters with the public; in particular, by taking seriously the public's concern with less serious offenses. In short, while the police knew that they were dependent on the community for information about crime, they never asked the public what was needed to obtain help beyond setting up 911 systems.

Second, the police rarely looked behind an offense to its precipitating causes. Nor did they think about crime prevention in terms of managing the precipitating causes. They knew, of course, that much crime was being produced by dangerous offenders, criminogenic situations, alcohol and drug abuse, and aggravating relationships. But they were ambivalent about acting on that knowledge. They tended to limit their responsibilities to applying the law to incidents to which they were summoned; they did not think in terms of applying instruments of civil law or the capacities of other city agencies to work on the proximate causes of crime. Criminal investigations emphasized legal evidence of guilt or innocence—not the question of precipitating causes.

There were many reasons to maintain this narrow focus on law enforcement. To a degree, it protected police organizations from criticisms that they were lawless and out of control. The police could explain that they merely enforced the laws and they exercised no discretion beyond this basic function. The narrow focus on law enforcement also protected the organization from failure in its basic crime control mission. If the police role was limited to applying the criminal law to offenses rather than to the more challenging goal of actually preventing and controlling crime, the police could succeed even if crime were not controlled. They could blame the other parts of the criminal justice system for their failures to deter and incapacitate the offenders whom the police had arrested. Finally, the narrow focus was consistent with the training and aspirations of the police themselves. Arresting people and using authority was real police work; mediating disputes, mobilizing communities, and badgering other city agencies for improved services was social work.

Whatever the reasons, the police remained reluctant to develop the internal capabilities needed to make their anecdotal impressions of precipitating causes systematic and powerful. Crime analysis sections merely kept statistics or characterized the location of crime; they did not identify dangerous offenders or trouble spots and avoided examining the role of alcohol and drugs in the serious crime problem. Nor did they propose alternative methods for dealing with crime problems. From the perspective of the police, it was far better to stay at the surface of social life and respond to crimes as they occurred rather than to intervene more widely and actively to manage the immediate conditions that were producing crimes.

Third, the police never fully exploited the self-defense capacities of the community itself. They did offer advice to merchants and citizen groups about how they could protect themselves from criminal victimization. And they helped organize neighborhood watch groups. But the main efforts went into helping the communities become more effective operational auxiliaries to the police departments. Citizens were encouraged to mark their property not only because it helped the police solve the crime, should the item be stolen, but also because it allowed the police to return the property to the owners. Crime watch groups were instructed to call the police rather than to intervene themselves. This was consistent with the desires of the police to maintain their monopoly on both expertise and operational capability in dealing with crime. They did not really want any growth in private security—whether it took the form of volunteer associations, such as the Guardian Angels, or commercialized operations, such as Burns Security Guards. Because of that interest, police commitment to building a community's self-defense capacities was always ambivalent. And, because they were ambivalent, the police did not think through the question of whether and how such efforts could actually help them control serious crime.

Problem-Solving and Community Approaches to Crime Control

In the 1980s, police departments throughout the country have begun to explore the crime-fighting effectiveness of tactics that build on previous approaches, but seek to extend them by looking behind the offenses to the precipitating causes of crimes, building closer relations with the community, and seeking to enhance the self-defense capacities of the communities themselves. These efforts are guided mostly by a theory of what might work and some illustrative examples. The theory is that the effectiveness of existing tactics can be enhanced if the police increase the quantity and quality of their contacts with citizens (both individuals and neighborhood groups) and include in their responses to crime problems thoughtful analyses of the precipitating causes of the offenses. The expectation is that this will both enhance the direct effectiveness of the police department and also enable the police department to leverage the resources of citizen groups and other public agencies to control crime. Some examples, drawn from recent experience, suggest the ways in which these new approaches can lead to enhanced crime control.

Enhanced Police Presence. From its inception, patrol has sought to prevent crime through the presence, or potential presence, of a conspicuous officer. Patrolling in cars is only one way to communicate police presence, however. Activities such as foot patrol, visiting citizens in their homes, and attending group meetings also increases the awareness of police to which all citizens respond—those intent on crime as well as those not. This presence both deters potential offenders from committing crimes and affords officers the opportunities to note criminal acts in progress.

Although the success of foot patrol tactics in controlling crime is counter-intuitive to those accustomed to patrol by automobile, confidence in this approach is common in England. There, when an anticrime unit is sent in to deal with a serious crime problem, as often as not it consists of foot patrol. The approach is successful because foot patrol officers have access to areas unavailable to officers in cars: walkways and areas between houses, for example. Unpublished work by Glenn Pierce suggests that some crimes, such as burglary, tend to be patterned within limited geographical and chronological space. If this is true, when combined with what is known about how burglars enter homes and businesses, properly targeted foot patrol might be the strongest potential anticrime tactic to deal with such crimes.

Better Surveillance and Deterrence of Dangerous Offenders. From the outset, police have sought to control crime through close surveillance of those who have committed crimes in the past. The problem has been to accurately identify those offenders. Police officers who work closely with a neighborhood are in a position to learn who behaves in criminal or delinquent ways within the community. By stationing themselves in particular locations, officers can surveil known troublemakers and forestall criminal behavior.

It is also legally and procedurally possible to consider assigning neighborhood police officers to the surveillance of probationers and parolees. Such surveillance would be more immediate and regular than that now provided by probation or parole officers. Aware that neighborhood police officers have easier access to information about their activities, people who were in the community on a conditional basis might be deterred from committing illegal acts.

Increased Access to Information. Community policing emphasizes the development of close communication between citizens and police. This communication helps police gather information for both *preventing* and *solving* crime. Familiarity with the social and physical characteristics of their beats also helps neighborhood police officers to understand linkages between various pieces of information gathered from their own observations and from other disparate sources. Work by Pate,[50] Greenwood, Chaiken and Petersilia,[51] Eck,[52] and Skogan and Antunes[53] suggests that use of information gathered by patrol officers is one of the most important ways in which police can improve their ability to apprehend offenders. In 1982, Baltimore County, Maryland, initiated a Citizen-Oriented Police Enforcement (COPE) unit, designed to bring the police into closer contact with the citizens and reduce their fears. A 1985 study showed that not only had COPE reduced fear, but also it had apparently produced a 12 percent reduction in the level of reported crime.[54]

Early Intervention to Prevent the Escalation of Disorder into Crime. In a widely read article, Kelling and Wilson argue that there is an important causal link between minor instances of disorder and the occurrence of serious crime.[55] Disorderly behavior—youths congregating, drunks lying down, prostitutes aggressively soliciting—left untended can escalate into serious crime. The implication is that intervention by police to stop uncivil behavior keeps it from escalating. Although this argument has intuitive appeal, little direct empirical evidence exists about exploiting its anticrime potential.

Crime Prevention Activities. An important part of community policing is providing anticrime consultation to citizens, businesses, and other community institutions. The recommendations range from home target hardening (locks, strengthened doors, etc.) to street and building design. A 1973 evaluation of Seattle's Community Crime Prevention Program, which used this approach, found a significant reduction in burglaries.[56]

Shoring Up Community Institutions. Institutions of neighborhood social control include families, churches, schools, local businesses, and neighborhood and community organizations. In many communities, the corrosive effects of social disorganization have seriously weakened such organizations. Police, working with such institutions and organizations, can reinforce their normative strength in a community. Although promising, it is unclear what impact the strengthening of community institutions has on serious crime. It is an attractive idea, however.

Problem Solving. Police have historically viewed calls for service and criminal events as individual incidents. Many such incidents are part of a chronic problem amenable to diagnosis and preventive intervention by either police or other agencies. Problem solving appears to be a promising approach to deter crime. When, in 1985, the Newport News Police Department turned to problem-oriented policing as an approach to dealing with crime, it was successful in dealing with three stubborn crime problems that had beset the community: a series of prostitution-related robberies, a rash of burglaries in a housing project, and larcenies from vehicles parked in downtown areas. In each case, the problem was solved not simply by solving the crimes and arresting offenders, nor by increasing levels of patrol (though both were done), but also by operating on the immediate conditions that were giving rise to the offenses.[57] These ideas, examples, and results lend plausibility to the notion that problem-solving or community policing can enhance the crime control capabilities of professional crime fighting. They do not prove the case, however.

A Strategic View of Crime Fighting

While police executives can produce increased levels of arrest and local reductions in crime through the creation of special programs, they are frustrated because they do not know how to produce reductions in citywide levels of crime. The main reason for this might be that their main force is not engaged in a serious crime-fighting effort even though it seems that it is. After all, it would be unreasonable to imagine that any single small program, typically engaging less than 5 percent of the force, could have much impact on aggregate levels of crime. The important question is, what is the remaining 95 percent of the force doing? For the most part, the answer is that they are deployed in patrol cars, responding to calls for service, and investigating crimes after they have occurred. These tactics have only limited effectiveness.

What remains unanswered is the consequence of shifting a whole department to a radically different style of policing. Moreover, the answer is hard to determine, since the period of transition would be quite awkward. In the short run, were officers taken from patrol and detective units to do problem-oriented or community policing, it is almost certain that response times would lengthen—at least until the problem-solving efforts reduced the demands for service by eliminating the precipitating problem that was producing the calls for service.[58] And even though an increase in response times does not necessarily indicate a real loss in crime-fighting effectiveness, it would be perceived as such because the public and the police have learned to equate rapid response to crime calls with crime control effectiveness.

What is tempting, of course, is to avoid choosing among these strategies and to adopt the strengths of these various approaches while avoiding their weaknesses. This would be reflected in decisions to establish special units to do problem solving or community policing within existing organizations whose traditions and main forces remained committed to reactive patrol and retrospective investigation.

But it may not be this easy. Indeed, experience demonstrates that it is not. Previous initiatives with team policing or split-force policing succeeded in building capacities for both styles of policing within the same department but tended to foster eventual competition and conflict.[59] The problem-solving and community policing aspects have usually eventually yielded to administrative demands to keep response times low or to officers' desires to avoid the demanding engagement with the community. The reason seems to be partly a matter of resources—there has never been enough manpower to maximize performance in both domains at once. But it also seems to be a matter of administrative style and structure. Problem-solving and community policing both require a greater degree of decentralization than does the current policing strategy. They depend more on the initiative of the officers. And they reach out for a close rather than a distant relationship with the community. These are all quite different than the administrative emphases of the current strategy, which prescribes centralization, control, and distance from the community.

So while logic and evidence suggest the crime control potential of adding problem-solving and community policing to the concept of rapid response and retrospective investigation, it is hard to add these functions without increasing the resources and significantly changing the administrative style of a police organization. That is hard for a police chief to decide to do without convincing evidence that it would work. The only things that make such a move easy to contemplate are (1) a deep sense that the current strategy and tactics have reached their limits; (2) the plausibility of the idea that increased effectiveness lies in working on proximate causes and mobilizing communities; and (3) the little bit of evidence we have that the alternative approach works. A few departments, such as Houston, Newport News, Baltimore County, and Philadelphia, have committed themselves to these alternative approaches. If they succeed over the next three to five years in reducing serious crime as well as in attracting citizen support, then the field will know that it has a better strategy of policing available than is now being used.

NOTES

1. For descriptions of these alternative strategies, see Robert C. Trojanowicz, "Community Policing vs. 'High Tech' Policing: What's in a Name?" (Unpublished paper, Michigan State University, April 1987); Herman Goldstein, *The Urban*

Police Function (Cambridge, Mass.: Ballinger Publishing, 1977); John Eck and William Spelman, "Solving Problems: Problem-Oriented Policing in Newport News" (Washington, D.C.: Police Executive Research Forum, January 1987).
  2. George L. Kelling and Mark H. Moore, "From Political to Reform to Community: The Evolving Strategy of Police" (Cambridge, Mass.: Program in Criminal Justice Policy and Management, John F. Kennedy School of Government, Harvard University, 1987).
  3. President's Commission on Law Enforcement and Administration of Justice, *Task Force Report: Science and Technology* (Washington, D.C.: U.S. Govt. Printing Office, 1967); Jan M. Chaiken and Warren Walker, *Patrol Car Allocation Model* (Santa Monica, Calif.: The Rand Corporation, 1985); Richard C. Larson, *Police Deployment from Urban Public Safety Systems,* vol. 1 (Lexington, Mass.: Lexington Books, 1978); David M. Kennedy, "Patrol Allocation in Portland, OR, Part A: PCAM in the Bureau," and "Patrol Allocation in Portland, OR, Part B, PCAM in the City" (Cambridge, Mass.: Case Program, John F. Kennedy School of Government, Harvard University, 1988).
  4. J. Thomas McEwen, Edward F. Connors III, and Marcia Cohen, *Evaluation of the Differential Police Response Field Test* (Washington, D.C.: U.S. Govt. Printing Office, 1986); Richard P. Grassie and John A. Hollister, *Integrated Criminal Apprehension Program: A Preliminary Guideline Manual for Patrol Operations Analysis* (Washington, D.C.: LEAA, U.S. Department of Justice, 1977).
  5. James Q. Wilson, "The Police and Crime," in *Thinking about Crime* (New York: Vintage Books, 1975), chap. 4. Larson, *Police Deployment from Urban Public Safety Systems.*
  6. Orlando W. Wilson, *The Distribution of the Police Patrol Force* (Chicago: Public Administration Services, 1941).
  7. Alfred Blumstein et al., *Deterrence and Incapacitation: Estimating the Effects of Criminal Sanctions on the Crime Rate* (Washington, D.C.: National Academy of Sciences, 1978).
  8. *Ibid.*
  9. Mark H. Moore, *Buy and Bust: The Effective Regulation of an Illicit Market in Heroin* (Lexington, Mass.: Lexington Books, 1977); Peter K. Manning, *The Narc's Game: Organizational and Informational Limits on Drug Law Enforcement* (Cambridge: MIT Press, 1980); Mark H. Moore, "Invisible Offenses: A Challenge to Minimally Intrusive Law Enforcement," in Gerald M. Caplan, ed., *Abscam Ethics* (Washington, D.C.: Police Foundation, 1983); Gary Marx, "Who Really Gets Stung? Some Issues Raised by the New Police Undercover Work," in Caplan, *Abscam Ethics.*
  10. George L. Kelling, "Juveniles and Police: The End of the Nightstick," in Francis X. Hartmann, ed., *From Children to Citizens,* vol. 2: *The Role of the Juvenile Court* (New York: Springer-Verlag, 1987).
  11. The exception is Marvin Wolfgang's work devoted to measuring crime seriousness as perceived by citizens. See Marvin E. Wolfgang and Thorsten Sellin, *The Measurement of Crime Seriousness* (New York: Wiley Publishing, 1964). See also Mark H. Moore et al., *Dangerous Offenders: The Elusive Target of Justice* (Cambridge, Mass.: Harvard University Press, 1984), chap. 2.
  12. Bureau of Justice Statistics, *The Severity of Crime* (Washington, D.C.: U.S. Department of Justice, January 1984), p. 5.
  13. Susan Estrich, *Real Rape* (Cambridge, Mass.: Harvard University Press, 1987).
  14. Bureau of Justice Statistics, *The Severity of Crime.*
  15. *Ibid.*
  16. For a view of crime as a dispute rather than an attack, see Donald Black, *The Manners and Customs of the Police* (New York: Academic Press, 1980), chap. 5. For important empirical evidence, see Vera Institute of Justice, *Felony Arrests: Their Prosecution and Disposition in the New York City Courts* (New York, 1981).

17. Bureau of Justice Statistics, "Households Touched by Crime: 1986," *BJS Bulletin* (Washington, D.C.: U.S. Department of Justice, June 1987).
18. Bureau of Justice Statistics, *Report to the Nation on Crime and Justice* (Washington, D.C.: U.S. Department of Justice, 1983).
19. Patrick W. O'Carroll and James A. Mercy, "Patterns and Recent Trends in Black Homicide," in Darnell F. Hawkins, ed., *Homicide among Black Americans* (Lanham, Maryland: University Press of America, 1986).
20. Bureau of Justice Statistics, "Households Touched by Crime."
21. James Q. Wilson, "Criminologists," in *Thinking about Crime* (New York: Vintage Books, 1975), chap. 3.
22. For a discussion of this concept and its importance to police strategies, see Moore et al., *Dangerous Offenders*, chap. 7.
23. Alfred Blumstein et al., *Criminal Careers and Career Criminals*, vol. 1 (Washington, D.C.: National Academy Press, 1986).
24. Jan Chaiken and Marcia Chaiken, *Varieties of Criminal Behavior* (Santa Monica, Calif.: The Rand Corporation, August 1982).
25. Peter W. Greenwood and Sue Turner, *Selective Incapacitation, Revisited for the National Institute of Justice* (Santa Monica, Calif.: The Rand Corporation, 1987).
26. Moore et al., *Dangerous Offenders.*
27. Glenn Pierce et al., "Evaluations of an Experiment in Proactive Police Intervention in the Field of Domestic Violence Using Repeat Call Analysis" (Boston: The Boston Fenway Program, Inc., May 13, 1987).
28. Lawrence W. Sherman, "Repeat Calls to Police in Minneapolis" (College Park, Maryland: University of Maryland, 1987).
29. This example of youth transportation comes from Christine Nixon's experience in New South Wales, Australia. For other examples, see John Eck and William Spelman, "Solving Problems: Problem-Oriented Policing."
30. Mark H. Moore, "Controlling Criminogenic Commodities: Drugs, Guns, and Alcohol," in James Q. Wilson, ed., *Crime and Public Policy* (San Francisco: Institute for Contemporary Studies Press, 1983).
31. Eric Wish, "Drug Use Forecasting System" (Unpublished working paper at the National Institute of Justice, Washington, D.C., January 1988).
32. *Ibid.*
33. Marvin Wolfgang, *Patterns in Criminal Homicide* (Montclair, New Jersey: Patterson Smith Publishing, 1975); James Collins, *Alcohol Use and Criminal Behavior: An Executive Summary* (Washington, D.C.: U.S. Department of Justice, 1981).
34. Mark H. Moore, "Drugs and Crime: A Policy Analytic Approach," Appendix to Report of the Panel on Drug Use and Criminal Behavior, *Drug Use and Crime* (Washington, D.C.: The National Institute on Drug Abuse and Research Triangle Institute, 1976).
35. David Levinson, "Alcohol Use and Aggression in American Subcultures," in Robin Room and Gary Collins, eds., *Alcohol and Disinhibition: Nature and Meaning of the Link* (Washington, D.C.: U.S. Department of Health and Human Services, 1983).
36. Moore, "Controlling Criminogenic Commodities."
37. Wolfgang, *Patterns in Criminal Homicide.*
38. M. Douglas Anglin and Yih-Ing Hser, "Treatment of Drug Abuse," manuscript to be published in Michael Tonry and James Q. Wilson, eds., *Drugs and Crime,* a special volume of *Crime and Justice: A Review of Research* (Chicago: University of Chicago Press, forthcoming).
39. Sherman, "Repeat Calls to Police in Minneapolis."
40. George L. Kelling, *Kansas City Preventive Patrol Experiment: A Summary Report* (Washington, D.C.: Police Foundation, 1974).

41. *Response Time Analysis* (Kansas City, Missouri: Kansas City Police Department, 1977).
42. Peter W. Greenwood, Jan M. Chaiken, and Joan Petersilia, *The Criminal Investigation Process* (Lexington, Mass.: D.C. Heath, 1977). John Eck, *Managing Case Assignments: Burglary Investigation Decision Model Replication* (Washington, D.C.: Police Executive Research Forum, 1979).
43. Moore, "Invisible Offenses."
44. Antony Pate, Robert Bowers, and Ron Parks, *Three Approaches to Criminal Apprehension in Kansas City: An Evaluation Report* (Washington, D.C.: Police Foundation, 1976).
45. Jerome E. McElroy, Colleen Cosgrove, and Michael Farrell, *Felony Case Preparation: Quality Counts,* Interim Report of the New York City Police Department Felony Case Preparation Project (New York: Vera Institute of Justice, 1981).
46. Grassie and Hollister, *Integrated Criminal Apprehension Program.*
47. Moore et al., *Dangerous Offenders,* chap. 7.
48. Marx, "Who Really Gets Stung?"
49. Wesley G. Skogan and George E. Antunes, "Information Apprehension, and Deterrence: Exploring the Limits of Police Productivity," *Journal of Criminal Justice,* 7(1979): 217–242.
50. Pate et al., *Three Approaches to Criminal Apprehension.*
51. Greenwood et al., *The Criminal Investigation Process.*
52. Eck, *Managing Case Assignments.*
53. Skogan and Antunes, "Information, Apprehension, and Deterrence."
54. Philip B. Taft, Jr., "Fighting Fear: The Baltimore County COPE Project" (Washington, D.C.: Police Executive Research Forum, February 1986), p. 20.
55. James Q. Wilson and George L. Kelling, "Broken Windows," *The Atlantic Monthly,* (March 1982): 29–38.
56. Betsey Lindsay and Daniel McGillis, "Citywide Community Crime Prevention: An Assessment of the Seattle Program," in Dennis P. Rosenbaum, ed., *Community Crime Prevention: Does It Work?* (Beverly Hills, Calif.: Sage Publications, 1986).
57. Eck and Spelman, "Solving Problems: Problem-Oriented Policing."
58. Calls for service declined in Flint, Michigan, after foot patrol was established and officers were handling less serious complaints informally. Robert Trojanowicz, *An Evaluation of the Neighborhood Foot Patrol Program in Flint, Michigan* (East Lansing: Michigan State University, 1982), pp. 29–30.
59. George L. Kelling and Mary Ann Wycoff, *The Dallas Experience: Human Resource Development* (Washington, D.C.: Police Foundation, 1978); James Tien et al., *An Alternative Approach in Police Patrol: The Wilmington Split-Force Experiment* (Cambridge, Mass.: Public Systems Evaluation, Inc., 1977).

ARTICLE 4

POLICE AND COMMUNITIES: THE QUIET REVOLUTION

George L. Kelling

A quiet revolution is reshaping American policing.

Police in dozens of communities are returning to foot patrol. In many communities, police are surveying citizens to learn what they believe to be their most serious neighborhood problems. Many police departments are finding alternatives to rapidly responding to the majority of calls for service. Many departments are targeting resources on citizen fear of crime by concentrating on disorder. Organizing citizens' groups has become a priority in many departments. Increasingly, police departments are looking for means to evaluate themselves on their contribution to the quality of neighborhood life, not just crime statistics. Are such activities the business of policing? In a crescendo, police are answering yes.

True, such activities contrast with popular images of police: the "thin blue line" separating plundering villains from peaceful residents and storekeepers and racing through city streets in high-powered cars with sirens wailing and lights flashing. Yet, in city after city, a new vision of policing is taking hold of the imaginations of progressive police and gratified citizens. Note the 1987 report of the Philadelphia Task Force. Dismissing the notion of police as Philadelphia's professional defense against crime, and its residents as passive recipients of police ministrations, the report affirms new police values:

> Because the current strategy for policing Philadelphia emphasizes crime control and neglects the Department's need to be accountable to the public

Reprinted from George L. Kelling, "Police and Communities: The Quiet Revolution," *Perspectives on Policing,* no. 1 (Washington, D.C.: National Institute of Justice, U.S. Department of Justice, and the Program in Criminal Justice Policy and Management, John F. Kennedy School of Government, Harvard University, June 1988).

and for a partnership with it, the task force recommends: The police commissioner should formulate an explicit mission statement for the Department that will guide planning and operations toward a strategy of *"community"* or *"problem-solving"* policing. Such a statement should be developed in consultation with the citizens of Philadelphia and should reflect their views (emphasis added).

These themes—problem solving, community policing, consultation, partnership, accountability—have swept through American policing so swiftly that Harvard University's Professor Mark H. Moore has noted that "we in academe have to scramble to keep track of developments in policing." Professor Herman Goldstein of the University of Wisconsin sees police as "having turned a corner" by emphasizing community accountability and problem solving.

THE NEW MODEL OF POLICING

What corner has been turned? What are these changes that are advancing through policing?

Broken Windows

In February 1982, James Q. Wilson and I published an article in *Atlantic [The Atlantic Monthly]* known popularly as "Broken Windows." We made three points.

1. Neighborhood disorder—drunks, panhandling, youth gangs, prostitution, and other urban incivilities—creates citizens' fear.
2. Just as unrepaired broken windows can signal to people that nobody cares about a building and can lead to more serious vandalism, untended disorderly behavior can also signal that nobody cares about the community and can lead to more serious disorder and crime. Such signals—untended property, disorderly persons, drunks, obstreperous youth, etc.—both create fear in citizens and attract predators.
3. If police are to deal with disorder to reduce fear and crime, they must rely on citizens for legitimacy and assistance.

"Broken Windows" gave voice to sentiments felt by both citizens and police. It recognized a major change in the focus of police. Police had believed that they should deal with serious crime yet were frustrated by lack of success. Citizens conceded to police that crime was a problem but were more concerned about daily incivilities that disrupted and often destroyed neighborhood social, commercial, and political life. "We [were] trying to get people to be concerned about crime problems," says Darrel Stephens, former chief in Newport News and now executive director of the Police Executive Research Forum,* "never understanding that daily living issues had a much greater impact on citizens and commanded their time and attention."

Many police officials, however, believed the broken windows metaphor went further. For them, it not only suggested changes in the focus of police work (disorder, for example), it also suggested major modifications in the overall strategy of police departments. What are some of these strategic changes?

Defense of a Community

Police are a neighborhood's primary defense against disorder and crime, right? This orthodoxy has been the basis of police strategy for a generation. What is the police job? Fighting crime. How do they do this? Patrolling in cars, responding to calls for service, and investigating crimes. What is the role of citizens in all of this? Supporting police by calling them if trouble occurs and by being good witnesses.

But using our metaphor, let us again ask the question of whether police are the primary defense against crime and disorder. Are police the "thin blue line" defending neighborhoods and communities? Considering a specific example, should police have primary responsibility for controlling a neighborhood youth who, say, is bullying other children?

Of course not. The first line of defense in a neighborhood against a troublesome youth is the youth's family. Even if the family is failing, our immediate answer would not be to involve police. Extended family—aunts, uncles, grandparents—might become involved. Neighbors and friends (of both the parents and [the] youth) often offer assistance. The youth's church or school might become involved.

On occasion police will be called: suppose that the youth is severely bullying other children to the point of injuring them. A bullied child's parents call the police. Is the bully's family then relieved of responsibility? Are neighbors? The school? Once police are called, are neighbors relieved of their duty to be vigilant and protect their own or other neighbors' children? Does calling police relieve teachers of their obligation to be alert and protect children from assault? The answer to all these questions is no. We expect families, neighbors, teachers, and others to be responsible and prudent.

If we believe that community institutions are the first line of defense against disorder and crime and are the source of strength for maintaining the quality of life, what should the strategy of police be? The old view was that they were a community's professional defense against crime and disorder: citizens should leave control of crime and maintenance of order to police. The new strategy is that police are to stimulate and but-

---

*Darrel Stephens went on to serve as police chief in St. Petersburg, Florida, building a model community policing program, and now serves as city manager for St. Petersburg.–*Ed.*

tress a community's ability to produce attractive neighborhoods and protect them against predators. Moreover, in communities that are wary of strangers, police serve to help citizens tolerate and protect outsiders who come into their neighborhoods for social or commercial purposes.

But what about neighborhoods in which things have gotten out of hand—where, for example, predators like drug dealers take over and openly and outrageously deal drugs and threaten citizens? Clearly, police must play a leading role defending such communities. Should they do so on their own, however?

Police have tried in the past to control neighborhoods plagued by predators without involving residents. Concerned, for example, about serious street crime, police made youths, especially minority youths, the targets of aggressive field interrogations. The results, in the United States during the 1960s and more recently in England during the early 1980s, were disastrous. Crime was largely unaffected. Youths already hostile to police became even more so. Worst of all, good citizens became estranged from police.

Citizens in neighborhoods plagued by crime and disorder were disaffected because they simply would not have police they neither knew nor authorized whizzing in and out of their neighborhoods "takin' names and kickin' ass." Community relations programs were beside the point. Citizens were in no mood to surrender control of their neighborhoods to remote and officious police who showed them little respect! Police are the first line of defense in a neighborhood? Wrong—citizens are!

Defending Communities—From Incidents to Problems

The strategy of assisting citizens maintain the quality of life in their neighborhoods dramatically improves on the former police strategy. To understand why, one has to understand in some detail how police work has been conducted in the past. Generally, the business of police for the past 30 years has been responding to calls for service. For example, a concerned and frightened citizen calls police about a neighborhood husband and wife who are fighting. Police come and intervene. They might separate the couple, urge them to get help, or, if violence has occurred, arrest the perpetrator. But basically, police try to resolve the incident and get back into their patrol cars so they are available for the next call. Beat officers may well know that this household has been the subject of fifty or one hundred calls to the police department during the past year. In fact, they have known intuitively what researchers Glenn Pierce in Boston and Lawrence Sherman in Minneapolis have confirmed through research: fewer than 10 percent of the addresses calling for police services generate over 60 percent of the total calls for service during a given year.

Indeed, it is very likely that the domestic dispute described above is nothing new for the disputing couple, the neighbors, or police. More likely than not, citizens have previously called police and they have responded. And, with each call to police, it becomes more likely that there will be another.

This atomistic response to incidents acutely frustrates patrol officers. Herman Goldstein describes this frustration: "Although the public looks at the average officer as a powerful authority figure, the officer very often feels impotent because he or she is dealing with things for which he or she has no solution. Officers believe this makes them look silly in the eyes of the public." But, given the routine of police work, officers have had no alternative to their typical response: go to a call, pacify things, and leave to get ready for another call. To deal with the problem of atomistic responses to incidents, Goldstein has proposed what he calls "problem-oriented policing."

Stated simply, problem-oriented policing is a method of working with citizens to help them identify and solve problems. Darrel Stephens, along with Chief David Couper of Madison, Wisconsin, and Chief Neil Behan of Baltimore County, Maryland, has pioneered in problem-oriented policing. Problems approached via problem-oriented policing include sexual assault and drunk driving in Madison; auto theft, spouse abuse, and burglary in Newport News; and street robbery and burglary in Baltimore County.

Stephens' goal is for "police officers to take the time to stop and think about what they were doing." Mark Moore echoes Stephens: "In the past there were a small number of guys in the police chief's office who did the thinking and everybody else just carried out their ideas. Problem solving gets thousands of brains working on problems."

THE DRIVE TO CHANGE

Why are these changes taking place now? There are three reasons:

1. Citizen Disenchantment with Police Services.   At first, it seems too strong to say "disenchantment" when referring to citizens' attitudes towards police. Certainly citizens admire and respect most police officers. Citizens enjoy contact with police. Moreover, research shows that most citizens do not find the limited capability of police to prevent or solve crimes either surprising or of particular concern. Nevertheless, there is widespread disenchantment with police tactics that continues to keep police officers remote and distant from citizens.

Minority citizens in inner cities continue to be frustrated by police who whisk in and out of their neighborhoods with little sensitivity to community norms and values. Regardless of where one asks, minorities want both the familiarity and accountability that characterize foot patrol. Working—and middle-class—communities of all races are demanding increased collaboration with police in the determination of police priorities in their neighborhoods. Community crime control has become a mainstay of their sense of neighborhood security and a means of lobbying for different police services. And many merchants and affluent citizens have felt so vulnerable that they have turned to private security for service and protection. In private sector terms, police are losing to the competition—private security and community crime control.

2. Research Conducted During the 1970s.   The 1970s research about police effectiveness was another stimulus to change. Research about preventive patrol, rapid response to calls for service, and investigative work—the three mainstays of police tactics—was uniformly discouraging.

Research demonstrated that preventive patrol in automobiles had little effect on crime, citizen levels of fear, or citizen satisfaction with police. Rapid response to calls for service likewise had little impact on arrests, citizen satisfaction with police, or levels of citizen fear. Also, research into criminal investigation effectiveness suggested that detective units were so poorly administered that they had little chance of being effective.

3. Frustration with the Traditional Role of the Police Officer.   Finally, patrol officers have been frustrated with their traditional role. Despite pieties that patrol has been the backbone of policing, every police executive has known that, at best, patrol has been what officers do until they become detectives or are promoted.

At worst, patrol has been the dumping ground for officers who are incompetent, suffering from alcoholism or other problems, or simply burned out. High status for police practitioners went to detectives. Getting "busted to patrol" has been a constant threat to police managers or detectives who fail to perform by some standard of judgment. (It is doubtful that failing patrol officers ever get threatened with being busted to the detective unit.)

Never mind that patrol officers have the most important mission in police departments: they handle the public's most pressing problems and must make complex decisions almost instantaneously. Moreover, they do this with little supervision or training. Despite this, police administrators treat patrol officers as if they did little to advance the organization's mission. The salaries of patrol officers also reflect their demeaned status. No wonder many officers have grown cynical and have turned to unions for leadership rather than to police executives. "Stupid management made unions," says Robert Kliesmet, the president of the International Union of Police Associations AFL-CIO.

The Basis for New Optimism

Given these circumstances, what is the basis of [the] current optimism of police leaders that they have turned the corner? Optimism arises from four factors:

1. Citizen Response to the New Strategy.   The overwhelming public response to community and problem-solving policing has been positive, regardless of where it has been instituted. When queried about how he knows community policing works in New York City, Lt. Jerry Simpson responds: "The district commanders' phones stop ringing." Simpson continues: "Commanders' phones stop ringing because problems have been solved. Even skeptical commanders soon learn that most of their troubles go away with community policing." Citizens like the cop on the beat and enjoy working with him or her to solve problems. Crisley Network in Boston—an agency that has established a network of neighborhood crime control organizations—puts it this way: "The cop on the beat, who meets regularly with citizen groups, is the single most important service that the Boston Police Department can provide."

Testimonies aside, perhaps the single most compelling evidence of the popularity of community or problem-solving policing is found in Flint, Michigan, where, it will be recalled, citizens have twice voted to increase their taxes to maintain neighborhood foot patrols—the second time by a two-to-one margin.

2. Ongoing Research on Police Effectiveness.   Research conducted during the early and mid-1970s frustrated police executives. It generally showed what did not work. Research conducted during the late 1970s and early 1980s was different. By beginning to demonstrate that new tactics did work, [the results of this research] fueled the move to rejuvenate policing. This research provided police with the following guidance:

- Foot patrol can reduce citizen fear of crime, improve the relationship between police and citizens, and increase citizen satisfaction with police. This was discovered in Newark, New Jersey, and [in] Flint. In Flint, foot patrol also reduced crime and calls for service. Moreover, in both cities, it increased officer satisfaction with police work.
- The productivity of detectives can be enhanced if patrol officers carefully interview neighborhood residents about criminal events and get the information to detectives, and detectives use it wisely, according to John Eck of PERF [Police Executive Research Forum].
- Citizen fear can be substantially reduced, researcher Tony Pate of the Police Foundation discovered in Newark, by police tactics that emphasize increasing the quantity and improving the quality of citizen–police interactions.
- Police anti-fear tactics can also reduce household burglaries, according to research conducted by Mary Ann Wycoff, also of the Police Foundation.
- Street-level enforcement of heroin and cocaine laws can reduce serious crime in the area of enforcement without [crime] being displaced to adjacent areas, according to an experiment conducted by Mark Leiman of Harvard University's Program in Criminal Justice Policy and Management.
- Problem-oriented policing can be used to reduce thefts from cars, problems associated with prostitution, and household burglaries, according to William Spelman and John Eck of PERF.

These positive findings about new police tactics provide police with both the motive and justification for continued efforts to rejuvenate policing.

3. Past Experiences Police Have Had with Innovation.   The desire to improve policing is not new with this generation of reformers. The 1960s and 1970s had their share of reformers as well. Robert Eichelberger of Dayton innovated with team policing (tactics akin in many ways to problem solving) and public policy making; Frank Dyson of Dallas, with team policing and generalist/specialist patrol officers; and Carl Gooden, with team policing in Cincinnati. There were many other innovators.

But innovators of this earlier era were handicapped by a lack of documented successes and failures of implementation. Those who experimented with team policing were not aware that elements of team policing were simply incompatible with preventive patrol and rapid response to calls for service. As a result, implementation of team policing followed a discouraging pattern. It would be implemented, officers and citizens would like it, it would have an initial impact on crime, and then business as usual would overwhelm it—the program would simply vanish.

Moreover, the lessons about innovation and excellence that Peters and Waterman brought together in *In Search of Excellence* were not available to police administrators. The current generation of reformers has an edge: they have availed themselves of the opportunity to learn from the documented successes and failures of the past. Not content with merely studying innovation and management in policing, Houston's Chief Lee Brown is having key personnel spend internships in private sector corporations noted for excellence in management.

4. The Values of the New Generation of Police Leaders.   The new breed of police leadership is unique in the history of American policing. Unlike the tendency in the past for chiefs to be local and inbred, chiefs of this generation are urbane and cosmopolitan.

Chief Lee Brown of Houston received a Ph.D. in criminology from the University of California–Berkeley; Chief Joseph McNamara of San Jose, California, has a Ph.D. from Harvard University and is a published novelist; Hubert Williams, formerly director of the Newark Police Department and now president of the Police Foundation, is a lawyer and has studied criminology in the Law School at Harvard University; Benjamin Ward, commissioner of the New York City Police Department, is an attorney and was commissioner of corrections in New York State.

These are merely a sample. The point is, members of this generation of police leadership are well educated and of diverse backgrounds. All of those noted above, as well as many others, have sponsored research and experimentation to improve policing.

PROBLEMS

We have looked at the benefits of community policing. What is the down side? What are the risks?

These questions led to the creation of the Executive Session on Community Policing in the Program in Criminal Justice Policy and Management of Harvard University's John F. Kennedy School of Government.

Funded by the National Institute of Justice and the Charles Stewart Mott and Guggenheim Foundations, the Executive Session has convened police and political elites with a small number of academics around the issue of community policing. Francis X. Hartmann, moderator of the Executive Session, describes the purpose of the meetings: "These persons with a special and important relationship to contemporary policing have evolved into a real working group, which is addressing the gap between the realities and aspirations of American policing. Community policing is a significant effort to fill this gap."

Among the questions the Executive Session has raised are the following:

1. *Police are a valuable resource in a community. Does community policing squander that resource by concentrating on the wrong priorities?* This question worries police. They understand that police are a valuable but sparse resource in a community. Hubert Williams, a pioneer in community policing, expresses his concern: "Are police now being put in the role of providing services that are statutorily the responsibilities of some other agencies?" Los Angeles' Chief Gates echoes Williams: "Hubie's right—you can't solve all the problems in the world and shouldn't try." Both worry that if police are spread too thin, by problem-solving activities, for example, that they will not be able to properly protect the community from serious crime.

This issue is now being heatedly debated in Flint. There, it will be recalled, citizens have passed two bills funding foot patrol—the second by a two-to-one majority. A report commissioned by city government, however, concludes, "The cost of the neighborhood foot patrol program exceeds the benefit it provides the citizens of Flint," and recommends abandoning the program when funding expires in 1988.

Why, according to the report, should foot patrol be abandoned? So more "effective" police work can be done. What is effective police work? Quick response to calls for service, taking reports, and increased visibility by putting police officers in cars. "It is simply wrong," says Robert Wasserman, noted police tactician and Research Fellow in the Program in Criminal Justice at Harvard, "to propose abandoning foot patrol in the name of short response time and visibility vis-à-vis patrolling in cars. Every shred of evidence is that rapid response and patrolling in cars doesn't reduce crime, increase citizen satisfaction, or reduce fear. Which is the luxury," Wasserman concludes, "a tactic like foot patrol that gives you two, and maybe three, of your goals, or a tactic like riding around in cars going from call to call that gives you none?" Experienced police executives share Wasserman's concerns. Almost without exception, they are attempting to find ways to get out of the morass that myths of the efficacy of rapid response have created for large-city police departments. It was Commissioner Ben Ward of New York City, for example, who put a cap on resources that can be used to respond to calls for service and is attempting to find improved means of responding to calls. Commissioner Francis "Mickey" Roache expresses the deep frustration felt by so many police: "I hate to say this, but in Boston we run from one call to another.

We don't accomplish anything. We're just running all over the place. It's absolutely insane."

A politician's response to the recommendation to end Flint's foot patrol program is interesting. Daniel Whitehurst, former mayor of Fresno, California, reflects: "I find it hard to imagine ending a program that citizens not only find popular but are willing to pay for as well."

"The overwhelming danger," Mark Moore concludes, "is that, in the name of efficiency, police and city officials will be tempted to maintain old patterns. They will think they are doing good but will be squandering police resources." "Chips" Stewart emphasizes the need to move ahead: "As comfortable as old tactics might feel, police must continue to experiment with methods that have shown promise to improve police effectiveness and efficiency."

2. How will community policing fit into police departments, given how they are now organized? Many police and academics believe this to be the most serious problem facing cities implementing community policing. Modern police departments have achieved an impressive capacity to respond quickly to calls for service. This has been accomplished by acquiring and linking elaborate automobile, telephone, radio, and computer technologies; by centralizing control and dispatch of officers; by pressing officers to be "in service" (rather than "out of service"); and by allocating police in cars throughout the city on the basis of expected calls for service.

Community policing is quite different: it is not incident or technology-driven; officers operate on a decentralized basis; and it allocates officers being in regular contact with citizens; and it allocates police on the basis of neighborhoods. The question is, how reconcilable are these two strategies? Some (Lawrence Sherman of the University of Maryland is one example) have taken a strong stance that radical alterations will be required if police are to respond more effectively to community problems. Others (Richard Larson of the Massachusetts Institute of Technology, for example) disagree, believing that community policing is reconcilable with rapid response technology—indeed, Professor Larson would emphasize that current computer technology can facilitate community policing.

3. Will community policing open the door to increased corruption or other inappropriate behavior by line officers? The initial news from Houston, New York, Flint, Newark, Los Angeles, Baltimore County, and other police departments that have experimented with community policing is good. Community policing has not led to increased problems of corruption or misbehavior.

Why is it, however, that policy makers fear that community policing has the potential to increase the incidents of police running amok? The answer? Community policing radically decentralizes police authority; officers must create for themselves the best responses to problems; and police become intimately involved with citizens.

These ingredients may not sound so troublesome in themselves—after all, many private and public sector organizations radically decentralize authority, encourage creativity, and are characterized by relative intimacy between service providers and consumers. Nevertheless, in police circles, such ingredients violate the orthodox means of controlling corruption. For a generation, police have believed that to eliminate corruption it is necessary to centralize authority, limit discretion, and reduce intimacy between police and citizens. They had good reason to [believe this]: early policing in the United States had been characterized by financial corruption, failure of police to protect the rights of all citizens, and zealotry.

But just as it is possible to squander police resources in the name of efficiency, it is also possible to squander police resources in the quest for integrity. Centralization, standardization, and remoteness may preclude many opportunities for corruption, but they may also preclude the possibility of good policing. For example, street-level cocaine and heroin enforcement by patrol officers, now known to have crime-reduction value, has been banned in cities because of fear of corruption. It is almost as if the purpose of police was to be corruption-free, rather than to do essential work. If, as it appears to be, it is necessary to take risks to solve problems, then so be it; police will have to learn to manage risks as well as do managers in other enterprises.

Does this imply softening on the issue of police corruption? Absolutely not. Police and city managers will have to continue to be vigilant: community policing exposes officers to more opportunities for traditional financial corruption; in many neighborhoods police will be faced with demands to protect communities from the incursions of minorities; and police will be tempted to become overzealous when they see citizens' problems being ignored by other agencies.

These dangers mean, however, that police executives will have to manage through values rather than merely policies and procedures, and by establishing regular neighborhood and community institution reporting mechanisms rather than centralized command and control systems.

Each of these issues—use of police resources, organizational compatibility, and corruption—is complicated. Some will be the subject of debate. Others will require research and experimentation to resolve. But most police chiefs will begin to address these issues in a new way. They will not attempt to resolve them in the ways of the past: in secret, behind closed doors. Their approach will reflect the values of the individual neighborhoods as well as the community as a whole.

Policing is changing dramatically. On the one hand, we wish policing to retain the old values of police integrity, equitable distribution of police resources throughout a community, and police efficiency, which characterized the old model of police. But the challenge of contemporary police and city executives is to redefine these concepts in light of the resurgence of neighborhood vitality, consumerism, and more realistic assessments of the institutional capacity of police.

The quiet revolution is beginning to make itself heard: citizens and police are joining together to defend communities.

A R T I C L E 5

THE NEW POLICING:
CONFRONTING COMPLEXITY

Herman Goldstein

Community policing is well on its way to becoming a common term in households across the nation. That is a satisfying development for many but causes some anxiety and discomfort for others. What accounts for the mixed reactions?

Under the rubric of community policing, progressive police administrators and interested citizens have been working hard for more than a decade to design and implement a form of policing that better meets the extraordinary demands on the police in the 1990s. Within these circles, the term "community policing" has been used to embrace and intricately web together initiatives that have long been advocated for modern-day policing. These efforts have stimulated more productive thought and experimentation than has occurred at any previous time in the history of policing in this country. They have also created a new feeling of excitement and optimism in a field that has desperately needed both. It is understandable, therefore, why the current wave of popular support for community policing is so welcome in many quarters. It gives a tremendous impetus to these new initiatives.

The downside of this new-found popularity is that "community policing" is widely used without any regard for its substance. Political leaders latch onto the label for the positive image it evokes but do not invest in the concept itself. Some police personnel resist community policing initiatives because of the belief that they constitute an effort to placate an overly demanding and critical segment of the community that is intent on exercising more control over police operations.

Reprinted from Herman Goldstein, "The New Policing: Confronting Complexity," *National Institute of Justice, Research in Brief* (Washington, D.C.: U.S. Department of Justice, December 1993).

Indeed, the popularity of the term has resulted in its being used to encompass practically all innovations in policing, from the most ambitious to the most mundane, from the most carefully thought through to the most casual. The label is being used in ways that increase public expectations that community policing will provide an instant solution not only for the problems of crime, disorder, and racial tension but for many of the other acute problems that plague our urban areas as well.

With such varied meanings and such broad expectations, the use of "community policing" creates enormous problems for those seriously interested in bringing about meaningful change in the American police. Carefully developed initiatives bearing the community policing label, fragile by their very nature, are endangered because superficial programs are so vulnerable to attack.

One reaction to this dilemma is to press for definition and simplification, to seek agreement on a pure model of community policing. This pressure for simplification is joined by well-intentioned practitioners who, understandably, want to know—in specific detail—what they are supposed to do. *Oversimplification,* however, can be a deadly enemy to progress in policing. The field already suffers because so much in policing is oversimplified.

Crime, violence, and disorder, for example, are simple, convenient terms, but they disguise amorphous, complex problems. Their common and indiscriminate use, especially in defining the responsibilities of the police, places a heavy burden on the police and complicates the police task. The police respond with law enforcement and patrol—equally simple terms commonly used by the public without any awareness of the methods they embrace and their value. If community policing takes its place alongside law enforcement or patrol as just another generic response to a simplistic characterization of the police function, not much will have been gained and the concept will quickly lose its credibility.

RETHINKING THE POLICE ROLE

The policing of a free, diverse, and vibrant society is an awesome and complex task. The police are called upon to deal with a wide array of quite different behavioral problems, each perplexing in its own way. The police have tremendous power—to deny freedom and to use force, even to take a life. Individual officers exercise enormous discretion in using their authority and in making decisions that affect our lives. The very quality of life in this country and the equilibrium of our cities depend upon the way in which the police function is carried out.

Given the awesome and complex nature of the police function, it follows that designing the arrangements and the organization to carry it out is equally complex. We are now in a period in which more attention is being given to the police function than at any prior time, a period in which we are rethinking, in all of its multiple dimensions, the arrangement for the policing of our society. We should not, therefore, lose patience because we have not yet come up with the perfect model; we should not get stalled trying to simplify change just to give uniform meaning to a single, catchy, and politically attractive term. We need to open up explorations rather than close them down. We need to better understand the complicated rather than search for the simple.

Some of the most common changes associated with community policing are already being implemented; for example, the permanent assignment of officers to specific beats with a mandate to get to know and relate to the community. There is now growing and persuasive support for decentralization, permanent assignments, and the development of "partnerships" between the police and the community. But these changes represent only a fragment of the larger picture.

Policing in the United States is much like a large, intricate, complex apparatus with many parts. Change of any one part requires changes in many others and in the way the parts fit and work together. For example, altering the way officers are assigned and how they patrol may be easy. But to gain full value from such changes and to sustain them, changes are also necessary in the organization and leadership of the police department—in the staffing, supervision, training, and recruitment, and in its internal working environment. Thus, a change in direction requires more than tinkering. It requires, if it is to be effective, simultaneous changes in many areas affecting the enterprise. This, in turn, requires careful planning and coordination. And perhaps most important, it requires time, patience, and learning from experience.

Moreover, to succeed in improving policing, we need to move beyond the exclusive focus on the police *agency.* There is an urgent need to alter the public's expectations of the police. And we need to revise the fundamental provisions that we as a society make for carrying out the police function. For example:

- Refine the authority granted the police (curtail it in some areas and expand it in others).
- Recognize the discretion exercised by the police and provide a means for its review and control.
- Provide the police with the resources that will enable them to get their job done.

We need, in other words, without compromising our commitment to democratic values, to bring expectations and capacity more into harmony so that a job increasingly labeled as "impossible" can be carried out.

THE NATURE OF CHANGE

To illustrate, in some detail, the complexity of change in policing, it is helpful to examine five spheres in which change is now occurring. What types of issues arise? And what is the interrelationship and interdependence among the factors involved in these changes?

1. Refining the Police Function and Public Expectations

The new form of policing expands the police function from crime fighting, without any abdication of that role, to include maintaining order, dealing with quality-of-life offenses, and fixing "broken windows"—all now recognized as being much more important than previously believed. The police have become more proactive, committed to preventing incidents rather than simply *reacting* to them. These shifts in emphasis appear to have gained widespread support.

But we need to be aware of the avalanche of business that this expansion of the police function invites, lest it constitute a serious self-inflicted wound. The volume and nature of the miscellaneous tasks that accrue to the police are many. Cutbacks in other government services only add to their number. In areas that are starved for social services, the slightest improvement in police response increases the demand on the police. As water seeks its own level, the vast array of problems that surface in a large urban area inevitably find their way to the agency most willing to accept them.

For example, consider the officer assigned to a specific neighborhood with a broad mandate to improve service. Within a very short period of time, that officer will be overwhelmed by the need for services that— despite the greatest creativity and resourcefulness—far exceeds his or her capacity to deliver.

Very often the police *can* do more to satisfy citizen needs. They can identify problems and take actions that result in mitigating or solving them when they are given the time and license to do so. But in the larger scheme of things, the need to reduce public expectations is every bit as important as the need to broaden the police function—not simply to make limited resources fit the demand, but for more complex reasons. Many of the most troublesome aspects of policing stem from the pressure that has been exerted on the police to appear omnipotent, to do more than they are authorized, trained, and equipped to do.

Police tend to like challenges. But the challenges to fill needs, to live up to expectations, can lead to the taking of shortcuts, the stretching of authority and, as a consequence, the potential for abuse of that authority. It is demoralizing to the thoughtful, dedicated officer to create the expectation that he or she can do more than take the edge off some of the more intractable problems that the police confront.

The new policing seeks to make the police job more achievable by realigning what the police do and do not do, by giving higher priority to some tasks and lower priority to others, by reducing public expectations and leveling with the public about police capacity, by engaging the public in taking steps to help themselves, and by connecting with other agencies and the private sector in ways that ensure that citizens referred to them will be helped. There is a need to invest much more in our individual communities in working through the questions that arise in trying to achieve this better alignment.

2. Getting Involved in the Substance of Policing

A common theme in initiatives under the community policing umbrella is the emphasis on improving relationships with the citizenry. Such improvement is vital in order to reduce tensions, develop mutual trust, promote the free exchange of information, and acquaint officers with the culture and lifestyle of those being policed.

Improved relationships are important. They would constitute a major advance in some cities. But many would argue that they merely lay a groundwork and create an environment in which to strive for more. When citizens ask if community policing works, they are not so much interested in knowing if the community likes the police or if the police are getting along with the community. Rather, they usually want to know if the community policing initiative has had an impact on the problems of concern to them: their fear of using the streets, the abandoned cars in the neighborhood, the gang that has been intimidating them. If the initiatives that have been taken do not go beyond improving relationships, there is a risk that community policing will become just another means by which police operate without having a significant, demonstrable impact on the problems the police are expected to handle.

This tendency in policing to become preoccupied with means over ends is obviously not new. It was this concern that gave rise to the work on problem-oriented policing. The police must give more substance to community policing by getting more involved in analyzing and responding to the specific problems citizens bring to their attention. This calls for a much heavier investment by the police in understanding the varied pieces of their business, just as the medical field invests in understanding different diseases. It means that police, more than anyone else, should have a detailed understanding of such varied problems as homicides involving teenage victims, drive-by shootings, and carjackings. And it means that a beat officer should have in-depth knowledge about the corner drug house, the rowdy teenage gang that assembles at the convenience store on Friday night, and the panhandler who harasses passersby on a given street corner. Analyzing each of these quite different problems in depth leads to the realization that what may work for one will not work for the other and that each may require a different combination of different responses. That is the beginning of wisdom in policing: One size clearly does not fit all.

Problem solving is being integrated into community policing initiatives in many jurisdictions. It dominates the commitment to change in some jurisdictions. Conference and training sessions for police have, with increased frequency, focused on such problems as the homeless, family violence, high-risk youth, child abuse, and school violence.

More of the momentum associated with community policing must be focused on these and similar problems. Smarter policing in this country requires a sustained effort within policing to research substantive problems, to make use of the mass of information and data on specific problems accumulated by individual police agencies, to experiment with different alternative responses, to evaluate these efforts, and to share the results of these evaluations with police across the nation. It would be useful to do more to reorient the work of research and development units in police departments and to entice some of the best minds in the field of criminology and related specialties to assist in these efforts. The police should not only make greater use of research done by others; they should themselves be engaged in research.

3. Rethinking the Relationship between the Police and the Criminal Justice System

Buried in all of the rhetoric relating to community policing is the fact that, with little notice and in subtle ways, the longstanding relationship between the police and the criminal justice system is being redefined. This is a radical change, but it is given scant attention in the literature on community policing. And the full consequences of the changes—and their relationship to some of the developments most commonly associated with community policing—have not been adequately explored.

The enforcement of criminal law is inherent in the police role. The great emphasis on enforcement affects the shape of their organizations, the attitudes and priorities of their personnel, and their relationship with the community. Significantly, police officers are referred to as "law enforcement officers." The felt need for objectivity and neutrality in law enforcement often results in the police being characterized as having no discretion. And the commitment to enforcement encourages the police to act in ways designed to inflate the public's impression of their capacity to enforce the law in the hope that their image alone will reduce crime and disorder.

Advanced forms of community policing reject many of the characteristics stemming from the emphasis on enforcement. A neighborhood police officer, for example, is expected to have a much broader interest than simply enforcing the criminal law, to exhaust a wide range of alternatives before resorting to arrest for minor offenses, to exercise broad discretion, and to depend more on resourcefulness, persuasion, or cajoling than on coercion, image, or bluff.

Reconciling these different perspectives has always been difficult. Some would even argue the two postures are incompatible. Simplistically, they are often distinguished as the "hard" and "soft" approaches in policing. But as a result of a sequence of developments in the past decade, the difference between the two approaches has diminished.

What has happened? So long as the police were intricately intertwined with the criminal justice system, they came to depend more heavily on the system. Thus, as violence and, especially, crimes associated with drugs increased, the police made more and more arrests of serious offenders. And to deal with disorder on the streets they arrested thousands of minor offenders as well, often stretching their authority somewhat (as police are pressured to do) in order to restore order. Predictably, the criminal justice system in most large urban areas, and many smaller ones as well, has been overwhelmed to the point that it is no longer possible for the system to accept some serious offenders, let alone minor offenders.

The consequences of recognizing that the capacity of the criminal justice system has limits are more far-reaching than is commonly recognized. Police can no longer use arrest, as they so freely did in the past, to deal with a wide variety of ambiguous situations. Moreover, the aura of authority on which the police have so heavily depended for getting so much of their job done, rooted in the capacity to arrest, has been greatly diminished. Police officers today simply do not appear as powerful and threatening to those who most frequently come in contact with them because they can no longer use the criminal justice system as they once did.

What does this mean for some of the central themes under the community policing umbrella? It means that there are new, pragmatic reasons for searching intensively for alternatives to the criminal justice system as the way in which to get the police job done.

It also means that there is now an added incentive to cultivate positive relationships with the community. The police need to replace the amorphous authority that they previously derived from the criminal justice system and on which they depended so heavily in the past. What better way to do this than arm themselves with what Robert Peel characterized in 1829 as that most powerful form of authority, the "public approval of their existence, actions, and behavior"?

The congested state of affairs in the criminal justice system means, too, that the police must reserve their use of that system for those situations in which it is most appropriate and potentially most effective. This latter need should lead the police and others committed to community policing to join [U.S.] Attorney General Janet Reno in speaking out for a more sensible national criminal justice policy that curbs the indiscriminate overuse of a system that will, if not checked, draw scarce funds away from preventive programs where those funds can do more good.

4. Searching for Alternatives

The diversification of policing—the move from primary dependence on the criminal law to the use of a wide range of different responses—is among the most significant changes under the community policing umbrella. It enables the police to move away from having to "use a hammer (the criminal justice system) to catch a fly"; it enables them to fine-tune their responses. It gives them a range of options (or tools) that in number and variety comes closer to matching the number and variety of problems they are expected to handle. These may include informal, common sense responses used in the past but never formally authorized.

The primary and most immediate objective in authorizing the police to use a greater range of alternatives is to improve police effectiveness. Quite simply, mediating a dispute, abating a nuisance, or arranging to have some physical barrier removed—without resorting to arrest—may be the best way to solve a problem.

But there are additional benefits in giving police officers a larger repertoire of responses. Currently, for example, one of the greatest impediments to improvement in policing is the strength of the police subculture. That subculture draws much of its strength from a secret shared among police: that they are compelled to bend the law and take shortcuts in order to get their job done. Providing the police with legitimate, clearcut means to carry out their functions enables them to operate more honestly and openly and, therefore, has the potential for reducing the strength and, as a consequence, the negative influence of the police subculture.

The diversification of options is also responsive to one of the many complexities in the staffing of police agencies. It recognizes, forthrightly, the important role of the individual police officer as a decision maker—a role the officer has always had but one that has rarely been acknowledged. Acknowledging and providing alternatives contribute toward redefining the job of a police officer by placing a value on thinking, on creativity, and on decision making. It credits the officer with having the ability to analyze incidents and problems and gives the officer the freedom to choose among various appropriate responses.

Changing to a system in which so much responsibility is invested in the lowest level employee, one who already operates with much independence on the streets, will not occur quickly or easily. And absent sufficient preparation, the results may be troublesome. This is especially so if officers, in their enthusiasm, blend together community support and their desire to please the community to justify using methods that are either illegal or improper. And implementation in a department that has a record of abuse or corruption is obviously much more problematic. Those concerned about control, however, must recognize that the controls on which we currently depend are much less effective than they are often thought to be. Preparations for the empowerment of officers requires changes in recruitment standards and training, establishing guidelines for the exercise of discretion, and inculcating values in officers that, in the absence of specific directions, guide their decision making. Meeting these needs in turn connects with the fifth and final dimension of change.

5. Changing the Working Environment in a Police Agency

If new forms of policing are to take hold, the working environment within police agencies must change. Much has been written about new management styles supportive of community policing. But with a few remarkable exceptions relatively little has actually been achieved. And where modest changes have been made they are often lost when a change in administration occurs or when the handling of a single incident brings embarrassment, resulting in a reversion to the old style of control.

"Working environment" means simply the atmosphere and expectations that superiors set in relating to their subordinates. In a tradition-bound department, managers, supported by voluminous, detailed rules, tend to exercise a tight, paramilitary, top-down form of control—perhaps reflecting the way in which they have historically sought to achieve control in the community.

The initiatives associated with community policing cannot survive in a police agency managed in traditional ways. If changes are not made, the agency sets itself up for failure. Officers will not be creative and will not take initiatives if a high value continues to be placed on conformity. They will not be thoughtful if they are required to adhere to regulations that are thoughtless. And they will not aspire to act as mature, responsible adults if their superiors treat them as immature children.

But properly trained and motivated officers, given the freedom to make decisions and act independently, will respond with enthusiasm. They will grasp the concept, appreciate its many dimensions, and skillfully fill their new roles. These officers will solve problems, motivate citizens to join together to do things for themselves, and create a feeling of security and goodwill. Equally important, the officers will find their work demanding but very satisfying. In rank-and-file officers, there exists an enormous supply of talent, energy, and commitment that, under quality leadership, could rapidly transform American policing.

The major impediment to tapping this wellspring has been a failure to engage and elicit a commitment from those having management and supervisory responsibilities. It is disheartening to witness a meeting of the senior staff of a police agency in which those in attendance are disconnected and often openly hostile to changes initiated by the chief executive and supported by a substantial proportion of the rank and file. It is equally disheartening to talk with police officers on the street and officers of lower supervisory rank who cite their *superior officer* as their major problem, rather than the complexity of their job.

Because the problem is of such magnitude, perhaps some bold—even radical—steps by legislative bodies and municipal chief executives may be necessary. Perhaps early retirement should be made more attractive for police executives who resist change. Perhaps consideration should be given to proposals recently made in England that call for the elimination of unnecessary ranks, and for making continuation in rank conditional on periodic review.

But before one can expect support for such measures, the public will need to be satisfied that police executives have exhausted whatever means are available to them for turning the situation around. When one looks at what has been done, it is troubling to find that a department's investment in the reorientation of management and supervisory personnel often consisted of no more than "a day at the academy"—and sometimes not even that. How much of the frustration in eliciting support from management and supervision stems from the fact that agencies have simply not invested enough in engaging senior officers, in explaining why change is necessary, and in giving these supervisors and managers the freedom required for them to act in their new role?

Some efforts to deal with the problem have been encouraging. The adoption of Total Quality Management [TQM] in policing has demonstrated very positive results and holds much promise. It ought to be encouraged. An important lesson can be learned from experiences with TQM. Training to support changes of the magnitude now being advocated in policing requires more than a one-shot effort consisting of a few classroom lectures. It requires a substantial commitment of time in different settings spread over a long period, a special curriculum, the best facilitators, and the development of problems, case studies, and exercises that engage the participants. It requires the development of teamwork in which subordinates contribute as much as superiors. And it requires that the major dimension of the training take the form of conscious change in the day-to-day interaction of personnel—not in a training setting, but on the job.

CONCLUSION

Dwelling on complexity is risky, for it can be overwhelming and intimidating. It is difficult. It turns many people off. But for those who get involved, the results can be very rewarding.

There have been extraordinary accomplishments in policing in the past two decades by police agencies that have taken on some of these difficult tasks. There is an enormous reservoir of ability and commitment in police agencies, especially among rank-and-file officers, and a willingness on the part of individual citizens and community groups at the grassroots level to engage with the police and support change. Viewed collectively, these achievements should be a source of optimism and confidence. By building on past progress and capitalizing on current momentum, change that is deeper and more lasting can be achieved.

But there is an even more compelling, overriding incentive to struggle with these complexities. We are being challenged today to commit ourselves anew to our unique character as a democracy, to the high value we as a nation place on diversity, ensuring equality, protecting individual rights, and guaranteeing that all citizens can move about freely and enjoy tranquil lives. The social problems that threaten the character of the nation are increasing, not decreasing. It will take major changes—apart from those in the police—to reduce these problems. In this turbulent period, it is more important than ever that we have a police capacity that is sensitive, effective, and responsive to the country's unique needs and that, above all else, is committed to protecting and extending democratic values. That is a high calling indeed.

PART 3

COMMUNITY POLICING:
A SYSTEMIC APPROACH

Community policing is first and foremost a philosophy, but it is also, more pragmatically, a systemic approach to policing. While guided by the philosophical underpinnings, community policing is adopted through changes in the way police conduct their business and how they interact with the community. It is imperative that a movement to community policing be complimented with changes in the way policing is performed, that all members of the police department be involved, and that every member of the community have an equal opportunity to become involved in the community policing initiatives. These various initiatives can be separated into three components: strategic-oriented policing, neighborhood-oriented policing, and problem-oriented policing. Strategic-oriented policing describes police-initiated activities that target specific criminal or order-maintenance problems to reduce the level of crime, fear of crime, or disorder. An example is police crackdowns. Neighborhood-oriented policing consists of any type of patrols that effectively bring the police and the community together, either through simple contact and interaction to actual participation in addressing the problems of crime and disorder. Finally, problem-oriented policing is the adoption of a problem-solving model to a police-community partnership, whereby they work together to identify problems in their community, create solutions to these problems, implement an agreed-upon solution, and evaluate the success of the solution. Taken together, these three components, adopted by all members of the police department and in concert with the community, create a systemic approach to change under the philosophy of community policing.

The first selection for this section is by Mark H. Moore and Robert C. Trojanowicz. In an earlier article they, along with George L. Kelling, discussed the implications of serious crime and policing (see part 2, article 3). In this article, they discuss the impact that fear of crime has on a community and hence, the impact it has, or should have, on policing. They then discuss a variety of police strategies for reducing fear of crime in the community, primarily through the three components of community policing.

The second selection is by George L. Kelling and Mark H. Moore. This article explores police strategies for dealing with crime from a historical perspective, leading up to what they term the "community problem-solving era." They then discuss the various changes police departments make under community policing, focusing on the three components.

The third selection is by the Community Policing Consortium, written and disseminated through a grant from the Bureau of Justice Assistance, U.S. Department of Justice. This article originally appeared as a monograph in August of 1994 and provides a basic foundation to understanding the systemic approach to policing. It specifically focuses on two of the components of community policing: neighborhood-oriented and problem-oriented policing. Because it has received a high level of exposure, because it has been well received by both academics and practitioners, and because it is a collaboration by a number of well-respected community policing researchers, "Understanding Community Policing" has become a classic in the community policing literature.

The fourth selection is by Malcolm K. Sparrow and has become a classic because it was one of the first articles to talk about implementing community policing and provided a nice comparison of traditional and community policing in box format. It is a short article, but one that has had a large impact upon a number of police practitioners attempting to implement the systemic approach to policing.

The fifth selection is by Lawrence W. Sherman from the University of Maryland. In this article, he describes the concept of a "police crackdown" and explains how these crackdowns can be employed successfully and what their drawbacks are. Police crackdowns have been widely employed as a community policing initiative to target crime and order-maintenance problems and is considered one form of strategic-oriented policing.

The final selection for this section is by John E. Eck and William Spelman. The cute title, referring to the late 1980s hit movie "Ghostbusters," may misrepresent a very important article detailing the pragmatic adoption of problem-oriented policing as originally articulated by Herman Goldstein (see part 1, article 2). In this article, the authors review two case studies, conducted in Baltimore, Maryland, and Newport News, Virginia, and describe how successful the problem-oriented approach to policing can be and why it has become, and needs to be, a key component of community policing.

POLICING AND THE FEAR OF CRIME

Mark H. Moore and Robert C. Trojanowicz

When crimes occur—when a ghetto teenager is shot to death in a gang war, when an elderly woman is mugged for her Social Security check, when a nurse is raped in a hospital parking lot, when one driver is punched by another in a dispute over a parking place, when a black family's new home is vandalized—society's attention is naturally focused on the victims and their material losses. Their wounds, bruises, lost property, and inconvenience can be seen, touched, and counted. These are the concrete signs of criminal victimization.

Behind the immediate, concrete losses of crime victims, however, is a different, more abstract crime problem—that of fear. For victims, fear is often the largest and most enduring legacy of their victimization. The raped nurse will feel vulnerable long after her cuts and bruises heal. The harassed black family suffers far more from the fear of neighborhood hostility than the inconvenience of repairing their property.

For the rest of us—the not-recently, or not-yet victimized—fear becomes a contagious agent spreading the injuriousness of criminal victimization. The gang member's death makes parents despair of their children's future. The mugging of the elderly woman teaches elderly residents to fear the streets and the teenagers who roam them. The fight over the parking place confirms the general fear of strangers. The harassment of the black family makes other minorities reluctant to claim their rights. In these ways, fear extends the damage of criminal victimization.

Reprinted from Mark H. Moore and Robert C. Trojanowicz, "Policing and the Fear of Crime," *Perspectives on Policing*, no. 3 (Washington, D.C.: National Institute of Justice, U.S. Department of Justice, and the Program in Criminal Justice Policy and Management, John F. Kennedy School of Government, Harvard University, June 1988).

Of course, fear is not totally unproductive. It prompts caution among citizens and thereby reduces criminal opportunities. Too, it motivates citizens to shoulder some of the burdens of crime control by buying locks and dogs, thereby adding to general deterrence. And fear kindles enthusiasm for publicly supported crime control measures. Thus, reasonable fears, channeled in constructive directions, prepare society to deal with crime. It is only when fear is unreasonable, or generates counterproductive responses, that it becomes a social problem.

This paper explores fear as a problem to be addressed by the police. It examines current levels and recent trends in the fear of crime; analyzes how fear is linked to criminal victimization; considers the extent to which fear is a distinct problem that invites separate control strategies; and assesses the positive and negative social consequences of fear. It then turns to what is known about the efficacy of police strategies for managing fear, i.e., reducing fear when it is irrational and destructive, and for channeling fear along constructive paths when it is reasonable and helpful in controlling crime.

THE FEAR OF CRIME

Society does not yet systematically collect data on fear. Consequently, our map of fear—its levels, trends, and social location—is sketchy. Nonetheless, its main features are easily identified.

First, fear is widespread. The broadest impact was registered by "The Figgie Report on Fear of Crime," released in 1980. Two-fifths of Americans surveyed reported that they were "highly fearful" they would become victims of violent crime.[1] Similar results were reported by the Harris poll of 1975, which found that 55 percent of all adults said they felt "uneasy" walking their own streets.[2] The Gallup poll of 1977 found that about 45 percent of the population (61 percent of the women and 28 percent of the men) were afraid to walk alone at night.[3] An eight-city victimization survey published in 1977 found that 45 percent of all respondents limited their activities because of fear of crime.[4] A statewide study in Michigan reported that 66 percent of respondents avoided certain places because of fear of crime.[5] Interviews with a random sample of Texans in 1978 found that more than half said that they feared becoming a serious crime victim within a year.[6]

Second, fear of crime increased from the late 1960s to the mid-1970s, then began decreasing during the mid-1970s. According to the 1968 Gallup poll, 44 percent of the women and 16 percent of the men said that they were afraid to walk alone at night. In 1977, when a similar question was asked, 61 percent of the women and 28 percent of the men reported they were afraid to walk alone at night—an increase of 17 percent for women and 12 percent for men.[7] In 1975, a Harris poll found that 55 percent of all adults felt "uneasy" walking their own streets. In 1985, this number had fallen to 32 percent—a significant decline.[8]

Third, fear is not evenly distributed across the population. Predictably, those who feel themselves most vulnerable are also the most fearful. Looking at the distribution of fear across the age and sex categories, the greatest levels of fear are reported by elderly women. The next most frightened group seems to be all other women. The least afraid are young men. Looking at race, class, and residence variables, blacks are more afraid of crime than whites, the poor are more afraid than the middle class or wealthy, and inner-city dwellers are more afraid than suburbanites.[9]

Indeed, while the current national trend may show a decline in fear, anecdotal evidence suggests that this trend has not yet reached America's ghettos. There, fear has become a condition of life. Claude Brown describes Harlem's problem in 1985:

> . . . In any Harlem building . . . every door has at least three locks on it. Nobody opens a door without first finding out who's there. In the early evening . . . you see people . . . lingering outside nice apartment houses, peeking in the lobbies. They seem to be casing the joint. They are actually trying to figure out who is in the lobby of their building. "Is this someone waiting to mug me? Should I risk going in, or should I wait for someone else to come?"
>
> If you live in Harlem, USA, you don't park your automobile two blocks from your apartment house, because that gives potential muggers an opportunity to get a fix on you. You'd better find a parking space within a block of your house, because if you have to walk two blocks you're not going to make it . . .
>
> In Harlem, elderly people walking their dogs in the morning cross the street when they see some young people coming . . . And what those elderly men and women have in the paper bags they're carrying is not just a pooper scooper—it's a gun. And if those youngsters cross the street, somebody is going to get hurt.[10]

These findings suggest that one of the most important privileges one acquires as one gains wealth and status in American society is the opportunity to leave the fear of crime behind. The unjust irony is that "criminals walk city streets, while fear virtually imprisons groups like women and the elderly in their homes."[11] James K. Stewart, Director of the National Institute of Justice, traces the important long-run consequences of this uneven distribution of fear for the economic development of our cities: if the inner-city populations are afraid of crime, then commerce and investment essentially disappear, and with them, the chance for upward social mobility.[12] If Hobbes is correct in asserting that the most fundamental purpose of civil government is to establish order and protect citizens from the fear of criminal attack that made life "nasty, brutish, and short" in the "state of nature," then the current level and distribution of fear indicate an important governmental failure.[13]

THE CAUSES OF FEAR

In the past, fear was viewed as primarily caused by criminal victimization. Hence, the principal strategy for controlling crime was reducing criminal victimization. More recently, we have learned that while fear of crime is associated with criminal victimization, the relationship is less close than originally assumed.[14]

The association between victimization and fear is seen most closely in the aggregate patterns across time and space. Those who live in areas with high crime rates are more afraid and take more preventive action than people living in areas where the risk of victimization is lower.[15] The trends in levels of fear seem to mirror (perhaps with a lag) trends in levels of crime.

Yet, the groups that are most fearful are not necessarily those with the highest victimization rates; indeed, the order is exactly reversed. Elderly women, who are most afraid, are the least frequently victimized. Young men, who are least afraid, are most often victimized.[16] Even more surprisingly, past victimization has only a small impact on levels of fear; people who have heard about others' victimizations are almost as fearful as those who have actually been victimized.[17] And when citizens are asked about the things that frighten them, there is little talk about "real crimes," such as robbery, rape, and murder. More often there is talk about other signs of physical decay and social disorganization, such as "junk and trash in vacant lots, boarded up buildings, stripped and abandoned cars, bands of teenagers congregating on street corners, street prostitution, panhandling, public drinking, verbal harassment of women, open gambling and drug use, and other incivilities."[18]

In accounting for levels of fear in communities, Wesley Skogan divides the contributing causes into five broad categories: (1) actual criminal victimization; (2) secondhand information about criminal victimization distributed through social networks; (3) physical deterioration and social disorder; (4) the characteristics of the built environment (i.e., the physical composition of the housing stock); and (5) group conflict.[19] He finds the strongest effects on fear arising from physical deterioration, social disorder, and group conflict.[20] The impact of the built environment is hard to detect once one has subtracted the effects of other variables influencing levels of fear. A review article by Charles Murray also found little evidence of a separate effect of the built environment on fear. The only exception to this general conclusion is evidence indicating that improved street lighting can sometimes produce significant fear reductions.[21]

The important implication of these research results is that fear might be attacked by strategies other than those that directly reduce criminal victimization. Fear might be reduced even without changes in levels of victimization by using the communications within social networks to provide accurate information about risks of criminal victimization and advice about constructive responses to the risk of crime; by eliminating the external signs of physical decay and social disorder; and by more effectively regulating group conflict between young and old, whites and minority groups, rich and poor. The more intriguing possibility, however, is that if fear could be rationalized and constructively channeled, not only would fear and its adverse consequences be ameliorated, but also real levels of victimization reduced. In this sense, the conventional understanding of this problem would be reversed: instead of controlling victimization to control fear, we would manage fear to reduce victimization. To understand this possibility, we must explore the consequences of fear—not only as ends in themselves, but also as means for helping society deal with crime.

THE ECONOMIC AND SOCIETAL CONSEQUENCES OF FEAR: COSTS AND BENEFITS

Fear is a more or less rational response to crime. It produces social consequences through two different mechanisms. First, people are uncomfortable emotionally. Instead of luxuriating in the peace and safety of their homes, they feel vulnerable and isolated. Instead of enjoying the camaraderie of trips to school, grocery stores, and work, they feel anxious and afraid. Since these are less happy conditions than feeling secure, fear produces an immediate loss in personal well-being.

Second, fear motivates people to invest time and money in defensive measures to reduce their vulnerability. They stay indoors more than they would wish, avoid certain places, buy extra locks, and ask for special protection to make bank deposits. Since this time, effort, and money could presumably be spent on other things that make people happier, such expenditures must also be counted as personal costs which, in turn, become social costs as they aggregate.

These are far from trivial issues. The fact that two-fifths of the population is afraid and that the nation continues to nominate crime as one of its greatest concerns means that society is living less securely and happily than is desirable. And if 45 percent of the population restricts its daily behavior to minimize vulnerability, and the nation spends more than $20 billion on private security protection, then private expenditures on reducing fear constitute a significant component of the national economy.[22] All this is in addition to the $40 billion that society spends publicly on crime control efforts.[23] In short, fear of crime claims a noticeable share of the nation's welfare and resources.

Fear has a further effect. Individual responses to fear aggregate in a way that erodes the overall quality of community life and, paradoxically, the overall capacity of society to deal with crime.[24] This occurs when the defensive reactions of individuals essentially compromise community life, or when they exacerbate the disparities between rich and poor by relying too much on private rather than public security.

Skogan has described in detail the mechanisms that erode community life:

> Fear . . . can work in conjunction with other factors to stimulate more rapid neighborhood decline. Together, the spread of fear and other local problems provide a form of positive feedback that can further increase levels of crime.

These feedback processes include (1) physical and psychological withdrawal from community life; (2) a weakening of the informal social control processes that inhibit crime and disorder; (3) a decline in the organizational life and mobilization capacity of the neighborhood; (4) deterioration of business conditions; (5) the importation and domestic production of delinquency and deviance; and (6) further dramatic changes in the composition of the population. At the end lies a stage characterized by demographic collapse.[25]

Even if fear does not destroy neighborhood life, it can damage it by prompting responses that protect some citizens at the expense of others, thereby leading to greater social disparities between rich and poor, resourceful and dependent, well-organized and anomic communities. For example, when individuals retreat behind closed doors and shuttered windows, they make their own homes safer. But they make the streets more dangerous, for there are fewer people watching and intervening on the streets. Or, when individuals invest in burglar alarms or private security guards rather than spending more on public police forces, they may make themselves safer, but leave others worse off because crime is deflected onto others.

Similarly, neighborhood patrols can make residents feel safe. But they may threaten and injure other law-abiding citizens who want to use the public thoroughfares. Private security guards sometimes bring guns and violence to situations that would otherwise be more peaceably settled. Private efforts may transform our cities from communities now linked to one another through transportation, commerce, and recreation, to collections of isolated armed camps, shocking not only for their apparent indifference to one another, but also ultimately for their failure to control crime and reduce fear. In fact, such constant reminders of potential threats may actually increase fear.

Whether fear produces these results or not depends a great deal on how citizens respond to their fears. If they adopt defensive, individualistic solutions, then the risks of neighborhood collapse and injustice are increased. If they adopt constructive, community-based responses, then the community will be strengthened not only in terms of its ability to defend itself, but also as an image of civilized society. Societies built on communal crime control efforts have more order, justice, and freedom than those based on individualistic responses. Indeed, it is for these reasons that social control and the administration of justice became public rather than private functions.

POLICE STRATEGIES FOR REDUCING FEAR

If it is true that fear is a problem in its own right, then it is important to evaluate the effectiveness of police strategies not only in terms of their capacity to control crime, but also in terms of their capacity to reduce fear. And if fear is affected by more factors than just criminal victimization, then there might be some special police strategies other than controlling victimization that could be effective in controlling the fear of crime.

Over the last 30 years, the dominant police strategy has emphasized three operational components: motorized patrol, rapid response to calls for service, and retrospective investigation of crimes.[26] The principal aim has been to solve crimes and capture criminals rather than reduce fear. The assumption has been that if victimization could be reduced, fear would decrease as well. Insofar as fear was considered a separate problem, police strategists assumed that motorized patrol and rapid response would provide a reassuring police omnipresence.[27]

To the extent that the police thought about managing citizens' individual responses to crime, they visualized a relationship in which citizens detected crime and mobilized the police to deal with it—not one in which the citizens played an important crime control role. The police advised shopkeepers and citizens about self-defense. They created 911 telephone systems to insure that citizens could reach them easily. And they encouraged citizens to mark their property to aid the police in recovering stolen property. But their primary objective was to make themselves society's principal response to crime. Everything else was seen as auxiliary.

As near monopolists in supplying enhanced security and crime control, police managers and union leaders were ambivalent about the issue of fear. On the one hand, as those responsible for security, they felt some obligation to enhance security and reduce fear. That was by far the predominant view. On the other hand, if citizens were afraid of crime and the police were the solution, the police department would benefit in the fight for scarce municipal funds. This fact has tempted some police executives and some unions to emphasize the risks of crime.[28]

The strategy that emphasized motorized patrol, rapid response, and retrospective investigation of crimes was not designed to reduce fear other than by a reduction in crime. Indeed, insofar as the principal objective of this strategy was to reduce crime, and insofar as citizens were viewed as operational auxiliaries of the police, the police could increase citizens' vigilance by warning of the risks of crime. Nevertheless, to the extent that reduced fear was considered an important objective, it was assumed that the presence and availability of police through motorized patrols and response to calls would achieve that objective.

The anticipated effects of this strategy on levels of fear have not materialized. There have been some occasions, of course, when effective police action against a serial murderer or rapist has reassured a terrorized community. Under ordinary circumstances, however, success of the police in calming fears has been hard to show. The Kansas City experiment showed that citizens were unaware of the level of patrol that occurred in their area. Consequently, they were neither reassured by increased patrolling nor frightened by reduced levels of patrol.[29] Subsequent work on response times revealed that fast responses did not necessarily reassure victims. Before victims even called the police, they often sought assistance and comfort from friends or relatives. Once they called, their satisfaction was related more to their expectations of when the police would arrive than to actual response time. Response time alone was not a significant factor in citizen satisfaction.[30] Thus, the dominant strategy of policing has not performed particularly well in reducing or channeling citizens' fears.

In contrast to the Kansas City study of *motorized* patrol, two field experiments have now shown that citizens are aware of increases or decreases in levels of *foot* patrol and that increased foot patrol reduces citizens' fears. After reviewing surveys of citizens' assessments of crime problems in neighborhoods that had enhanced, constant, or reduced levels of foot patrol, the authors of *The Newark Foot Patrol Experiment* concluded:

> . . . persons living in areas where foot patrol was created perceived a notable decrease in the severity of crime-related problems.[31]

And:

> Consistently, residents in beats where foot patrol was added see the severity of crime problems diminishing in their neighborhoods at levels greater than the other two [kinds of] areas.[32]

Similarly, a foot patrol experiment in Flint, Michigan, found the following:

> Almost 70 percent of the citizens interviewed during the final year of study felt safer because of the Foot Patrol Program. Moreover, many qualified their response by saying that they felt especially safe when the foot patrol officer was well known and highly visible.[33]

Whether foot patrol can work in less dense cities and whether it is worth the cost remain arguable questions. But the experimental evidence clearly supports the hypothesis that fear is reduced among citizens exposed to foot patrol.

Even more significantly, complex experiments in Newark and Houston with a varied mix of fear reduction programs showed that at least some programs could successfully reduce citizens' fears. In Houston, the principal program elements included:

1. a police community newsletter designed to give accurate crime information to citizens;
2. a community organizing response team designed to build a community organization in an area where none had existed;
3. a citizen contact program that kept the same officer patrolling in a particular area of the city and directed him to make individual contacts with citizens in the area;
4. a program directing officers to re-contact victims of crime in the days following their victimization to reassure them of the police presence; and

5. establishing a police community contact center staffed by two patrol officers, a civilian coordinator, and three police aides, within which a school program aimed at reducing truancy and a park program designed to reduce vandalism and increase use of a local park were discussed, designed, and operated.[34]

In Newark, some program elements were similar, but some were unique. Newark's programs included the following:

1. a police community newsletter;
2. a coordinated community policing program that included a directed police-citizen contact program, a neighborhood community police center, neighborhood cleanup activities, and intensified law enforcement and order maintenance;
3. a program to reduce the signs of crime that included: a) a directed patrol task force committed to foot patrol, radar checks on busy roads, bus checks to enforce city ordinances on buses, and enforcement of disorderly conduct laws; and b) a neighborhood cleanup effort that used police auspices to pressure city service agencies to clean up neighborhoods, and to establish a community work program for juveniles that made their labor available for cleanup details.[35]

Evaluations of these different program elements revealed that programs "designed to increase the quantity and improve the quality of contacts between citizens and police" were generally more successful in reducing citizens' fears.[36] This meant that the Houston Citizen Contact Patrol, the Houston Community Organizing Response Team, the Houston Police Community Station, and the Newark Coordinated Community Policing Program were all successful in reducing fear.

Other approaches that encouraged close contact, such as newsletters, the victim re-contact program, and the signs-of-crime program, did not produce clear evidence of fear reduction in these experiments. The reasons that these programs did not work, however, may have been specific to the particular situations rather than inherent in the programs themselves. The victim re-contact program ran into severe operating problems in transmitting information about victimization from the reporting officers to the beat patrol officers responsible for the re-contacts. As a result, the contacts came far too long after the victimization. Newsletters might be valuable if they were published and distributed in the context of ongoing conversations with the community about crime problems. And efforts to eliminate the signs of crime through order maintenance and neighborhood cleanup might succeed if the programs were aimed at problems identified by the community. So, the initial failures of these particular program elements need not condemn them forever.

The one clear implication of both the foot patrol and fear reduction experiments is that closer contact between citizens and police officers reduces fear. As James Q. Wilson concludes in his foreword to the summary report of the fear reduction experiment:

> In Houston . . . opening a neighborhood police station, contacting the citizens about their problems, and stimulating the formation of neighborhood organizations where none had existed can help reduce the fear of crime and even reduce the actual level of victimization.[37]

In Newark, many of the same steps—including opening a storefront police office and directing the police to make contacts with the citizens in their homes—also had beneficial effects.

The success of these police tactics in reducing fear, along with the observation that fear is a separate and important problem, suggests a new area in which police can make a substantial contribution to the quality of life in the nation's cities. However, it seems likely that programs like those tried in Flint, Newark, and Houston will not be tried elsewhere unless mayors and police administrators begin to take fear seriously as a separate problem. Such programs are expensive and take patrol resources and managerial attention away from the traditional functions of patrol and retrospective investigations of crime. Unless their effects are valued, they will disappear as expensive luxuries.

On the other hand, mayors and police executives could view fear as a problem in its own right and as something that inhibits rather than aids effective crime control by forcing people off the streets and narrowing their sense of control and responsibility. If that were the case, not only would these special tactics become important, but the overall strategy of the department might change. That idea has led to wider and more sustained attacks on fear in Baltimore County and Newport News.

In Baltimore County, a substantial portion of the police department was committed to the Citizen-Oriented Police Enforcement (COPE) unit—a program designed to improve the quantity and quality of contacts between citizens and the police and to work on problems of concern to citizens.[38] A major objective was to reduce fear. The effort succeeded. Measured levels of fear dropped an average of 10 percent for the various projects during a six-month period.[39] In Newport News, the entire department shifted to a style of policing that emphasized problem solving over traditional reactive methods.[40] This approach, like COPS, took citizens' fears and concerns seriously, as well as serious crime and calls for service.

These examples illustrate the security-enhancing potential of problem-solving and community approaches to policing. By incorporating fear reduction as an important objective of policing, by changing the activities of the police to include more frequent, more sustained contacts with citizens; and by consultation and joint planning, police departments seem to be able not only to reduce fear, but to transform it into something that helps to build strong social institutions. That is the promise of these approaches.

CONCLUSION

Fear of crime is an important problem in its own right. Although levels of fear are related to levels of criminal victimization, fear is influenced by other factors, such as a general sense of vulnerability, signs of physical and social decay, and intergroup conflict. Consequently, there is both a reason for fear and an opportunity to work directly on that fear, rather than indirectly through attempts to reduce criminal victimization.

The current police strategy, which relies on motorized patrol, rapid responses to calls for service, and retrospective investigations of crimes, seems to produce little reassurance to frightened citizens, except in unusual circumstances when the police arrest a violent offender in the middle of a crime spree. Moreover, a focus on controlling crime rather than increasing security (analogous to the medical profession's focus on curing disease rather than promoting health) leads the police to miss opportunities to take steps that would reduce fear independently of reducing crime. Consequently, the current strategy of policing does not result in reduced fear. Nor does it leave much room for fear reduction programs in the police department.

This is unfortunate, because some fear reduction programs have succeeded in reducing citizens' fears. Two field experiments showed that foot patrol can reduce fear and promote security. Programs that enhance the quantity and quality of police contacts with citizens through neighborhood police stations and through required regular contacts between citizens and police have been successful in reducing fear in Houston and Newark.

The success of these particular programs points to the potential of a more general change in the strategy of policing that (1) would make fear reduction an important objective and (2) would concentrate on improving the quantity and quality of contacts between citizens and police at all levels of the department. The success of these approaches has been demonstrated in Baltimore County and Newport News.

Based on this discussion, it is apparent that a shift in strategy would probably be successful in reducing fear, and that would be an important accomplishment. What is more speculative (but quite plausible) is that community policing would also be successful in channeling the remaining fear along constructive rather than destructive paths. Criminal victimization would be reduced, and the overall quality of community life would be enhanced beyond the mere reduction in fear.

NOTES

1. *The Figgie Report on Fear of Crime: America Afraid, Part 1: The General Public* (Research and Forecasts, Inc., sponsored by A-T-O Inc., Willoughby, Ohio, 1980), p. 29.

2. Louis Harris, "Crime Rates: Personal Uneasiness in Neighborhoods," *Chicago Tribune*, 6 June 1975.

3. *Gallup Poll Public Opinion,* vol. 5: 1977 (New York: Random House, 1977), pp. 1240–41.

4. James Garofalo, *Public Opinion about Crime: The Attitudes of Victims and Non-Victims in Selected Cities* (Washington, D.C.: U.S. Govt. Printing Office, 1977).

5. "The Michigan Public Speaks Out on Crime" (Detroit, Michigan: Market Opinion Research, 1977).

6. R. H. C. Teske Jr. and N. L. Powell, "Texas Crime Poll—Spring 1978," *Survey* (Huntsville, Texas: Sam Houston State University Criminal Justice Center, 1978), p. 19.

7. *Gallup Poll Public Opinion,* vol. 3: 1935–1971 (New York: Random House, 1972), pp. 2164–65; *Gallup Poll Public Opinion,* vol. 5: 1977 (New York: Random House, 1977), pp. 1240–41.

8. Louis Harris, "Crime Rates: Personal Uneasiness in Neighborhoods," *Chicago Tribune,* 6 June 1975; Louis Harris, "Crime Fears Decreasing," *Harris Survey* (Orlando, Florida: Tribune Media Services, Inc., 21 March 1985).

9. Wesley G. Skogan and Michael G. Maxfield, *Coping with Crime: Individual and Neighborhood Reactions,* vol. 124 (Beverly Hills, California: Sage Publications, 1981), pp. 74–77.

10. Claude Brown in "Images of Fear," *Harper's* 270 (May 1985): 44.

11. Robert C. Trojanowicz et al., "Fear of Crime: A Critical Issue in Community Policing" (unpublished paper, Program in Criminal Justice Policy and Management, John F. Kennedy School of Government, Harvard University, Cambridge, 29 September 1987), p. 1.

12. James K. Stewart, "The Urban Strangler: How Crime Causes Poverty in the Inner City," *Policy Review* 37 (summer 1986): 6–10.

13. Thomas Hobbes, *Leviathan* (New York: Penguin Publishing, 1981).

14. Wesley Skogan, "Fear of Crime and Neighborhood Change," in Albert J. Reiss Jr. and Michael Tonry, *Communities and Crime,* vol. 8 of *Crime and Justice: A Review of Research* (Chicago: The University of Chicago Press, 1986), p. 210.

15. Skogan and Maxfield, *Coping with Crime,* pp. 194–98.

16. Skogan and Maxfield, *Coping with Crime,* chapter 5.

17. Skogan, "Fear of Crime and Neighborhood Change," p. 211.

18. *Ibid.,* p. 212.

19. *Ibid.,* p. 210–15.

20. *Ibid.,* p. 222.

21. Charles A. Murray, "The Physical Environment and Community Control of Crime," in James Q. Wilson, ed., *Crime and Public Policy* (San Francisco: Institute for Contemporary Studies, 1983), p. 115.

22. William C. Cunningham and Todd Taylor, *The Hallcrest Report: Private Security and Police in America* (Portland, Oregon: Chancellor Press, 1985).

23. National Institute of Justice, *Crime and Protection in America: A Study of Private Security and Law Enforcement Resources and Relationships* (Washington, D.C.: U.S. Department of Justice, May 1985).

24. For a discussion of the importance of "eyes on the street," see Jane Jacobs, *The Death and Life of Great American Cities* (New York: Random House, 1961).

25. Skogan, "Fear of Crime and Neighborhood Change," p. 215.

26. George L. Kelling and Mark H. Moore, "From Political to Reform to Community: The Evolving Strategy of Police" (working paper, Program in Criminal Justice Policy and Management, John F. Kennedy School of Government, Harvard University, Cambridge, October 1987).

27. O. W. Wilson, *Distribution of Police Patrol Forces* (Chicago: Public Administration Services, 1941).

28. For an example of the use of fear to build support for the police, see the discussion of the "fear city" campaign in *The Newark Foot Patrol Experiment* (Washington, D.C.: Police Foundation, 1981), pp. 120–21.

29. Kelling et al., *Kansas City Preventive Patrol Experiment.*

30. Antony Pate et al., *Police Response Time: Its Determinants and Effects* (Washington, D.C.: Police Foundation, 1987).

31. *The Newark Foot Patrol Experiment,* p. 72.

32. *Ibid.,* p. 123.

33. Robert Trojanowicz, *An Evaluation of the Neighborhood Foot Patrol Program in Flint, Michigan* (East Lansing: Michigan State University, 1982), p. 86.

34. Antony Pate et al., *Reducing Fear of Crime in Houston and Newark,* pp. 7–10.

35. *Ibid.,* pp. 10–18.

36. *Ibid.,* p. 35.

37. James Q. Wilson, in Pate et al., *Reducing Fear of Crime in Houston and Newark,* p. ii.

38. Philip B. Taft Jr., "Fighting Fear: The Baltimore County COPE Project" (Washington, D.C.: Police Executive Research Forum, February 1986).

39. *Ibid.,* p. 20.

40. John E. Eck and William Spelman, "Solving Problems: Problem-Oriented Policing in Newport News" (Washington, D.C.: Police Executive Research Forum, January 1987).

ARTICLE 7

THE EVOLVING STRATEGY OF POLICING

George L. Kelling and Mark H. Moore

Policing, like all professions, learns from experience. It follows, then, that as modern police executives search for more effective strategies of policing, they will be guided by the lessons of police history. The difficulty is that police history is incoherent, its lessons hard to read. After all, that history was produced by thousands of local departments pursuing their own visions and responding to local conditions. Although that varied experience is potentially a rich source of lessons, departments have left few records that reveal the trends shaping modern policing. Interpretation is necessary.

METHODOLOGY

This essay presents an interpretation of police history that may help police executives [who are] considering alternative future strategies of policing. Our reading of police history has led us to adopt a particular point of view. We find that a dominant trend guiding today's police executives—a trend that encourages the pursuit of independent, professional autonomy for police departments—is carrying the police away from achieving their maximum potential, especially in effective crime fighting. We are also convinced that this trend in policing is weakening *public* policing relative to *private* security as the primary institution providing security to society. We believe that this has dangerous long-term

Reprinted from George L. Kelling and Mark H. Moore, "The Evolving Strategy of Policing," *Perspectives on Policing,* no. 4 (Washington, D.C.: National Institute of Justice, U.S. Department of Justice, and the Program in Criminal Justice Policy and Management, John F. Kennedy School of Government, Harvard University, June 1988).

implications not only for police departments but also for society. We think that this trend is shrinking rather than enlarging police capacity to help create civil communities. Our judgment is that this trend can be reversed only by refocusing police attention from the pursuit of professional autonomy to the establishment of effective problem-solving partnerships with the communities they police.

Delving into police history made it apparent that some assumptions that now operate as axioms in the field of policing (for example, that effectiveness in policing depends on distancing police departments from politics; or that the highest priority of police departments is to deal with serious street crime; or that the best way to deal with street crime is through directed patrol, rapid response to calls for service, and skilled retrospective investigations) are not timeless truths, but rather choices made by former police leaders and strategists. To be sure, the choices were often wise and far-seeing as well as appropriate to their times. But the historical perspective shows them to be choices nonetheless, and therefore open to reconsideration in the light of later professional experiences and changing environmental circumstances.

We are interpreting the results of our historical study through a framework based on the concept of "corporate strategy."[1] Using this framework, we can describe police organizations in terms of seven interrelated categories:

- The sources from which the police construct the legitimacy and continuing power to act on society
- The definition of the police function or role in society
- The organizational design of police departments
- The relationships the police create with the external environment
- The nature of police efforts to market or manage the demand for their services
- The principal activities, programs, and tactics on which police agencies rely to fulfill their mission or achieve operational success
- The concrete measures the police use to define operational success or failure

Using this analytic framework, we have found it useful to divide the history of policing into three different eras. These eras are distinguished from one another by the apparent dominance of a particular strategy of policing. The political era, so named because of the close ties between police and politics, dated from the introduction of police into municipalities during the 1840s, continued through the Progressive period and ended during the early 1900s. The reform era developed in reaction to the political. It took hold during the 1930s, thrived during the 1950s and 1960s, [and] began to erode during the late 1970s. The reform era now seems to be giving way to an era emphasizing community problem solving.

By dividing policing into these three eras dominated by a particular strategy of policing, we do not mean to imply that there were clear boundaries between the eras. Nor do we mean that in those eras everyone policed in the same way. Obviously, the real history is far more complex than that. Nonetheless, we believe that there is a certain professional ethos that defines standards of competence, professionalism and excellence in policing; that at any given time, one set of concepts is more powerful, more widely shared, and better understood than others; and that this ethos changes over time. Sometimes, this professional ethos has been explicitly articulated, and those who have articulated the concepts have been recognized as the leaders of their profession. O. W. Wilson, for example, was a brilliant expositor of the central elements of the reform strategy of policing. Other times, the ethos is implicit—accepted by all as the tacit assumptions that define the business of policing and the proper form for a police department to take. Our task is to help the profession look to the future by representing its past in these terms and trying to understand what the past portends for the future.

THE POLITICAL ERA

Historians have described the characteristics of early policing in the United States, especially the struggles between various interest groups to govern the police.[2] Elsewhere, the authors of this paper analyzed a portion of American police history in terms of its organizational strategy.[3] The following discussion of elements of the police organizational strategy during the political era expands on that effort.

Legitimacy and Authorization

Early American police were authorized by local municipalities. Unlike their English counterparts, American police departments lacked the powerful, central authority of the crown to establish a legitimate, unifying mandate for their enterprise. Instead, American police derived both their authorization and resources from local political leaders, often ward politicians. They were, of course, guided by the law as to what tasks to undertake and what powers to utilize. But their link to neighborhoods and local politicians was so tight that both Jordan[4] and Fogelson[5] refer to the early police as adjuncts to local political machines. The relationship was often reciprocal: Political machines recruited and maintained police in office and on the beat, while police helped ward political leaders maintain their political offices by encouraging citizens to vote for certain candidates, discouraging them from voting for others, and, at times, by assisting in rigging elections.

The Police Function

Partly because of their close connection to politicians, police during the political era provided a wide array of services to citizens. Inevitably police departments were involved in crime prevention and control and order maintenance, but they also provided a wide variety of social services. In the late nineteenth century, municipal police departments ran soup lines; provided temporary lodging for newly arrived immigrant workers in station houses[6]; and assisted ward leaders in finding work for immigrants, both in police and other forms of work.

Organizational Design

Although ostensibly organized as a centralized, quasi-military organization with a unified chain of command, police departments of the political era were nevertheless decentralized. Cities were divided into precincts, and precinct-level managers often, in concert with the ward leaders, ran precincts as small-scale departments—hiring, firing, managing, and assigning personnel as they deemed appropriate. In addition, decentralization combined with primitive communications and transportation to give police officers substantial discretion in handling their individual beats. At best, officer contact with central command was maintained through the call box.

External Relationships

During the political era, police departments were intimately connected to the social and political world of the ward. Police officers often were recruited from the same ethnic stock as the dominant political groups in the localities, and continued to live in the neighborhoods they patrolled. Precinct commanders consulted often with local political representatives about police priorities and progress.

Demand Management

Demand for police services came primarily from two sources: ward politicians making demands on the organization and citizens making demands directly on beat officers. Decentralization and political authorization encouraged the first; foot patrol, lack of other means of transportation, and poor communications produced the latter. Basically, the demand for police services was received, interpreted, and responded to at the precinct and street levels.

Principal Programs and Technologies

The primary tactic of police during the political era was foot patrol. Most police officers walked beats and dealt with crime, disorder, and other problems as they arose, or as they were guided by citizens and precinct superiors. The technological tools available to police were limited. However, when call boxes became available, police administrators used them for supervisory and managerial purposes; and, when early automobiles became available, police used them to transport officers from one beat to another.[7] The new technology thereby increased the range, but did not change the mode, of patrol officers.

Detective divisions existed but without their current prestige. Operating from a caseload of "persons" rather than offenses, detectives relied on their caseloads to inform on other criminals.[8] The "third degree" was a common means of interviewing criminals to solve crimes. Detectives were often especially valuable to local politicians for gathering information on individuals for political or personal, rather than offense-related, purposes.

Measured Outcomes

The expected outcomes of police work included crime and riot control, maintenance of order, and relief from many of the other problems of an industrializing society (hunger and temporary homelessness, for example). Consistent with their political mandate, police emphasized maintaining citizen and political satisfaction with police services as an important goal of police departments.

In sum, the organizational strategy of the political era of policing included the following elements:

- Authorization—primarily political
- Function—crime control, order maintenance, broad social services
- Organizational design—decentralized and geographical
- Relationship to environment—close and personal
- Demand—managed through links between politicians and precinct commanders, and face-to-face contacts between citizens and foot patrol officers
- Tactics and technology—foot patrol and rudimentary investigations
- Outcome—political and citizen satisfaction with social order

The political strategy of early American policing had strengths. First, police were integrated into neighborhoods and enjoyed the support of citizens—at least the support of the dominant and political interests of an area. Second, and probably as a result of the first, the strategy provided useful services to communities. There is evidence that it helped contain riots. Many citizens believed that police prevented crimes or solved crimes when they occurred.[9] And the police assisted immigrants in establishing themselves in communities and finding jobs.

The political strategy also had weaknesses. First, intimacy with community, closeness to political leaders, and a decentralized organizational structure, with its inability to provide supervision of officers, gave rise to police corruption. Officers were often required to enforce unpopular laws foisted on immigrant ethnic neighborhoods by crusading reformers (primarily of English and Dutch background) who objected to ethnic values.[10] Because of their intimacy with the community, the officers were vulnerable to being bribed in return for nonenforcement or lax enforcement of laws. Moreover, police closeness to politicians created such forms of political corruption as patronage and police interference in elections.[11] Even those few departments that managed to avoid serious financial or political corruption during the late nineteenth and early twentieth centuries (Boston, for example) succumbed to large-scale corruption during and after Prohibition.[12]

Second, close identification of police with neighborhoods and neighborhood norms often resulted in discrimination against strangers and others who violated those norms, especially minority ethnic and racial groups. Often ruling their beats with the "ends of their nightsticks," police regularly targeted outsiders and strangers for rousting and "curbstone justice."[13]

Finally, the lack of organizational control over officers resulting from both decentralization and the political nature of many appointments to police positions caused inefficiencies and disorganization. The image of Keystone Cops—police as clumsy bunglers—was widespread and often descriptive of realities in American policing.

THE REFORM ERA

Control over police by local politicians, conflict between urban reformers and local ward leaders over the enforcement of laws regulating the morality of urban migrants, and abuses (corruption, for example) that resulted from the intimacy between police and political leaders and citizens produced a continuous struggle for control over police during the late nineteenth and twentieth centuries.[14] Nineteenth-century attempts by civilians to reform police organizations by applying external pressures largely failed; twentieth-century attempts at reform, originating from both internal and external forces, shaped contemporary policing as we knew it through the 1970s.[15]

Berkeley's police chief, August Vollmer, first rallied police executives around the idea of reform during the 1920s and early 1930s. Vollmer's vision of policing was the trumpet call: Police in the post-flapper generation were to remind American citizens and institutions of the moral vision that had made America great and of their responsibilities to maintain that vision.[16] It was Vollmer's protégé, O. W. Wilson, however, who, taking guidance from J. Edgar Hoover's shrewd transformation of the corrupt and discredited Bureau of Investigation into the honest and prestigious Federal Bureau of Investigation (FBI), became the principal administrative architect of the police reform organizational strategy.[17]

Hoover wanted the FBI to represent a new force for law and order, and saw that such an organization could capture a permanent constituency that wanted an agency to take a stand against lawlessness, immorality, and crime. By raising eligibility standards and changing patterns of recruitment and training, Hoover gave the FBI agents stature as upstanding moral crusaders. By committing the organization to attacks on crimes such as kidnaping, bank robbery, and espionage—crimes that

attracted wide publicity and required technical sophistication, dogged-
ness, and a national jurisdiction to solve—Hoover established the organization's reputation for professional competence and power. By establishing tight central control over his agents, limiting their use of
controversial investigation procedures (such as undercover operations),
and keeping them out of narcotics enforcement, Hoover was also able to
maintain an unparalleled record of integrity. That, too, fitted the image of
a dogged, incorruptible crime-fighting organization. Finally, lest anyone
fail to notice the important developments within the Bureau, Hoover developed impressive public relations programs that presented the FBI and
its agents in the most favorable light. (For those of us who remember the
1940s, for example, one of the most popular radio phrases was "The FBI
in peace and war"—the introductory line in a radio program that portrayed a vigilant FBI protecting us from foreign enemies as well as villains on the "10 Most Wanted" list, another Hoover/FBI invention.)

Struggling as they were with reputations for corruption, brutality,
unfairness, and downright incompetence, municipal police reformers
found Hoover's path a compelling one. Instructed by O. W. Wilson's texts
on police administration, they began to shape an organizational strategy
for urban police analogous to the one pursued by the FBI.

Legitimacy and Authorization

Reformers rejected politics as the basis of police legitimacy. In their
view, politics and political involvement was the *problem* in American
policing. Police reformers therefore allied themselves with Progressives.
They moved to end the close ties between local political leaders and police. In some states, control over police was usurped by state government. Civil service eliminated patronage and ward influences in hiring
and firing police officers. In some cities (Los Angeles and Cincinnati, for
example), even the position of chief of police became a civil service position to be attained through examination. In others (such as Milwaukee), chiefs were given lifetime tenure by a police commission, to be removed from office only for cause. In yet others (Boston, for example),
contracts for chiefs were staggered so as not to coincide with the mayor's
tenure. Concern for separation of police from politics did not focus only
on chiefs, however. In some cities, such as Philadelphia, it became illegal for patrol officers to live in the beats they patrolled. The purpose of
all these changes was to isolate police as completely as possible from political influences.

Law, especially criminal law, and police professionalism were established as the principal bases of police legitimacy. When police were
asked why they performed as they did, the most common answer was
that they enforced the law. When they chose not to enforce the law—for
instance, in a riot when police isolated an area rather than arrested
looters—police justification for such action was found in their claim to
professional knowledge, skills, and values, which uniquely qualified
them to make such tactical decisions. Even in riot situations, police re-

jected the idea that political leaders should make tactical decisions; that was a police responsibility.[18]

So persuasive was the argument of reformers to remove political influences from policing, that police departments became one of the most autonomous public organizations in urban governments.[19] Under such circumstances, policing a city became a legal and technical matter left to the discretion of professional police executives under the guidance of law. Political influence of any kind on a police department came to be seen as not merely a failure of police leadership but as corruption in policing.

The Police Function

Using the focus on criminal law as a basic source of police legitimacy, police in the reform era moved to narrow their functioning to crime control and criminal apprehension. Police agencies became *law enforcement agencies*. Their goal was to control crime. Their principal means was the use of criminal law to apprehend and deter offenders. Activities that drew the police into solving other kinds of community problems and relied on other kinds of responses were identified as "social work," and became the object of derision. A common line in police circles during the 1950s and 1960s was, "If only we didn't have to do social work, we could really do something about crime." Police retreated from providing emergency medical services as well—ambulance and emergency medical services were transferred to medical, private, or firefighting organizations.[20] The 1967 President's Commission on Law Enforcement and Administration of Justice ratified this orientation: heretofore, police had been conceptualized as an agency of urban government; the President's Commission reconceptualized them as part of the criminal justice system.

Organizational Design

The organization form adopted by police reformers generally reflected the *scientific* or *classical* theory of administration advocated by Frederick W. Taylor during the early twentieth century. At least two assumptions attended classical theory. First, workers are inherently uninterested in work and, if left to their own devices, are prone to avoid it. Second, since workers have little or no interest in the substance of their work, the sole common interest between workers and management is found in economic incentives for workers. Thus, both workers and management benefit economically when management arranges work in ways that increase workers' productivity and link productivity to economic rewards.

Two central principles followed from these assumptions: division of labor and unity of control. The former posited that if tasks can be broken into components, workers can become highly skilled in particular components and thus more efficient in carrying out their tasks. The latter posited that the workers' activities are best managed by a *pyramid of control,* with all authority finally resting in one central office.

Using this classical theory, police leaders moved to routinize and standardize police work, especially patrol work. Police work became a form of crimefighting in which police enforced the law and arrested criminals if the opportunity presented itself. Attempts were made to limit discretion in patrol work: a generation of police officers was raised with the idea that they merely enforced the law.

If special problems arose, the typical response was to create special units (e.g., vice, juvenile, drugs, tactical) rather than to assign them to patrol. The creation of these special units, under central rather than precinct command, served to further centralize command and control and weaken precinct commanders.[21]

Moreover, police organizations emphasized control over workers through bureaucratic means of control: supervision, limited span of control, flow of instructions downward [of] and information upward in the organization, establishment of elaborate record-keeping systems requiring additional layers of middle managers, and coordination of activities between various production units (e.g., patrol and detectives), which also required additional middle managers.

External Relationships

Police leaders in the reform era redefined the nature of a proper relationship between police officers and citizens. Heretofore, police had been intimately linked to citizens. During the era of reform policing, the new model demanded an impartial law enforcer who related to citizens in professionally neutral and distant terms. No better characterization of this model can be found than televisions's Sergeant Friday, whose response, "Just the facts, ma'am," typified the idea: impersonal and oriented toward crime solving rather than responsive to the emotional crisis of the victim.

The professional model also shaped the police view of the role of citizens in crime control. Police redefined the citizen role during an era when there was heady confidence about the ability of professionals to manage physical and social problems. Physicians would care for health problems, dentists for dental problems, teachers for educational problems, social workers for social adjustment problems, and police for crime problems. The proper role of citizens in crime control was to be relatively passive recipients of professional crime control services. Citizens' actions on their own behalf to defend themselves or their communities came to be seen as inappropriate, smacking of vigilantism. Citizens met their responsibilities when a crime occurred by calling police, deferring to police actions, and being good witnesses if called upon to give evidence. The metaphor that expressed this orientation to the community was that of the police as the "thin blue line." It connotes the existence of dangerous external threats to communities, portrays police as standing between that danger and good citizens, and implies both police heroism and loneliness.

Demand Management

Learning from Hoover, police reformers vigorously set out to sell their brand of urban policing.[22] They, too, performed on radio talk shows, consulted with media representatives about how to present police, engaged in public relations campaigns, and in other ways presented this image of police as crime fighters. In a sense, they began with an organizational capacity—anticrime police tactics—and intensively promoted it. This approach was more like selling than marketing. Marketing refers to the process of carefully identifying consumer needs and then developing goods and services that meet those needs. Selling refers to having a stock of products or goods on hand irrespective of need and selling them. The reform strategy had as its starting point a set of police tactics (services) that police promulgated as much for the purpose of establishing internal control of police officers and enhancing the status of urban police as for responding to community needs or market demands.[23] The community "need" for rapid response to calls for service, for instance, was largely the consequence of police selling the service as efficacious in crime control rather than of a direct demand from citizens.

Consistent with this attempt to sell particular tactics, police worked to shape and control demand for police services. Foot patrol, when demanded by citizens, was rejected as an outmoded, expensive frill. Social and emergency services were terminated or given to other agencies. Receipt of demand for police services was centralized. No longer were citizens encouraged to go to "their" neighborhood police officers or districts; all calls went to a central communications facility. When 911 systems were installed, police aggressively sold 911 and rapid response to calls for service as effective police service. If citizens continued to use district, or precinct, telephone numbers, some police departments disconnected those telephones or got new telephone numbers.[24]

Principal Programs and Technologies

The principal programs and tactics of the reform strategy were preventive patrol by automobile and rapid response to calls for service. Foot patrol, characterized as outmoded and inefficient, was abandoned as rapidly as police administrators could obtain cars.[25] The initial tactical reasons for putting police in cars had been to increase the size of the areas police officers could patrol and to take the advantage away from criminals who began to use automobiles. Under reform policing, a new theory about how to make the best tactical use of automobiles appeared.

O. W. Wilson developed the theory of preventive patrol by automobile as an anticrime tactic.[26] He theorized that if police drove conspicuously marked cars randomly through city streets and gave special attention to certain "hazards" (bars and schools, for example), a feeling of police omnipresence would be developed. In turn, that sense of omnipresence would both deter criminals and reassure good citizens. Moreover, it was hypothesized that vigilant patrol officers moving rapidly through city streets would happen upon criminals in action and be able to apprehend them.

As telephones and radios became ubiquitous, the availability of cruising police came to be seen as even more valuable: if citizens could be encouraged to call the police via telephones as soon as problems developed, police could respond rapidly to calls and establish control over situations, identify wrong-doers, and make arrests. To this end, 911 systems and computer-aided dispatch were developed throughout the country. Detective units continued, although with some modifications. The "person" approach ended and was replaced by the case approach. In addition, forensic techniques were upgraded and began to replace the old "third degree" or reliance on informants for the solution of crimes. Like other special units, most investigative units were controlled by central headquarters.

Measured Outcomes

The primary desired outcomes of the reform strategy were crime control and criminal apprehension.[27] To measure achievement of these outcomes, August Vollmer, working through the newly vitalized International Association of Chiefs of Police, developed and implemented a uniform system of crime classification and reporting. Later, the system was taken over and administered by the FBI, and the *Uniform Crime Reports* became the primary standard by which police organizations measured their effectiveness. Additionally, individual officers' effectiveness in dealing with crime was judged by the number of arrests they made; other measures of police effectiveness included response time (the time it takes for a police car to arrive at the location of a call for service) and "number of passings" (the number of times a police car passes a given point on a city street). Regardless of all other indicators, however, the primary measure of police effectiveness was the crime rate as measured by the *Uniform Crime Reports.*

In sum, the reform organizational strategy contained the following elements:

- Authorization—law and professionalism
- Function—crime control
- Organizational design—centralized, classical
- Relationship to environment—professionally remote
- Demand—channeled through central dispatching activities
- Tactics and technology—preventive patrol and rapid response to calls for service
- Outcome—crime control

In retrospect, the reform strategy was impressive. It successfully integrated its strategic elements into a coherent paradigm that was internally consistent and logically appealing. Narrowing police functions to crime fighting made sense. If police could concentrate their efforts on prevention of crime and apprehension of criminals, it followed that they could be more effective than if they dissipated their efforts on other problems. The model of police as impartial, professional law enforcers was attractive because it minimized the discretionary excesses which developed during the political era. Preventive patrol and rapid response to calls for service were intuitively appealing tactics, as well as means to control officers and shape and control citizens demands for service. Further, the strategy provided a comprehensive, yet simple, vision of policing around which police leaders could rally.

The metaphor of the thin blue line reinforced their need to create isolated independence and autonomy in terms that were acceptable to the public. The patrol car became the symbol of policing during the 1930s and 1940s; when equipped with a radio, it was at the limits of technology. It represented mobility, power, conspicuous presence, control of officers, and professional distance from citizens.

During the late 1960s and 1970s, however, the reform strategy ran into difficulty. First, regardless of how police effectiveness in dealing with crime was measured, police failed to substantially improve their record. During the 1960s, crime began to rise. Despite large increases in the size of police departments and in expenditures for new forms of equipment (911 systems, computer-aided dispatch, etc.), police failed to meet their own or public expectations about their capacity to control crime or prevent its increase. Moreover, research conducted during the 1970s on preventive patrol and rapid response to calls for service suggested that neither was an effective crime control or apprehension tactic.[28]

Second, fear rose rapidly during this era. The consequences of this fear were dramatic for cities. Citizens abandoned parks, public transportation, neighborhood shopping centers, and churches, as well as entire neighborhoods. What puzzled police and researchers was that levels of fear and crime did not always correspond: crime levels were low in some areas, but fear high. Conversely, in other areas, levels of crime were high, but fear low. Not until the early 1980s did researchers discover that fear is more closely correlated with disorder than with crime.[29] Ironically, order maintenance was one of those functions that police had been downplaying over the years. They collected no data on it, provided no training to officers in order-maintenance activities, and did not reward officers for successfully conducting order-maintenance tasks.

Third, despite attempts by police departments to create equitable police-allocated systems and to provide impartial policing to all citizens, many minority citizens, especially blacks during the 1960s and 1970s, did not perceive their treatment as equitable or adequate. They protested not only police mistreatment, but lack of treatment—inadequate or insufficient services—as well.

Fourth, the civil rights and anti-war movements challenged police. This challenge took several forms. The legitimacy of police was questioned: students resisted police, minorities rioted against them, and the public, observing police via live television for the first time, questioned their tactics. Moreover, despite police attempts to upgrade personnel through improved recruitment, training, and supervision, minorities and then women insisted that they had to be adequately represented in policing if police were to be legitimate.

Fifth, some of the myths that undergirded the reform strategy— police officers use little or no discretion and the primary activity of police is law enforcement—simply proved to be too far from reality to be sustained. Over and over again, research showed that use of discretion characterized policing at all levels and that law enforcement comprised but a small portion of police officers' activities.[30]

Sixth, although the reform ideology could rally police chiefs and executives, it failed to rally line officers. During the reform era, police executives had moved to professionalize their ranks. Line officers, however, were managed in ways that were antithetical to professionalization. Despite pious testimony from police executives that "patrol is the backbone of policing," police executives behaved in ways that were consistent with classical organizational theory—patrol officers continued to have low status; their work was treated as if it were routinized and standardized; and petty rules governed issues such as hair length and off-duty behavior. Meanwhile, line officers received little guidance in use of discretion and were given few, if any, opportunities to make suggestions about their work. Under such circumstances, the increasing "grumpiness" of officers in many cities is not surprising, nor is the rise of militant unionism.

Seventh, police lost a significant portion of their financial support, which had been increasing or at least constant over the years, as cities found themselves in fiscal difficulties. In city after city, police departments were reduced in size. In some cities, New York for example, financial cutbacks resulted in losses of up to one-third of departmental personnel. Some, noting that crime did not increase more rapidly or arrests decrease during the cutbacks, suggested that New York City had been overpoliced when at maximum strength. For those concerned about levels of disorder and fear in New York City, not to mention other problems, that came as a dismaying conclusion. Yet it emphasizes the erosion of confidence that citizens, politicians, and academicians had in urban police—an erosion that was translated into lack of political and financial support.

Finally, urban police departments began to acquire competition: private security and the community crime control movement. Despite the inherent value of these developments, the fact that businesses, industries, and private citizens began to search for alternative means of protecting their property and persons suggest a decreasing confidence in either the capability or the intent of the police to provide the services that citizens want.

In retrospect, the police reform strategy has characteristics similar to those that Miles and Snow[31] ascribe to a defensive strategy in the private sector. Some of the characteristics of an organization with a defensive strategy are (with specific characteristics of reform policing added in parentheses):

- Its market is stable and narrow (crime victims).
- Its success is dependent on maintaining dominance in a narrow, chosen market (crime control).

- It tends to ignore developments outside its domain (isolation).
- It tends to establish a single core technology (patrol).
- New technology is used to improve its current product or service rather than to expand its product or service line (use of computers to enhance patrol).
- Its management is centralized (command and control).
- Promotions generally are from within (with the exception of chiefs, virtually all promotions are from within).
- There is a tendency toward a functional structure with high degrees of specialization and formalization.

A defensive strategy is successful for an organization when market conditions remain stable and few competitors enter the field. Such strategies are vulnerable, however, in unstable market conditions and when competitors are aggressive. The reform strategy was a successful strategy for policing during the relatively stable period of the 1940s and 1950s. Police were able to sell a relatively narrow service line and maintain dominance in the crime control market. The social changes of the 1960s and 1970s, however, created unstable conditions. Some of the more significant changes included: the civil rights movement; migration of minorities into cities; the changing age of the population (more youths and teenagers); increases in crime and fear; increased [supervision] of police actions by courts; and the decriminalization and deinstitutionalization movements. Whether or not the private sector defensive strategy properly applies to police, it is clear that the reform strategy was unable to adjust to the changing social circumstances of the 1960s and 1970s.

THE COMMUNITY PROBLEM-SOLVING ERA

All was not negative for police during the late 1970s and early 1980s, however. Police began to score victories that they barely noticed. Foot patrol remained popular, and in many cities, citizen and political demands for it intensified. In New Jersey, the state funded the Safe and Clean Neighborhoods Program, which funded foot patrol in cities, often over the opposition of local chiefs of police.[32] In Boston, foot patrol was so popular with citizens that when neighborhoods were selected for foot patrol, politicians often made the announcements, especially during election years. Flint, Michigan, became the first city in memory to return to foot patrol on a citywide basis. It proved so popular there that citizens twice voted to increase their taxes to fund foot patrol—most recently by a two-thirds majority. Political and citizen demands for foot patrol continued to expand in cities throughout the United States. Research into foot patrol suggested it was more than just politically popular, it contributed to city life: it reduced fear, increased citizen satisfaction with police, improved police attitudes toward citizens, and increased the morale and job satisfaction of police.[33]

Additionally, research conducted during the 1970s suggested that one factor could help police improve their record in dealing with crime: information. If information about crimes and criminals could be obtained from citizens by police, primarily patrol officers, and could be properly managed by police departments, investigative and other units could significantly increase their effect on crime.[34]

Moreover, research into foot patrol suggested that at least part of the fear reduction potential was linked to the order-maintenance activities of foot patrol officers.[35] Subsequent work in Houston and Newark indicated that tactics other than foot patrol that, like foot patrol, emphasized increasing the quantity and improving the quality of police-citizen interactions had outcomes similar to those of foot patrol (fear reduction, etc.).[36] Meanwhile, many other cities were developing programs [that], though not evaluated, [were] similar to those in the foot patrol, Flint, and fear reduction experiments.[37]

The findings of foot patrol and fear reduction experiments, when coupled with the research on the relationship between fear and disorder, created new opportunities for police to understand the increasing concerns of citizens' groups about disorder (gangs, prostitutes, etc.) and to work with citizens to do something about it. Police discovered that when they asked citizens about their priorities, citizens appreciated the inquiry and also provided useful information—often about problems that beat officers might have been aware of, but about which departments had little or no official data (e.g., disorder). Moreover, given the ambiguities that surround both the definitions of disorder and the authority of police to do something about it, police learned that they had to seek authorization from local citizens to intervene in disorderly situations.[38]

Simultaneously, Goldstein's problem-oriented approach to policing[39] was being tested in several communities: Madison, Wisconsin; Baltimore County, Maryland; and Newport News, Virginia. Problem-oriented policing rejects the fragmented approach in which police deal with each incident, whether citizen- or police-initiated, as an isolated event with neither history nor future. Pierce's findings about calls for service illustrate Goldstein's point: 60 percent of the calls for service in any given year in Boston originated from 10 percent of the households calling the police.[40] Furthermore, Goldstein and his colleagues in Madison, Newport News, and Baltimore County discovered the following: police officers enjoy operating with a holistic approach to their work; they have the capacity to do it successfully; they can work with citizens and other agencies to solve problems; and citizens seem to appreciate working with police—findings similar to those of the foot patrol experiments (Newark and Flint)[41] and the fear reduction experiments (Houston and Newark).[42]

The problem confronting police, policymakers, and academicians is that these trends and findings seem to contradict many of the tenets that dominated police thinking for a generation. Foot patrol creates new intimacy between citizens and police. Problem solving is hardly the routinized and standardized patrol modality that reformers thought was necessary to maintain control of police and limit their discretion. Indeed, use of discretion is the *sine qua non* of problem-solving policing. Relying on citizen endorsement of order-maintenance activities to justify police action acknowledges a continued or new reliance on political authorization for police work in general. And, accepting the quality of urban life as an outcome of good police service emphasizes a wider definition of the police function and the desired effects of police work.

These changes in policing are not merely new police tactics, however. Rather, they represent a new organizational approach, properly called a community strategy. The elements of that strategy are:

Legitimacy and Authorization

There is renewed emphasis on community, or political, authorization for many police tasks, along with law and professionalism. Law continues to be the major legitimating basis of the police function. It defines basic police powers, but it does not fully direct police activities in efforts to maintain order, negotiate conflicts, or solve community problems. It becomes one tool among many others. Neighborhood, or community, support and involvement are required to accomplish those tasks. Professional and bureaucratic authority, especially that which tends to isolate police and insulate them from neighborhood influences, is lessened as citizens contribute more to definitions of problems and identification of solutions. Although in some respects similar to the authorization of policing's political era, community authorization exists in a different political context. The civil service movement, the political centralization that grew out of the Progressive era, and the bureaucratization, professionalization, and unionization of police stand as counterbalances to the possible recurrence of the corrupting influences of ward politics that existed prior to the reform movement.

The Police Function

As indicated above, the definition of police function broadens in the community strategy. It includes order maintenance, conflict resolution, problem solving through the organization, and provision of services, as well as other activities. Crime control remains an important function, with an important difference, however. The reform strategy attempts to control crime directly through preventive patrol and rapid response to calls for service. The community strategy emphasizes crime control *and prevention* as an indirect result of, or an equal partner to, the other activities.

Organizational Design

Community policing operates from organizational assumptions different from those of reform policing. The idea that workers have no legitimate, substantive interest in their work is untenable when programs such as those in Flint, Houston, Los Angeles, New York City, Baltimore County, Newport News, and others are examined. Consulting with community groups, problem solving, maintaining order, and other such activities are antithetical to the reform ideal of eliminating officers' discretion through routinization and standardization of police activities. Moreover, organizational decentralization is inherent in community policing: the involvement of police officers in diagnosing and responding to neighborhood and community problems necessarily pushes operational and tactical decision making to the lower levels of the organization. The creation of neighborhood police stations (storefronts, for example), reopening of precinct stations, and establishment of beat offices (in schools, churches, etc.) are concrete examples of such decentralization.

Decentralization of tactical decision making to precinct or beat levels does not imply abdication of executive obligations and functions, however. Developing, articulating, and monitoring organizational strategy remains the responsibility of management. Within this strategy, operational and tactical decision making is decentralized. This implies what may at first appear to be a paradox: while the number of managerial levels may decrease, the number of managers may increase. Sergeants in a decentralized regime, for example, have managerial responsibilities that exceed those they would have in a centralized organization.

At least two other elements attend this decentralization: increased participative management and increased involvement of top police executives in planning and implementation. Chiefs have discovered that programs are easier to conceive and implement if officers themselves are involved in their development through task forces, temporary matrix-like organizational units, and other organizational innovations that tap the wisdom and experience of sergeants and patrol officers. Additionally, police executives have learned that good ideas do not translate themselves into successful programs without extensive involvement of the chief executive and his close agents in every stage of planning and implementation, a lesson learned in the private sector as well.[43]

One consequence of decentralized decision making, participative planning and management, and executive involvement in planning is that fewer levels of authority are required to administer police organizations. Some police organizations, including the London Metropolitan Police (Scotland Yard), have begun to reduce the number of middle-management layers, while others are contemplating doing so. Moreover, as in the private sector, as computerized information gathering systems reach their potential in police departments, the need for middle managers whose primary function is data collection will be further reduced.

External Relationships

Community policing relies on an intimate relationship between police and citizens. This is accomplished in a variety of ways: relatively long-term assignments of officers to beats, programs that emphasize familiarity between citizens and police (police knocking on doors, consultations, crime control meetings for police and citizens, assignment to officers of "caseloads" of households with ongoing problems, problem solving, etc.), revitalization or development of Police Athletic League programs, educational programs in grade and high schools, and other programs. Moreover, police are encouraged to respond to the feelings and fears of citizens that result from a variety of social problems or from victimizations.

Further, the police are restructuring their relationship with neighborhood groups and institutions. Earlier, during the reform era, police had claimed a monopolistic responsibility for crime control in cities, communities, and neighborhoods; now they recognize serious competitors in the "industry" of crime control, especially private security and the community crime control movement. Whereas in the past police had dismissed these sources of competition or, as in the case of community crime control, had attempted to co-opt the movement for their own purposes,[44] now police in many cities (Boston, New York, Houston, and Los Angeles, to name a few) are moving to structure working relationships or strategic alliances with neighborhood and community crime-control groups. Although there is less evidence of attempts to develop alliances with the private security industry, a recent proposal to the National Institute of Justice envisioned an experimental alliance between the Fort Lauderdale, Florida, Police Department and the Wackenhut Corporation in which the two organizations would share responses to calls for service.

Demand Management

In the community problem-solving strategy, a major portion of demands is decentralized, with citizens encouraged to bring problems directly to beat officers or precinct offices. Use of 911 is discouraged, except for dire emergencies. Whether tactics include aggressive foot patrol as in Flint or problems solving as in Newport News, the emphasis is on police officers' interacting with citizens to determine the types of problems they are confronting and to devise solutions to those problems. In contrast to reform policing with its selling orientation, this approach is more like marketing: customer preferences are sought, and satisfying customer needs and wants, rather than selling a previously packaged product or service, is emphasized. In the case of police, they gather information about citizens' wants, diagnose the nature of the problem, devise possible solutions, and then determine which segments of the community they can best serve and which can be best served by other agencies and institutions that provide services, including crime control.

Additionally, many cities are involved in the development of demarketing programs.[45] The most noteworthy example of demarketing is in the area of rapid response to calls for service. Whether through the development of alternatives to calls for service, educational programs designed to discourage citizens from using the 911 system, or, as in a few cities, simply not responding to many calls for service, police actively attempt to demarket a program that had been actively sold earlier. Often demarketing 911 is thought of as a negative process. It need not be so, however. It is an attempt by police to change social, political, and fiscal circumstances to bring consumers' wants in line with police resources and to accumulate evidence about the value of particular police tactics.

Tactics and Technology

Community policing tactics include foot patrol, problem solving, information gathering, victim counseling and services, community organizing
and consultation, education, walk-and-ride and knock-on-door programs, as well as regular patrol, specialized forms of patrol, and rapid
response to emergency calls for service. Emphasis is placed on information sharing between patrol and detectives to increase the possibility of
crime solution and clearance.

Measured Outcomes

The measures of success in the community strategy are broad: quality of
life in neighborhoods, problem solution, reduction in fear, increased
order, citizen satisfaction with police services, as well as crime control.
In sum, the elements of the community strategy include:

- Authorization—community support (political), law, profession-
alism
- Function—crime control, crime prevention, problem solving
- Organizational design—decentralized, task forces, matrices
- Relationship to environment—consultative, police defend values
of law and professionalism, but listen to community concerns
- Demand—channeled through analysis of underlying problems
- Tactics and technology—foot patrol, problem solving, etc.
- Outcomes—quality of life and citizen satisfaction

CONCLUSION

We have argued that there were two stages of policing in the past, political and reform, and that we are now moving into a third, the community era. To carefully examine the dimensions of policing during each of
these eras, we have used the concept of organizational strategy. We believe that this concept can be used not only to describe the different
styles of policing in the past and the present, but also to sharpen the understanding of police policy makers of the future.

For example, the concept helps explain policing's perplexing experience with team policing during the 1960s and 1970s. Despite the popularity of team policing with officers involved in it and with citizens, it
generally did not remain in police departments for very long. It was unusually planned and implemented with enthusiasm and maintained for
several years. Then, with little fanfare, it would vanish—with everyone
associated with it saying regretfully that for some reason it just did not
work as a police tactic. However, a close examination of team policing reveals that it was a strategy that innovators mistakenly approached as a tactic. It had implications for authorization (police turned to neighborhoods
for support), organizational design (tactical decisions were made at lower

levels of the organization), definition of function (police broadened their service role), relationship to environment (permanent team members responded to the needs of small geographical areas), demand (wants and needs came to team members directly from citizens), tactics (consultation with citizens, etc.), and outcomes (citizen satisfaction, etc.). What becomes clear, though, is that team policing was a competing strategy with different assumptions about every element of police business. It was no wonder that it expired under such circumstances. Team and reform policing were strategically incompatible—one did not fit into the other. A police department could have a small team policing unit or conduct a team policing experiment, but business as usual was reform policing.

Likewise, although foot patrol symbolizes the new strategy for many citizens, it is a mistake to equate the two. Foot patrol is a tactic, a way of delivering police services. In Flint, its inauguration has been accompanied by implementation of most of the elements of a community strategy, which has become business as usual. In most places, foot patrol is not accompanied by the other elements. It is outside the mainstream of "real" policing and often provided only as a sop to citizens and politicians who are demanding the development of different policing styles. This certainly was the case in New Jersey when foot patrol was evaluated by the Police Foundation.[46] Another example is in Milwaukee, where two police budgets are passed: the first is the police budget; the second, a supplementary budget for modest levels of foot patrol. In both cases, foot patrol is outside the mainstream of police activities and conducted primarily as a result of external pressures placed on departments.

It is also a mistake to equate problem solving or increased order-maintenance activities with the new strategy. Both are tactics. They can be implemented either as part of a new organizational strategy, as foot patrol was in Flint, or as an "add-on," as foot patrol was in most of the cities in New Jersey. Drawing a distinction between organizational add-ons and a change in strategy is not an academic quibble; it gets to the heart of the current situation in policing. We are arguing that policing is in a period of transition from a reform strategy to what we call a community strategy. The change involves more than making tactical or organizational adjustments and accommodations. Just as policing went through a basic change when it moved from the political to the reform strategy, it is going through a similar change now. If elements of the emerging organizational strategy are identified and the policing institution is guided through the change rather than left blindly thrashing about, we expect that the public will be better served, policy makers and police administrators more effective, and the profession of policing revitalized.

A final point: the classical theory of organization that continues to dominate police administration in most American cities is alien to most of the elements of the new strategy. The new strategy will not accommodate to the classical theory: the latter denies too much of the real nature of police work, promulgates unsustainable myths about the nature and quality of police supervision, and creates too much cynicism in officers attempting to do creative problem solving. Its assumptions about workers are simply wrong.

Organizational theory has developed well beyond the stage it was at during the early 1900s, and policing does have organizational options that are consistent with the newly developing organizational strategy. Arguably, policing, which was moribund during the 1970s, is beginning a resurgence. It is overthrowing a strategy that was remarkable in its time, but which could not adjust to the changes of recent decades. Risks attend the new strategy and its implementation. The risks, however, for the community and the profession of policing, are not as great as attempting to maintain a strategy that faltered on its own terms during the 1960s and 1970s.

NOTES

1. Kenneth R. Andrews, *The Concept of Corporate Strategy* (Homewood, Illinois: Richard D. Irwin, Inc., 1980).
2. Robert M. Fogelson, *Big-City Police* (Cambridge, Harvard University Press, 1977); Samuel Walker, *A Critical History of Police Reform: The Emergence of Professionalism* (Lexington, Mass.: Lexington Books, 1977).
3. Mark H. Moore and George L. Kelling, "To Serve and Protect: Learning from Police History," *The Public Interest* 7 (winter 1983).
4. K. E. Jordan, *Ideology and the Coming of Professionalism: American Urban Police in the 1920s and 1930s* (dissertation, Rutgers University, 1972).
5. Fogelson, *Big-City Police.*
6. Eric H. Monkkonen, *Police in Urban America, 1860–1920* (Cambridge, Mass.: Cambridge University Press, 1981).
7. *The Newark Foot Patrol Experiment* (Washington, D.C., Police Foundation, 1981).
8. John Eck, *Solving Crimes: The Investigation of Burglary and Robbery* (Washington, D.C.: Police Executive Research Forum, 1984).
9. Thomas A. Reppetto, *The Blue Parade* (New York: The Free Press, 1978).
10. Fogelson, *Big-City Police.*
11. *Ibid.*
12. George L. Kelling, "Reforming the Reforms: The Boston Police Department" (occasional paper, Joint Center for Urban Studies of M.I.T. and Harvard, Cambridge, 1983).
13. George L. Kelling, "Juveniles and Police: The End of the Nightstick," in *From Children to Citizens, Vol. II: The Role of the Juvenile Court,* Francis X. Hartmann, ed., (New York: Springer-Verlag, 1987).
14. Walker, *A Critical History of Police Reform: The Emergence of Professionalism.*
15. Fogelson, *Big-City Police.*
16. Kelling, "Juveniles and Police: The End of the Nightstick."
17. Orlando W. Wilson, *Police Administration* (New York: McGraw Hill, 1950).
18. "Police Guidelines," John F. Kennedy School of Government Case Program #C14-75-24, 1975.
19. Herman Goldstein, *Policing a Free Society* (Cambridge, Mass.: Ballinger, 1977).
20. Kelling, "Reforming the Reforms: The Boston Police Department."
21. Fogelson, *Big-City Police.*
22. William H. Parker, "The Police Challenge in Our Great Cities," *The Annals* 29 (January 1954): 5–13.
23. For a detailed discussion of the differences between selling and marketing, see John L. Crompton and Charles W. Lamb, *Marketing Government and Social Services* (New York: John Wiley and Sons, 1986).

24. Commissioner Francis "Mickey" Roache of Boston has said that when the 911 system was instituted there, citizens persisted in calling "their" police—the district station. To circumvent this preference, district telephone numbers were changed so that citizens would be inconvenienced if they dialed the old number.
25. *The Newark Foot Patrol Experiment.*
26. Orlando W. Wilson, *Police Administration.*
27. A. E. Leonard, "Crime Reporting as a Police Management Tool," *The Annals* 29 (January 1954).
28. George L. Kelling et al., *The Kansas City Preventive Patrol Experiment: A Summary Report* (Washington, D.C.: Police Foundation, 1974); William Spelman and Dale K. Brown, *Calling the Police* (Washington, D.C.: Police Executive Research Forum, 1982).
29. *The Newark Foot Patrol Experiment;* Wesley Skogan and Michael G. Maxfield, *Coping with Crime* (Beverly Hills, Calif.: Sage, 1981); Robert Trojanowicz, *An Evaluation of the Neighborhood Foot Patrol Program in Flint, Michigan* (East Lansing: Michigan State University, 1982).
30. Mary Ann Wycoff, *The Role of Municipal Police Research as a Prelude to Changing It* (Washington, D.C.: Police Foundation, 1982); Goldstein, *Policing a Free Society.*
31. Raymond E. Miles and Charles C. Snow, *Organizational Strategy, Structure and Process* (New York: McGraw-Hill, 1978).
32. *The Newark Foot Patrol Experiment.*
33. *The Newark Foot Patrol Experiment;* Trojanowicz, *An Evaluation of the Neighborhood Foot Patrol Program in Flint, Michigan.*
34. Tony Pate et al., *Three Approaches to Criminal Apprehension in Kansas City: An Evaluation Report* (Washington, D.C., Police Foundation, 1976); Eck, *Solving Crimes: The Investigation of Burglary and Robbery.*
35. James Q. Wilson and George L. Kelling, "Police and Neighborhood Safety: Broken Windows," *The Atlantic Monthly* (March 1982): 29–38.
36. Tony Pate et al, *Reducing Fear of Crime in Houston and Newark: A Summary Report* (Washington, D.C.: Police Foundation, 1986).
37. Jerome H. Skolnick and David H. Bayley, *The New Blue Line: Police Innovation in Six American Cities* (New York: The Free Press, 1986); Albert J. Reiss Jr., *Policing a City's Central District: The Oakland Story* (Washington, D.C.: National Institute of Justice, March 1985).
38. Wilson and Kelling, "Police and Neighborhood Safety: Broken Windows."
39. Herman Goldstein, "Improving Policing: A Problem-Oriented Approach," *Crime and Delinquency* (April 1979): 236–258.
40. Glenn Pierce et al., "Evaluation of an Experiment in Proactive Police Intervention in the Field of Domestic Violence Using Repeat Call Analysis" (Boston, Mass.: The Boston Fenway Project, Inc., 13 May 1987).
41. *The Newark Foot Patrol Experiment;* Trojanowicz, *An Evaluation of the Neighborhood Foot Patrol Program in Flint, Michigan.*
42. Pate et al., *Reducing Fear of Crime in Houston and Newark: A Summary Report.*
43. James R. Gardner, Robert Rachlin, and H. W. Allen Sweeney, eds., *Handbook of Strategic Planning* (New York: John Wiley and Sons, 1986).
44. Kelling, "Juveniles and Police: The End of the Nightstick."
45. Crompton and Lamb, *Marketing Government and Social Services.*
46. *The Newark Foot Patrol Experiment.*

Article 8

Understanding Community Policing: A Framework for Action

Community Policing Consortium

INTRODUCING COMMUNITY POLICING

The movement toward community policing has gained momentum in recent years as police and community leaders search for more effective ways to promote public safety and to enhance the quality of life in their neighborhoods. Chiefs, sheriffs, and other policing officials are currently assessing what changes in orientation, organization, and operations will allow them to benefit the communities they serve by improving the quality of the services they provide.

Community policing encompasses a variety of philosophical and practical approaches and is still evolving rapidly. Community policing strategies vary depending on the needs and responses of the communities involved; however, certain basic principles and considerations are common to all community policing efforts.

To date, no succinct overview of community policing exists for practitioners who want to learn to use this wide-ranging approach to address the problems of crime and disorder in their communities. "Understanding Community Policing," prepared by the Community Policing Consortium, is the beginning of an effort to bring community policing into focus. The document, while not a final product, assembles and examines the critical components of community policing to help foster the learning process and to structure the experimentation and modification required to make community policing work.

Reprinted from Community Policing Consortium, "Understanding Community Policing: A Framework for Action" (Washington, D.C.: Bureau of Justice Assistance, August 1994).

TRACING THE ROOTS OF COMMUNITY POLICING

There are compelling reasons why law enforcement leaders believe the time has come to alter the policies and practices of their organizations. These reasons are rooted in the history of policing and police research during the last quarter of a century, in the changing nature of communities, and in the shifting characteristics of crime and violence that affect these communities.

Policing strategies that worked in the past are not always effective today. The desired goal, an enhanced sense of safety, security, and well-being, has not been achieved. Practitioners agree that there is a pressing need for innovation to curb the crises in many communities. Both the level and nature of crime in this country and the changing character of American communities are causing police to seek more effective methods. Many urban communities are experiencing serious problems with illegal drugs, gang violence, murders, muggings, and burglaries. Suburban and rural communities have not escaped unscathed. They are also noting increases in crime and disorder.

In addition, the social fabric of our country has changed radically. The family unit is not as stable as it once was. Single working parents find it extremely difficult to spend enough time with their children, and churches and schools have been unable to fill this void. Immigrants, ethnic groups, and minorities, while adding to the diverse nature of American communities, often have different interests and pursue disparate goals.

Governments at all levels are having increased difficulty balancing budgets, which frequently forces police departments to allocate dwindling resources to growing problems.

In this rapidly changing environment, where police cope with an epidemic drug problem, gang activity, and increased levels of violence, the concept of community policing is taking hold. Police leaders using this commonsense approach to the problems of crime and disorder, an approach that may very well enhance and maximize performance and resources, have struck a responsive chord in both national and local governments and in communities across the nation.

Government and community leaders are beginning to recognize that they also must accept responsibility for keeping their neighborhoods safe. Communities must take a unified stand against crime, violence, and disregard for the law and must make a commitment to increasing crime prevention and intervention activities. Police agencies must help build stronger, more self-sufficient communities—communities in which crime and disorder will not thrive.

Community policing is democracy in action. It requires the active participation of local government, civic and business leaders, public and private agencies, residents, churches, schools, and hospitals. All who share a concern for the welfare of the neighborhood should bear responsibility for safeguarding that welfare. Community policing is being advocated by leaders at the highest levels of government—including President Clinton and U.S. Attorney General Reno, who describes it as the "changing of policing." In addition, it has been suggested that community policing can play a primary role in changing the way all government services are provided at the community level.

The implementation of community policing necessitates fundamental changes in the structure and management of police organizations. Community policing differs from traditional policing in how the community is perceived and in its expanded policing goals. While crime control and prevention remain central priorities, community policing strategies use a wide variety of methods to address these goals. The police and the community become partners in addressing problems of disorder and neglect (e.g., gang activity, abandoned cars, and broken windows) that, although perhaps not criminal, can eventually lead to serious crime. As links between the police and the community are strengthened over time, the ensuing partnership will be better able to pinpoint and mitigate the underlying causes of crime.

Police are finding that crime-control tactics need to be augmented with strategies that prevent crime, reduce the fear of crime, and improve the quality of life in neighborhoods. Fear of crime has become a significant problem in itself. A highly visible police presence helps reduce fear within the community, fear which has been found to be ". . . more closely correlated with disorder than with crime."[1] However, because fear of crime can limit activity, keep residents in their homes, and contribute to empty streets, this climate of decline can result in even greater numbers of crimes. By getting the community involved, police will have more resources available for crime-prevention activities, instead of being forced into an after-the-fact response to crime.

Analyses of crime statistics show that the current emphasis on crime fighting has had a limited effect on reducing crime. In addition, the concept of centralized management of most police organizations has often served to isolate police from the communities they serve. This isolation hampers crime-fighting efforts. Statistics on unreported crime suggest that in many cases police are not aware of existing problems. Without strong ties to the community, police may not have access to pertinent information from citizens that could help solve or deter crime.

Helpful information will be forthcoming from community members when police have established a relationship of trust with the community they serve. Establishing this trust will take time, particularly in communities where internal conflicts exist or where relations with the police have been severely strained. Community policing offers a way for the police and the community to work together to resolve the serious problems that exist in these neighborhoods. Only when community members believe the police are genuinely interested in community perspectives and problems will they begin to view the police as a part of that community.

Experience and research reveal that "community institutions are the first line of defense against disorder and crime. . . ."[2] Thus, it is essential that the police work closely with all facets of the community to identify concerns and to find the most effective solutions. This is the essence of community policing.

The Role of the Police: A Historical Perspective

When Sir Robert Peel established the London Metropolitan Police, he set forth a number of principles, one of which could be considered the seed of community policing: ". . . the police are the public and the public are the police."[3] For a number of reasons, the police lost sight of this relationship as the central organizing concept for police service. Researchers have suggested that the reform era in government, which began in the early 1900s, coupled with a nationwide move toward professionalization, resulted in the separation of the police from the community.[4] Police managers assigned officers to rotating shifts and moved them frequently from one geographical location to another to eliminate corruption. Management also instituted a policy of centralized control, designed to ensure compliance with standard operating procedures and to encourage a professional aura of impartiality.

This social distancing was also reinforced by technological developments. The expanding role of automobiles replaced the era of the friendly foot patrol officer. By the 1970s, rapid telephone contact with police through 911 systems allowed them to respond quickly to crimes. Answering the overwhelming number of calls for service, however, left police little time to prevent crimes from occurring. As increasingly sophisticated communications technology made it possible for calls to be transmitted almost instantaneously, officers had to respond to demands for assistance regardless of the urgency of the situation. Answering calls severely limited a broad police interaction with the community. The advent of the computer also contributed to the decrease in police contact with the community. Statistics, rather than the type of service provided or the service recipients, became the focus for officers and managers. As computers generated data on crime patterns and trends, counted the incidence of crimes, increased the efficiency of dispatch, and calculated the rapidity and outcome of police response, rapid response became an end in itself.

Random patrolling also served to further break the link between communities and police. Police were instructed to change routes constantly, in an effort to thwart criminals. However, community members also lost the ability to predict when they might be able to interact with their local police.

The height of police isolation came in an era of growing professionalization, when the prevailing ideology was that the professional knew best and when community involvement in crime control was seen by almost everyone as unnecessary.

The movement to end police corruption, the emphasis on professionalization, and the development of new technology occurred in an era of growing crime and massive social change. Police had trouble communicating with all members of the socially and culturally diverse communities they served. The police and the public had become so separated from one another that in some communities an attitude of "us versus them" prevailed between the police and community members. One observer of the urban scene characterized the deteriorating police-community relationship this way: "For the urban poor the police are those who arrest you."[5]

A Social and Professional Awakening

The burst of ideas, arguments, and protests during the 1960s and 1970s mushroomed into a full-scale social movement. Antiwar protestors, civil rights activists, and other groups began to demonstrate in order to be heard. Overburdened and poorly prepared police came to symbolize what these groups sought to change in their government and society. Focusing attention on police policies and practices became an effective way to draw attention to the need for wider change. Police became the targets of hostility, which ultimately led police leaders to concerned reflection and analysis.

In this era of protest, citizens began to take a stronger hand in the development of policies and practices that affected their lives. The police force's inability to handle urban unrest in an effective and appropriate manner brought demands by civic leaders and politicians for a reexamination of police practices. Between 1968 and 1973, three Presidential Commissions made numerous recommendations for changes in policing—recommendations that were initially responded to by outside organizations. Agencies of the U.S. Department of Justice, in collaboration with countless police departments throughout the country who were open to research and innovation, played a major role in stimulating, supporting, and disseminating research and technical assistance. Millions of dollars were spent to foster and support criminal justice education. In addition, these federal agencies supported a wide variety of police training, conferences, research, and technology upgrading.

A number of organizations within the policing field also became committed to improving policing methods in the 1970s. Among those on the forefront of this movement for constructive change were the Police Foundation, the Police Executive Research Forum, the National Organization of Black Law Enforcement Executives, the Urban Sheriffs' Group of the National Sheriffs' Association, and the International Association of Chiefs of Police. These organizations conducted much of the basic research that led police to reevaluate traditional policing methods.

The Role of Research in Policing

Increases in federal funding and the growth of criminal justice education resulted in the rapid development of research on policing. Many of the research findings challenged prevailing police practices and beliefs. Federally funded victimization surveys documented the existence of unreported crime. Practitioners had to acknowledge that only a fraction of crimes were being reported, and, therefore, began seeking ways to improve their image and to interact more effectively with the communities they served.

An early research study was the Kansas City Preventive Patrol Experiment. This field experiment found that randomized patrolling had a limited impact on crime or citizens' attitudes and caused police leaders to begin thinking about alternative ways to use their patrol personnel.[6] Another study by the Kansas City Police Department assessed the value of rapid response by police and concluded that in most cases rapid response did not help solve crimes.[7] The study revealed that a large portion of serious crimes are not deterred by rapid response. The crime sample that was analyzed indicated that almost two-thirds of these crimes were not reported quickly enough for rapid response to be effective. While a prompt police response can increase the chance of making an on-scene arrest, the time it takes a citizen to report a crime largely predetermines the effect that police response time will have on the outcome. This study revealed a need for formal call-screening procedures to differentiate between emergency and nonemergency calls. More efficient dispatching of calls could make additional time available for patrol officers to interact with the community.

This study led to further research that also demonstrated the value of response strategies that ensured that the most urgent calls received the highest priority and the most expeditious dispatch. Studies of alternative responses to calls for service found that community residents would accept responses other than the presence of police immediately on the scene if they were well informed about the types of alternatives used.[8]

Differential police response strategies were also examined by the Birmingham, Alabama, Police Department.[9] The objectives of the project were to increase the efficiency with which calls for service were managed and to improve citizen satisfaction with police service. The study included the use of call-prioritization codes, call-stacking procedures, both police and nonpolice delayed-response strategies, and teleservice. The alternate strategies were found to be successful in diverting calls from mobilized field units without a loss in citizen satisfaction.

The Directed Patrol study assessed how to use most effectively the time made available by more efficient call-response measures.[10] The study suggested that, rather than performing randomized patrols when not handling calls, the officers' time could be more profitably spent addressing specific criminal activities. To direct officers' attention and to help them secure time, the department instituted support steps that included crime analysis, teleservice, and walk-in report-handling capabilities.

The San Diego Police Department conducted several significant research studies during the 1970s. These included an evaluation of one-officer versus two-officer patrol cars, an assessment of the relationship between field interrogations of suspicious persons and criminal deterrence, and a community-oriented policing (COP) project,[11] which was the first empirical study of community policing. The COP project required patrol officers to become knowledgeable about their beats through "beat-profiling" activities, in which officers studied the topographics, demographics, and call histories of their beats. Officers were also expected to develop "tailored patrol" strategies to address the types of crime and citizen concerns revealed by their profiling activities.

Officers participating in the COP project concluded that random patrolling was not as important as previously thought. They also concluded that developing stronger ties with members of the community was more important than once believed. In addition, the project demonstrated that interaction with the community could improve the attitudes of officers toward their jobs and toward the communities they served and could encourage the officers to develop creative solutions to complex problems.

Many of the findings from this study have a direct bearing on contemporary community policing efforts. First, by getting to know members of the community, the officers were able to obtain valuable information about criminal activity and perpetrators. They were also able to obtain realistic assessments of the needs of community members and their expectations of police services. The study also exposed the need to reevaluate the issue of shift rotation. Officers must be assigned to permanent shifts and beats if they are to participate in community activities. Finally, the COP project demonstrated the critical role that shift lieutenants and sergeants play in program planning and implementation. The exclusion of supervisors in training and development efforts ultimately led to the demise of the COP program in San Diego.

In 1979, Herman Goldstein developed and advanced the concept of "problem-oriented policing" (POP), which encouraged police to begin thinking differently about their purpose.[12] Goldstein suggested that problem resolution constituted the true, substantive work of policing and advocated that police identify and address root causes of problems that lead to repeat calls for service. POP required a move from a reactive, incident-oriented stance to one that actively addressed the problems that continually drained police resources. In a study of POP implementation in Newport News, Virginia, POP was found to be an effective approach to addressing many community problems, and important data about POP design and implementation was gathered.[13] Other research indicated that police could identify the "hot spots" of repeat calls in a community and thereby devise strategies to reduce the number of calls.[14]

While much of the policing research conducted in the 1970s dealt with patrol issues, the Rand Corporation examined the role of detectives.[15] This study concluded that detectives solved only a small percentage of the crimes analyzed and that the bulk of the cases solved hinged on information obtained by patrol officers. This dramatically challenged traditional thinking about the roles of detectives and patrol officers in the handling of investigative functions. The implication was that patrol officers should become more actively involved in criminal investigations. The implementation of appropriate training would allow patrol officers to perform some early investigating that could help in obtaining timely case closures, thereby reducing the tremendous caseloads of detectives and allowing them to devote more time to complex investigations.

The Newark Foot Patrol Experiment suggested that police could develop more positive attitudes toward community members and could promote positive attitudes toward police if they spent time on foot in their neighborhoods.[16] Foot patrol also eased citizen fear of crime: ". . . persons living in areas where foot patrol was created perceived a notable decrease in the severity of crime-related problems."[17] Experimental foot patrols in Flint, Michigan, also elicited citizen approval. Residents said foot patrols made them feel safer and residents ". . . felt especially safe when the foot patrol officer was well known and highly visible."[18] In addition, it is worth noting that in both cities the use of foot patrols increased officer satisfaction with police work.[19]

The fear reduction studies provided empirical data on the effectiveness of key community policing tactics (e.g., community organizing, door-to-door contacts, neighborhood mini-stations, and intensified enforcement coupled with community involvement) in reducing fear among residents, improving community conditions, and enhancing the image of the police.[20] Driving this study was the notion that if fear could be reduced, community residents would be more inclined to take an active role in preserving safety and tranquility within their neighborhoods.

Police Response to the Need for Change

A number of dynamic police leaders participated in various Presidential Commissions during the 1960s and 1970s. They also contributed their time and expertise to the newly created police organizations that were working to bring about improvements in policing policies. However, many of these police leaders found themselves alone when they tried to infuse their own departments with this spirit of change. Community policing implementation was impeded by centralized management practices and traditional operating assumptions.

Many experienced police managers and officers found it difficult to accept this challenge to the practices and procedures that had always guided their actions. Thus, it was not surprising that these innovations were often overwhelmed by traditional policies and that the innovators were frequently suspected of being manipulated by outsiders or of pursuing their personal career agendas at the expense of the organization.

Many of today's police managers have supplemented their professional education by studying literature developed since the 1970s. Once considered radical, many of the strategies that evolved from this research on policing are now considered necessary for improving performance. Ideas that were raised 20 years ago have been modified and expanded to fit current conditions.

Police executives realize that it is no longer sufficient to think in terms of making only minor alterations to traditional management and operational practices. Management's current challenge is to meet the escalating and varied demands for service with more effective delivery strategies to optimize staff and resources, to encourage innovative thinking, and to involve the community in policing efforts.

Following the lead of corporate America, police managers are beginning to adopt the principles associated with total quality or participatory management. There is growing recognition in policing that employees should have input into decisions about their work. Management practices that restrict the flow of communication and stifle innovation are giving way to the belief that those actually working in the community can best understand its needs and develop ways to meet them. Police also realize that not only the service providers but also the service recipients must define priorities and join forces with others to find inventive, long-term solutions to deepening problems of crime and violence.

Today the movement for change within policing is led aggressively by policing practitioners themselves. The current shift to community policing reflects the conscious effort of a profession to reexamine its policies and procedures. Incorporating the core components of community policing with existing policing methods is the first step in this ongoing process.

DEFINING THE CORE COMPONENTS OF COMMUNITY POLICING

The growing trend within communities to participate in the fight against crime and disorder has paralleled a growing recognition by police that traditional crime-fighting tactics alone have a limited impact on controlling crime. Community policing is the synthesis of these two movements.

The foundations of a successful community policing strategy are the close, mutually beneficial ties between police and community members. Community policing consists of two complementary core components, community partnership and problem solving. To develop community partnership, police must develop positive relationships with the community, must involve the community in the quest for better crime control and prevention, and must pool their resources with those of the community to address the most urgent concerns of community members. Problem solving is the process through which the specific concerns of communities are identified and through which the most appropriate remedies to abate these problems are found.

Community policing does not imply that police are no longer in authority or that the primary duty of preserving law and order is subordinated. However, tapping into the expertise and resources that exist within communities will relieve police of some of their burdens. Local government officials, social agencies, schools, church groups, business people—all those who work and live in the community and have a stake in its development—will share responsibility for finding workable solutions to problems that detract from the safety and security of the community.

The Concept of Community

The goal of community policing is to reduce crime and disorder by carefully examining the characteristics of problems in neighborhoods and then applying appropriate problem-solving remedies. The "community" for which a patrol officer is given responsibility should be a small, well-defined geographical area. Beats should be configured in a manner that preserves, as much as possible, the unique geographical and social characteristics of neighborhoods while still allowing efficient service.

Patrol officers are the primary providers of police services and have the most extensive contact with community members. In community policing efforts, they will provide the bulk of the daily policing needs of the community, and they will be assisted by immediate supervisors, other police units, and appropriate government and social agencies. Upper level managers and command staff will be responsible for ensuring that the entire organization backs the efforts of patrol officers.

Effective community policing depends on optimizing positive contact between patrol officers and community members. Patrol cars are only one method of conveying police services. Police departments may supplement automobile patrols with foot, bicycle, scooter, and horseback patrols, as well as adding "mini-stations" to bring police closer to the community. Regular community meetings and forums will afford police and community members an opportunity to air concerns and find ways to address them.

Officers working long-term assignments on the same shift and beat will become familiar figures to community members and will become aware of the day-to-day workings of the community. This increased police presence is an initial move in establishing trust and serves to reduce fear of crime among community members, which, in turn, helps create neighborhood security. Fear must be reduced if community members are to participate actively in policing. People will not act if they feel that their actions will jeopardize their safety.

Although the delivery of police services is organized by geographic area, a community may encompass widely diverse cultures, values, and concerns, particularly in urban settings. A community consists of more than just the local government and the neighborhood residents. Churches, schools, hospitals, social groups, private and public agencies, and those who work in the area are also vital members of the community. In addition, those who visit for cultural or recreational purposes or provide services to the area are also concerned with the safety and security of the neighborhood. Including these "communities of interest" in efforts to address problems of crime and disorder can expand the resource base of the community.

Concerns and priorities will vary within and among these communities of interest. Some communities of interest are long-lasting and were formed around racial, ethnic, or occupational lines or [around] a common history, church, or school. Others form and reform as new problems are identified and addressed. Interest groups within communities can be in opposition to one another—sometimes in violent opposition. Intracommunity disputes have been common in large urban centers, especially in times of changing demographics and population migrations.

These multiple and sometimes conflicting interests require patrol officers to function not only as preservers of law and order, but also as skillful mediators. Demands on police from one community of interest can sometimes clash with the rights of another community of interest. For example, a community group may oppose certain police tactics used to crack down on gang activity, which the group believes may result in discriminatory arrest practices. The police must not only protect the rights of the protesting group, but must also work with all of the community members involved to find a way to preserve neighborhood peace. For this process to be effective, community members must communicate their views and suggestions and back up the negotiating efforts of the police. In this way, the entire community participates in the mediation process and helps preserve order. The police must encourage a spirit of cooperation that balances the collective interests of all citizens with the personal rights of individuals.

The conflicts within communities are as important as the commonalities. Police must recognize the existence of both to build the cooperative bonds needed to maintain order, provide a sense of security, and control crime. Police must build lasting relationships that encompass all elements of the community and center around the fundamental issues of public safety and quality of life. The key to managing this difficult task is trust.

Community Partnership: Core Component One

Establishing and maintaining mutual trust is the central goal of the first core component of community policing—community partnership. Police recognize the need for cooperation with the community. In the fight against serious crime, police have encouraged community members to come forth with relevant information. In addition, police have spoken to neighborhood groups, participated in business and civic events, worked with social agencies, and taken part in educational and recreational programs for school children. Special units have provided a variety of crisis intervention services. So how then do the cooperative efforts of community policing differ from the actions that have taken place previously? The fundamental distinction is that, in community policing, the police become an integral part of the community culture, and the community assists in defining future priorities and in allocating resources. The difference is substantial and encompasses basic goals and commitments.

Community partnership means adopting a policing perspective that exceeds the standard law enforcement emphasis. This broadened outlook recognizes the value of activities that contribute to the orderliness and well-being of a neighborhood. These activities could include helping accident or crime victims, providing emergency medical services, helping resolve domestic and neighborhood conflicts (e.g., family violence, landlord-tenant disputes, or racial harassment), working with residents and local businesses to improve neighborhood conditions, controlling automobile and pedestrian traffic, providing emergency social services and referrals to those at risk (e.g., adolescent runaways, the homeless, the intoxicated, and the mentally ill), protecting the exercise of constitutional rights (e.g., guaranteeing a person's right to speak, protecting lawful assemblies from disruption), and providing a model of citizenship (e.g., helpfulness, respect for others, honesty, and fairness).

These services help develop trust between the police and the community. This trust will enable the police to gain greater access to valuable information from the community that could lead to the solution and prevention of crimes, will engender support for needed crime-control measures, and will provide an opportunity for officers to establish a working relationship with the community. The entire police organization must be involved in enlisting the cooperation of community members in promoting safety and security.

Building trust will not happen overnight; it will require ongoing effort. But trust must be achieved before police can assess the needs of the community and construct the close ties that will engender community support. In turn, this cooperative relationship will deepen the bonds of trust.

To build this trust for an effective community partnership, police must treat people with respect and sensitivity. The use of unnecessary force and arrogance, aloofness, or rudeness at any level of the agency will dampen the willingness of community members to ally themselves with the police.

The effective mobilization of community support requires different approaches in different communities. Establishing trust and obtaining cooperation are often easier in middle-class and affluent communities than in poorer communities, where mistrust of police may have a long history. Building bonds in some neighborhoods may involve supporting basic social institutions (e.g., families, churches, schools) that have been weakened by pervasive crime or disorder.[21] The creation of viable communities is necessary if lasting alliances that nurture cooperative efforts are to be sustained. Under community policing, the police become both catalysts and facilitators in the development of these communities.

Community policing expands police efforts to prevent and control crime. The community is no longer viewed by police as a passive presence or a source of limited information, but as a partner in this effort. Community concerns with crime and disorder thus become the target of efforts by the police and the community working in tandem.

The close alliance forged with the community should not be limited to an isolated incident or series of incidents, nor confined to a specific time frame. The partnership between the police and the community must be enduring and balanced. It must break down the old concepts of professional versus civilian, expert versus novice, and authority figure versus subordinate. The police and the community must be collaborators in the quest to encourage and preserve peace and prosperity.

The more conspicuous police presence of the long-term patrol officer in itself may encourage community response. But it is not sufficient. The entire police organization must vigorously enlist the cooperation of community residents in pursuing the goals of deterring crime and preserving order. Police personnel on every level must join in building a broad rapport with community members. For the patrol officer, police–community partnership entails talking to local business owners to help identify their problems and concerns, visiting residents in their homes to offer advice on security, and helping to organize and support neighborhood watch groups and regular community meetings. For example, the patrol officer will canvass the neighborhood for information about a string of burglaries and then revisit those residents to inform them when the burglar is caught. The chief police executive will explain and discuss controversial police tactics so that community members understand the necessity of these tactics for public and officer safety. The department management will consult community members about gang suppression tactics, and every level of the department will actively solicit the concerns and suggestions of community groups, residents, leaders, and local government officials. In this police–community partnership, providing critical social services will be acknowledged as being inextricably linked to deterring crime, and problem solving will become a cooperative effort.

Problem Solving: Core Component Two

Problem solving is a broad term that implies more than simply the elimination and prevention of crimes. Problem solving is based on the assumption that "crime and disorder can be reduced in small geographic areas by carefully studying the characteristics of problems in the area, and then applying the appropriate resources. . . ." and on the assumption that "individuals make choices based on the opportunities presented by the immediate physical and social characteristics of an area. By manipulating these factors, people will be less inclined to act in an offensive manner."[22]

The problem-solving process is explained further:

> The theory behind problem-oriented policing is simple. Underlying conditions create problems. These conditions might include the characteristics of the people involved (offenders, potential victims, and others), the social setting in which these people interact, the physical environments, and the way the public deals with these conditions.
>
> A problem created by these conditions may generate one or more incidents. These incidents, while stemming from a common source, may appear to be different. For example, social and physical conditions in a deteriorated apartment complex may generate burglaries, acts of vandalism, intimidation of pedestrians by rowdy teenagers, and other incidents. These incidents, some of which come to police attention, are symptoms of the problems. The incidents will continue so long as the problem that creates them persists.[23]

As police recognize the effectiveness of the problem-solving approach, there is a growing awareness that community involvement is essential for its success. Determining the underlying causes of crime depends, to a great extent, on an in-depth knowledge of community. Therefore, community participation in identifying and setting priorities will contribute to effective problem-solving efforts by the community and the police. Cooperative problem solving also reinforces trust, facilitates the exchange of information, and leads to the identification of other areas that could benefit from the mutual attention of the police and the community. The problem-solving process, like community partnership, is self-renewing.

For this process to operate effectively, the police need to devote attention to and recognize the validity of community concerns. Neighborhood groups and the police will not always agree on which specific problems deserve attention first. Police may regard robberies as the biggest problem in a particular community, while residents may find derelicts who sleep in doorways, break bottles on sidewalks, and pick through garbage cans to be the number one problem. Under community policing, the problem with derelicts should also receive early attention from the police with the assistance of other government agencies and community members. For example, one police captain reported the following:

> What we found . . . was that maybe some things that we thought were important to them really weren't that important, and other things we didn't think were important at all, were very important . . . Like abandoned cars: in one of our areas, that was a very important thing. They were really bugged about all these abandoned cars, and they thought it was a bad police department that wouldn't take care of them. When we started removing the cars their opinion of us went up, even though because we'd changed priorities we were putting fewer drug addicts in jail.[24]

Therefore, in addition to the serious crime problems identified by police, community policing must also address the problems of significant concern to the community. Community policing in effect allows community members to bring problems of great concern to them to the attention of the police. Once informed of community concerns, the police must work with citizens to address them, while at the same time encouraging citizens to assist in solving the problems of concern to the police.

The nature of community problems will vary widely and will often involve multiple incidents that are related by factors including geography, time, victim or perpetrator group, and environment. Problems can affect a small area of a community, an entire community, or many communities. Community problems might include the following:

- An unusually high number of burglaries that are creating great anxiety and fear among residents in an apartment complex
- Panhandling that creates fear in a business district
- Prostitutes in local parks or on heavily traveled streets
- Disorderly youth who regularly assemble in the parking lot of a convenience store
- An individual who persistently harasses and provokes community members[25]

In community policing, the problem-solving process is dependent on input from both the police and the community. Problem solving can involve:

- Eliminating the problem entirely. This type of solution is usually limited to disorder problems. Examples include eliminating traffic congestion by erecting traffic control signs and destroying or rehabilitating abandoned buildings that can provide an atmosphere conducive to crime.

- Reducing the number of the occurrences of the problem. Drug-dealing and the accompanying problems of robbery and gang violence will be decreased if the police and community work together to set up drug counseling and rehabilitation centers. Longer range solutions might include intensifying drug education in schools, churches, and hospitals.
- Reducing the degree of injury per incident. For example, police can teach store clerks how to act during a robbery in order to avoid injury or death and can advise women in the community on ways to minimize the chances of being killed or seriously injured if attacked.
- Improving problem handling. Police should always make an effort to treat people humanely (e.g., show sensitivity in dealing with rape victims and seek ways to ease their trauma, or increase effectiveness in handling runaway juveniles, drug addicts, and drunk drivers by working with other agencies more closely).
- Manipulating environmental factors to discourage criminal behavior. This can include collaborative efforts to add better lighting, remove overgrown weeds and trim shrubbery, and seal off vacant apartment buildings.

There are as many solutions as there are problems. These solutions range from simple, inexpensive measures to complex, long-term answers that will require significant investment of staff and resources. Problem solving is limited only by the imagination, creativity, perseverance, and enthusiasm of those involved. Community policing allows solutions to be tailor-made to the specific concerns of each community. The best solutions are those that satisfy community members, improve safety, diminish anxiety, lead to increased order, strengthen the ties between the community and the police, and minimize coercive actions. The following example describes such a solution:

A patrol officer faced with chronic nighttime robberies of convenience stores discovered that a major contributing factor was that cash registers could not be seen from the street, either because of their location within the store or because of posters plastered on front windows. The officer did not identify the "root cause" or ultimate cause of crime, but instead identified an underlying condition that, once addressed, held promise of reducing the number of future convenience store robberies.

To identify this underlying problem, the patrol officer talked with and solicited suggestions from convenience store owners and employees, other members of the business community, and community residents. The officer's identification of a contributing cause of the robberies is a high-leverage accomplishment in terms of its likely positive impact on the frequency of future robberies. Evidence of police concern and soliciting input from the community also reinforces cooperative ties.[26]

Patrol officers serve as catalysts for joint police and community problem-solving endeavors. They are involved with the community on a day-to-day basis, understand its unique physical and social characteristics, are aware of local problems, and, when needed, can help community members articulate their needs. Many problems within the community can be successfully handled by patrol officers or their immediate supervisors and members of the community—e.g., determining that better lighting would decrease the incidence of muggings at a local park.

All levels of the police organization should contribute to problem solving, depending on the scope and seriousness of the problem. For example, crafting a solution to widespread incidents of spousal assault taking place in several communities in an agency's jurisdiction might involve multiple levels of police management. Patrol officers may have noticed a correlation between spousal assaults and excessive drinking by the perpetrators, especially at illegal after-hours clubs. The officers, their supervisors, and community members might explore ways to close down these clubs with the help of local zoning and city planning boards. Perpetrators with alcohol problems might be required to attend rehabilitation programs run by a city agency. Meanwhile, mid- and senior-level police managers and community leaders might confer with women's groups and other social agencies about providing temporary housing and counseling for victims and their families. In addition, members of the community might be able to repair an abandoned building to house the victims.

The problem-solving process relies on the expertise and assistance of an array of social and government agencies and community resources. At the senior command level, police managers might combine forces with a civil abatement agency to condemn and board up crack houses. One police officer seeking a systemwide approach to the problem of spousal assault formed a team comprised of units from the police department and representatives from women's shelters, the YWCA, nearby military bases, the prosecutor's office, newspapers, hospitals, and social agencies. A tremendous amount of leverage can be attained through the collaboration and partnership of this type of far-ranging alliance.

Community policing puts new emphasis on tackling the underlying causes of crime by addressing problems at the grassroots level. To maximize the time that the patrol officer can spend interacting with community members, community policing encourages the use of the 911 system only for true emergencies. Nonemergency calls should be handled through other means, including delays in responding and report handling by the police station or sheriff's office over the telephone or by mail.

These alternative measures require a wide base of support within the community. To obtain this support, the police must instruct residents on the nature of an emergency and on alternative responses to nonemergencies. Alternative responses will need to be thoroughly explained before community members will accept them. The residents should be secure in the knowledge that the police response will be appropriate for the urgency of the demand for service, and that the reduction in the volume of

911 calls will allow officers to spend more time in the community and will maximize the use of the residents' tax dollars.

Implications for Management and the Organizational Structure

Effective community partnership and problem solving will require the mastery of new responsibilities and the adoption of a flexible style of management. Community policing emphasizes the value of the patrol function and the patrol officer as an individual. Patrol officers have traditionally been accorded low status despite the scope and sensitivity of the tasks they perform. Community policing requires the shifting of initiative, decision making, and responsibility downward within the police organization. The neighborhood officer or deputy sheriff becomes responsible for managing the delivery of services to a community, and ". . . everything of a policing nature [in that community] 'belongs' to that person."[27]

With this responsibility comes wide-ranging discretionary and decision-making power. Under community policing, patrol officers are given broader freedom to decide what should be done and how it should be done in their communities—they assume managerial responsibility for the delivery of police services to their assigned area. Patrol officers are the most familiar with the needs and strengths of their communities and are thus in the best position to forge the close ties with the community that lead to effective solutions to local problems.

The shift in status and duties of the patrol officer is critical to the community partnership and problem-solving components of community policing. Assignment stability of these neighborhood officers is also essential if they are to develop close working relationships within their communities because

> . . . they are expected to engage in activities other than simply reacting to calls for service. Having officers periodically rotate among the shifts impedes their ability to identify problems. It also discourages creative solutions to impact the problems, because the officers end up rotating away from the problems. Thus, a sense of responsibility to identify and resolve problems is lost. Likewise, management cannot hold the officers accountable to deal with problems if the officers are frequently rotated from one shift to another.[28]

The enhanced role of the patrol officer has enormous organizational and managerial implications. The entire police organization must be structured, managed, and operated in a manner that supports the efforts of the patrol officer and that encourages a cooperative approach to solving problems. Under community policing, command is no longer centralized, and many decisions now come from the bottom up instead of from the top down. Greater decision-making power is given to those closest to the situation with the expectation that this change will improve the overall performance of the agency. This transformation in command structure is not only sound management, but is also crucial to the creation of meaningful and productive ties between the police and the community. To establish a partnership with the community,

> . . . the police must move to empower two groups: the public itself and the street officers who serve it most closely and regularly. Only when the public has a real voice in setting police priorities will its needs be taken seriously; only when street officers have the operational latitude to take on the problems they encounter with active departmental backing will those needs really be addressed.[29]

Community policing alters the contemporary functions of supervisors and managers. Under community policing, management serves to guide, rather than dominate, the actions of patrol officers and to ensure that officers have the necessary resources to solve the problems in their communities. Creativity and innovation must be fostered if satisfactory solutions to long-standing community problems are to be found. The transition to community policing requires recognizing that the new responsibilities and decision-making power of the neighborhood patrol officers must be supported, guided, and encouraged by the entire organization. In addition, it requires establishing clearly stated values that provide both the police organization and the public with a clear sense of policing's expanded focus and direction.

Values: The Guiding Principles

Community policing is ultimately about values—specifically, the change in values that is needed to adapt policing to these changing times. Values must be ingrained in the very culture of the organization and must be reflected in its objectives, in its policies, and in the actions of its personnel.

> Values are the beliefs that guide an organization and the behavior of its employees. . . . The most important beliefs are those that set forth the ultimate purposes of the organization. . . . They provide the organization with its raison d'etre for outsiders and insiders alike and justify the continuing investment in the organization's enterprise. . . . [They] influence substantive and administrative decisions facing the organization, they lend a coherence and predictability to top management's actions and the responses to the actions of employees. This helps employees make proper decisions and use their discretion with confidence that they are contributing to rather than detracting from organizational performance.[30]

A clear statement of beliefs and goals gives direction to the organization and helps ensure that values are transformed into appropriate actions and behaviors. The entire agency must be committed to the values embodied by such a mission statement. This mission statement should be widely disseminated both inside and outside the police organization to garner public support and to facilitate accountability. In the move to community policing, where problem-solving efforts and accountability are shared by the police, the local government, and the community, explicitly defined values become critically important in assigning responsibility and attracting and mobilizing support and resources. Community policing

> . . . relies heavily on the articulation of policing values that incorporate citizen involvement in matters that directly affect the safety and quality of neighborhood life. The culture of the police department therefore becomes one that not only recognizes the merits of community involvement but also seeks to organize and manage departmental affairs in ways that are consistent with such beliefs.[31]

An organization's mission statement should be simple, direct, and unassuming. Values must be unequivocally communicated so that officers understand the influence on their actions:

> Planners need to assess what specific behaviors by organizational members support or undermine the stated values. This assessment requires that the values be defined in operational terms such that an observer can know whether any particular employee action is on target or off target. . . . Planners must also think clearly about how management will know whether the desired changes are taking place; feedback and evaluative steps must be developed.[32]

Community policing relies on the establishment of a clear, unambiguous link of values to behaviors. By creating a system of performance measurement, specific operational meaning can be given to seemingly abstract values. The guiding values central to community policing are trust, cooperation, communication, ingenuity, integrity, initiative, discretion, leadership, responsibility, respect, and a broadened commitment to public safety and security. A succinct mission statement that embodies these values and that is widely communicated to personnel, local government, and members of the community will form the basis of assessment systems that match actions and behaviors to the goals of community policing.

IMPLEMENTING A COMMUNITY POLICING STRATEGY

The implementation of a community policing strategy is a complicated and multifaceted process that, in essence, requires planning and managing for change. Community policing cannot be established through a mere modification of existing policy; profound changes must occur on every level and in every area of a police agency—from patrol officer to chief executive and from training to technology. A commitment to community policing must guide every decision and every action of the department.

Some Implementation Basics

Implementation plans will vary from agency to agency and from community to community. The most appropriate implementation method will depend, in part, on internal and external conditions facing the agency. For example, a chief executive who comes into an organization that is ripe for change at a time when confidence in the police is low may find that the organization will respond favorably to innovative policies. On the other hand, a chief executive who inherits a smoothly running organization may find it more difficult to implement change.[33]

One factor that will affect the approach to implementation is the extent of change that is required. In some agencies, current operations procedures and management practices may already conform closely to community policing, while in others extensive changes may be necessary. This will affect how a chief guides the organization toward the goals of community policing. A thorough assessment of current programs will help identify what will be required to integrate community partnership and problem-solving strategies and expanded crime control and prevention tactics with preexisting policies. Identifying priorities for change will also permit police agencies to establish interim milestones for monitoring progress.

Another essential element of successful implementation is communication. Communication must be timely, comprehensive, and direct. The chief executive must explain the concepts of community policing thoroughly to the entire police organization, the local political leadership, public and private agencies, and the community at large. All participants must understand their role in community policing efforts. Regular communication will encourage active participation and decrease resistance and opposition. Lines of communication must be maintained both within the police organization and between the police and participants within the community. Successful implementation requires the smooth flow of information.

The implementation of a community policing strategy must be a dynamic and flexible process. Ongoing input, evaluation, and feedback from both inside and outside the police organization are essential to making community policing work. All phases of community policing implementation must be carefully planned and properly timed to maximize success; even good ideas can fail if they are poorly executed.

Planning must be responsive to changing needs, conditions, and priorities. A strong research and planning capability that is open to suggestion and criticism will allow refinements and revisions to be made during the implementation process. Such flexibility is crucial to the success of community policing.

There are numerous ways in which police management can steer agencies toward community policing. The following can be adapted to the circumstances of different organizations and communities.

City and Community Resources

The long-term success of community policing in transforming the law enforcement profession depends on the willingness of local governments to pursue effective integration. Elected and appointed administrators must understand the law enforcement agency's implementation strategy and participate in its development. Mayors, city managers, legislative representatives, and other government executives must not be passive partners in this process; they must guide the expansion of this movement toward "community-oriented government" at the local level. Just as the police need to determine the best ways to respond to and solve problems of crime and violence, political leaders and service providers need to find ways to direct all available resources at these critical social problems. Law enforcement agencies alone do not have the resources to address all contemporary problems; however, community policing can be a catalyst for mobilizing resources at the national, state, and local levels to impact these problems more successfully.

Collaboration between the police agency and local government officials is essential, since officers and supervisors will routinely seek assistance from local government departments for services from sanitation to health. Regular communication with the heads of government agencies will help secure their assistance and will allow them to prepare their personnel for the additional service requests that will be received.

Nongovernment agencies and institutions constitute another important community asset. The chief or sheriff should enlist the support of these private agencies in community policing efforts. One department invited representatives from these organizations to participate in training sessions on community-oriented policing.[34]

Depending on the nature and scope of the problem addressed, the composition of problem-solving teams could be restricted to police personnel or could include representatives from the community, government agencies, and social agencies. The department must develop close cooperative links with all community policing partners who contribute to the problem-solving process, and explicit procedures must be established that facilitate the appropriate use of resources.

Every member of the police organization can contribute to the development of a comprehensive list of available government and private resources. This list should include names, addresses, phone numbers, and a description of services. This information should be easily accessible to allow patrol officers, supervisors, and dispatchers to provide references to community members.

Plan of Action: Three Options

There is no "right" way to implement community policing. Each of the following three approaches has strengths and weaknesses.

Plan, then implement.   This method entails developing a detailed long-range plan, with tasks and timelines, and assigning officers to execute the plan. This approach clearly delineates a set of strategies and actions that impart a sense of direction to implementation efforts; however, the initial planning stage for a large agency can take months or even years, and even a very detailed plan will be unable to predict the obstacles that will arise. In the absence of experience-based feedback, some part of the implementation process may be miscalculated.

Planning can also be complicated by the size of the staff involved. Keeping the planning staff relatively small may prevent the process from becoming unwieldy; however, it may not adequately represent all levels of command, function, and experience within the organization, thus creating the risk that the plan will not be well implemented. Planning can also become excessive and may stifle enthusiasm.

Plan and implement. In this approach, planning and action occur simultaneously. While the planning process continues, the agency begins to implement certain aspects of the program. This method allows the agency to get started quickly, involves more personnel at the outset, and permits future planning to benefit from feedback. However, the agency risks false starts, confusion, and major blunders unless effective, rapid, and regular communication takes place between planners and implementers.

Implement with little planning. The third option is for an agency with little preparation or knowledge of the nature of community policing to quickly launch into the action phase and then, on the basis of feedback, to retool the effort and begin the cycle again. This process is continuous, with each reevaluation cycle advancing the idea of community policing a bit further within the organization. This approach assumes that a limited knowledge of community policing may prevent agencies from initially planning in a meaningful way. Advocates note that the almost immediate action will catch officers' attention at all organizational levels and will harness the existing enthusiasm to help mobilize support. However, the constant shifts in goals and actions can be highly unsettling to the organization and the community it serves.

Among the factors to be considered when selecting a method of implementation are the extent of change in current agency operations that will be required, the size of the organization, the staff the agency can assign to implementation efforts, the readiness of the organization for the new approach, and the expectations of the community. The method of planning and implementing simultaneously will probably prove most effective for the majority of agencies implementing community policing.

Scope of Initial Implementation Efforts

Initial implementation of community policing can involve the entire agency or only a special unit or district. Agency-wide commitment will require a reevaluation of all aspects of operations. Many systems will need to be restructured to facilitate new job responsibilities and to foster productive partnerships with the community. Initiating changes of this magnitude will require patience, perseverance, and total commitment.

For these reasons, organization-wide implementation may not be feasible for agencies in which current methods of policing are deeply ingrained. Effective implementation will require time to train personnel, establish bonds with the community, and create appropriate support systems. The amount of time required will depend on the current orientation of the organization, its existing relationship with the community, and the resources available.

Implementation of community policing through a special, well-trained unit often offers early indications of success and focuses the attention of the community and media on the beneficial nature of community policing. However, care must be taken to avoid creating divisions within the agency. If community policing is perceived as merely a special-unit function, its eventual implementation throughout the agency could be significantly impaired. In addition, launching community policing through a special unit can lead to the misconception that the new policing style does not have to be integrated with all other facets of operations.

Implementation within one or more districts or areas can serve to demonstrate success and generate valuable data for expanding community policing agencywide, but this may also require more time and effort than implementation within a special unit. However, officers in the targeted district can help train others as community policing expands throughout the organization. Another advantage of district implementation is that it requires the cooperative efforts of all levels of management. The community policing district must not be perceived as a mere adjunct to existing police procedures.

The effectiveness of the implementation of community policing throughout the organization will depend on the manner in which community policing goals are communicated initially. If agency leaders imply that community policing in the special unit or district constitutes a test to determine whether the approach should be expanded agency-wide, competition and divisiveness can result. Managers should state unequivocally that the special unit or district is not a test site, but is the starting point for the agency-wide implementation of community policing.

No matter which approach is selected, feedback is essential. Without adequate feedback, agencies can encounter implementation problems that could have been avoided. Mistakes are bound to occur during implementation of community policing. Recognizing mistakes, handling them in a timely manner, and learning from them should be built into well-planned feedback procedures.

Mobilizing Support

The police executive will be called on to display exemplary leadership in the move to community policing. Change must come from the top down. The behavior of the chief executive will set the tone and pattern for the entire organization. Management must create a new, unified organizational outlook, and strategies must be developed to deal effectively with obstacles to change.

For the police it is an entirely different way of life. . . . The task facing the police chief is nothing less than to change the fundamental culture of the organization. . . . Throughout the period of change the office of the chief executive is going to be surrounded by turbulence, like it or not. It will require personal leadership of considerable strength and perseverance.[35]

Early mobilization of support for community policing is critical. Internally, the chief or sheriff must develop support at all levels of the organization; externally, the chief executives must gather support from the local government, public and private agencies, the media, and other policing agencies in the region. The cooperation of the local mayor or city manager is imperative to the successful implementation of a community policing strategy, as is the cooperation of local government decision makers and community organizations. A lack of commitment from any of these key groups could result in failure.

A certain amount of opposition to community policing should be anticipated, both inside and outside the agency. Elected officials may be too impatient to await the results of a community policing effort or may prefer to have a newer version of current policing procedures. Some groups within the community may be suspicious of the concept in general.

Resistance within the agency is inevitable as restructuring occurs. During the implementation of any change, employees may feel threatened and seek ways to resist.[36] This will be especially true if community policing is incorrectly perceived as being "soft on crime" and as making social service activities the patrol officers' primary responsibility.

Those at the highest level of command must be aware of the concerns of mid-level managers, who may be particularly sensitive to the shifts in decision-making responsibility and to the wider discretion accorded patrol officers.

Teamwork, flexibility, mutual participation in decision making, and citizen satisfaction are concepts that initially may threaten the supervisor who is more comfortable with the authoritarian role and routinized operations inherent in traditional policing. Thus, the education of supervisors in new styles of leadership and management must be given a high priority if they are to carry out their responsibility for the success of community policing.[37]

Keeping all personnel well informed, involving them in ongoing planning and implementation, soliciting their input and suggestions, and encouraging feedback in all areas of implementation are essential to obtaining organization-wide support. Management must instill the agency with a new spirit of trust and cooperation that will be carried over into the relationships between the agency and its community policing partners. The early cooperation and influence of management is key to gaining support throughout the ranks.

Chiefs who do not invest in assessing and responding to the honest attitudes of managers, who do not invest in defining the new roles managers are expected to play, and who do not provide their managers with the training they need to effectively fill these new roles are likely to be frustrated in their efforts to implement change. In their frustration with managers, they will be tempted to bypass them and to go straight to the first-line officers with implementation plans. . . . But without the support of the supervisors and managers, few first-line officers will be willing to risk changing their behaviors.[38]

Agency leaders can also move to counter intra-agency resistance by building a strong external constituency.[39] The chief or sheriff might make a public commitment to community policing and elicit from special interest groups a statement of their concerns. The chief may be able to support the work of commissions and committees that support ideas for change. These efforts would allow the top management to approach the organization backed by a public mandate for community policing.

In anticipation of a move to community policing, a chief might also disband some squads that emphasize traditional methods of policing, redesign evaluation systems to give credit for contributions to the nature and quality of community life, expand training to include community partnership and problem-solving strategies, and establish new communication channels with other public service organizations.[40]

Timing

Timing is an important factor in the implementation process. Implementation that moves too slowly may dampen enthusiasm and reduce momentum, while implementation that moves too quickly may create confusion and resentment and may threaten the success of the project through the use of hurried and ill-conceived methods. Community policing requires major changes in operations, including decentralization of activities and facilities, role changes for most personnel, new training, revised schedules, and an altered call-response system. All of these changes require careful consideration and coordination.

The order of some changes will have an inherent logic; it simply won't make sense to undertake some before making others. However, the ordering of some of the objectives may be optional. When this is the case, it may make sense to postpone the more difficult until later in the change timetable. Easy "wins" may make the best openers. These would be changes for which it should be possible to build the broadest base of support. . . . Meeting some of the easier goals may help prepare the organization for the more difficult ones.[41]

Correct timing is often a matter of making the most of available opportunities. Police management should be ready to take advantage of any opportunity that could champion the cause of community policing.

> Those opportunities can be defined as events that throw the spotlight on police policy and provide a "case in point" justification for a reform proposal. Ironically, opportunities often come disguised as crises, and managers must resist the instinctive impulse to think first of damage control. Managers interested in reform will embrace crises and make the most of them. . . .[42]

Managing Internal Change

Community policing necessitates the introduction of fundamental and comprehensive change to the police agency. Organizational efforts must support the evolving responsibilities of patrol officers. For example, information systems should move beyond the efficient processing of criminal offense reports to the delivery of timely and accurate information to officers. Training will govern the pace of change and should affect more than just the new recruits. Performance evaluation should no longer be a mere feedback mechanism, but instead should be a tool to facilitate the change process. Successful implementation of community policing entails careful examination of the following organizational issues.

Deployment of Personnel

Permanent or long-term shifts and beat assignments must be instituted if patrol officers are to form lasting and productive partnerships with the community. Community policing depends on this stability. In addition, community boundaries should be carefully drawn to preserve the integrity of existing neighborhoods and to encourage cooperation within the community.

A comprehensive analysis of workloads across shifts and areas is essential to guide the deployment of personnel. This analysis should include data for each community covering the following areas:

- The frequency and nature of calls for service
- The frequency and nature of criminal activity
- The expectations for response time
- The estimated time needed for community partnership and problem-solving activities

Some agencies will need to increase the number of officers who are assigned to patrol operations and to readjust existing patrol assignments. Criminal investigation units may need to be surveyed to determine if efforts are being duplicated, which could allow some officers to return to patrol. Civilians could also be hired for support positions not requiring policing skills, in order to reassign police personnel to community patrols.

Supervision

Consistent supervision is necessary for effective community policing. Supervision will suffer if sergeants or lieutenants have schedules that only partially overlap those of the patrol officers. Close collaboration between patrol officers and their supervisors is as critical to successful community policing as the partnership between the officer and the community members.

While patrol officers need consistent supervision, "The attitude that police officers must be guided and directed at every turn must be discarded . . . ."[43] Supervisors should function as mentors, motivators, and facilitators. Community policing's broad approach to problem solving can enhance communication and interaction between departmental levels. If middle managers are made an integral part of the problem-solving process, they will become another resource for patrol officers, rather than just another level of supervision.[44] By acting as liaisons, running interference, and suggesting appropriate auxiliary support, supervisors can help patrol officers respond to a wide variety of service demands.

Among the community policing responsibilities for first-line supervisors and mid-level managers are the following:

- Maintaining beat integrity
- Overseeing the creation of beat profiles
- Working with officers and community residents to create a system for the allocation and utilization of resources
- Working with officers and community members to develop, implement, and manage problem-solving systems
- Assessing results and providing feedback on accomplishments and progress made in addressing problems of crime and disorder

Supervisors should also bring patrol officers into the management process, facilitate group cohesiveness, and assist personnel in reaching their maximum potential.

Mid-level managers should eliminate impediments to the process of problem solving and to the attainment of results. They must learn to manage multi-functional teams and to assume more responsibility for strategic planning, as well as become actively involved in mobilizing the community in crime-prevention activities.

Mid-level managers should conduct regular meetings with their staff to discuss plans, activities, and results. They should evaluate the progress or failure of strategies, programs, or responses based on performance indicators supplied by officers, supervisors, and community members. Managers have a responsibility to enrich the jobs of their personnel by delegating authority, acting as mentors, and overseeing training and education. They also must meet frequently with their superiors to provide updates, seek direction and guidance, and help expand strategies to address crime and disorder within communities.

Human Resource Development

Training is key to the effective implementation of community policing. Training should communicate and reinforce the changes taking place in organizational values and policies, and should help build consensus, resolve, and unity both inside and outside [of] the police organization.

Community policing skills should be integrated into the training curricula, not treated as a separate component of the training program. Training in community policing should supplement law enforcement techniques with communication and leadership skills that will encourage participation from the community. All personnel must become skilled in the techniques of problem solving, motivating, and team building. Training should involve the entire agency and should include civilian personnel who can enlist participation in community meetings, help the police organization sharpen its marketing message, and incorporate sophisticated technology into the organization's service-oriented operations.

Initial training efforts should be directed at managers and supervisors, who may feel their authority is being eroded by the modified priorities of the organization.[45] More important, they must be relied on to transmit and translate the new concepts to those they supervise.

The training of mid-level managers should emphasize their role in facilitating the problem-solving process by coaching, coordinating, and evaluating the efforts of patrol officers. To prepare mid-level managers for their community policing responsibilities, one agency chief required all personnel with the rank of sergeant and above to attend training sessions that had three goals: to show supervisors how to manage officers' time so that problems could be addressed without diminishing police capability for handling calls, to describe how problems should be analyzed, and to ensure that all trainees knew what was expected of them and their officers.[46]

Patrol officers must also receive extensive training that encourages and develops both initiative and discretionary ability—a dramatic departure from traditional thinking. They must develop planning, organization, problem-solving, communication, and leadership skills through ongoing, thorough training. Eventually, these officers will be able to assist in the training of others.

Performance Evaluation and Reward

Performance evaluation can be a valuable management tool for facilitating change and can help communicate agency priorities to employees. Systems for evaluating personnel performance should reflect the goals of community policing. "Emphasizing quality over quantity represents a major difference between traditional policing and community-oriented policing."[47] Patrol officers could be evaluated on how well they know their beats—a prerequisite for identification of problems—and how effectively they and their supervisors have adopted problem-solving techniques. Other relevant performance measures include the extent to which personnel have formed partnerships with the community and the nature of their contributions to this team effort. Since officers are working as part of a team, they should not be evaluated as if they were operating alone.

The occasional mistake made by an officer seeking to solve community issues in a proactive manner would be an inappropriate measure of performance. "Managers cannot have it both ways. They cannot ask officers to be risk-takers and then discipline them when occasional mistakes occur."[48] The insight, initiative, and creativity shown by personnel should be considered in the performance appraisal; the motivation behind the action also must be considered. Mistakes made in an honest attempt to solve a problem should not be evaluated in the same manner as mistakes made through carelessness, lack of commitment, or deliberate disregard for policing policies.

Retaining the services of personnel who are skilled in community policing depends, in large part, on appropriate rewards for solid performance. Rewards must be consistent with the values and methods associated with community policing. Patrol officers and supervisors should be evaluated and rewarded for exceptional skills in problem solving or community mobilization efforts, rather than on the number of calls handled or parking tickets issued.

Rewards also include the establishment of well-defined and suitable career paths for all personnel. Specific career development opportunities should reward past effort and allow room for growth, especially for patrol officers. The backbone of community policing is the patrol officer, and the status, pay, and working conditions of this position should encourage people to spend an entire career in patrol. "In effect, what is needed is a system that rewards advancement through skill levels in the same job as much or more than it rewards advancement through the ranks."[49]

Management should also consider expanding the criteria for the existing award program and placing more emphasis on community partnership and problem-solving skills. Some departments have invited community members to help select police award recipients. Others have added awards for community members who participate in police efforts. These awards will help solidify commitments and encourage continued cooperation among community policing participants.

Workload Control and Information Systems

The efficient management of service calls is essential for officers to have sufficient time to interact and work with community members to solve problems of crime and disorder. Most agencies control 911 calls for service by determining which calls demand an immediate response and which can be handled with alternate responses or through a referral to another agency. Nonemergency calls can be handled by delayed officer response, by telephone, by mail, or by having the caller come to the station. Research shows that the public will not insist on an immediate response to a nonemergency service request if the alternative response is both appropriate and performed as described.[50]

The problem-solving orientation of community policing requires a greater emphasis on analytic skills and expert systems management to obtain the most valuable information support. Information support will have to be provided for problems that have not been previously studied and for the incorporation of data from outside the department.[51] Analysis must go beyond identifying and forecasting crime patterns; tactical analysis should be supplemented with strategic analysis.

> . . . strategic analysis seeks to identify factors that contribute to crime and non-crime problems. Strategic analysis is a natural by-product of the problem-oriented approach. . . . Strategic analysts should attempt to identify why problems exist in neighborhoods as well as identify the conditions that contribute to and perpetuate crime. This information will certainly prove useful in the planning and implementation of tactical responses and crime prevention strategies.[52]

Strategic analysis will require that information be collected by a number of unconventional methods, e.g., conducting neighborhood victimization surveys, canvassing rehabilitation centers and hospitals, interacting with school officials, and assessing the impact of environmental changes on criminal activity.

Technology tends to heighten the isolation of the police from the public; therefore, management must ensure that technological innovations are integrated into community policing activities in a way that fosters meaningful cooperation and aids in the process of problem solving. Modern CAD (computer-aided dispatch) systems can assist in prioritizing police response to service requests. Cellular telephones, pagers, fax machines, and voice mail can also relieve the overburdened 911 systems and provide vital communication links between communities and the police. In addition, geocoding and mapping technology can prove invaluable to the problem-solving process.

> Advancements in technology now allow computerized maps of neighborhood activity. [In a test] using personal computers with specially designed software, community groups were able to map data provided by daily police reports. . . . This strategy holds considerable promise for mapping less-serious incivilities (not only the dramatic incidents) that lower the quality of neighborhood life. . . . Research suggests that releasing local crime statistics to the public will not increase the public's fear of crime so long as the statistics are accompanied by specific, feasible crime prevention recommendations.[53]

All data should be made available through an integrated management information system that can be conveniently accessed by patrol officers, supervisors, command staff, and support personnel. This might entail the use of laptop computers and other mobile communications equipment. Wide dissemination and information sharing are essential components of community policing. Pertinent and appropriate information should be made available to members of the community whenever possible. For example, statistics showing an increase in burglaries or rapes in a specific section of town should be shared with the community to further the problem-solving process.

Facilities

Effective community collaboration and interaction will require patrol officers to be more accessible to community members. "Storefront" police offices or "mini-stations" within neighborhoods can be established quite inexpensively, particularly with assistance from the community. The duties of staffing storefront facilities can be shared among officers, civilian employees, and community residents. These sites provide officers and citizens with the opportunity to discuss problems and plan activities. One police jurisdiction operated a storefront station at a shopping mall, while another used a closed-down roadhouse in a rural area to provide residents with easier access to police services. Some deputies in sparsely populated rural areas are allowed to report in by phone, instead of driving many miles to attend roll call, so that contact with community residents can be maximized. In a sense, the deputies' homes become satellite stations, allowing them greater access to the community.

Facilitating the Implementation Process

Astute chief executives will realize that leadership ability can be found at many levels, both inside and outside the police organization. They should enlist the help of people whose ideas, drive, and ability will help spur the progress of community policing. However, police executives must take responsibility for directing implementation efforts and outlining the parameters for addressing the various facets of community policing. Strong and continued leadership from the top of the organization will reduce confusion and disagreement at lower levels.

Police chiefs will not be able to manage the entire implementation process; therefore, a team or committee, one or more internal coordinators, and outside sources such as consultants should be designated by the chief.

Members of an implementation team, task force, or committee will also have other responsibilities; therefore, an internal coordinator may be needed to provide daily support for team efforts. For greater effectiveness, internal coordinators should be recruited from the command level of the organization to avoid communication problems.

Outside consultants can also facilitate implementation because they are frequently able to gain access to all levels of the organization more easily than an internal coordinator. Consultants can bring a wealth of experience to the implementation process, including knowledge about the implementation of community policing strategies and suggestions for gathering relevant information. Occasionally consultants may encounter resistance within agencies that are not accustomed to external assistance. Executives loaned from private sector companies also may be useful to police organizations. "The private sector uses such programs to allow one or more employees to work, with pay, for a not-for-profit or community organization for as long as a year at a time."[54]

To ensure a smooth transition to community policing, top management should consider creating a broad-based implementation team. An agency-wide team, which could be divided into a number of committees, should adequately represent all levels of the agency in experience and function. An even broader team might include representatives from local government, police unions, other agencies, and members of the community whose assistance would be instrumental to the success of a community policing strategy.

Officers on the implementation team must be allowed to participate outside the traditional lines of authority.[55] This means that while a chairperson will direct and coordinate each committee's activities, there should be no rank within committees. The police chief must have frequent contact with all committees. In addition, the efforts of committees should be coordinated by one or more facilitators who share the chief's thinking and understand the ultimate goals of community policing.

Marketing: Selecting a Message and an Image

Before implementing a community policing strategy, the agency should communicate the concept of community policing to its own personnel and to the community, including political and business leaders and the media. Different emphases and images may be appropriate for different audiences; however, a message to one group should not contradict or neutralize an equally valid message to another.

For example, messages to officers focusing on problem solving and arrests might conflict with images directed at the general public showing officers distributing teddy bears to preschoolers. Both messages and roles are valid; one emphasizes problem solving as a valuable anticrime tool, while the other shows the benefits of trust-building and partnerships with the community.

To avoid sending contradictory messages, agencies should settle on a dominant theme and communicate it consistently both internally and externally. For example, the theme might emphasize a new "customer service" orientation to policing, focus on partnership building, or highlight the prospects community policing holds for creating secure neighborhoods. Subsidiary points—problem solving, community contact, or ridding neighborhoods of signs of neglect or disorder—could be grouped under the umbrella of this central theme. An excellent example of a central theme is the "Together We Can" slogan that will steer the marketing of community policing efforts in Chicago.

Marketing involves communicating through symbols, stories about real-life situations, and testimonials by those whom the community and officers respect. Marketing messages are conveyed internally through memos, roll-call briefings, newsletters, and special videos, and in person by command staff and chief executives, among others. Externally, they are publicized through public forums, posters, flyers, meetings, public service announcements, and the officers' personal contact with community members.

Although the use of a label or acronym to help market community policing seems a small matter, it needs careful consideration.

> If employees are generally supportive of the change, then the label provides
> a positive rallying symbol. . . . If, on the other hand, there is substantial
> resistance to the change, then the label becomes a negative rallying symbol.
> . . . People begin to play games with the acronym. Neighborhood-Oriented
> Policing becomes "Nobody On Patrol" or "NOPE."[56]

The media must be included early in the implementation process to market successfully the idea of community policing. Media involvement ensures a wide dissemination of the community policing message and encourages the media to stay involved in future community policing efforts; the media also will be less apt to "derail" if there is a bump in the crime statistics or if some community policing policies are less effective than hoped. If the budget allows, media consultants can be useful. The agency's internal media relations unit should thoroughly understand the chief executive's vision of community policing and communicate it clearly in news releases and interviews. All who are marketing the concept must be careful not to claim more for community policing than it can deliver.

ASSESSING THE PROGRESS OF COMMUNITY POLICING

A critical aspect of implementation is the assessment of community policing efforts, both in terms of achieving necessary change within the organization itself and accomplishing external goals (such as establishing working relationships with the community and reducing levels of crime, fear, and disorder). Ongoing assessment meets a number of fundamental needs.

Every government and public agency, including the police, should be able to give an accurate account of its current activities to policymakers and taxpayers. Thus, ongoing assessment of policy and performance should be a primary function of any policing organization. Assessment becomes even more vital when an organization is undergoing the comprehensive changes that a shift to community policing will entail. Constant assessment of the process of change is needed for managers to determine how to keep the implementation process on track. The most effective strategies also need to be identified so managers can make informed choices about where to allocate limited resources.

Ongoing assessment helps give the organization a clear sense of direction and allows management to focus efforts on the most productive and efficient practices. Therefore, assessment is indispensable in determining which elements of community policing should be maintained, altered, or eliminated, and offers key decision makers in the jurisdiction a way to gauge the impact and cost-effectiveness of community policing efforts.

Assessment will help determine whether necessary changes in the support systems are taking place and whether appropriate efforts are being made to accomplish the stated goals. Assessment also can help communicate agency expectations to employees.

Giving community members a way to measure the success of community policing efforts is critical to maintaining strong ties, ensuring continued participation, and documenting the progress made. Conversely, evaluations of the community policing strategy from government and community leaders will affect how future cooperative efforts are constructed. Thorough assessment helps make police more responsive to the community's needs, which should strengthen the trust and partnership on which community policing is based.

Developing a sound assessment program should begin with a strategic plan that outlines the goals, methods, objectives, and timetables, and assigns personnel for internal and external changes. These goals and responsibilities will form the basis of performance assessment and will allow police leadership to detect failures and roadblocks, as well as to chart progress and document accomplishments.

Assessing Internal Changes

Large gaps can exist between policy and actions, therefore, management must take nothing for granted in the implementation of community policing policies and procedures. The chief executive should constantly ask, "How is the implementation going? Is it on track? What problems are occurring? What help is needed?"

In smaller organizations, these questions can be answered through a process called "management by walking around" in which the chief visits key managers and implementation groups to get on-the-spot reports on implementation efforts. The chief should also consult patrol officers to obtain their views on the implementation process. In every organization, the chief executive should hold regular meetings with the personnel responsible for overseeing community policing implementation and should ask for reports on efforts with the goal of both reinforcing accountability and allowing for immediate discussion of problems. Regular reports on progress and problems relating to specific community policing objectives and timetables should be supplied by members of the implementation team.

Assessment of the more intangible internal changes, for example, the decentralization of management, can be complex. The chief executive and the head of the implementation team could meet regularly with groups of managers and supervisors to discuss changes in decision-making authority. Periodic personnel surveys can also help determine what modifications have occurred in management style, which obstacles stand in the way of change, and how agency leadership can facilitate the necessary adjustments in the roles of managers, supervisors, and patrol officers.

Three Criteria for Assessment

Evaluating the impact of community policing is critical for many reasons. Key decision makers must be able to judge the strategy's impact and cost-effectiveness, and the police organization must be able to measure the success or failure of its policies and activities. As with implementation methods, assessment measures will vary depending on the size of the organization and the nature of its current policies. Ongoing monitoring will expedite the implementation process, attract support, aid problem solving, and reveal new opportunities for productive partnerships with the community.

In the past, police efforts usually have been evaluated on a traditional and narrow set of criteria (e.g., crime statistics, the number of 911 calls, the length of police response, the number of arrests and citations). These assessments were often taken only at times of serious crime increases.

Many of the traditional methods of assessment remain valid but can measure only the effectiveness of crime-fighting tactics and cannot gauge the effect of crime-prevention efforts. Changes in the scope of policing necessitate a revised system for evaluating the performance of individuals, as well as agencies. As police take a proactive role in deterring crime, a broader set of assessment criteria, which incorporate traditional measures of crime-fighting activities with those that encompass community partnership and problem-solving activities, will be needed.

Traditional crime-control activities should become only one of the ways in which the community policing strategy and individual officers are assessed. Many indications of the success of community policing efforts are intangible (e.g., absence of fear, quality of interaction with community members); therefore, assessing a community policing strategy is a qualitative as well as a quantitative process. The values that the department promotes will form the basis of sound qualitative measures of effectiveness. Assessment should reward organizational and individual behavior that assists in deterring crime and solving other neighborhood problems. Creativity, initiative, and ingenuity should be emphasized in the evaluation of individual officers. Three major criteria—effectiveness, efficiency, and equity—can be used to provide the quantitative and qualitative measures needed to assess the success of a community policing strategy.

Effectiveness. An effective community policing strategy will reduce neighborhood crime, decrease citizens' fear of crime, and enhance the quality of life in the community. An important goal of community policing is to provide higher quality service to neighborhoods; therefore, customer satisfaction becomes an important measure of effectiveness. The perception of progress among community members and ongoing feedback from all elements of the community are essential parts of the assessment process. Randomly and routinely conducted surveys will inform the agency of the public view of police performance and the level of fear and concern and will make the agency aware of the extent to which community members feel as if they are participants in the community policing effort.

One of the core components of community policing is community partnership. Therefore, an early measure of effectiveness will be the number and type of community partnerships that have been formed. The cooperation and participation of community members is necessary to deter crime and reduce the fear of crime in the neighborhood. Assessing the effectiveness of community policing efforts includes determining whether problems have been solved and judging how well the managers and patrol officers have applied the community partnership and problem-solving components of community policing described previously.

Assessment should measure whether a problem was solved and how this was accomplished. As stated earlier, the number of arrests made is only one possible measure of effective problem solving; solving problems often does not involve arrest and, in many cases, does not guarantee that a problem will disappear completely. For example, the officer who determined that one of the underlying causes of an increase in convenience store robberies was that cash registers could not be seen by passersby did not eradicate the burglary. However, his efforts did provide valuable information that could help deter future robberies. Satisfactory assessment measures for community policing must give proper credit to officers like this who successfully abate a problem through means other than arrest. The officer's contribution to solving the problem and his consultations with members of the community showed the concern and effectiveness of police officers and created the goodwill for the department that is crucial to the success of community policing.

The number and type of problems solved and the creativity and scope of the solutions will provide a way to measure community policing's effectiveness. Not all of the problems will involve criminal activity, and many will not even be considered a priority by the police agency. However, where serious crime is not involved, the concerns and fears of community members should order the priorities of the agency.

In community policing, officers may act as facilitators to mobilize community support. They may also function as mediators in disputes between individuals or organizations, or take responsibility for referring a problem to the appropriate social or government agency. The effective use of government and community agencies in problem solving is an indication that community policing policies are working. Thus, the mobilization and intelligent use of community resources in solving problems and the sensitive handling of dissension become important factors in assessing the performance of officers and the success of the program.

Increased levels of community participation in crime reduction and prevention efforts is another indication of program success. Community members will not act if they are afraid or suspicious. Community members should become more willing to work with the police in a variety of ways, ranging from converting abandoned buildings to community assets to involving police actively in neighborhood watch groups. They might also be more comfortable providing information on criminal activity in the area. In fact, calls to report crime may increase considerably during the early phases of community policing implementation, as community confidence in police capability rises and community trust increases. However, the number of 911 calls will likely decrease over time, which will provide a quantitative measure of the strategy's effect. For instance, emergency calls in the pioneering Flint, Michigan, foot patrol district dropped 43 percent over the course of the experiment.[57]

A concrete indication of community policing's success is the commitment of an increased level of community resources devoted to crime reduction efforts. Active consultation and financial participation by public and private agencies, schools, and the business community will demonstrate that community partnership efforts are working. Communities also should begin to initiate and conduct projects with minimal guidance from the police.

Renewed activity within the community also will demonstrate the effectiveness of community policing efforts, particularly in areas where citizens have been afraid to leave their homes. Reduction in fear can also result in the perception among residents that crime is on the wane, whether or not this is statistically accurate. An increased willingness of citizens to walk to schools and parks, patronize stores, and go to restaurants and movies will signal a general decrease in fear of crime. In turn, the very fact that community members are reclaiming their streets will help deter future criminal activity and create more vigorous neighborhoods.

Improved quality of life is difficult to measure but is an important goal of community policing and will be reflected in comments from community members. Ridding the streets of gangs, drunks, panhandlers, and prostitutes—perhaps with the help of public and private social agencies—will enhance the quality of life. Removing signs of neglect (e.g., abandoned cars, derelict buildings, and garbage and debris) will offer tangible evidence that community policing efforts are working to bring about increased order in the community.

In community policing, the police function includes the provision of services that in the recent past have been regarded as outside policing's purview. These services include aiding accident and crime victims, arbitrating neighborhood and domestic disputes, and providing emergency medical and social services. An analysis of the nature of calls for police service (e.g., a lower percentage of calls reporting criminal activity in proportion to calls requesting social assistance) will provide a measure of how well the strategy is working.

Efficiency.   Efficiency means getting the most results with available resources. To measure the efficiency of community policing, the resources of the police agency, local government and private agencies, citizen groups, the business community, and the neighborhood must first be defined. The assessment must then determine whether these resources are being used to their fullest to solve any given problem. Agencies that can successfully enhance and realign their resources by forming community partnerships will be able to make community policing more efficient and cost-effective.

Two major shifts must occur within the police organization if community policing is to work efficiently. Staunch partnerships and collaborative efforts must first be established with the community. The command structure of the police organization must then be decentralized so that problem solving, decision making, and accountability are spread to all levels of the organization. Such decentralization challenges personnel to be more creative and more effective because the decisions they make are more timely and influenced by firsthand knowledge of the facts.[58] Decentralization also gives higher level managers more time to formulate strategies that will improve the organization's performance.

In a decentralized policing organization, neighborhood patrol officers are responsible for the daily policing needs of the community, with guidance and backing from supervisors. Their long-term shifts and neighborhood patrol assignments give them the opportunity to function more efficiently and successfully.

Patrol officers who handle daily police functions can form stronger bonds with the community. This "pride of ownership" motivates both parties to solve the problems that affect the security and harmony of the neighborhood. Patrol officers will experience greater job satisfaction as they accept higher levels of responsibility and accountability. Officers are often able to resolve issues quickly, allowing them to see the immediate results of their efforts. With high morale and greater job satisfaction, patrol officers will more effectively mobilize the community. If they are highly motivated, given the necessary support, and appropriately rewarded for their efforts, the job satisfaction they experience will help make the community policing strategy a success.

The roles and responsibilities of all personnel in the police organization are altered so that the leadership and ingenuity officers display will become important factors in determining the efficiency of the program. Assessment and reward procedures must therefore be revised accordingly.

Community help will increase the efficiency of the program and relieve some of the strain of tight police budgets. Partnerships in the community can bring fresh resources to problems, even those traditionally considered "police-only" business. According to one sheriff, "There is virtually no limitation on how much more effective and efficient a sheriff's office can become, working collectively as a partner with community members while, at the same time, saving resources, dollars, and frustration on the part of constituents."[59]

Decentralized decision making and community partnership engenders new organizational and resource issues that must be addressed to operate the system efficiently. Budgets must reflect the goals of community policing by allocating money and resources in proportion to the results achieved. With decentralization, police officers who have the greatest responsibility for the daily policing operations will have more direct input into budgetary decisions and greater accountability for financial decisions, actions taken, and results achieved.

Efficiency must be built into each aspect of the community policing strategy—from the creation of community boundaries that cultivate productive alliances to the adoption of technologies that increase communication. Expanded and thorough training is paramount in an efficient shift to community policing. Intensive training, although initially costly in terms of dollars and time, will eventually make the process more efficient, as well-trained and experienced personnel share practical knowledge with colleagues.

Efficiency in larger agencies may be increased by redefining job functions at all management levels. For example, one large jurisdiction implementing community policing required sergeants to coordinate officer decision making across beats as necessary and to confer with their lieutenants on decisions that involved a large or long-term commitment of resources. Lieutenants in turn apprised their respective captains about happenings on beats across their districts. Such amended roles for mid-level managers may promote efficiency through fewer levels of supervision. While an important supervisory role is to help maximize the amount of time neighborhood officers can spend in their communities, community policing will require supervisors to coordinate problem-solving activities within and across communities, help secure resources, evaluate activities and decisions, and provide guidance and support to neighborhood officers.

Also central to achieving efficiency in time and dollars is controlling calls for service. Sophisticated technological advances can help prioritize calls and facilitate communication among community policing partners. Alternative response strategies for nonemergency calls include a delayed-officer response and officer response by appointment. Low-priority situations can be handled by telephone, walk-in, and mail-in reporting. "All indications are that these systems save an enormous amount of time, reduce officer frustration, and are equally satisfactory to the callers."[60]

Effectiveness and efficiency are important yardsticks by which to measure community policing's achievements, but equity, the third major criterion for judging progress, has the greatest impact on the success of community policing.

Equity. Equity is grounded firmly in the Constitution of the United States, which all police officers are sworn to uphold. A foremost tenet of community policing is equity; that is, all citizens should have a say in how they are governed. Officers may relate better to citizens as individuals because they cooperate closely with and are recognized as an integral part of the community. Community policing can thus become a force for enhancing democratic principles.

Community policing provides an opportunity to emphasize uncompromising integrity, unyielding standards of fairness, and unwavering equality, because officers have to work closely with the community and will be increasingly confronted with ethical dilemmas.

Equity, as understood in community policing activities, has three dimensions: equal access to police services by all citizens, equal treatment of all individuals under the U.S. Constitution, and equal distribution of police services and resources among communities.

Equal access to police services.   All citizens, regardless of race, religion, personal characteristics, or group affiliation, must have equal access to police services for a full and productive partnership with a community. The paramount commitment of community policing should be respect for all citizens and sensitivity to their needs. Neighborhood officers must not discriminate against any community members. Supervisors should help ensure that police services are readily available throughout the community.

In addition, lines of communication must be kept open with all partners in the community policing effort. Favoritism of one group over another will severely hamper future cooperative efforts. Groups who are more vocal than others cannot be permitted to use community policing to serve their own purposes. Police must prevent such behavior before it adversely affects the trust that has been established within and among communities.

Equal treatment under the constitution.   Police must treat all individuals according to the constitutional rights that officers are sworn to protect and enforce. Careful attention to the constitutional rights of citizens, victims, or perpetrators will help to engender bonds of trust between the police and community. Police must treat all persons with respect and impartiality—including the homeless, the poor, and the mentally or physically handicapped. They must reject stereotypes, ignore skin color, and use reason and persuasion rather than coercion wherever possible, because inequitable or harsh treatment can lead to frustration, hostility, and even violence within a community. Such unethical behavior will imperil the trust so necessary to community policing.

Some contemporary community activists and leaders have experienced past confrontations with the police, which may present serious challenges to implementing community policing and involving the community in policing efforts.

Equal distribution of police services and resources among communities. Because community policing customizes policing services to the needs of each community, services should be distributed equitably among poor and minority communities. Care must be taken, however, to ensure that this is the case.

For equitable distribution of resources among communities, each community must articulate its needs and be willing to work with the police to ensure its share of police services. Each neighborhood officer must listen to the community members and be willing to work with the community members to meet those needs. Poor and minority neighborhoods can present particular challenges for some patrol officers, who may have to bridge differences of race and class before a level of trust and cooperation can be established.

Some neighborhoods may appear unwilling to help police in their efforts to improve life in the community. Officers must realize that sometimes "the community seems so helpless because it feels abandoned and would discover new strengths if only the police could make an effective alliance with important community elements. . . . Departments that have taken early steps [into community policing] are full of stories of apparently lost neighborhoods that flowered under new police attention."[61]

One community must not be given preference over another; all communities must have equal access to police services. Equity, however, may not always mean equal distribution of police services and resources. Wealthier communities are often able to contribute more resources to the problem-solving process than can poorer communities. Crime rates will also be higher in some communities, requiring more police intervention and a larger share of police resources to decrease crime and transform neighborhoods from places of fear into city or county assets.

Refining the Assessment Process

Assessment of community policing is an ongoing process that should include a reevaluation of the assessment measures themselves. With more experience in community policing, a police agency will be able to develop measures that accurately chart successes and failures and indicate where changes need to be made.

The values of the policing organization must guide the move to community policing and shape every decision made and every action taken. Above all, police organizations must be responsive to community priorities and demands for service from the beginning of the community policing effort.

CONCLUSION

Police agencies should not allow political leaders and the public to develop unrealistic expectations for community policing in terms of crime deterrence or speed of implementation. Community policing calls for long-term commitment; it is not a quick fix. Achieving ongoing partnerships with the community and eradicating the underlying causes of crime will take planning, flexibility, time, and patience. Management can measure progress by their success in meeting interim goals and must reinforce the concept inside and outside the organization that success is reached through a series of gradual improvements.

Local political leadership may be eager for fast results, but police leadership must make it clear to city and county officials that implementing community policing is an incremental and long-term process. Political and community leaders must be regularly informed of the progress of community policing efforts to keep them interested and involved. The police organization, from the chief executive down, must stress that the success of community policing depends on sustained joint efforts of the police, local government, public and private agencies, and members of the community. This cooperation is indispensable to deterring crime and revitalizing our neighborhoods.

NOTES

1. George L. Kelling, and Mark H. Moore, "The Evolving Strategy of Policing," *Perspectives on Policing* (Washington, D.C.: National Institute of Justice and John F. Kennedy School of Government, Harvard University, 1988), p. 8. Based on *The Newark Foot Patrol Experiment* (Washington, D.C.: Police Foundation, 1981).
2. As quoted in George L. Kelling, "Police and Communities: The Quiet Revolution," *Perspectives on Policing* (Washington, D.C.: National Institute of Justice and John F. Kennedy School of Government, Harvard University, 1988), p. 2.
3. Chris Braiden, "Enriching Traditional Police Roles," in *Police Management: Issues and Perspectives* (Washington, D.C.: Police Executive Research Forum, 1992), p. 108.
4. George L. Kelling, and Mark H. Moore, "The Evolving Strategy of Policing," *Perspectives on Policing* (Washington, D.C.: National Institute of Justice and John F. Kennedy School of Government, Harvard University, 1988), pp. 4–5.
5. Michael Harrington, *The Other America: Poverty in the United States* (New York: Macmillan,1981), p. 16.
6. George L. Kelling, Antony Pate, Duane Dieckman, and Charles E. Brown, *The Kansas City Preventive Patrol Experiment: A Technical Report* (Washington, D.C.: Police Foundation, 1974), pp. iii, 533–5.
7. Kansas City Police Department, *Response Time Analysis: Volume II, Part I—Crime Analysis* (Washington, D.C.: U.S. Gov. Printing Office, 1980), p. iii.
8. John E. Eck, and William Spelman, "A Problem-Oriented Approach to Police Service Delivery," in *Police and Policing: Contemporary Issues,* Dennis Jay Kenney, ed. (New York: Praeger, 1989), p. 101.
9. Michael T. Farmer, ed., *Differential Police Response Strategies* (Washington, D.C.: Police Executive Research Forum, 1981), p. 3.
10. Kansas City Police Department, *Directed Patrol: A Concept in Community-Specific, Crime-Specific, and Service-Specific Policing* (Kansas City, Missouri: Kansas City Police Department, 1974), p. 465.
11. John E. Boydstun and Michael E. Sherry, *San Diego Community Profile: Final Report* (Washington, D.C.: Police Foundation, 1975), p. 83.
12. Herman Goldstein, "Improving Policing: A Problem-Oriented Approach," *Crime and Delinquency* 25 (1979): 241–3.
13. John E. Eck, and William Spelman, *Problem Solving: Problem-Oriented Policing in Newport News* (Washington, D.C.: Police Executive Research Forum, 1987), pp. 81, 99.

14. Lawrence W. Sherman, Patrick R. Gartin, and Michael E. Buerger, "Hot Spots of Predatory Crime: Routine Activities and the Criminology of Place," *Criminology* 27 (1989): 39.

15. Peter W. Greenwood, and Joan Petersilia, *The Criminal Investigation Process—Vol. I: Summary and Policy Implications* (Santa Monica: Rand Corporation, 1975), p. v. See also Peter W. Greenwood, Jan M. Chaiken, and Joan Petersilia, *The Criminal Investigation Process* (Lexington, Mass.: DC Heath, 1977).

16. George L. Kelling, *The Newark Foot Patrol Experiment* (Washington, D.C.: Police Foundation, 1981), pp. 94–96.

17. Robert C. Trojanowicz, "An Evaluation of a Neighborhood Foot Patrol Program," *Journal of Police Science and Administration* 11 (1983): 410–419.

18. Robert C. Trojanowicz, *An Evaluation of the Neighborhood Foot Patrol Program in Flint, Michigan* (East Lansing: Michigan State University, 1982) p. 86. See also Robert C. Trojanowicz, "An Evaluation of a Neighborhood Foot Patrol Program," *Journal of Police Science and Administration* 11 (1983).

19. George L. Kelling, "Police and Communities: The Quiet Revolution," *Perspectives on Policing* (Washington, D.C.: National Institute of Justice and John F. Kennedy School of Government, Harvard University, 1988), p. 5.

20. Antony M. Pate, Mary Ann Wycoff, Wesley G. Skogan, and Lawrence W. Sherman, *Reducing Fear of Crime in Houston and Newark: A Summary Report* (Washington, D.C.: Police Foundation, 1986), p. 3.

21. Mark H. Moore, Robert Trojanowicz, and George L. Kelling, "Crime and Policing," *Perspectives on Policing* (Washington, D.C.: National Institute of Justice and John F. Kennedy School of Government, Harvard University, 1988) p. 10.

22. John E. Eck, and William Spelman, et al. *Problem Solving: Problem-Oriented Policing in Newport News* (Washington, D.C.: Police Executive Research Forum, 1987), pp. xvi–xvii. See also Ronald V. Clarke, "Situational Crime Prevention: Its Theoretical Basis and Practical Scope," in *Crime and Justice: An Annual Review of Research,* Michael Tonry and Norval Morris, eds. (Chicago: University of Chicago Press, 1983).

23. John E. Eck, and William Spelman, et al., *Problem Solving: Problem-Oriented Policing in Newport News* (Washington, D.C.: Police Executive Research Forum, 1987), p. xvi.

24. Malcolm K. Sparrow, Mark H. Moore, and David M. Kennedy, *Beyond 911: A New Era in Policing.* (New York: Basic Books, 1990), pp. 175–176.

25. Herman Goldstein, *Problem-Oriented Policing* (New York: McGraw Hill, 1990), pp. 66–67.

26. Dietz and Baker, "Murder at Work," *American Journal of Public Health* 77 (1987): 273–274.

27. Chris R. Braiden, "Enriching Traditional Roles," *Police Management: Issues and Perspectives,* Larry T. Hoover, ed. (Washington, D.C.: Police Executive Research Forum, 1992), p. 101.

28. Timothy N. Oettmeier, and William H. Bieck, *Developing a Policing Style for Neighborhood Policing: Executive Session #1 (Houston: Houston Police Department, 1987), pp. 12–13.*

29. Malcolm K. Sparrow, Mark H. Moore, and David M. Kennedy, *Beyond 911: A New Era for Policing* (New York: Basic Books, 1990), pp. 182–183.

30. Robert Wasserman, and Mark H. Moore, "Values in Policing," *Perspectives on Policing* (Washington, D.C.: National Institute of Justice and John F. Kennedy School of Government, Harvard University, 1988), pp. 1,3.

31. Lee P. Brown, "Community Policing: A Practical Guide for Police Officials," *Perspectives on Policing* (Washington, D.C.: National Institute of Justice and John F. Kennedy School of Government, Harvard University, 1989), p. 5.

32. Gary W. Cordner, Craig B. Fraser, and Chuck Wexler, "Research, Planning, and Implementation," in *Local Government Police Management,* 3d ed., William A. Geller, ed. (Washington, D.C.: International City Management Association, 1991), pp. 346–347.
33. Malcolm K. Sparrow, "Implementing Community Policing," *Perspectives on Policing* (Washington, D.C.: National Institute of Justice and John F. Kennedy School of Government, Harvard University, 1988), p. 2.
34. David C. Couper, and Sabine H. Lobitz, *Quality Policing: The Madison Experience* (Washington, D.C.: Police Executive Research Forum, 1991), p. 67.
35. Malcolm K. Sparrow, "Implementing Community Policing," *Perspectives on Policing* (Washington, D.C.: National Institute of Justice and John F. Kennedy School of Government, Harvard University, 1988), p. 2.
36. Gary W. Cordner, Craig B. Fraser, and Chuck Wexler, "Research, Planning and Implementation," in *Local Government Police Management,* 3d ed., William A. Geller, ed. (Washington, D.C.: International City Management Association, 1991).
37. Edwin Meese III, "Community Policing and the Police Officer," *Perspectives on Policing* (Washington, D.C.: National Institute of Justice and John F. Kennedy School of Government, Harvard University, 1991), p. 7.
38. Mary Ann Wycoff and Timothy Oettmeier (forthcoming, 1994).
39. Malcolm K. Sparrow, "Implementing Community Policing," *Perspectives on Policing* (Washington, D.C.: National Institute of Justice and John F. Kennedy School of Government, Harvard University, 1988), p. 3.
40. *Ibid.*
41. Mary Ann Wycoff and Timothy Oettmeier (forthcoming, 1994).
42. Lawrence W. Sherman and Anthony V. Bouza in Gary W. Cordner, Craig B. Fraser, and Chuck Wexler, "Research, Planning and Implementation," in *Local Government Police Management,* 3d ed., William A. Geller, ed. (Washington, D.C.: International City Management Association, 1991), sidebar.
43. Timothy N. Oettmeier and William H. Bieck, *Integrating Investigative Operations through Neighborhood-Oriented Policing: Executive Session #2* (Houston: Houston Police Department, 1988), p. 35.
44. Malcolm K. Sparrow, "Implementing Community Policing," *Perspectives on Policing* (Washington, D.C.: National Institute of Justice and John F. Kennedy School of Government, Harvard University, 1988), p. 6.
45. Timothy N. Oettmeier and William H. Bieck, *Integrating Investigative Operations through Neighborhood-Oriented Policing: Executive Session #2* (Houston: Houston Police Department, 1988).
46. John E. Eck and William Spelman, *Problem Solving: Problem-Oriented Policing in Newport News* (Washington, D.C.: Police Executive Research Forum, 1987), pp. 104–6.
47. Joseph E. Brann and Suzanne Whalley, "COPPS: The Transformation of Police Organizations," in *Community-Oriented Policing and Problem Solving* (Sacramento: Attorney General's Crime Prevention Center, 1992), p. 74.
48. George L. Kelling, Robert Wasserman, and Hubert Williams, "Police Accountability and Community Policing," *Perspectives on Policing* (Washington, D.C.: National Institute of Justice and John F. Kennedy School of Government, Harvard University, 1988), p. 6.
49. Mark H. Moore and Darrel W. Stephens, *Beyond Command and Control: The Strategic Management of Police Departments* (Washington, D.C.: Police Executive Research Forum, 1991), p. 94
50. John E. Eck and William Spelman, "A Problem-Oriented Approach to Police Service Delivery," *Police and Policing: Contemporary Issues,* Dennis Jay Kenney, ed. (New York: Praeger, 1989), p. 101.

51. Malcolm Sparrow, "Information Systems and the Development of Policing," *Perspectives on Policing* (Washington, D.C.: National Institute of Justice and John F. Kennedy School of Government, Harvard University, 1993), p. 4.
52. Timothy N. Oettmeier and William H. Bieck, *Integrating Investigative Operations through Neighborhood-Oriented Policing: Executive Session #2* (Houston: Houston Police Department, 1988), p. 64.
53. Dennis P. Rosenbaum, Eusevio Hernandez, and Sylvester Daughtry Jr, "Crime Prevention, Fear Reduction, and the Community," *Local Government Police Management,* William A. Geller, ed. (Washington, D.C.: International City Management Association, 1991), p. 116.
54. Hubert Williams, "External Resources," *Local Government Police Management,* William A. Geller, ed. (Washington, D.C.: International City Management Association, 1991), p. 465.
55. Robert C. Wadman and Robert K. Olson, *Community Wellness: A New Theory of Policing* (Washington, D.C.: Police Executive Research Forum, 1990), p. 61.
56. Mary Ann Wycoff and Timothy Oettmeier (forthcoming, 1994).
57. Robert C. Trojanowicz, "An Evaluation of a Neighborhood Foot Patrol Program," *Journal of Police Science and Administration* 11 (1983): 417.
58. Mark H. Moore and Darrel W. Stephens, *Beyond Command and Control: The Strategic Management of Police Departments* (Washington, D.C.: Police Executive Research Forum, 1991), p. 76.
59. Robert J. Prinslow, "Community Policing in Marion County, Oregon," *Roll Call,* special ed. (June 1993): 9.
60. Herman Goldstein, *Problem-Oriented Policing* (New York: McGraw Hill, 1990), pp. 20–21.
61. Malcolm Sparrow, Mark H. Moore, and David M. Kennedy, *Beyond 911: A New Era for Policing* (USA: Basic Books, 1990), p. 180.

BIBLIOGRAPHY

Advisory Commission on Intergovernmental Relations. *The New Grass Roots Government.* Washington, D.C.: U.S. Gov. Printing Office, 1972.
———. *State–Local Relations in the Criminal Justice System.* Washington, D.C.: U.S. Gov. Printing Office, 1971.
Allevato, S. *Developing of a Law Enforcement Plan for California Cities Committed to Quality Service through Community-Oriented Policing.* Sacramento: California Commission on Peace Officer Standards and Training, 1989.
American Association of Retired Persons, Criminal Justice Services Program Department. Neighborhood Watch—Communities Combat Crime. Washington, D.C.: American Association of Retired Persons, 1983.
Banas, Dennis, and Robert C. Trojanowicz. *Uniform Crime Reporting and Community Policing—An Historical Perspective.* East Lansing, Mich.: National Neighborhood Foot Patrol Center, Michigan State University, School of Criminal Justice, 1985.
Bayley, David H. *The Best Defense.* Washington, D.C.: Police Executive Research Forum, 1992.
———. *Model of Community Policing: The Singapore Story.* Washington, D.C.: U.S. Department of Justice, Office of Justice Programs, National Institute of Justice, 1989.
Behan, Cornelius J. "Responding to Change and Managing Crimewarps." *American Journal of Police* 9, no. 3 (1990).

Belknap, J., Merry Morash, and Robert C. Trojanowicz. *Implementing a Community Policing Model for Work With Juveniles—An Exploratory Study.* East Lansing, Mich.: National Neighborhood Foot Patrol Center, Michigan State University, School of Criminal Justice, 1986.

Bittner, Egon. *Aspects of Police Work.* Boston: Northeastern University Press, 1990.

Blumstein, Alfred, and Jacqueline Cohen. *Criminal Careers and Career Criminals.* Washington, D.C.: National Academy of Sciences, 1986.

Blumstein, Alfred, Jacqueline Cohen, and Daniel Nagin. *Deterrence and Incapacitation: Estimating the Effects of Criminal Sanctions on Crime Rates.* Washington, D.C.: National Academy of Sciences, 1978.

Bowman, Gary W., Simon Hakim et al., eds. *Privatizing the United States Justice System Police, Adjudication, and Corrections Services from the Private Sector.* Jefferson, N.C.: McFarland Company, Inc., 1992.

Boydstun, John E., and Michael E. Sherry. *San Diego Community Profile, Final Report.* Washington, D.C.: Police Foundation, 1975.

Brann, Joseph E., and Suzanne Whalley. "COPPS: The Transformation of Police Organizations." *Community-Oriented Policing and Problem Solving.* Sacramento: California Attorney General's Crime Prevention Center, 1992.

Brown, Lee P. "Neighborhood-Oriented Policing." *American Journal of Police* 9, no. 3 (1990). Special issue.

———. "Community Policing: A Practical Guide for Police Officials." *Perspectives on Policing.* Washington, D.C.: U.S. Department of Justice, Office of Justice Programs, National Institute of Justice; and John F. Kennedy School of Government, Harvard University, 1989.

Bureau of Justice Statistics. "Prisoners in 1992." *Bureau of Justice Statistics Bulletin* (May 1992).

———. *The Prosecution of Felony Arrests.* Washington, D.C.: U.S. Department of Justice, Office of Justice Programs, 1992.

———. "State and Local Police Departments, 1990." *Bureau of Justice Statistics Bulletin* (February 1992).

———. *Sourcebook of Criminal Justice Statistics, 1991.* Washington, D.C.: U.S. Department of Justice, Office of Justice Programs, 1992.

———. *Criminal Victimization in the United States, 1991.* Washington, D.C.: U.S. Department of Justice, Office of Justice Programs, 1992.

C. F. Productions, Inc. *Crime File: Drugs, Community Response.* Washington, D.C.: U.S. Department of Justice, Office of Justice Programs, National Institute of Justice, 1990.

Chamber of Commerce of the United States. *Marshaling Citizen Power against Crime.* Washington, D.C., 1970.

———. *Forward Thrust—A Process for Mobilizing Total Community Resources.* Washington, D.C., 1969.

———. *Developing Voluntary Leadership.* Washington, D.C., n.d.

Chen, M. M. "System Approach of Needs-Oriented Police Planning: An Empirical Study." *Police Studies* 13, no. 4 (winter 1990).

Clarke, Ronald V. "Situational Crime Prevention: Its Theoretical Bases and Practical Scope." *Crime and Justice: An Annual Review of Research* 4 (1983).

Community Patrol Officer Program: A Pilot Program in Community Oriented Policing in the 72d Precinct, Interim Progress Report. New York: Vera Institute of Justice, 1984.

Community Policing—Making the Case for Citizen Involvement. Rockville, Md.: Charles Stewart Mott Foundation, 1987.

Cordner, Gary W. "Fear of Crime and the Police—An Evaluation of a Fear-Reduction Strategy." *Journal of Police Administration* 14, no. 3 (September 1986).

Cordner, Gary W., and Donna C. Hale, eds. *What Works in Policing: Operations and Administration Examined.* Cincinnati, Ohio: Anderson Publishing Company, 1992.

Couper, David C., and Sabine H. Lobitz. *Quality Policing: The Madison Experience.* Washington, D.C.: Police Executive Research Forum, 1991.

Cox, S. M. "Policing Into the 21st Century." *Police Studies* 13, no. 4 (winter 1990).

Craven, D. *Oregon Serious Crime Survey: Attitudes about Crime.* Washington, D.C.: U.S. Department of Justice, Office of Justice Programs, National Institute of Justice, 1989.

Criswell, D., and V. King. "Houston's Field Training Practicum." *Field Training Quarterly* 5, no. 2 (second quarter, 1988).

Cumming, Elaine, Ian Cumming, and Laural Edell. "Policeman as Philosopher, Guide, and Friend." *Social Problems* 12 (1965).

Daly, N. C., and P. J. Morehead. *Evaluation of Community Policing: Final Report of the Community Survey and Police Department Internal Survey.* St. Petersburg, Fla.: St. Petersburg Police Department, 1992.

Delaware Statistical Analysis Center. *East Side Wilmington Anti-Drug Abuse Program Evaluation.* Rockville, Md.: U.S. Department of Justice, Office of Justice Programs, National Institute of Justice, 1990.

Donovan, E. J., and W. F. Walsh. "Private Security and Community Policing: Evaluation and Comment." *Journal of Criminal Justice* 17, no. 3 (1989).

Dunham, Roger G., and Geoffrey Alpert, eds. *Critical Issues in Policing: Contemporary Readings.* Prospect Heights, Ill.: Waveland Press Inc., 1989.

Eck, John E., and William Spelman. *Problem Solving: Problem-Oriented Policing in Newport News.* Washington, D.C.: U.S. Department of Justice, Office of Justice Programs, National Institute of Justice, and Police Executive Research Forum, 1987.

————. "Who Ya Gonna Call? The Police as Problem-Busters." *Crime and Delinquency* 33 (1987).

Esbensen, F. "Foot Patrol: Of What Value?" *American Journal of Police* 6, no. 1 (spring 1987).

Espinosa, G., and R. Wittmier. "Police Bicycle Patrols: An Integral Part of Community Policing." *Campus Enforcement Journal* 21, no. 6 (November–December 1991).

Farmer, Michael T., ed. *Differential Police Response Strategies.* Washington, D.C.: Police Executive Research Forum, 1981.

Farrell, Michael J. *Community Patrol Officer Program: Community-Oriented Policing in New York City Police Department, Interim Progress Report Number 2.* New York: Vera Institute of Justice, 1986.

Fleissner, D., N. Feden, E. Scotland, and D. Klinger. *Community Policing in Seattle: A Descriptive Study of the South Seattle Crime Reduction Project.* Rockville, Md.: U.S. Department of Justice, Office of Justice Programs, National Institute of Justice, 1991.

Freeman, Michael A. "Community-Oriented Policing." *MIS Report. International City Management Association* 24, no. 9 (September 1989).

Friedmann, Robert R. "Community Policing: Promises and Challenges." *Journal of Contemporary Criminal Justice* 6, no. 2 (May 1990).

Geller, William A., ed. *Local Government Police Management.* Washington, D.C.: International City Management Association, 1991.

————. *Police Leadership in America.* New York: Praeger Publishers, 1985.

Goldstein, Herman. *Problem-Oriented Policing.* New York: McGraw Hill, Inc., 1990.

————. "Improving Policing: A Problem-Oriented Approach." *Crime and Delinquency* 25 (1979).

Greene, Jack R. "Foot Patrol and Community Policing: Past Practices and Future Prospects." *American Journal of Police* 6, no. 1 (spring 1987).

Greene, Jack R., and Stephan D. Mastrofski. *Community Policing: Rhetoric or Reality.* New York: Praeger Publishers, 1988.

Greenwood, Peter W., Jan M. Chaiken, and Joan Petersilia. *The Criminal Investigation Process.* Lexington: DC Heath, 1977.

Greenwood, Peter W., and Joan Petersilia. *The Criminal Investigation Process—Vol. I: Summary and Policy Implications.* Santa Monica, Calif.: Rand Corporation, 1975.

Gruber, C. A. "Neighborhood Policing." *Law Enforcement Technology* 19, no. 5 (May 1992).

Hall, D. L. "Community Policing: An Overview of the Literature." *Public Policy Report* 1, no. 1 (June 1990).

Hand, Learned. *The Contribution of an Independent Judiciary to Civilization.* 1942.

Hansen, K. J. *Exploratory Study of the Extension of Local Empowerment through Community Policing.* Washington, D.C.: U.S. Department of Justice, Office of Justice Programs, National Institute of Justice, 1991.

Harrington, Michael. *The Other America: Poverty in the United States.* New York: Macmillan, 1981.

Hayward Police Department. *Community Policing and Problem Solving (COPPS).* Hayward: Hayward Police Department, 1991.

Hermanson, S. *Police–Community Relations: A Survey Measuring Citizens' Attitudes Towards and Perceptions of the Louisville Police Department.* Louisville, Ky.: University of Louisville Urban Studies Center, College of Urban and Public Affairs, 1982.

Herzberg, F. "One More Time, How Do You Motivate Employees?" *Harvard Business Review* (January–February 1968).

Hoover, Larry T., ed. *Police Management: Issues and Perspectives.* Washington, D.C.: Police Executive Research Forum, 1992.

Independent Commission on the Los Angeles Police Department. *Report of the Independent Commission on the Los Angeles Police Department.* Los Angeles, 1991.

Institute for Law and Social Research. *Expanding the Perspective of Crime Data: Performance Implications for Policymakers.* Washington, D.C.: Law Enforcement Assistance Administration, 1977.

International City Management Association. *Source Book: Community-Oriented Policing: An Alternative Strategy.* Washington, D.C.: U.S. Department of Justice, Office of Justice Programs, National Institute of Justice, 1991.

Jackson, F. *Directory of City Policing Programs, Vol. 3.* Rockville, Md.: U.S. Department of Justice, Office of Justice Programs, National Institute of Justice, 1989.

Jacobs, Jane. *The Death and Life of Great American Cities.* New York: Vintage, 1961.

Jensen, F. P. *Evaluating Police Effectiveness by the Year 2001.* Sacramento: California Commission on Peace Officer Standards and Training, 1992.

Johnson, J. *Police Officers A to Z.* New York: Walker, 1986.

Johnson, M. C. *Effectiveness of the Addition of Foot Patrol in Montclair, N.J.* Ann Arbor, Mich.: University Microfilms, 1980.

Kansas City Police Department. *Response Time Analysis: Vol. II—Part I, Crime Analysis.* Washington, D.C.: U.S. Govt. Printing Office, 1980.

———. *Directed Patrol: A Concept in Community-Specific, Crime-Specific, and Service-Specific Policing.* Kansas City, Mo.: Kansas City Police Department, 1974.

Kelling, George L. "Police and Communities: The Quiet Revolution." *Perspectives on Policing.* Washington, D.C.: U.S. Department of Justice, Office of Justice Programs, National Institute of Justice; and John F. Kennedy School of Government, Harvard University, 1988.

————. "Acquiring a Taste for Order—The Community and Police." *Crime and Delinquency* 33, no. 1 (January 1987).

————. *Foot Patrol—Crime File Series Study Guide.* Rockville, Md.: U.S. Department of Justice, Office of Justice Programs, National Institute of Justice, 1986.

————. "Conclusions." *The Newark Foot Patrol Experiment.* Washington, D.C.: The Police Foundation, 1981.

————. *Foot Patrol.* Washington, D.C.: U.S. Department of Justice, Office of Justice Programs, National Institute of Justice, 1986.

Kelling, George L., Robert Wasserman, and Hubert Williams. "Police Accountability and Community Policing." *Perspectives on Policing.* Washington, D.C.: U.S. Department of Justice, Office of Justice Programs, National Institute of Justice; and John F. Kennedy School of Government, Harvard University, 1988.

Kelling, George L., and Mark H. Moore. "The Evolving Strategy of Policing." *Perspectives on Policing.* Washington, D.C.: U.S. Department of Justice, Office of Justice Programs, National Institute of Justice; and John F. Kennedy School of Government, Harvard University, 1988.

Kelling, George L., Anthony Pate, Duane Dieckman, and Charles E. Brown. *The Kansas City Preventive Patrol Experiment: A Technical Report.* Washington, D.C.: Police Foundation, 1974.

Kennedy, David M. "The Strategic Management of Police Resources." *Perspectives on Policing.* Washington, D.C.: U.S. Department of Justice, Office of Justice Programs, National Institute of Justice; and John F. Kennedy School of Government, Harvard University, 1993.

Kennedy, L. W. "Evaluation of Community-Based Policing in Canada." *Canadian Police College Journal,* no. 4 (1991).

Kenney, Dennis Jay, ed. *Police and Policing: Contemporary Issues.* New York: Praeger Publishers, 1989.

Manning, Peter K. "Community Policing." *American Journal of Police* 3, no. 2 (spring 1984).

Manual for the Establishment and Operation of a Foot Patrol Program—Books in Brief. Rockville, Md.: National Criminal Justice Reference Service, 1985.

Maryland Department of Public Safety and Correctional Services. *Maryland's Law Enforcement Strategy in Partnership with the People.* Rockville, Md.: National Criminal Justice Reference Service, 1992.

McDonald, P., and Robert Wasserman. *High Performance Police Management: A Source Book.* Rockville, Md.: Police Management Association, and U.S. Department of Justice, Office of Justice Programs, National Institute of Justice, 1988.

McElroy, Jerome E., Colleen A. Cosgrove, and Susan Sadd. *An Examination of the Community Patrol Officer Program (CPOP) in New York City.* New York: Vera Institute of Justice, 1989.

McEwen, Thomas, John Eck et al. *Evaluation of Community Crime/Problem Resolution through Police Directed Patrol: Executive Summary.* Alexandria, Va.: Institute for Law and Justice; and Washington, D.C.: Police Executive Research Forum, 1989.

McEwen, Thomas, Edward F. Connors III, and Marcia I. Cohen. *Evaluation of the Differential Police Response Field Test.* Washington, D.C.: U.S. Govt. Printing Office, 1986.

Meese, Edwin III. "Community Policing and the Police Officer." *Perspectives on Policing.* Washington, D.C.: U.S. Department of Justice, Office of Justice Programs, National Institute of Justice; and John F. Kennedy School of Government, Harvard University, 1991.

Moore, Mark H., and Darrel W. Stephens. *Beyond Command and Control: The Strategic Management of Police Departments.* Washington, D.C.: Police Executive Research Forum, 1991.

Moore, Mark H., and Robert C. Trojanowicz. "Policing and the Fear of Crime." *Perspectives on Policing.* Washington, D.C.: U.S. Department of Justice, Office of Justice Programs, National Institute of Justice; and John F. Kennedy School of Government, Harvard University, 1988.

————. "Corporate Strategies for Policing." *Perspectives on Policing.* Washington, D.C.: U.S. Department of Justice, Office of Justice Programs, National Institute of Justice; and John F. Kennedy School of Government, Harvard University, 1988.

Moore, Mark H., Robert C. Trojanowicz, and George L. Kelling. "Crime and Policing." *Perspectives on Policing.* Washington, D.C.: U.S. Department of Justice, Office of Justice Programs, National Institute of Justice; and John F. Kennedy School of Government, Harvard University, 1988.

More, Harry W. *Special Topics in Policing.* Cincinnati, Ohio: Anderson Publishing Company, 1992.

Morris, Edward K., and Curtis J. Braukmann, eds. *Behavioral Approaches to Crime and Delinquency: A Handbook of Application, Research, and Concepts.* New York: Plenum Press, 1987.

National Advisory Commission on Civil Disorders. *Report of the National Advisory Commission on Civil Disorders.* Washington, D.C.: U.S. Govt. Printing Office, 1992.

National Advisory Commission on Criminal Justice Standards and Goals. *Community Crime Prevention.* Washington, D.C.: U.S. Govt. Printing Office, 1973.

National Institute of Justice. *Community Policing in Seattle: A Model Partnership between and Police, Research-in-Brief.* Washington, D.C.: U.S. Department of Justice, Office of Justice Programs, 1992.

Needle, Jerome A., and Raymond T. Galvin. "Community Policing: An Inevitable Progression." *Community Policing: Issues and Options* 1, no. 9 (October 1993).

Newport News Police Department Patrol Division. *COPP (Community Oriented Police Patrol).* Rockville, Md.: U.S. Department of Justice, Office of Justice Programs, National Institute of Justice, 1984.

Oettmeier, Timothy N., and William H. Bieck. *Integrating Investigative Operations Through Neighborhood-Oriented Policing: Executive Session #2.* Houston: Houston Police Department, 1987.

————. *Developing a Policing Style for Neighborhood Policing: Executive Session #1.* Houston: Houston Police Department, 1987.

Pate, Antony, and Sampson Annan. *Baltimore Community Policing Experiment Part 1—Technical Report; and Part 2—Appendixes.* Rockville, Md.: U.S. Department of Justice, Office of Justice Programs, National Institute of Justice, 1989.

————. *Baltimore Community Policing Experiment: Summary Report.* Rockville, Md.: U.S. Department of Justice, Office of Justice Programs, National Institute of Justice, 1989.

Pate, Antony, Mary Ann Wycoff, Wesley Skogan, and Lawrence W. Sherman. *Reducing Fear of Crime in Houston and Newark.* New York: AMS Press Inc., 1987.

————. *Reducing Fear of Crime in Houston and Newark: A Summary Report.* Washington, D.C.: Police Foundation, 1986.

Pate, Antony, and Wesley Skogan. *Coordinated Community Policing—The Newark Experience Technical Report.* Rockville, Md.: U.S. Department of Justice, Office of Justice Programs, National Institute of Justice, 1985.

Pate, Antony, P.J. Lavrakas, Mary Ann Wycoff, Wesley Skogan, and Lawrence Sherman. *Neighborhood Police Newsletters—Experiments in Newark and Houston Technical Report.* Rockville, Md.: U.S. Department of Justice, Office of Justice Programs, National Institute of Justice, 1985.

Pate, Antony, Robert Bowers, and Ron Parks. *Three Approaches to Criminal Apprehension in Kansas City: An Evaluation Report.* Washington, D.C.: Police Foundation, 1976.

Payne, Dennis M., and Robert C. Trojanowicz. *Performance Profiles of Foot Versus Motor Officers.* East Lansing, Mich.: National Neighborhood Foot Patrol Center, Michigan State University, School of Criminal Justice, 1985.

Peak, Ken, Robert Bradshaw, and Ronald Glensor. "Improving Citizen Perceptions of the Police: 'Back to the Basics' with a Community Policing Strategy." *Journal of Criminal Justice* 20, no. 1 (1992).

Philadelphia Police Study Task Force. *Philadelphia and Its Police: Toward a New Partnership.* Philadelphia: Philadelphia Police Study Task Force, 1987.

Police Foundation. Foot Patrol—Crime Files Series. Rockville, Md.: U.S. Department of Justice, Office of Justice Programs, National Institute of Justice, 1984.

President's Commission on Law Enforcement and Administration of Justice. *Task Force Report: The Police.* Washington, D.C.: U.S. Govt. Printing Office, 1967.

———. *The Challenge of Crime in a Free Society.* Washington, D.C.: U.S. Govt. Printing Office, 1967.

Punch, Maurice, ed. *Control in the Public Organization.* Cambridge, Mass.: MIT Press, 1983.

Reiner, R. "Watershed in Policing." *Political Quarterly* (April–June 1985).

Reiss, Albert J. Jr. *Private Employment of Public Force.* Washington, D.C.: U.S. Department of Justice, Office of Justice Programs, National Institute of Justice, 1988.

———. *Police a City's Central District: The Oakland Story.* Washington, D.C.: U.S. Govt. Printing Office, 1985.

———. *The Police and the Public.* New Haven, Conn.: Yale University Press, 1971.

Richardson, J. *Exploratory Study of Present and Potential Relations between Community Policing and Neighborhood Justice Centers.* Washington, D.C.: U.S. Department of Justice, Office of Justice Programs, National Institute of Justice, 1991.

Riechers, L. M., and R. R. Roberg. "Community Policing: A Critical Review of Underlying Assumptions." *Journal of Police Science and Administration* 17, no. 2 (June 1990).

Ripley, J. P. "Crime Prevention through Community Relations." *Innovations in South Carolina Law Enforcement.* Rockville, Md.: U.S. Department of Justice, Office of Justice Programs, National Institute of Justice, 1982.

Ruane, J. M., and K. A. Cerulo. "Police and Community Mental Health Centers (CMHCs): The Transition From Penal to Therapeutic Control." *Law and Police* 12, no. 2 (April 1990).

Rush, Thomas Vale. "A Study of Police–Citizen Transactions" (dissertation). Philadelphia: Temple University, 1974.

Scanlon, Robert A., ed. *Law Enforcement Bible.* South Hackensack, N.J.: Stoeger Publishing Company, 1982.

Schnelle, John F., Robert E. Kirchner Jr., Joe D. Casey, Paul H. Uselton Jr., and M. Patrick McNees. "Patrol Evaluation Research: A Multiple Baseline Analysis of Saturation Police Patrolling During Day and Night Hours." *Journal of Applied Behavior Analysis* 10 (1977).

Schwab, S. *Restructuring Small Police Agencies: A Transition toward Customer Service.* Sacramento: California Commission on Peace Officer Standards and Training (POST), 1992.

Scott, Eric J. "The Impact of Victimization on Fear." *Crime and Delinquency* 31 (1981).

Sechrest et al. "Rehabilitation of Criminal Offenders" *Crime and Delinquency* 2 (1979).

Sherman, Lawrence W. *Neighborhood Safety—Crime File Series Study Guide.* Rockville, Md.: U.S. Department of Justice, Office of Justice Programs, National Institute of Justice, 1986.

Sherman, Lawrence W., Patrick R. Gartin, and Michael E. Buerger. "Hot Spots of Predatory Crime: Routing Activities and the Criminology of Place." *Criminology* 27, no. 1 (1989).

Skogan, Wesley G., and George E. Attunes. "Information, Apprehension, and Deterrence: Exploring the Limits of Police Productivity." *Journal of Criminal Justice* 7 (1979).

Skolnick, Jerome H., and David H. Bayley. *New Blue Line: Police Innovation in Six American Cities.* New York: Free Press, 1986.

Smith, Douglas A. "Neighborhood Context of Police Behavior." In *Communities and Crime,* Albert J. Reiss Jr. and Michael Tonry, eds. Chicago: University of Chicago Press, 1986. (See NCJ 103315.)

Sparrow, Malcolm K. "Information Systems and the Development of Policing." *Perspectives on Policing.* Washington, D.C.: U.S. Department of Justice, Office of Justice Programs, National Institute of Justice; and John F. Kennedy School of Government, Harvard University, 1993.

———. "Implementing Community Policing." *Perspectives on Policing.* Washington, D.C.: U.S. Department of Justice, Office of Justice Programs, National Institute of Justice; and John F. Kennedy School of Government, Harvard University, 1988.

Sparrow, Malcolm K., Mark H. Moore, and David M. Kennedy. *Beyond 911: A New Era for Policing.* New York: Basic Books, Inc., 1990.

Staff report to the National Commission on the Causes and Prevention of Violence. *Law and Order Reconsidered.* Washington, D.C.: U.S. Govt. Printing Office, 1969.

Stratta, E. "Lack of Consultation." *Policing* 6, no. 3 (autumn 1990).

Taylor, M. "Constraints to Community-Oriented Policing." *Police Journal* 15, no. 2 (April 1992).

Toch, Hans, and J. Douglas Grant. *Police as Problem Solvers.* New York: Plenum Publishing Corporation, 1991.

Trojanowicz, Robert C. *Preventing Civil Disturbances: A Community Policing Approach.* Washington, D.C.: U.S. Department of Justice, Office of Justice Programs, National Institute of Justice, 1989.

———. *An Evaluation of a Neighborhood Foot Patrol Program in Flint, Michigan.* East Lansing, Mich.: Michigan State University, 1982.

———. "An Evaluation of a Neighborhood Foot Patrol Program." *Journal of Police Science Administration* 11, no. 4 (December 1983).

Trojanowicz, Robert C., and Bonnie Bucqueroux. *Toward Development of Meaningful and Effective Performance Evaluations.* East Lansing, Mich.: National Center for Community Policing, Michigan State University School of Criminal Justice, 1992.

———. *Community Policing and the Challenge of Diversity.* Washington, D.C.: U.S. Department of Justice, Office of Justice Programs, National Institute of Justice, 1991.

———. *Community Policing.* Cincinnati, Ohio: Anderson Publishing Company, 1990.

Trojanowicz, Robert C., and Mark H. Moore. *The Meaning of Community in Community Policing.* East Lansing, Mich.: Michigan State University, National Neighborhood Foot Patrol Center, School of Criminal Justice, 1988.

Trojanowicz, Robert C., and David Carter. *Philosophy and Role of Community Policing.* Rockville, Md.: U.S. Department of Justice, Office of Justice Programs, National Institute of Justice, 1988.

Trojanowicz, Robert C., B. Benson, and Susan Trojanowicz. *Community Policing: University Input Into Campus Police Policy-Making.* East Lansing, Mich.: National Neighborhood Foot Patrol Center, Michigan State University, School of Criminal Justice, 1988.

Trojanowicz, Robert C., Richard Gleason, Bonnie Pollard, and David Sinclair. *Community Policing: Community Input Into Police Policy-Making.* East Lansing, Mich.: National Neighborhood Foot Patrol Center, Michigan State University, School of Criminal Justice, 1987.

Trojanowicz, Robert C., and Bonnie Pollard. *Community Policing: The Line Officer's Perspective.* East Lansing, Mich.: National Neighborhood Foot Patrol Center, Michigan State University, School of Criminal Justice, 1986.

Trojanowicz, Robert C., Marilyn Steele, and Susan Trojanowicz. *Community Policing: A Taxpayer's Perspective.* East Lansing, Mich.: National Neighborhood Foot Patrol Center, Michigan State University, School of Criminal Justice, 1986.

Trojanowicz, Robert C., Bonnie Pollard, Francine Colgan, and Hazel A. Harden. *Community Policing Programs—A Twenty-Year View.* East Lansing, Mich.: National Neighborhood Foot Patrol Center, Michigan State University, School of Criminal Justice, 1986.

Trojanowicz, Robert C., and Jerome Belknap. *Community Policing: Training Issues.* East Lansing, Mich.: National Neighborhood Foot Patrol Center, Michigan State University, School of Criminal Justice, 1986.

Trojanowicz, Robert C., and Dennis W. Banas. *Perceptions of Safety: A Comparison of Foot Patrol Versus Motor Patrol Officers.* East Lansing, Mich.: National Neighborhood Foot Patrol Center, Michigan State University, School of Criminal Justice, 1985.

———. *Job Satisfaction: A Comparison of Foot Patrol versus Motor Patrol Officers.* East Lansing, Mich.: National Neighborhood Foot Patrol Center, Michigan State University, School of Criminal Justice, 1985.

———. *Impact of Foot Patrol on Black and White Perceptions of Policing.* East Lansing, Mich.: National Neighborhood Foot Patrol Center, Michigan State University, School of Criminal Justice, 1985.

Trojanowicz, Robert C., and Hazel A. Harden. *Status of Contemporary Community Policing Programs.* East Lansing, Mich.: National Neighborhood Foot Patrol Center, Michigan State University, School of Criminal Justice, 1985.

Trojanowicz, Robert C., and P. R. Smyth. *Manual for the Establishment and Operation of a Foot Patrol Program.* East Lansing, Mich.: National Neighborhood Foot Patrol Center, Michigan State University, School of Criminal Justice, 1984.

Tucson Police Department. *Tucson Police Department Enhanced Crime Prevention Program, Final Report.* Tucson, Ariz.: Tucson Police Department, 1991.

Turner, B. "Community Policing: Beyond Neighborhood Watch." *Research Update* 2, no. 4 (fall 1991).

Uchida, Craig, Brian Forst, and Sampson Annan. *Modern Policing and the Control of Illegal Drugs: Testing New Strategies in Two American Cities.* Washington, D.C.: Police Foundation, 1992.

United States Conference of Mayors. *Directory of City Policing Programs, Vol. IV.* Rockville, Md.: U.S. Department of Justice, Office of Justice Programs, National Institute of Justice, 1990.

University of South Carolina College of Criminal Justice. *Innovations in South Carolina Law Enforcement, 1985.* Rockville, Md.: U.S. Department of Justice, Office of Justice Programs, National Institute of Justice, 1985.

Vaughn, J.R. "Community-Oriented Policing . . . You Can Make It Happen." *Law and Order* 39, no. 6 (June 1991).

Wadman, Robert C., and Robert K. Olson. *Community Wellness: A New Theory of Policing.* Washington, D.C.: Police Executive Research Forum, 1990.

Ward, J. "Community Policing on the Home Front." *CJ the Americas* 5, no. 2 (April–May 1992).

Wasserman, Robert, and Mark H. Moore. "Values in Policing." *Perspectives on Policing.* Washington, D.C.: U.S. Department of Justice, Office of Justice Programs, National Institute of Justice; and John F. Kennedy School of Government, Harvard University, 1988.

Webber, Alan M. "Crime and Management: An Interview with New York City Police Commissioner Lee P. Brown." *Harvard Business Review* 69 (May–June 1991).

Weisburd, David, Jerome McElroy, and Patricia Hardyman. "Challenges to Supervision in Community Policing: Observations on a Pilot Project." *American Journal of Police* 7, no. 2 (1988).

Whitaker, Gordon P., ed. *Understanding Police Agency Performance.* Washington, D.C.: Govt. Printing Office, 1984.

Wiatrowski, M., and J. Vardalis. "Experiment in Community Policing in Delray Beach, Florida." *Police Journal* 63, no. 2 (April–June 1990).

Williams, Hubert, and Patrick V. Murphy. "The Evolving Strategy of Police: A Minority View." *Perspectives on Policing.* Washington, D.C.: U.S. Department of Justice, Office of Justice Programs, National Institute of Justice; and John F. Kennedy School of Government, Harvard University, 1990.

Wilson, James Q., and George L. Kelling. "Broken Windows." *The Atlantic Monthly* (March 1982).

———. "Making Neighborhoods Safe." *The Atlantic Monthly* 263, no. 2 (February 1989).

Witte, Jeffrey E., Lawrence F. Travis III, and Robert H. Langworthy. "Participatory Management in Law Enforcement: Police Officer, Supervisor, and Administrator Perceptions." *American Journal of Police* 9, no. 4 (1990).

Wycoff, Mary Ann, and Timothy N. Oettmeier. *Planning and Implementation Issues for Community-Oriented Policing: The Houston Experience.* Washington, D.C.: U.S. Department of Justice, Office of Justice Programs, National Institute of Justice, forthcoming.

Wycoff, Mary Ann, and Wesley G. Skogan. *Citizen Contact Patrol—The Houston Field Test.* Washington, D.C.: Police Foundation; and Rockville, Md.: U.S. Department of Justice, Office of Justice Programs, National Institute of Justice, 1985.

———. *Community Policing: Quality from the Inside, Out.* Washington, D.C.: U.S. Department of Justice, Office of Justice Programs, National Institute of Justice, forthcoming.

Wycoff, Mary Ann, Wesley G. Skogan, Anthony M. Pate, and Lawrence W. Sherman. *Police-Community Stations: The Houston Field Test, Executive Summary.* Rockville, Md.: U.S. Department of Justice, Office of Justice Programs, National Institute of Justice, 1985.

———. *Police as Community Organizers—The Houston Field Test, Executive Summary.* Rockville, Md.: U.S. Department of Justice, Office of Justice Programs, National Institute of Justice, 1985.

Wycoff, Mary Ann, and Wesley G. Skogan. *Police as Community Organizers—The Houston Field Test, Technical Report.* Washington, D.C.: Police Foundation; and Rockville, Md.: U.S. Department of Justice, Office of Justice Programs, National Institute of Justice, 1985.

Article 9

Implementing Community Policing

Malcolm K. Sparrow

A simple lesson, well understood by truck drivers, helps to frame the problem for this paper: greater momentum means less maneuverability. This professional truck driver does not drive his 50-ton trailer-truck the same way that he drives his sports car. He avoids braking sharply. He treats corners with far greater respect. And he generally does not expect the same instant response from the trailer, with its load, that he enjoys in his car. The driver's failure to understand the implications and responsibilities of driving such a massive vehicle inevitably produces tragedy: if the driver tries to turn too sharply, the cab loses traction as the trailer's momentum overturns or jackknifes the vehicle.

Police organizations also have considerable momentum. Having a strong personal commitment to the values with which they have "grown up," police officers will find any hint of proposed change in the police culture extremely threatening. Moreover, those values are reflected in many apparently technical aspects of their jobs—systems for dispatching patrols, patrol officers constantly striving to be available for the next call, incident logging criteria, etc. The chief executive who simply announces that community policing is now the order of the day, without a carefully designed plan for bringing about that change, stands in danger both of "losing traction" and of throwing his entire force into confusion.

The concept of community policing envisages a police department striving for an absence of crime and disorder and concerned with, and sensitive to, the quality of life in the community. It perceives the community as an agency and partner in promoting security rather than as a

Reprinted from Malcolm K. Sparrow, "Implementing Community Policing,"
Perspectives on Policing, no. 9 (Washington, D.C.: National Institute of Justice, U.S.
Department of Justice, and the Program in Criminal Justice Policy and Management,
John F. Kennedy School of Government, Harvard University, November 1988).

passive audience. This is in contrast to the traditional concept of policing that measures its successes chiefly through response times, the number of calls handled, and detection rates for serious crime. A fuller comparison between traditional and community policing models is given in the appendix in a question-and-answer format [see pp. 182–183].

The task here is to focus attention upon some of the difficulties inherent in a change of policing style, rather than to defend or advocate community policing. So we will address some general problems of institutional change, albeit within the context of a discussion of policing styles.

Those who accept the desirability of introducing community policing confront a host of difficult issues: What structural changes are necessary, if any? How do we get the people on the beat to behave differently? Can the people we have now be forced into the new mold, or do we need to recruit a new kind of person? What should we tell the public, and when? How fast can we bring about this change? Do we have enough external support?

These are the problems of implementation. The aim of this paper is to assist in their resolution. You will find here, however, no particular prescription—no organizational chart, no list of objectives, no sample press releases. Such a prescription could not satisfy any but the most particular of circumstances. The intent here is to explore some general concepts in organizational behavior, to uncover particular obstacles to desired change that might be found within police departments, and then to find the most effective means for overcoming the obstacles.

DANGERS OF UNDERESTIMATING THE TASK: CHANGING A CULTURE

Even the superficial review of community policing in the appendix indicates the magnitude of the task facing a chief executive. Implementing community policing is not a simple policy change that can be effected by issuing a directive through the normal channels. It is not a mere restructuring of the force to provide the same service more efficiently. Nor is it a cosmetic decoration designed to impress the public and promote greater cooperation.

For the police it is an entirely different way of life. It is a new way for police officers to see themselves and to understand their role in society. The task facing the police chief is nothing less than to change the fundamental culture of the organization. This is especially difficult because of the unusual strength of police cultures and their great resistance to change.

The unusual strength of the police culture is largely attributable to two factors. First, the stressful and apparently dangerous nature of the police role produces collegiate bonds of considerable strength, as officers feel themselves besieged in an essentially hostile world. Second, the long hours and the rotating shifts kill most prospects for a normal (wider) social life; thus, the majority of an officer's social life is confined to his or her own professional circle.

Altering an organizational philosophy is bound to take considerable time. Another analogy may be helpful: the greater the momentum of a ship, the longer it takes to turn. One comforting observation is that a huge ship can nevertheless be turned by a small rudder. It just takes time, and it requires the rudder to be set steadfastly for the turn throughout the whole turning point.

It is worth pointing out, also, that there will be constant turbulence around a rudder when it is turning the ship—and no turbulence at all when it is not. This analogy teaches us something if the office of the chief executive is seen as the rudder responsible for turning the whole organization. The lessons are simple. First, the bigger the organization, the longer it will take to change. Second, throughout the period of change the office of the chief executive is going to be surrounded by turbulence, like it or not. It will require personal leadership of considerable strength and perseverance.

RENDERING APPEARANCE SUSCEPTIBLE TO CHANGE

A chief executive may be fortunate enough to inherit an organization that is already susceptible to change. For instance, he may arrive shortly after some major corruption scandal or during a period when external confidence in the police department is at rock bottom. In such a case, the chief executive is fortunate in that leadership is required and expected of him. His organization is poised to respond quickly to his leadership on the grounds that the new chief, or his new policies, may represent the best or only hopes of rescue.

A chief executive who inherits a smoothly running bureaucracy, complacent in the status quo, has a tougher job. The values and aspirations of the traditional policing style will be embodied in the bureaucratic mechanisms—all of which superficially appear to be functioning well. The need for change is less apparent.

The task of the chief executive, in such a situation, is to expose the defects that exist within the present system. That will involve challenging the fundamental assumptions of the organization, its aspirations and objectives, the effectiveness of the department's current technologies, and even its view of itself. The difficulty for the chief is that raising such questions, and questioning well-entrenched police practices, may look and feel destructive rather than constructive. Managers within the department will feel uneasy and insecure, as they see principles and assertions for which they have stood for many years being subjected to unaccustomed scrutiny.

The process of generating a questioning, curious, and ultimately innovative spirit within the department seems to necessarily involve this awkward stage. It looks like an attempt by the chief to deliberately upset his organization. The ensuing uncertainty will have a detrimental effect upon morale within the department, and the chief has to pay particular attention to that problem. Police officers do not like uncertainty within their own organization; they already face enough of that on the streets.

The remedy lies in the personal commitment of the chief and his senior managers. Morale improves once it is clear that the change in direction and style is taking root rather than [being] a fleeting fancy, that the chief's policies have some longevity, and that what initially appeared to be destructive cynicism about police accomplishments is, in fact, a healthy, progressive, and forgiving openmindedness.

The chief executive is also going to require outside help in changing the organization. For instance, the chief may be able to make a public commitment to a new kind of policing long before he can convince his organization to adopt it. He may be able to create a public consensus that many of the serious policing problems of the day are direct results of the fact that the new kind of policing was not practiced in the past. He may be able to educate the public, or the mayor, about the shortcomings of existing practices even before his staff is prepared to face up to them.

He may identify pressure groups that he can use to his advantage by eliciting from them public enunciation of particular concern. He may be able to foster and empower the work of commissions, committees, or inquiries that help to make his organization vulnerable to change. He can then approach his own organization backed by a public mandate— and police of all ranks will, in due course, face questions from the public itself that make life very uncomfortable for them if they cling to old values.

The chief may even accentuate his staff's vulnerability to external pressures by removing the protection provided by a public information officer and insisting that the news media be handled by subordinate officers. In so doing, the chief would have to accept that some mistakes will inevitably be made by officers inexperienced with media affairs. High-level tolerance of those early errors will be critical to middle management's acceptance of the new openness. They will need to feel that they are working within a supportive, challenging, coaching environment—not that they are being needlessly exposed to personal risk.

TWO KINDS OF IMBALANCE

Two different types of imbalance within the organization may help render it suceptible to change: "directed imbalance" and "experimental imbalance."

Directed imbalance. Return for a moment to physical analogies and consider the process of turning a corner on a bicycle. Without thinking, the rider prepares for the turn by leaning over to the appropriate side. Small children learning to ride a bicycle quickly discover the perils of not leaning enough, or too much, for the desired turn. The characteristics of the imbalance, in this instance, are that it is necessary and that it makes sense only in the context of the anticipated change in direction. It is, nevertheless, imbalance—because the machine will fall over if the turn is not subsequently made. Inevitable disaster follows, conversely, from making the turn without the preparatory leaning.

Directed imbalances within a police organization will be those imbalances that are created in anticipation of the proposed changes in orientation. They will be the changes that make sense only under the assumption that the whole project will be implemented and that it will radically alter organizational priorities.

Examples of such directed imbalance would be the movement of the most talented and promising personnel into the newly defined jobs; making it clear that the route to promotion lies within such jobs; disbanding those squads that embody and add weight to the traditional values; recategorizing the crime statistics according to their effect on the community; redesigning the staff evaluation system to take account of contributions to the nature and quality of community life; providing in-service training in problem-solving skills for veteran officers and managers; altering the nature of the training given to new recruits to include problem-solving skills; establishing new communication channels with other public services; and contracting for annual community surveys for a period of years.

Experimental Imbalances.   This differs from directed imbalance in its incorporation of trial and error—lots of trials and a tolerance of error. The benefits of running many different experiments in different parts of the organization are more numerous than they might, at first sight, appear. There is the obvious result of obtaining experimental data to be used in planning for the future. There is also the effect of creating a greater willingness to challenge old assumptions and hence a greater susceptibility to change at a time when the organization needs to change most rapidly.

There is also the effect of involving lots of officers in a closer and more personal way. It does not matter so much what it is that they are involved in—it is more important that they feel involved and that they feel they are subject to the attention of headquarters. They will then be much more disposed to try to understand what the values of headquarters really are.

Also, officers will see lots of apparently crazy ideas being tried and may, in time, realize that they have some ideas of their own that are slightly less crazy. Perhaps for the first time they will be willing to put their ideas forward, knowing that they will not be summarily dismissed. The resourcefulness of police officers, so long apparent in their unofficial behavior, can at last be put to the service of the department. Creativity blossoms in an experimental environment that is tolerant of unusual ideas.

MANAGING THROUGH VALUES

Existing police structures tend to be mechanistic and highly centralized. Headquarters is the brain that does the thinking for the whole organization. Headquarters, having thought, disseminates rules and regulations in order to control practice throughout the organization. Headquarters must issue a phenomenal volume of policy, as it seeks to cover every new and possible situation. A new problem, new legislation, or new idea eventually produces a new wave of instructions sent out to divisions from headquarters.

The 1984 publication in Britain of the "Attorney General's New Guidelines on Prosecution and Cautioning Practice" provides a useful example. The purpose of the guidelines was to introduce the idea that prosecutions should be undertaken when, and only when, prosecution best serves the public interest. As such, the guidelines represent a broadening of police discretion. In the past, police were authorized to caution only juveniles and senior citizens. Under the new guidelines offenders of any age may be cautioned in appropriate circumstances. Unfortunately, the order was issued in some county forces through some 30 pages of detailed, case-by-case instructions distributed from headquarters. The mass of instructions virtually obscured the fact that broader discretion was being granted.

Police officers have long been accustomed to doing their jobs "by the book." Detailed instruction manuals, sometimes running into hundreds, even thousands, of pages have been designed to prescribe action in every eventuality. Police officers feel that they are not required to exercise judgment so much as to know what they are supposed to do in a particular situation. There is little creativity and very little problem solving. Most of the day is taken up just trying not to make mistakes. And it is the voluminous instruction manuals which define what is, and what is not, a mistake. Consequently, heavy reliance is placed upon the prescriptions of the manuals during disciplinary investigations and hearings.

How does the traditional management process feel from the receiving (operational) end? Sometimes like this: "It all comes from headquarters; it is all imposed; it is all what somebody else has thought up—probably somebody who has time to sit and think these things up." New ideas are never conceived, evaluated, and implemented in the same place, so they are seldom "owned" or pursued enthusiastically by those in contact with the community.

Why is this state of affairs a hindrance to the ideals of community policing? Because it allows for no sensitivity either on a district level (i.e., to the special needs of the community) or on an individual level (i.e., to the particular consideration of one case). It operates on the assumption that wealthy suburban districts need to be policed in much the same way as public housing apartments. While patrol officers may be asked to behave sensitively to the needs of the community and to the individuals with whom they deal, there is little organizational support for such behavior.

Of course, there remains a need for some standing orders, some prepared contingency plans, and some set procedures. But such instructions can come to be regarded as a resource rather than as a constraining directive. In the past, instruction manuals have been used as much to allocate blame retrospectively after some error has come to light as to facilitate the difficult work of patrol officers. Many departments, in implementing community policing (which normally involves a less militaristic and more participatory management style), have de-emphasized their instruction manuals.

The instruction manual of the West Midlands Police Force in England had grown to four volumes, each one over three inches thick, totaling more than 2,000 pages of instructions. In June 1987, under the direction of Chief Constable Geoffrey Dear, they scrapped it. They replaced it with a single-page "Policy Statement" which gave 11 brief "commandments." These commandments spoke more about initiative and "reasonableness of action" than about rules or regulations. All officers were issued pocket-size laminated copies of this policy statement so that, at any time, they could remind themselves of the basic tenets of their department.

The old manual had contained some useful information that could not be found elsewhere. This was extracted, condensed, and preserved in a new, smaller, "advice manual." It was only one-third the size of the old manual and, significantly, was distributed with an explicit promise that it would never be used in the course of disciplinary investigations or hearings. The ground-level officers were able to accept it as a valuable resource, whereas they had regarded the old manual as a constant threat, omniscient but unfeeling.

The Chief Constable had set up a small team to be responsible for introducing the new policy statement and advice manual. One year after the first distribution of these two documents to the force, the feelings of that team were that the ground-level officers accepted the change and appreciated it, but that some of the mid-level managers found the implied management style harder to accept and were reluctant to discard their old manuals.[1]

Another trend in the management of policing is for procedures "set in stone" to be played down in favor of accumulated experience. There are growing repositories of professional experience, either in the form of available discussion forums for officers trying new techniques, or in the form of case studies where innovations and their results are described.[2] One difficulty here is that police officers have to be persuaded that it is helpful, rather than harmful, to record their failures as well as their successes—and for that they will need a lot of reassurance.

Senior managers have begun to emphasize the ideals, ethics, and motivations that underlie the new image of policing, as opposed to the correctness or incorrectness of procedures. Disciplinary inquiries, therefore, come to rest less firmly on the cold facts of an officer's conduct and more upon his intentions, his motivations, and the reasonableness and acceptability of his judgment in the particular situation.

The relationship between headquarters and district commands may also need to change. The role of headquarters will be to preach the values and state the principles and broad objectives and then to allow the districts a great deal of discretion in deciding on particular programs suited to their geographical area. Similarly, management within any one division or district should be, as far as possible, through values and principles rather than rules and regulations; individual officers can then be encouraged to use their own judgment in specific cases.

The nature of the rank structure itself can be a principal obstacle to the effective communication of new values throughout the organization, primarily because it consists of many thin layers. A typical British police force (say of 3,000 officers) has nine layers of rank. The larger metropolitan forces have even more. In the larger American forces, the number of ranks can vary from 9 to 13, depending on the size of the department. This is in contrast to the worldwide Roman Catholic Church (with over 600 million members), which does a fairly good job of disseminating values with only five layers. We know from physics that many thin layers are the best formula for effective insulation; for instance, we are told that the best protection from cold weather is to wear lots of thin layers of clothing rather than a few thick ones.

Certainly such a deep rank structure provides a very effective natural barrier, insulating the chief officer from his patrol force. It makes it possible for the police chief to believe that all his officers are busily implementing the ideas which, last month, he asked his deputy to ask his assistants to implement—while, in fact, the sergeant is telling his officers that the latest missive from those cookies at headquarters "who have forgotten what this job is all about" shouldn't actually affect them at all.

During a period of organizational reorientation, the communication between the chief and the rank and file needs to be more effective than that—and so will need to be more direct. The insulating effects of the rank structure will need to be overcome if there is to be any hope of the rank and file understanding what their chief officers are trying to get them to think about. It means that the chief must talk to the officers, and must do so at length. Some chiefs have found it valuable to publish their own value statements and give all patrol officers personal copies. Alternatively, the chief may choose to call meetings and address the officers himself.

This is not proposed as a permanent state of affairs, as clearly the rank structure has its own values and is not to be lightly discarded. During the period of accelerated change, however, the communication between the top and the bottom of the organization has to be unusually effective. Hence, it is necessary to ensure that the message is not filtered, doctored, or suppressed (either by accident or as an act of deliberate sabotage) by intermediate ranks during such times.

The likelihood of a change in policy and style surviving in the long term probably depends as much on its acceptance by middle management as on anything else. The middle managers, therefore, have to be coached and reeducated; they have to be given the opportunity and incentive for critical self-examination and the chance to participate in the reappraisal of the organization. Some chiefs have invested heavily in management retraining, seminars, and retreats, taking care to show their personal commitment to those enterprises.

TERRITORIAL RESPONSIBILITY

One of the most obvious structural changes that has normally accompanied a move toward community policing is the assignment of officers to beats. It is important to understand how such a move fits into the general scheme of things. At first sight it appears that patrol officers who drive cars on shift work have territorial responsibility; for eight hours a day they cover an area. It fact, there are two senses in which that particular area is not the officer's professional territory. First, officers know that they may be dispatched to another area at any time should the need arise. Second, they are not responsible for anything that occurs in their area when they are off duty. The boundaries of their professional territories are more clearly defined by the time periods when they are on duty than by a geographical area. The fact that a professional territory spans a period of time rather than an area clearly has the effect of forcing the officer's concern to be largely focused on incidents rather than on the long-term problems of which the incidents may be symptoms. The patrol officers are bound to remain reactive rather than proactive. Long-term problems remain outside their responsibility.

In contrast, when patrol officers are given an area and told "this is yours and nobody else's," their professional territory immediately becomes geographical. The 24-hour demand on police resources requires that some calls in their area will be dealt with by other personnel. But the beat officers know that they have principal responsibility for a street or streets. They have the opportunity and obligation to have an impact on difficult problems. The more-committed beat officers demand to know what happened on their beat while they were off duty; they tend to make unsolicited followup visits and struggle to find causes of incidents that would otherwise be regarded as haphazard.

It is fairly easy to see how the chief officer, district commanders, and individual beat officers can have a clear territorial responsibility. What about the remainder in middle management? There is danger that community contact and concern will be the preserve of the highest and lowest ranks of the service, with the middle ranks living a cozy internal life of administration.

Middle-ranking officers can continue to be a barrier to the dissemination of the new values unless they too are made to live by them. This is perhaps best accomplished by making each rank correspond to some level of aggregation of beats or of community concerns. Thus middle managers should interact as fully with the community as the most senior and most junior officers. They thereby become a meaningful resource for the patrol officers rather than just one more level of supervision. They then can provide contextual frameworks at successively higher levels to assist subordinates in the understanding and resolution of particular community problems.

RESISTANCE AND SABOTAGE

The most robust resistance to any change in values within an organization will come from those parts that stand to benefit most by the perpetuation of the old set of values. In introducing the ideals of community policing, the chief should anticipate substantial resistance from particular areas, the first of which is the detective branch.

The idea that crime investigation is the single most important function of the police makes the criminal investigation division the single most important unit within the organization; it gives a detective higher status than a patrol officer. Should we expect the detective branch to applaud an absence of crime? It seems that their values are sometimes shaped to prefer an abundance of crime, provided it is all solved. It seems that special attention may have to be given to dismantling the detectives' view of what is, and what is not, important. Certainly the detective branch typically views the introduction of community policing as a matter for the patrol officers—"our job is still to solve crimes."

Detectives' perception of their job will remain "my job is to solve crime" until they are removed from the group that reinforces that perception. Their goals will remain the same until their professional territory is redefined. Their professional territories, if the detectives are to adopt and understand the ideals of community policing, should be defined segments of the community.

The detectives may, or may not, share their segments with uniformed officers; they may, or may not, retain the title of detective. Such considerations will depend, to an extent, on the particular constraints imposed by union power. But they have to be incorporated into the community policing system. They have to be encouraged to work closely within neighborhood policing units. Thus the valuable intelligence that detectives gain through crime investigation can be fed back into the patrol operation. Also, the detectives are made to feel that crime prevention is their principal obligation, and not the preserve either of the patrol force or of a dedicated, but peripheral, unit.

The essential change, whatever the prevailing circumstances, is that the detectives' professional territory has to be extended some considerable distance beyond the instances of reported crime. The detectives may end up looking more like "district investigators" than members of an elite, and separate, unit.

A second area of resistance will probably be the bureaucratic administration. It will include many key personnel who have been able to do their job comfortably and mechanically for many years. Such jobs will include the purchase of equipment and supplies, the recruiting and training of staff, and perhaps most importantly, the preparation and administration of annual budgets. The chief officers may have the authority to allocate police resources as they think best, but they are frequently frustrated by administrators who find some bureaucratic reason for not releasing funds for particular purposes or by the creation of other bureaucratic obstacles.

A fundamental reappraisal of organizational priorities is likely to "upset the apple cart" in these areas in a manner that bureaucrats will find difficult to tolerate. Such staff members need to be converted. The practical application is that such personnel must be included in the audience when the new organizational values are being loudly proclaimed. If they are left out at the beginning, they may well become a significant stumbling block at some later stage.

CONCLUSION

One final cautionary note: the principal task facing police leaders in changing the orientation of their organizations has been identified as the task of communicating new values. In order to stand a chance of communicating values effectively, you need to believe in them yourself and be part of a community that believes in them too.

NOTES

1. The Metropolitan Police Department (London) is in the process of making a similar change, moving away from a comprehensive instruction manual and toward clear, brief statements of the principles for action.
2. Much of this work stemmed from initiatives funded by the National Institute of Justice, the Police Executive Research Forum, the Police Foundation, and concerned philanthropic foundations.

APPENDIX

TRADITIONAL VS. COMMUNITY POLICING: QUESTIONS AND ANSWERS

Question	Traditional	Community Policing
Who are the police?	A government agency principally responsible for law enforcement	Police are the public and the public are the police: the police officers are those who are paid to give full-time attention to the duties of every citizen
What is the relationship of the police force to other public service departments?	Priorities often conflict	The police are one department among many responsible for improving the quality of life
What is the role of the police?	Focusing on solving crimes	A broader problem-solving approach
How is police efficiency measured?	By detection and arrest rates	By the absence of crime and disorder
What are the highest priorities?	Crimes that are high value (e.g., bank robberies) and those involving violence	Whatever problems disturb the community most

Question	Traditional	Community Policing
What, specifically, do police deal with?	Incidents	Citizens' problems and concerns
What determines the effectiveness of police?	Response times	Public cooperation
What view do police take of service calls?	Deal with them only if there is no real police work to do	Vital function and great opportunity
What is police professionalism?	Swift, effective response to serious crime	Keeping close to the community
What kind of intelligence is most important?	Crime intelligence (study of particular crimes or series of crimes)	Criminal intelligence (information about the activities of individuals or groups)
What is the essential nature of police accountability?	Highly centralized; governed by rules, regulations, and policy directives; accountable to the law	Emphasis on local accountability to community needs
What is the role of headquarters?	To provide the necessary rules and policy directives	To preach organizational values
What is the role of the press liaison department?	To keep the "heat" off operational officers so they can get on with the job	To coordinate an essential channel of communication with the community
How do the police regard prosecutions?	As an important goal	As one tool among many

ARTICLE 10

POLICE CRACKDOWNS

Lawrence W. Sherman

Can you increase the deterrent effect of policing without increasing the police budget? Few people would say so. But it may well be possible.

The key to success may be rotating, rather than permanent, patrol priorities and plans. By frequent changes in targets, but with major enforcement efforts—crackdowns—during a brief time period, police may get a "free bonus" of deterrence each time they replace one target with another. By the time potential criminals figure out that police have switched targets, a police department may be ready to switch back again.

Crackdowns constitute one of the most widespread developments in American policing in the 1980s. Drunk driving, domestic violence, public drug markets, street-walking prostitutes, illegal parking, and even unsafe bicycle riding have all been targets for publicly announced police crackdowns. What all these problems have in common is that they occur in such volume that police usually ignore most individual transgressions. What the crackdowns have in common is a sharp increase in law enforcement resources applied to the previously underenforced laws, with a clear goal of deterring the misconduct.

Crackdowns can be defined as increases in either the certainty or severity of official police reaction to a specific type of crime or all crime in a specific area. More precisely, police crackdowns constitute a sudden, usually proactive, change in activity. The activity is intended to drastically increase either the communicated threat or actual certainty of apprehension. Crackdowns are aimed at specific types of offenses or at all offenses in certain specific areas.

Crackdowns must be distinguished from formal police personnel allocation decisions. The distribution of officers around a city is normally

Reprinted from Lawrence W. Sherman, "Police Crackdowns," *Research in Action* (Washington, D.C.: National Institute of Justice, March/April 1990).

unequal per square mile, since it is guided by such factors as the relative density of population, number of calls for service, and amount of reported crime in each area. Simply adjusting the allocation as those factors change is not a crackdown but a finetuning of permanent triage priorities.

Crackdowns focus on specific target problems,[1] and these provide the sole justification for reallocating police resources outside the usual formula.

The notion that crackdowns might have lingering, or "residual," deterrent effects even after the crackdown is over has led to an analysis of some cities' experience with crackdowns and a review of 18 case studies of police crackdowns (see box). The evidence from the case studies supports the notion of residual deterrence—that is, some crime reduction persists after a crackdown is over. Moreover, there is some decay of initial crackdown impact even if police resources remain in the targeted area.

By constantly changing crackdown targets, police may reduce crime more through the accumulations of residual deterrence at several locations than through initial deterrence at a single location. And by limiting the time period devoted to each target, police might also avoid wasting scarce resources trying to sustain initial deterrent effects in the face of inevitable decay.

This article examines the basic reasoning for this hypothesis. Its purpose is not to advocate crackdowns but rather to consider how they might be employed and evaluated more effectively.

MANAGING THE SCARCITY PROBLEM

A basic theory of criminal justice is that crime can be deterred through certain punishment. But in modern America there is too much crime and too little law enforcement to make punishment very certain. The chances of being arrested for any given crime are very low because offenders have ample opportunity to choose a time and place that existing police resources cannot cover.

Despite continuing debate about the crime problem, few communities have raised budgets to make police more effective in arresting offenders. After 1978, in fact, the total number of police officers in big cities began to decline while reports of both serious and minor crimes increased substantially.[2]

Given this situation of scarce resources, policy makers have two choices. They can constantly shift priorities as this article suggests but as rarely happens in practice. Or they can adopt the more common method of simply setting permanent triage priorities, whereby some kinds of offenses are ignored or given very little attention so that resources can be concentrated on more serious problems.

In some cities, for example, police will not investigate burglaries unless the loss exceeds $5,000. In other cities, marijuana smoking and public drinking have been virtually decriminalized by police limitations.

Police crackdowns can target specific neighborhoods or specific offenses, and their duration can range from a few weeks to several years. The following, selected from the 18 case studies reviewed for this article, illustrate this range. Initial and residual deterrent effects varied, sometimes based on factors outside the scope of the crackdowns themselves.

Drug crackdown, Washington, D.C.
A massive police presence—60 police officers per day and a parked police trailer—in the Hanover Place neighborhood open-air drug market provided an effective initial deterrent.

Lynn, Massachusetts, open-air heroin market.
A 4-year crackdown using four to six police officers led to 140 drug arrests in the first 10 months and increased demand for drug treatment.

Operation Clean Sweep, Washington, D.C.
The city allocated 100 to 200 officers—many on overtime—to 59 drug markets, making 60 drug arrests a day. Tactics included roadblocks, observation of open-air markets, "reverse buy" sell-and-bust by undercover officers, and seizure of cars.

Repeat Call Address Policing (RECAP) Experiment, Minneapolis.
A special unit of 5 police officers attempted to reduce calls for service from 125 residential addresses, increasing their presence with landlords and tenants. This short-term targeting of resources led to a 15 percent drop in calls from these addresses, compared to 125 control addresses.

Nashville, Tennessee, patrol experiment.
A sharp increase in moving patrol at speeds under 20 miles per hour in four high-crime neighborhoods netted a measurable decrease in Part I index crime during two short crackdowns (11 days and 15 days).

Disorder crackdown in Washington, D.C.
Massive publicity accompanied a crackdown on illegal parking and disorder that was attracting street crime to the Georgetown area of the city. Police raised their weekend manpower 30 percent and installed a trailer at a key intersection to book arrestees.

New York City subway crackdown.
This massive crackdown involved increasing the number of police officers from 1,200 to 3,100, virtually guaranteeing an officer for every train and every station. Crime fell during the first 2 years of the crackdown but rose again during the following 6 years.

Cheshire, England, drunk-driving crackdowns.
During two short-term crackdowns, one accompanied by continuing publicity, police increased Breathalyzer tests up to sixfold between 10 PM and 2 AM. Significant deterrent effects continued up to 6 months after the crackdowns ceased.

London prostitution crackdown.
Stepped up arrests of prostitutes, pimps, and brothel keepers—combined with cautions of their customers—succeeded in reducing "curb-crawling" with no displacement.

New Zealand drunk-driving crackdowns.
Deterrent effects of two short-term crackdowns were felt even before they began because of intensive publicity about the impending crackdowns and stepped-up administration of Breathalyzer tests.

And until quite recently, police, prosecutors, and judges rarely took any action against minor domestic violence. These practical compromises were all seen as necessary ways to have enough law enforcement personnel and prison space for armed robbers, narcotics pushers, rapists, and murderers.[3]

One consequence of this triage approach is endless wrangling over what the priorities should be. Thus, an early 1986 *New York Times* editorial took New York's police commissioner to task for failing to enforce bicycle traffic laws after three deaths and many injuries to pedestrians. The commissioner's public response was that he could not spare the personnel from dealing with the "crack" epidemic. Nonetheless, by July of that year, New York police had launched an unannounced crackdown on cyclists, issuing 3,633 summonses in two weeks and prompting Buffalo, New York, police to follow suit.[4]

These sporadic pressures on policy are nothing new. Like the exhausted parent, police fail to crack down out of sheer poverty of resources rather than poverty of desire. But when political pressures or the news media focus attention on some law that has been little enforced, police resources may be temporarily diverted from normal priorities to deal with that long-ignored problem.

The effect is almost a change in the interpretation of the criminal law, a virtual admission that the offense had previously received too low a priority. The crackdown communicates to the lawbreaking public a statement that, in effect, the law is back on the books. Indeed, when Milwaukee police cracked down on misdemeanor domestic violence in May 1986 by adopting a new arrest policy, street officers often explained to the arrestees that the arrest was the result of a new law.

CHARACTERISTICS OF CRACKDOWNS

Police crackdowns have three possible tactical elements: presence, sanctions, and media threats.

- *Presence* is simply an increased ratio of police officers per potential offender, either in places or in situations. Increased presence can be accomplished either through uniformed presence (which communicates a visible threat to potential offenders) or through plainclothes surveillance (which may make potential offenders less certain about the risk of apprehension).
- *Sanctions* denote any coercive police imposition on offenders or potential offenders: stopping cars or pedestrians for identification checks, issuing warnings, mounting roadblock checkpoints, conducting Breathalyzer tests, making arrests, and so on.
- *Media threats* are announced intentions to increase the certainty of sanctions. They are reported in newspapers, public service announcements on television and radio, or even through billboard campaigns.

OPERATION PRESSURE POINT

In early 1984, a newly appointed New York City police commissioner launched "Operation Pressure Point," a two-year crackdown on the Lower East Side drug markets. Prior to the crackdown, the area had offered many blatant drug bazaars, with customers attracted from all over the New York area. Heroin buyers could be seen standing in long lines stretching around street corners.

The crackdown, at a cost of $12 million per year, used more than 150 uniformed officers, most of them rookies. The crackdown began with a high volume of drug arrests—65 per day for the first six weeks, then dropping to 20 per day. This rate continued until at least August 1986, by which time the police had made 21,000 drug-related arrests in the target area.

Tactics included observation-of-sale arrests, undercover buys, raids on dealing locations, arrests for unrelated misdemeanors and violations, tips from informers, and a "hotline" phone number.

The initial deterrent effect was a 47 percent reduction in robberies in 1984 compared to 1983 and a 62 percent reduction (from 34 to 13) in homicides during the same period. This initial effect was maintained until at least the first eight months of 1986, with a 40 percent reduction in robbery and a 9 percent reduction in homicides compared to the first eight months of 1983. While no displacements to the immediate vicinity were found, other parts of Manhattan experienced a growth in drug markets.

In practice, these tactical elements are combined in different ways. The interaction between presence and sanctions, for example, is ironically perverse: greater presence can produce more sanctions, but sanctions can reduce presence by taking police away to process arrests. In a 1985 parking violation crackdown in the Georgetown district of Washington, D.C.,[5] police avoided this dilemma by installing a booking center in a trailer parked on the street on weekend nights, saving the police a two-mile drive to the station for each arrest. Conversely, visible presence can reduce the number of sanctions imposed as would-be violators change their behavior in the face of almost certain arrest.

Area crackdowns tend to emphasize presence, while offense-specific crackdowns emphasize sanctions. Whether a media campaign is added to the other elements of a crackdown may depend on public interest in the problem as well as business interest in providing such advertising services free of charge.

A backoff is the usual sequel to a crackdown. For reasons of necessity (which may be a virtue), crackdowns rarely last forever. On rare occasions, some crackdowns may become part of the permanent triage, realigning the previous priority system. But most will eventually terminate in a backoff, which can be defined as a reduction in the visible threat or actual certainty of apprehension created by the crackdown. Backoffs can occur suddenly or gradually. They can result from explicit police management decisions or uncorrected informal action of enforcement personnel, and they can take place through reduced presence or by reduced sanctioning.

CHANGING POLICIES OR INCREASING POLICE PRESENCE

Police crackdowns take two frequently overlapping forms. One is a policy change about how to handle specific offenses, such as arresting wife beaters rather than counseling them, or towing illegally parked cars rather than just ticketing them. The other is an increase in police presence in specific geographical areas, constituting a temporary state of full enforcement of every law on the books for those particular areas. Both kinds of crackdowns attempt to communicate a more powerful threat of apprehension and punishment than "normal" policing.

Both kinds of crackdowns are highly controversial, although the geographically focused approach is probably more vulnerable to charges that police violate civil liberties. Most of the controversy centers on the effectiveness of the crackdowns: Are they worth the cost in tax dollars and public inconvenience? Vocal constituencies may strongly support crackdowns, but critics often argue that police crackdowns are undertaken for political purposes or as an excuse for police to earn overtime pay. Police themselves at times have raised doubts about the crime reduction effects of crackdowns.

Similarly, academic observers have been skeptical about the effects of police crackdowns. The leading student of drunk driving enforcement has argued that such crackdowns fail to create lasting deterrence,[6] while a leading police scholar has suggested that massive, sudden increases in police patrol can deter street crimes temporarily but not over the long run.[7]

DISTINGUISHING AMONG DIFFERENT DETERRENT EFFECTS

All these debates fail to make important distinctions among the different kinds of deterrent effects crackdowns can produce. They fail to separate any initial deterrence in the immediate wake of a crackdown from the possible residual deterrence after the crackdown has been withdrawn. They also fail to take account of the varying speed with which any initial deterrence decays during or after the crackdown.

There is evidence that some crackdowns do initially deter or at least displace some kinds of offenses. However, it is hard to sustain many crackdowns over a long period, either because police eventually start backing off or because potential offenders gradually realize that their chances of being caught are not as great as they had thought. None of the successful short-term crackdowns reviewed in our study appeared to suffer deterrence decay, suggesting that the decay problems may be limited to longer crackdowns. Yet even in longer-term crackdowns, deterrence may take as long as two years to diminish under the right conditions.

The slow decay constitutes a bonus residue of deterrence from the crackdown period. This residue fits the growing body of theory and evidence about how people make decisions under conditions of uncertainty, since intermittent, unpredictable crackdowns make risks of apprehension far more uncertain than could any system of fixed police priority—including long-term crackdowns. But systematic empirical evidence for the residual deterrence hypothesis is still quite meager.

One NIJ [National Institute of Justice] experiment testing the residual deterrence hypothesis has just been completed by the Minneapolis Police Department and the Crime Control Institute.[8] This "hot spots" patrol experiment randomly assigned 55 high-crime areas to receive up to 3 hours of extra, unpredictable time of patrol car presence each day and 55 other high-crime areas to receive normal patrol. The experiment is now being evaluated in terms of crime reports, calls for service, and more than 6,000 hours of systematic observation of the level of disorder.

CRACKDOWN EFFECTS

The effects of crackdowns revolve around five key questions:

- Was there any initial deterrent effect?
- Was there any increase in crime?
- Was there apparent local displacement?
- Did the initial deterrence decay?
- Was there any residual deterrence after the backoff?

Any crime reduction is arguably a general deterrent effect, even though it fails to distinguish between the reduction in the general crime rate and reduction in the criminal activity of individual active offenders.[9]

Interpreting any crime reduction as deterrence is problematic in other ways. A reduction could have been caused by incapacitation of a few active offenders early on in the crackdown. Or it could have been caused by changing transportation patterns, declining area population, or other factors.[10] But over short periods, with large enough numbers of offenses, it seems reasonable for police to interpret a crime reduction as a deterrent effect.

The more important point is the distinction between initial and residual deterrence. If a crime reduction is achieved while the crackdown tactic—presence, sanctions, or publicity—is still in operation, then it is plausibly an initial deterrence effect. But if the crime reduction is sustained after the tactic is terminated or reduced, then it is plausibly a residual deterrent effect. The perceived risk of apprehension that "hangs over" could influence decisions not to commit offenses after the risk (or the communicated threat) is actually reduced, at least until other evidence indicates that the risk has returned to its prior level. Decay, or a gradual decline from initial changes, is therefore a central concept for crackdowns in at least three ways.

Crackdown Decay.   Since a crackdown requires greater police effort, the tendency to regress to the former level of effort may cause the implementation of the crackdown itself to decay. Fewer arrests are made, fewer people are stopped, more officers are diverted to other duties—all of which could be planned by police commanders or just carried out by the lower ranks.

Initial Deterrence Decay.   With or without a decay of police effort, an initial crime reduction might decay as potential offenders learn through trial and error that they have overestimated the certainty of getting caught.

Residual deterrence decay.   The same learning process can take place gradually after the effort is actually reduced, with the residual deterrence slowly declining as word-of-mouth communication and personal experience show that it is once again "safe" to break the law.

CONCLUSIONS

The data gathered at the 18 sites suggest that crackdowns cause an initial shock to potential offenders. We cannot know how many of the cases where deterrence decayed might have shown residual deterrence if the crackdowns had been stopped sooner. But we can speculate that the rebounding crime rates might have looked much the same without continued expenditure of police resources. Aiming for residual deterrence could make wider use of crackdowns far more feasible than trying to achieve sustained deterrence over time.

NOTES

1. John Eck and William Spelman, *Problem Solving: Problem-Oriented Policing in Newport News* (Washington, D.C.: Police Executive Research Forum, 1987).
2. U.S. Department of Justice, Bureau of Justice Statistics, *Police Employment and Expenditure Trends* (Washington, D.C.: U.S. Govt. Printing Office, 1986).
3. Federal Bureau of Investigation, *Crime in America: The Uniform Crime Reports (annual)* Washington, D.C.: Federal Bureau of Investigation, 1978–1988).
4. Mary Connelly, Caryle C. Douglas, and Laura Mansnerus, "Cracking Down on City Cyclists," *New York Times* (August 24, 1986, eastern ed.).
5. Lawrence W. Sherman, Anne Roschelle, Patrick R. Gartin, Deborah Linnell, and Clare Coleman, "Cracking Down and Backing Off: Residual Deterrence" (report submitted to the National Institute of Justice, Washington, D.C., by the Center for Crime Control, University of Maryland, 1986).

6. H. Laurence Ross, *Deterring the Drinking Driver: Legal Policy and Social Control* (Lexington, Mass.: D.C. Heath, 1981).

7. James Q. Wilson, *Thinking about Crime,* 2nd ed. (New York: Basic Books, 1983) p. 64.

8. Lawrence W. Sherman, and David Weisburd, "Policing the Hot Spots of Crime: An Experimental Research Design" (unpublished manuscript, Crime Control Institute, 1988).

9. Alfred Blumstein, Jacqueline Cohen, Jeffrey Roth, and Christy Visher, eds., *Criminal Careers and "Career Criminals,"* 2 vols. (Washington, D.C.: National Academy Press, 1986).

10. Thomas Cook and Donald T. Campbell, *Quasi-Experimentation: Design and Analysis Issues for Field Settings* (Chicago: Rand-McNally, 1979).

Article 11

Who Ya Gonna Call? The Police as Problem-Busters

John E. Eck and William Spelman

Charlie Bedford couldn't sleep. Most nights, his residential Newport News street was quiet, marred only by the low rumble of an occasional truck on Jefferson Avenue two blocks away. But lately, Friday and Saturday nights had been different: groups of a dozen or more rowdy teenagers kept him awake, with their loud music and their horseplay. There had been no violence. But there had been some vandalism, and the kids seemed unpredictable. More disturbing, the kids came from another section of town, miles away. One sleepless Friday night it became too much. Charlie Bedford called the cops.[1]

Problems like Mr. Bedford's plague many urban neighborhoods. Disorderly behavior and other incivilities make life difficult for residents while creating fears of more serious harm. Wilson and Kelling (1982) have suggested that without intervention, citizens' fear may spark disinvestment in neighborhoods, leading to decay, more crime, and more fear. Because of concerns like these, incivilities have become a focus of researcher interest and police action.[2]

The increased interest in social order, fear, and community policing is the latest development of a continuing discussion about the role of the police in the community. The last two decades have seen a variety of proposals to bring the police closer to the community—community relations units, team policing, neighborhood watch, and foot patrol, among others. At the same time there has been equal interest in police operational effectiveness, especially with regard to crime control; directed patrol, case screening, crime analysis, and differential response were but a few of the ideas proposed and tested. For the most part, these two lines of thinking have developed independently. But we can help the Charlie Bedfords of our communities by combining the two areas. To see why, let us take a closer look at what might be called "community policing" and "crime control policing."

COMMUNITY POLICING

Largely as a result of the riots of the 1960s, police began to examine their ties to the communities they served. Black and Hispanic communities were concerned largely with controlling police use of force. The police were concerned with defusing the dissension, creating a more favorable image for themselves. Perhaps because these aims were so politically charged, these first attempts were formal, involving new bureaucratic structures such as community relations units and civilian review boards. Both were limited: community relations units had little effect on the behavior of street officers; line officers objected so strenuously to civilian review boards that most were dismantled or rendered impotent shortly after they were implemented (Goldstein, 1977).

Dissatisfied, some police administrators began efforts aimed at bringing police closer to people. The most ambitious of these efforts, team policing, typically involved a radical restructuring of the police bureaucracy. The hierarchical structure of policing was to be abandoned; decision making was to be decentralized; police officers were to be well-rounded generalists, rather than specialized technicians. These operational changes were to put police decision making closer to the communities served. In practice, team policing proved too hard to implement, and few efforts survive today. But three team policing strategies survived: storefront police stations. foot patrol, and community crime watch.

Storefront police stations put police officers in the community at all times, forcing them to deal with the public constantly. And, presumably, members of the public would be more willing to walk into a station located in an unpretentious setting in their own neighborhood if they wished to provide information or make a complaint. Storefronts were often well accepted by the communities they served and increased the amount of communication between police and citizens. There were indications that they helped to reduce fear of crime too. But officers who did not staff the storefronts often regarded these jobs as "public relations," far removed from "real police work."[3]

Foot patrols cast police in the most traditional of roles. Because they are in direct contact with the public at almost all times, foot officers become informal authority figures, wielding the (usually) discreet threat of force to get results (Kelling, 1987). The bulwark of policing at the turn of the century, foot patrols were enjoying a comeback as early as the mid-1960s. The trend has become more pronounced in the last few years. Evaluations of foot patrol programs conflict over whether they reduce serious crime (Trojanowicz, n.d.; Police Foundation, 1981; Williams and Pate, 1987). However, they agree that foot patrols lead to increased contact between police and citizens, often leaving the citizens feeling safer and more satisfied with their police services. Perhaps more important, foot patrol officers learned more about the neighborhood's problems; the best foot patrol officers tried to solve them.

Finally, community crime watches emerged as an important means of police–citizen communication in the 1970s. At first, police just provided citizens with crime prevention information. Later, police grew more ambitious and tried to organize communities. Organized communities were supposed to exert more control over rowdy youths and wayward adults, thus reducing illegal and threatening behavior. Despite some initial successes (for example, Cirel et al., 1977), crime watch programs have led to few sustained crime reductions nor do they seem to make people feel much safer. Indeed, there are indications that the organizing tactics usually used by police leave people more afraid than before (Lavrakas, 1985; Rosenbaum, 1987).

Most evidence suggests that storefronts, foot patrols, and crime watches do little to control crime. But they are all successful in increasing communication between the police and the public, and sometimes they have made people feel safer. Surely this is a gain, particularly in light of research that suggests that citizens may be more harmed by fear of crime than by victimization itself (Taub, Taylor, and Dunham, 1984; Greenberg, Rohe, and Williams, 1984). To the degree that fear of crime is a vague and somewhat irrational sense of unease, sighting an officer on foot, in a local station, or standing before a neighborhood meeting can help to reduce it. But most research indicates that fear of crime is quite rational, grounded in reasonable perceptions of vulnerability (Skogan, 1987; Fowler and Mangione, 1974). To the degree that fear of crime is rational, we can expect that fear will return to its prior levels, so long as the conditions that cause it do not change. Indeed, there are indications that fear-reduction strategies based on increased police–public communication are effective only in the short run (Fowler and Mangione, 1983).

The community policing projects also showed the disparity between the problems people face and the problems police attack. Most citizens' concerns are not directly related to crime. Trash on the streets, noise, abandoned and ill-maintained buildings, barking dogs, and the like form the bulk of calls for police service. In many areas, residents judge these problems to be more serious than street crime (Spelman, 1983). Still, police are oriented to crime control. Given the attention police have paid to crime over the years, one would expect that they would have learned to control it. In fact, the opposite is true.

CRIME CONTROL POLICING

Also as a result of the riots of the 1960s, researchers began to examine the ability of the police to control crime. Over the next two decades, researchers steadily undermined five basic premises of police crime control practice.

First, the Kansas City Preventive Patrol Experiment questioned the usefulness of random patrol in cars (Kelling et al., 1974). Second, studies of response time undermined the premise that the police must rapidly send officers to all calls (Kansas City Police Department, 1980; Spelman and Brown, 1984). Third, research suggested and experiments confirmed that the public does not always expect fast response by police to nonemergency calls (Farmer, 1981; McEwen, Connors, and Cohen, 1984). Fourth, studies showed that officers and detectives are limited in their abilities to successfully investigate crimes (Greenwood, Petersilia, and Chaiken, 1977; Eck, 1982). And fifth, research showed that detectives need not follow up every reported unsolved crime (Greenberg, Yu, and Lang, 1973; Eck, 1979). In short, most serious crimes were unaffected by the standard police actions designed to control them. Further, the public did not notice reductions in patrol, response speed to nonemergencies, or lack of follow-up investigations.

Random, unmanaged patrol operations did not seem to work. Special units, although occasionally successful, were expensive and could not be used routinely. But, police administrators reasoned, perhaps the problem was not that patrol and investigation tactics did not work. Perhaps they just needed to be managed better.

Research was showing that patrol officers and detectives had time available that could be better used (Gay, Schell, and Schack, 1977; Greenwood, Petersilia, and Chaiken, 1977). And additional time could be created, since citizens did not notice changes in patrol or detective operations. To free up patrol officer time, differential police response strategies were developed. Citizen calls that could be handled over the phone, through the mail, or by the caller appearing at a police station were diverted from patrol officers to civilians. Nonemergency calls requiring an officer received a scheduled response instead of an immediate dispatch (Farmer, 1981; McEwen, Connors, and Cohen, 1984). To free up detective time, crimes that had no leads, short of murder or rape, were no longer investigated once a patrol officer had completed the initial investigation. Managers would direct investigative efforts so that the free time could be used effectively in the fight against crime (Eck, 1982). To direct these efforts, information about crime and criminals was needed. Crime analysis seemed to be the answer.

Crime analysis units used police records describing initial and follow-up investigations, arrests of offenders, and police encounters with suspicious persons to analyze the nature of crime and criminals (Reinier et al., 1976). The crimes that analysts reviewed were usually burglaries, robberies, and, in a few agencies, rapes and auto thefts. Crime analysts looked for patterns. They plotted the locations and times of burglaries to direct patrol officers to the most likely targets. They mapped robberies to deploy stakeouts by patrol officers and detectives. They collated offender descriptions to identify suspects for detectives. In some agencies, crime analysts even gave information about crime patterns to neighborhood watch groups.

These efforts showed that collecting and analyzing information about crimes may improve police operations. But it is doubtful whether they reduce crime (Gay, Beall, and Bowers, 1984). Crime analysis units have too many limitations to have more than a marginal influence on crime or any other problem. One limitation is particularly critical: crime analysis is an attempt to find out where to apply established police responses. The responses are set before problems are understood; the same responses are used on widely differing problems. Instead, the aim should be to understand a problem and then determine what is needed to solve it.

Street operations do need more and better management. In order to manage, police managers need better information about local problems. But they must understand the problem before designing a solution. They must look for solutions to such problems as vandalism, rowdy behavior, drug use, drunkenness, and noise.

Community policing has used the same responses—foot patrol, storefront stations, and neighborhood watch—to address a wide variety of community concerns. Crime control policing has applied another standard set of procedures—patrol, investigations, surveillance, and stakeouts—to a wide variety of crime problems. In neither form of policing has there been a systematic attempt to tailor the responses to the characteristics of each particular problem.

> Sergeant Hogan was on duty when Mr. Bedford called. He assigned the problem to Officer Paul Summerfield. Summerfield suspected that the source of the problem might be a roller skating rink. The rink had been trying to increase business by offering reduced rates and transportation on Friday and Saturday nights. At two in the morning, as he drove north along Jefferson Avenue to the rink, Summerfield saw several large groups of youths walking south. Other kids were hanging around at the rink. Summerfield talked to several of them and found that they were waiting for a bus. The other kids, he was told, had become impatient and begun the three-mile walk home. Summerfield talked to the rink owner. The owner had leased the bus to pick up and drop off kids who lived far from the rink. But there were always more kids needing rides at the end of the night than the bus had picked up earlier.
>
> Officer Summerfield returned to the skating rink early the next evening. He saw 50 or so youngsters get out of the bus rented by the skating rink. But he saw others get out of the public transit buses that stopped running at midnight. And he saw parents in pajamas drop their kids off, then turn around and go home. Clearly the rink's bus would be unable to take home all the kids who would be stranded at closing time. Summerfield left, perplexed.

PROBLEM-ORIENTED POLICING

How could Officer Summerfield solve this problem? Herman Goldstein, in an article in this journal*, has described an approach that could help (Goldstein, 1979). According to Goldstein, police have lost sight of

---

*Crime & Delinquency.–Ed.

their objectives in their efforts to improve management. They must begin focusing on problems the public expects them to solve. Problems are "the incredibly broad range of troublesome situations that prompt citizens to turn to the police." Management improvements, though important, are only a means for improving police capacities to solve problems. Goldstein described three key elements of this problem-oriented approach.

First, problems must be defined more specifically. Broad legal definitions, such as burglary or robbery, should be replaced by descriptions that include such characteristics as location, time, participants' behaviors and motivation, and so on.

Second, information about problems must be collected from sources outside the police agency and not just from internal sources. The officers who have to deal with problems are a good source of information that is seldom exploited. But businesses, other government agencies, and private citizens can often provide data needed to understand problems fully.

Third, police agencies must engage in a broad search for solutions, including alternatives to the criminal justice process. The best solutions often involve public and private individuals and organizations who have a stake in seeing the problem resolved.

The Baltimore County Police Department and the Newport News Police Department have begun to implement problem-oriented policing. Let us look at how these agencies diagnose problems and try to resolve them.

Baltimore County.   Two sensational murders within a week brought fear of violent crime among Baltimore County residents to a head in August 1981. The incidents were unrelated and unlikely to be repeated, and the murderers were soon caught and eventually imprisoned for their acts. Still, the public's concern did not subside. In response, the Baltimore County Council provided its police department with 45 new officers.

Realizing that these officers would be spread very thin in a 1,700-officer department, Chief Cornelius Behan and his command staff decided to concentrate them into a special 45-officer unit to combat fear of crime—the Citizen-Oriented Police Enforcement (COPE) unit.

In 1981, no one knew much about fighting fear of crime. As a result, COPE officers confined their activities in target neighborhoods to directed patrol, motorcycle patrol, and community crime prevention. Despite some modest successes, COPE managers were dissatisfied with their efforts. Chief Behan had given them a charge to be innovative; so far, they had done little that had not been done many times before.

Gary Hayes, the late executive director of the Police Executive Research Forum and a friend of Chief Behan's, was asked to help. Hayes arranged for Herman Goldstein to train COPE supervisors in the theory and practice of problem solving. Almost immediately, COPE began to take on a sense of direction it had lacked in its first year of operation.

COPE's approach to problem solving relies heavily on a unique combination of creativity and standard procedures. A problem is usually referred to COPE by another unit of the police department or by another county agency. An initial assessment of the nature of the problem is made, and one officer is assigned to lead the solution effort. COPE officers then conduct a door-to-door survey of residents and businesses in the problem neighborhood. The officers also solicit other opinions: patrol officers, detectives, and officials from other agencies are often important sources of information. The results are used to define the problem more specifically and to identify aspects of the problem the police never see.

The COPE officers assigned to solve the problem then meet to consider the data they have collected and to brainstorm possible solutions. Next they design an action plan, which details the solutions to be attempted and a timetable for implementing them. Once the solutions are in place, COPE officers often conduct a second survey to see whether they have been successful.

Three years after its inception, these procedures have become the COPE unit's primary approach to reducing fear. But this is not the only method of solving problems; in Newport News, a complementary approach was designed.

Newport News.   In 1984 the National Institute of Justice funded the Police Executive Research Forum to develop and test a new approach to crime analysis. Darrel Stephens, then chief of the Newport News, Virginia, Police Department, was particularly interested in this approach, and Goldstein consulted with the project staff and officials of the Newport News police.

There are several differences between the Newport News Police Department's project and the Baltimore County COPE project. First, problem-oriented policing is an agencywide strategy in Newport News. All department members, including supervisors, are responsible for identifying, analyzing, and solving problems. Second, any type of problem is fair game, whether it is crime, fear, or another disorder. Third, less emphasis is placed on procedures in Newport News. Instead, a department task force under the guidance of Chief Stephens developed a "problem analysis model," a set of guidelines for data collection and thinking.

But the Newport News approach has many similarities with Baltimore County's. Both departments emphasize careful definition and analysis of problems prior to developing solutions. Evaluating solutions is also stressed. In both departments, supervisors encourage officers analyzing problems to look beyond the police department for information. This means talking to residents, business people, offenders, city agency personnel, and anyone else who could know something about the problem. Similarly, supervisors encourage officers to work with people and organizations outside policing to develop solutions. Criminal justice responses, although not discouraged, are seen as only one option among many.

PROBLEM-ORIENTED POLICING AT WORK

Let us look at how these two agencies have handled several common problems. Much attention has been devoted to crime and fear in residential neighborhoods, so we will first look at two problems of this type. Problems occur in nonresidential areas as well; we next describe an effort to solve a problem occurring in a downtown area with few residents and little commercial activity. Finally, some problems are not confined to a small geographic area but affect people everywhere. As our last case study shows, the problem-oriented approach can be applied equally well to problems like these.

Neighborhood Problems

Loch Raven Apartments (Baltimore County). Residents of the Loch Raven Apartments were shocked and frightened when beset by a spate of street robberies in 1984. While patrol officers and detectives tried to solve the crimes, COPE was called in to deal with the problem of fear. Officer Wayne Lloyd was assigned to lead the effort.

Officer Lloyd first coordinated a door-to-door survey of Loch Raven residents. He found that most of the residents were elderly women who felt particularly vulnerable to street attacks. Most were unwilling to leave their apartments after dark. Their feelings were exacerbated by the conditions of the complex: many street and building lights were broken; unkempt trees and shrubs created many hiding places; rats, stray dogs, and unrepaired structural damage all contributed to the feeling—widespread among residents—that they were trapped.

Reasoning that many solutions were needed for so complex a problem, Lloyd and his colleagues found a way to get almost everyone involved. Representatives of two local neighborhood associations agreed to help Loch Raven Apartments residents form their own association. The police convinced a variety of organizations to assist the new neighborhood group: a local printer produced crime prevention information free of charge; a local church donated its meeting facilities; a local baker contributed free donuts. Other agencies helped in other ways. Alerted to the poor lighting situation, Baltimore Gas and Electric repaired its street lights and installed new ones. The walkways and hallways of Loch Raven Apartments were visited by representatives of numerous local agencies, including the Animal Control, Health, Fire, and Housing Departments. The apartment manager bowed to the accumulated pressures and began to refurbish the buildings.

Perhaps because of the deterrent effect of patrolling dog catchers, building inspectors, and the like, the string of robberies stopped completely. Burglaries in the complex, running at a rate of six per month prior to the COPE unit's intervention, dropped to one every two months; it has remained at that level ever since. Perhaps most important, COPE provided the residents with better living conditions and a new community association that can help them obtain further improvements.

As the Loch Raven case illustrates, the police can draw upon the resources of many other public and private agencies in their problem-solving efforts. These "hidden allies" may only need guidance as to where they can be most effective. In this case, a variety of agencies respected the COPE unit's opinion that Loch Raven was a trouble spot that deserved their attention.

The Belmont Treehouse (Baltimore County).   No one ever seemed to use the Belmont Community Park. Casual passersby would rarely see a child in this playground or a jogger on one of the park's tree-shaded walks. Had they looked closely, they might have seen the reason: rowdy youths frequented one corner of the park. They used drugs and drank, and resisted all attempts by patrol officers to remove them. Neighborhood residents kept their children—and themselves—far away, fearing intimidation and exposure to alcohol and drugs. Residents had complained to various local government agencies for years with no response. Finally, one of the residents read about COPE in his community newspaper and called the unit.

COPE Officers Sam Hannigan and James Chaconas were assigned to handle the Belmont problem. Their survey of neighborhood residents revealed that the problem did not focus on the park, after all; instead, it centered on a shed, dubbed the "treehouse," that older youths constructed in the vacant, wooded lot next door. The treehouse was often used as a crash pad and drinking place by a few local teenagers.

Hannigan and Chaconas felt that the public nature of the drinking and drug abuse was mostly responsible for the residents' fears. So, at the suggestion of several neighborhood residents, they decided to make the drinking and drug abuse less visible by removing the treehouse.

Their first efforts went nowhere. The County Roads Department agreed that the treehouse posed a hazard and was in violation of city codes. They refused to take the problem seriously, however, since no one lived there. The Health and Fire Departments felt the same way. Even if they had been willing to condemn the shack, the formal process would have taken months.

Instead, the officers decided to work with the owner. They searched through tax records to find the owner of the vacant lot. When interviewed at his home, the owner readily admitted that the treehouse was a nuisance and a hazard and that he had no use for it whatever. Still, he feared retaliation from the kids who had constructed it and was unable to pay the costs of demolishing the building.

Hannigan and Chaconas discussed the situation with Central COPE Lieutenant Veto Mentzell. They agreed that the two officers should demolish the treehouse themselves. Two employees of the County Roads Commission agreed to help out. Next Saturday morning, the four, armed with saws and sledgehammers, quickly reduced the treehouse to rubble. Then they carted the pieces to a waiting county truck and took them to the dump.

The kids still drink and use drugs, and most of them have stayed in the neighborhood. They now meet in private places, however, where they are not visible to their neighbors. Most important, residents are no longer subject to their unpredictable, loud, and threatening behavior. The Belmont Neighborhood Association reports that residents are less fearful. One tangible result of the fear reduction is that, for the first time in years, the park is filled with children.

The Belmont case shows that an apparently intractable problem— here, fear created by teenage drinking and drug abuse—can be ameliorated with a little analysis and through some simple actions. The Treehouse case took two weeks from start to finish. The key was to accept the neighborhood's definition of the problem (threatening public behavior) rather than the usual police definition (illegal drinking and drug abuse).

A Nonneighborhood Problem

Not all problems occur in areas used by people who have common concerns. Some parts of cities have no real community of interests. Our next example shows how the problem-oriented approach can be applied in this sort of area.

Thefts from Vehicles (Newport News). For years, thefts from vehicles parked near the Newport News Shipyards have constituted around 10 percent of all index crime reported in Newport News. In 1984, 738 such thefts were reported; dollar losses from the thefts—not including damage to the vehicles—totaled nearly $180,000. Patrol Officer Paul Swartz was assigned to analyze the issues involved and to recommend solutions. He reviewed offense and arrest reports for the parking lot area going back three years and began tracking current cases. Because of these efforts, he was able to identify several parking areas where large numbers of thefts had taken place. These theft-prone areas became the focus of patrol efforts. Swartz also interviewed patrol officers and detectives familiar with the area and talked to members of the Shipyard's security force. As a result, Swartz identified a couple of brothers who stole from vehicles in the northern lots and a few individual offenders who stole in the southern lots.

Swartz gave the descriptions of the known offenders to the officers patrolling the lots. These officers began to stop and talk to suspects when they were seen in the area. Meanwhile, Swartz interviewed several thieves already convicted and sentenced for breaking into vehicles in these parking lots. He promised the offenders that nothing said in the interviews would be used against them. Swartz learned that drugs were a prime target of the northern thieves, but stereo equipment and auto parts were also targets. They especially looked for "muscle" cars, cars with bumper stickers advertising local rock and roll stations, or cars with other evidence that the owner might be a marijuana smoker or cocaine user (for example, a roach clip or a feather hanging from the rearview mirror). The southern thieves did not focus on drugs but instead concentrated on car stereo equipment and auto parts. Swartz also learned the names, descriptions, and addresses of other thieves; he confirmed that a few were particularly frequent offenders. This information was passed on to other street officers, who made several in-progress arrests. The detectives and the prosecutor worked to ensure that the most frequent offenders were convicted and sentenced to several months in jail.

As of this writing, the department is still developing a long-term solution to this problem. It will probably include working with the Shipyard and its workers to develop a theft prevention strategy. In the interim, there has been a 55 percent decrease in the number of these thefts

since April 1985 (from 51 per month to 23 per month), when the field interrogations and arrests of the repeat offenders began.

This is an example of using previously untapped information. Some
street officers had knowledge of who was involved in the thefts, but this
information was never put to use until Swartz began his analysis. Offenders were another source of information that had not been used before. As with the community problems described above, collecting information about nonneighborhood problems gives the police the ability to
design a response that has a good chance of solving the problems. In this
case, the solution involved standard police practices, but they were the
practices that fit the need.

A Jurisdictionwide Problem

In addition to problems occurring in small geographic areas, police must
deal with problems that affect their entire jurisdictions. Among these
problems are some of the most troublesome issues confronting the police: juvenile runaways, drunk driving, and spouse abuse, for example.
The last example describes how an officer dealt with a jurisdictionwide
problem.

Domestic Violence (Newport News).   Marvin Evans was a Newport News
homicide detective. He was also a member of the task force that designed
the department's approach to problem-oriented policing. Frustrated with
investigating murders after they had been committed, Evans decided to
find a way to prevent them. His analysis of homicide data indicated that
most occurred in the southern part of the city; but, more important, half
were the direct result of domestic violence, and half of these cases involved couples who had come to police attention previously. When
Evans reviewed national research on domestic violence he found that his
findings were typical. This encouraged him to look into the handling of
these cases locally. So he began interviewing counselors at the local
woman's shelter, assistant state's attorneys, judges, ministers, and anyone else who had an interest in the problem.

Since his fellow officers had an important role in dealing with this
issue, he sought their views. Evans used a survey to determine how officers handled domestic cases and their knowledge of the available options. He found that officers were unaware of the fact that they could file
a complaint that could result in a warrant, even if the victim refused. He
found that officers did not like handling domestic violence cases because
those officers who did handle these cases spent many frustrating hours
processing them.

So Evans decided to bring together a group of interested people who
could design a better way of handling these cases. This group included
representatives of the local woman's shelter, the state's attorney's office,
the circuit court, churches, the local newspaper, the Army, and other organizations, as well as the police.

The result of their efforts was a comprehensive plan for handling
family violence in the city. The objective was to keep families together

while showing both the abuser and the victim how to handle stressful situations without resorting to violence. Although a mandatory arrest policy was adopted for specific types of circumstances (incidents involving injuries, the presence of a weapon, or a prior history of violence, for example), arrest was not seen as an end in itself, but as a means to provide treatment that could preserve the valuable aspects of the families involved. To support this strategy, the state's attorney's office and the court agreed that they would not drop charges if the victim refused to prosecute. Instead, they would use the threat of legal sanctions to get both parties into counseling.

The program was pretested in the fall of 1985, and officers were instructed as to its operation. In January, the program was officially begun, and in February, the local newspaper published a 20-page special section on domestic violence. Virtually all aspects were covered, from the causes of domestic violence as seen by victims, offenders, and researchers to the responses to domestic violence by the police, courts, and counselors. This example shows that line officers can identify problems, conduct an analysis, and organize a communitywide response. In this case, the solution included the entire city. In addition to mobilizing many private and public organizations to help reduce domestic killings and assaults, Evans was able to convince the local newspaper to show the public what they could do to curb domestic violence.

SUMMARY

As these cases illustrate, the problem-oriented approach can be applied to a wide variety of problems. Problem solving can assist in the resolution of neighborhood problems, but it is equally applicable to problems that affect areas with no residential population or to citywide problems. Problem-oriented policing relies on and supports community policing, but it is not synonymous with community policing.

Moreover, the experience of Baltimore County and Newport News shows that police officers have the skill and interest needed to conduct thorough studies of problems and to develop creative solutions. Training and management direction can improve officers' problem diagnosis and analysis skills. And officers involved in problem solving seem to enjoy improving the quality of life of the citizens whom they serve. For many, problem solving is more satisfying than traditional police work because they can see the results of their work more clearly (Cordner, 1985).

The case studies also demonstrate that police have the time available to handle their current workload and to solve problems as well. Differential patrol response, investigative case screening, and similar practices can free up time for nontraditional activities.

The additional free time can be structured in a variety of ways. Baltimore County adopted one approach—it created a special unit. Newport News adopted a different approach—it had all department members solve problems, part of the time. In Newport News, problem-solving time was structured in two ways. For a few problems, an officer was temporarily assigned to attack the problem full time. (For example, Officer Swartz was assigned full time to the parking lots problem.) For most others, an officer was assigned to handle the problem in addition to his or her other duties. (Detective Evans created a domestic violence program while investigating homicides, for instance.) Each of the three methods offers its own set of costs and benefits, and it is too soon to tell which methods are best. Most likely, different methods will work better for different problems and police agencies.

Finally, the case studies make it clear that problem-oriented policing is a state of mind and not a program, technique, or procedure. The keys are clear-headed analysis of the problem and an uninhibited search for solutions. These can be achieved by applying standard operating procedures (as is typically the case in Baltimore County) or a looser analytic model (as in Newport News). There probably is no single best method for developing this state of mind. The best method for any given agency will depend on the characteristics of the agency.

Long-Run Considerations

As problem-oriented policing becomes standard practice in more and more departments, we can expect to see three other fundamental changes in the way police do business. The problem-oriented police department will probably have to change its internal management structure. The role of the police will change, and with it their relationship with community and other parts of the city bureaucracy. Finally, although problem solving creates the opportunity for greatly increased benefits, it also brings with it the potential for increased risks. Let us consider these long-run considerations in more detail.

Management Structure. As we have emphasized, the point of problem solving is to tailor the police response to the unique circumstances of each problem. Inevitably, this means that decision-making authority must be decentralized; the discretion of line officers and their supervisors—those members of the department who know most about each problem—must increase. As a result, we can expect that mid- and upper-level managers will need to develop new methods of structuring this increased discretion.

Decentralizing authority will affect all levels of the hierarchy, but it will probably affect line supervisors—sergeants—the most. As a result, agencies adopting a problem-oriented approach will have to provide much more extensive policy guidance and training to their sergeants. Problem solving puts a dual burden on these officials. On the one hand, they must make many of the tough, operational decisions. Line supervisors—those members of the department who know most about each of their officers, set priorities among different problems, facilitate work with other divisions of the police department and outside agencies, and make sure their officers solve the problems they are assigned. On the other hand, the sergeants must also provide leadership, encouraging creative analysis and response. So a first-line supervisor under problem solving might come to resemble the editor of a newspaper or the manager of an R&D unit more than an army sergeant.[4] Indeed, in Baltimore County there are indications that this is beginning to happen (Taft, 1986).

Police Role.   It is almost certain that problem solving will influence the police officers who undertake it to reconsider their role in society. As we have described above, identifying, studying, and solving problems requires that officers make more contacts with people and organizations outside the police agency. As they do this, they will become exposed to a wider variety of interests and perspectives. Many officers will discover that they can accomplish more by working with these individuals and groups. As a consequence, they will begin to take a broader, more informed view of the problems they must handle.

This is all to the good, but few improvements are without complications. A police agency taking on a complex problem may find itself in the midst of a contentious community power struggle. This could undermine the authority of the agency in other, less controversial areas. As a result, police agencies may avoid important but controversial problems. On the other hand, the problem-oriented police agency may find that it must get involved in controversial problems to avoid favoring one side over another.

Political problems will probably not be limited to police-community relations. Solving problems will require police agencies to work closely with a host of other public agencies as well. This raises the issue of "turf." Other public agencies may view a problem-solving endeavor as encroachment, rather than collaboration. This is especially likely when the problem is largely due to the failure of another agency to do its job. Even if police are successful in avoiding conflict with other agencies and with the public, problem solving will almost certainly increase the political complexity of managing a police agency.

Increased Risks and Benefits.   The case studies described above suggest that police agencies who take on a broader, problem-solving role can be more effective than before. But they may also do more harm than before, either through inadvertent mistakes or through outright abuses of authority.

Even creative responses based on careful analysis will sometimes fail. Some responses may even make matters worse. This has always been true of police work or the work of any government agency. Currently, however, failures to handle calls adequately seldom result in difficulties for the public at large. Few people are involved in each incident, and the scope of police intervention is usually very limited. The consequences of a failure to solve a problem may be much more serious: Problems involve many people; ill-advised responses may have far-reaching social implications.

Abuse of authority presents an even thornier issue. The police will be actively intervening in situations they had previously left alone, presenting more opportunities for abuse.

At the same time, however, the problem-oriented approach encourages police to analyze problems in detail and solicit the cooperation of outside organizations and individuals before responding. This will help to reduce the likelihood of both errors and abuses. In addition, because problem-oriented policing emphasizes noncoercive responses, inappropriate use of force and sanctions should become less likely. Mistakes and abuses will persist, of course; whether they are more or less benign than present mistakes and abuses remains to be seen.

In any case, it is clear that the limits of police authority will become more and more an issue as problem solving becomes standard practice. Who will set these limits? The short answer is, some combination of the same actors who already set and enforce police standards: informal pressure from private citizens in their contacts with individual officers; elected officials; the staff of other public and private agencies; and the police themselves. What limits will be established is an open question, considered at greater length elsewhere (Goldstein, 1987). One thing is certain: problem solving will require a new consensus on the role, authority, and limitations of the police in each jurisdiction that tries it.

Full implementation of problem solving will be a slow and sometimes difficult process. No agency will be able to "adopt" problem solving simply by making a few changes in standard operating procedures or just by telling officers to go to it. If it becomes a fad—if police managers try to implement it too quickly, without doing the necessary spadework—problem-oriented policing will fail. As Charlie Bedford's case shows, however, careful planning can yield great benefits for an agency that works to solve its community's problems.

> Officer Summerfield consulted Sergeant Hogan. They agreed that the skating rink owner should be asked to bus the kids home. Summerfield returned to the rink and spoke with the owner. The owner agreed to lease more buses. By the next weekend, the buses were in use and Summerfield and Hogan saw no kids disturbing Mr. Bedford's neighborhood.
>
> Sergeant Hogan summed it up: "Look, we can have the best of both worlds. People here can get their sleep and the kids can still have fun. But we can't do it by tying up officers and chasing kids every Friday and Saturday night. There has to be a way of getting rid of the problem once and for all."

NOTES

1. This case study and those that follow are true. Names of citizens have been changed, but names of police officials and places have not been. The information on which these case studies are based came from two projects being conducted by the authors. The Newport News study was funded by the National Institute of Justice under grant 84-IJCX-0040. The Baltimore County project was funded in part by the Florence V. Burden Foundation. The opinions expressed in this article are those of the authors and not necessarily those of the National Institute of Justice, the Burden Foundation, the police agencies described, or the Police Executive Research Forum.

2. See, for example, Skogan and Maxfield (1981); Skogan (1987); Police Foundation (1981); Williams and Pate (1987); Brown and Wycoff (1987).
3. For descriptions and evaluations of the effectiveness of storefronts in Detroit and Houston, see Holland (1985) and Brown and Wycoff (1987).
4. For examples of supervision in an R&D unit and a high-tech firm, see Kidder (1981) and Auletta (1984). For a broader discussion of this management style, see Drucker (1985) and Peters and Waterman (1982).

REFERENCES

Auletta, Ken. 1984. *The art of corporate success: The story of Schlumberger.* New York: Penguin.
Brown, Lee and Mary Ann Wycoff. 1987. Policing Houston: Reducing fear and improving service. *Crime & Delinquency* 33, (1).
Cirel, Paul et al. 1977. *Community crime prevention program, Seattle, Washington: An exemplary project.* Washington, D.C.: Department of Justice, National Institute of Justice.
Cordner, Gary W. 1985. *The Baltimore County Citizen-Oriented Police Enforcement (COPE) project. Final evaluation.* Final report to the Florence V. Burden Foundation. Baltimore: Criminal Justice Department, University of Baltimore.
Drucker, Peter F. 1985. *Innovation and entrepreneurship: Practice and principles.* New York: Harper & Row.
Eck, John E. 1979. *Managing case assignments: The burglary investigation decision model replication.* Washington, D.C.: Police Executive Research Forum.
——. 1982. *Solving crimes: The investigation of burglary and robbery.* Washington, D.C.: Police Executive Research Forum.
Farmer, Michael, ed. 1981. *Differential police response strategies.* Washington, D.C.: Police Executive Research Forum.
Fowler, Floyd J., Jr., and Thomas W. Mangione. 1974. The nature of fear. Center for Survey Research working paper. Boston: Center for Survey Research, University of Massachusetts and Joint Center for Urban Studies, Massachusetts Institute of Technology and Harvard University.
——. 1983. *Neighborhood crime, fear and social control: A second look at the Hartford program.* Washington, D.C.: U.S. Govt. Printing Office.
Gay, William G., Theodore M. Beall, and Robert A. Bowers. 1984. *A four-site assessment of the integrated criminal apprehension program.* Washington, D.C.: University City Science Center.
Gay, William G., Theodore H. Schell, and Stephen Schack. 1977. *Prescriptive package: Improving patrol productivity. Volume I, routine patrol.* Washington, D.C.: U.S. Govt. Printing Office.
Goldstein, Herman. 1977. *Policing a free society.* Cambridge, Mass.: Ballinger.
——. 1979. Improving policing: A problem-oriented approach. *Crime & Delinquency* 25: 236–258.
——. 1987. Toward community-oriented policing: Potential basic requirements and threshold questions. *Crime & Delinquency* 33(1).
Greenberg, Bernard, Oliver S. Yu, and Karen Lang. 1973. *Enhancement of the investigative function. Volume I, Analysis and conclusions.* Final Report, Phase I. Springfield, Va.: National Technical Information Service.
Greenberg, Stephanie W., William M. Rohe, and Jay R. Williams. 1984. *Safe and secure neighborhoods: Physical characteristics and informal territorial control in high- and low-crime neighborhoods.* Washington, D.C.: U.S. Govt. Printing Office.

Greenwood, Peter, Joan Petersilia, and Jan Chaiken. 1977. *The criminal investigation process.* Lexington, Mass.: D.C. Heath.
Holland, Lawrence H. 1985. Police and the community: The detroit ministation experience. *FBI Law Enforcement Bulletin* 54 (February): 1–6.
Kansas City Police Department. 1980. *Response time analysis. volume II, Part I. Crime analysis.* Washington, D.C.: U.S. Govt. Printing Office.
Kelling, George L. 1987. Acquiring a taste for order: The community and police. *Crime & Delinquency* 33(1).
Kelling, George L. et al. 1974. *The Kansas City preventive patrol experiment: A technical report.* Washington, D.C.: Police Foundation.
Kidder, Tracy. 1981. *Soul of a new machine.* New York: Avon.
Lavrakas, Paul J. 1985. Citizen self-help and neighborhood crime prevention policy. In *American violence and public policy.* Lynn A. Curtis, ed. New Haven: Yale University Press.
McEwen, J. Thomas, Edward F. Connors, and Marcia I. Cohen. 1984. *Evaluation of the differential police response field test.* Alexandria, Va.: Research Management Associates.
Peters, Thomas J., and Robert H. Waterman. 1982. *In search of excellence: Lessons from America's best-run companies.* New York: Warner.
Police Foundation. 1981. *The Newark foot patrol experiment.* Washington, D.C.: Author.
Reinier, G. Hobart, M. R. Greenlee, and M. H. Gibbens. 1976. *Crime analysis in support of patrol.* National Evaluation Program: Phase I Report. Washington, D.C.: U.S. Govt. Printing Office.
Rosenbaum, Dennis P. 1987. The theory and research behind neighborhood watch: Is it a sound fear and crime reduction strategy? *Crime & Delinquency* 33(1).
Skogan, Wesley G. 1987. The impact of victimization on fear. *Crime & Delinquency* 33(1).
——— and Michael G. Maxfield. 1981. *Coping with crime: Individuals and neighborhood reactions.* Beverly Hills, Calif.: Sage.
Spelman, William. 1983. *Reactions to crime in Atlanta and Chicago: A police-oriented reanalysis.* Final report to the National Institute of Justice. Cambridge: Harvard Law School.
——— and Dale K. Brown. 1984. *Calling the police: Citizen reporting of serious crime.* Washington, D.C.: U.S. Govt. Printing Office.
Taft, Philip B., Jr. 1986. *Fighting fear: The Baltimore County C.O.P.E. project.* Washington, D.C.: Police Executive Research Forum.
Taub, Richard, D. Garth Taylor, and Jan Dunham. 1984. *Patterns of neighborhood change: Race and crime in urban America.* Chicago: University of Chicago Press.
Trojanowicz, Robert C. n.d. *An evaluation of the neighborhood foot patrol program in Flint, Michigan.* East Lansing, Mich.: Neighborhood Foot Patrol Center, Michigan State University.
Williams, Hubert, and Antony M. Pate. 1987. Returning to first principles: Reducing the fear of crime in Newark. *Crime & Delinquency* 33(1).
Wilson, James Q., and George L. Kelling. 1982. Broken windows: The police and neighborhood safety. *The Atlantic Monthly* (March): 29–38.

PART 4

ORGANIZATION AND
MANAGEMENT

A critical aspect of the implementation of community policing lies in the organizational structure and management style of police supervisors within the police department. If a police agency attempts to implement community policing while retaining the traditional para-military structure, chain-of-command procedures and continues to utilize an authoritarian style of top-down management, community policing will be destined to fail. Because community policing is a philosophy and is value driven, hence driving the changes in the way police conduct their business and relate with the community, so too should these values drive change in the way management conducts their business and relates with the line officers. The articles in this section attempt to deal with the systemic changes that are called for under community policing.

The first article in this section is by Robert Wasserman and Mark H. Moore. In this article, they tie the philosophy of community policing (specifically, the values) to the concept of management. They discuss not just that certain values are needed but how values can be used as a management tool and how these values can be implemented by management.

The second article is by David M. Kennedy. In this article, he discusses how the police organization must utilize and deploy police resources more strategically in order to be more successful under the community policing model. He discusses past failures with police resource allocation, discusses how this allocation can and has changed with the community policing movement, and makes recommendations for where police agencies can go to find new untapped resources.

The third article in this section is by Mark H. Moore and Robert C. Trojanowicz. They discuss corporate strategies and management practices and describe how these can be used to compliment the changes needed in police management under community policing. What is especially nice about this article is their discussion of professional crime fighting, strategic policing, problem-solving policing, and community policing.

Ultimately, what they describe is a synthesis of these concepts (primarily as the total concept of community policing) and how management can generate solutions for the implementation of these concepts by employing various corporate strategies.

The fourth article in this section is written by George L. Kelling, one of the originators of the community policing concept, and William J. Bratton, former New York City Police Commissioner. This article first provides a historical overview of police management in the past, looking at the various management methods employed to control the organization. They then look at how these methods have not been highly successful and discuss new methods to help control the organization. The most important aspect of this article is its focus on mid-level management.

The final article in this section is an article written by George L. Kelling, Robert Wasserman, and Hubert Williams. They answer the primary criticism of community policing, that by enhancing the relationship between the police and the public, police officers will become more corrupt. They detail the historical reasons for police neutrality and organizational centralization, which were to deal with the problems of political corruption, and then move to a better understanding of why community policing is not a method of policing that will incite a reoccurrence of this corruption. They specifically point to the values that should be driving community policing, the accountability of the police to the community under community policing, and various administrative mechanisms that management has at their disposal, such as training, audits, and peer control.

ARTICLE 12

VALUES IN POLICING

Robert Wasserman and Mark H. Moore

This paper explores the role that the explicit statement of police values can have on the pursuit of excellence within police departments. Values are the beliefs that guide an organization and the behavior of its employees. The most important beliefs are those that set forth the ultimate purposes of the organization. They provide the organization with its raison d'être for outsiders and insiders alike and justify the continuing investments in the organization's enterprise.[1]

Often, however, the beliefs about purposes are hopelessly entangled with assumptions about the nature of the organization's environment, the principal means for achieving its purposes, and the sorts of relationships and expectations that exist within the organization. For example, in policing, the strong belief among many police officers that they stand as the front line of defense against community lawlessness—reflecting what is often a rather narrow definition of order—conditions the organizational environment within which the police operate. These beliefs can easily become the prevalent values of the force.

All organizations have values. One can see these values expressed through the actions of the organization—the things that are taken seriously and the things that are rejected as irrelevant, inappropriate, or dangerous. Jokes, solemn understandings, and internal explanations for actions also express values.

Police departments are powerfully influenced by their values. The problem is that police departments, like many organizations, are guided by implicit values that are often at odds with explicit values. This breeds

Reprinted from Robert Wasserman and Mark H. Moore, "Values in Policing,"
Perspectives on Policing, no. 8 (Washington, D.C.: National Institute of Justice, U.S. Department of Justice, and the Program in Criminal Justice Policy and Management, John F. Kennedy School of Government, Harvard University, November 1988).

confusion, distrust, and cynicism rather than clarity, commitment, and high morale. Almost as bad, the explicit values articulated by some police organizations are unsuited to the challenges confronting today's police departments. Finally, there is a reluctance on the part of some police executives to rely on explicit statements of values as an important management tool for enhancing the performance of their organizations. Still, more police executives are working towards superior police performance by articulating a new set of values and by using these as a primary management tool.

"Value orientation" has been neither the driving force nor the basis of organizational life in American policing. Should the American police organization have a set of organizational values that are explicitly acknowledged and well known throughout the organization? Should police officers recognize that their survival in the police department rests on whether they embody these organizational values in their actions? This paper examines these questions.

How Are Values Articulated and Expressed?   Some organizations state their values directly to clientele or employees. Even so, customers, clients, and organizational authorizers (community residents, mayors, and city council members in the municipal setting, and bankers and institutional investors in the corporate sphere) become aware of an organization's values only through the actions of members of the organization or the work of public relations officials.

American corporations are far more sophisticated in communicating values than are government organizations. In industry, values often are expressed through corporate value statements, public advertising, and management pronouncements.[2] Yet, while public relations may create an illusion that a particular set of values is important to the corporation, actual consumer experience often determines eventually the true nature of the corporation's values.

There is often a disparity between the values explicitly established by an organization and those that are actually embraced and pursued. In such cases, corporate management focuses on one set of values while employees adopt an entirely different set. This occurs either because of the failure of management to communicate organizational values or because stated organizational values fail to take into account the reality of the workplace.

The disparity is particularly common in American policing. Mayors and city managers often give their police executives a dual set of objectives, such as "clean up the gangs in the park" and "don't break the law in doing it." Since cleaning up the park has primary importance, and the police are unsupported in developing tools and tactics necessary to solve the underlying problems creating the situation, the mayoral concern with "don't break the law" implicitly becomes "don't tell me about it if you must break the law."

Major corporations have had to deal with the same pressures and ambiguities. In the case of a large producer of orange juice, maintaining profitability was translated by midlevel managerial employees as being more important than product quality, thus making it acceptable to water down the juice as long as it went undiscovered.

In many organizations, values are taken for granted until a crisis centers public attention on the disparity between the organization's stated values and those actually pursued. High-performing commercial organizations consciously strive to ensure that values expressed by employee actions and comments match the values of the organization. Many other organizations, however, function with a dual standard of public relations pronouncements and actual workplace values.

Values as a Management Tool.   The explicit statement and frequent pronouncement of organizational values becomes an important management tool in three circumstances: first, when management's explicit values are so well incorporated in the administrative systems and culture of an organization that they become workplace values; second, when management's values seem well suited to the challenges and tasks facing the organization, and their pursuit will lead to organizational success; and third, when the organization's operations are such that management through values is superior to any other kind of management control.

Values play this important role for several reasons. To the extent that the values actually influence substantive and administrative decisions facing the organization, they lend a coherence and predictability to top management's actions and the responses to the actions of employees. This helps employees make proper decisions and use their discretion with confidence that they are contributing to rather than detracting from organizational performance. That means that the necessity for strong control is lessened. Explicit values also lend significance and meaning to the activity of employers. They transform small transactions and events into expressions of personal commitment to particular values. Finally, explicit statements of values invite broad public support and facilitate accountability. To the extent that the values are attractive to shareholders, customers, and employees in the private sector, and to constituents, clients, and employees in the public sector, a flow of resources to the organization is initiated. To the extent that the values are actually expressed in organizational actions, accountability is preserved, and the flow of resources sustained.[3]

Note that management through values is a particularly important tool for organizations that find it difficult to codify procedures or measure their performance. This occurs in organizations where outputs are hard to define, adaptations of operations to individual cases are often necessary, and technical innovations are occurring. It also occurs in organizations where operations make close supervision impossible. The reason is that in such organizations, the principal alternative methods of control are obviously infeasible.

Values in Policing.   Policing styles reflect a department's values. A police agency that independently adopts an aggressive tactical orientation has a far different set of values than a police agency that carefully engages neighborhood residents in planning for crime control activities. The values inherent in policing before the reform efforts of the 1930s often reflected political and personal priorities of employees or special interest groups rather than a commitment to broad principles of professionalism.

Sometimes the values of police organizations have been publicly stated. O. W. Wilson, for example, published a set of values for the Wichita Police Department when he was the city's chief of police; he did the same for Chicago when he served as that city's police superintendent.[4] It is more usual, however, for the values that drive policing to be unstated. A number of police agencies, such as Los Angeles, have carefully incorporated values into their rules and procedural directives. Other police agencies, such as Madison (Wisconsin) and Houston, have articulated individual value statements reflecting organizational commitments.

Much of the current discussion about improving police performance is concerned about the values that should guide policing. To understand that discussion, it is useful to contrast the values of professional crime-fighting policing with the values of community problem-solving policing.

The Values of Professional Crime-Fighting Policing.   Over the last four decades, as police departments have become increasingly professional, several key values have emerged to justify and guide the performance of police agencies. While often unstated, these values include the following:

- Police authority is based solely in the law. Professional police organizations are committed to enforcement of that law as their primary objective.
- Communities can provide police with assistance in enforcing the law. Helpful communities will provide police with information to assist them (the police) in carrying out their mission.
- Responding to citizen calls for service is the highest police priority. All calls must receive the fastest response possible.
- Social problems and other neighborhood issues are not the concern of the police unless they threaten breakdown of public order.
- Police, being experts in crime control, are best suited to develop police priorities and strategies.

Other values reflect the common belief among police officers (and some chief police executives) that police departments exist to advance the profession of policing, not to serve as an important part of maintaining democratic values and improving the quality of life in urban communities. From these perspectives, there is little interest in, or respect for, the community basis for police authority.

The Values of Community Policing.   In the ongoing dialogue about community policing, there are two important new developments. A number of chiefs of police have defined a set of values reflecting internal (employee and administration) and external (community and government) consensus about the nature of the police function and operation of the police agency.

Second, from the discussion of values, these chiefs have discovered that communities are more thoughtful and receptive to discussion of police priorities and strategies if that discussion occurs within the larger context of mission and value consideration. No longer is the chief of police considered out of place when he suggests to his community that public consideration of policing values and standards is in order. The experiences of these chiefs has shown that the development of value statements can be illuminating to both the community and members of the police department.

In 1982, for example, Lee P. Brown, Houston's chief of police, made public a statement of the values of the Houston Police Department. This statement set forth the commitments of the police department in several critical areas, such as policymaking, community access to decision making, standards of integrity, and field strategy development. As Chief Brown noted, the statement established the criteria for evaluating the performance of the department.

The value statement for the Houston Police Department includes the following:

- The Houston Police Department will involve the community in all policing activities that directly impact the quality of community life.
- The Houston Police Department believes that policing strategies must preserve and advance democratic values.
- The Houston Police Department believes that it must structure service delivery in a way that will reinforce the strengths of the city's neighborhoods.
- The Houston Police Department believes that the public should have input into the development of policies that directly impact the quality of neighborhood life.
- The Houston Police Department will seek the input of employees into matters that impact employee job satisfaction and effectiveness.

By publicly stating values, the beliefs underpinning organizational actions, Chief Brown wished to have both the community and the police department focus on important issues of police authority, standards, and operational limits. Indeed, he believed public acknowledgment of community-oriented values was an important step in his move to change the culture of the Houston Police Department from a defensive orientation designed to protect internal organizational patterns to an externally directed community-positive orientation.

The developing emphasis on community policing has generated a substantial amount of discussion about values because, by definition, community policing reflects a set of values rather than a technical orientation toward the police function. It reflects a concern with the quality of police service delivery, the relationship between the police and the community, and the relationship within the police agency between management

and employees. As opposed to the more traditional perspective of professional crime-fighting policing, which emphasizes the maintenance of
internal organizational controls, community policing emphasizes service
output, the quality of results, and the impact of police services on the
state of urban living.

There have been several examples of values that reflect this orientation. In Boston, Commissioner Francis M. Roache has set forth the following commitment for the police department:

> The department is committed to the positive evolution, growth, and
> livability of our city.

Sir Kenneth Newman, former commissioner of the Metropolitan Police in London, England, set forth the following values for that department:

> In pursuing the aim and duty of maintaining a peaceful community,
> members of the Metropolitan Police view their role as one involving
> cooperation with others in the creation and maintenance of a way of life in
> communities which strikes the optimum balance between the collective
> interests of all citizens and the personal rights of all individuals.
>   The aim of the Metropolitan Police will, therefore, be to work with
> other agencies to develop what is known as a "situational" or "problem-
> solving" approach to crime prevention.

Discussions of the Executive Session on Community Policing at Harvard University's John F. Kennedy School of Government have produced
a set of values that represents the key characteristics of community policing. These characteristics are embodied in the following principles:

> Community policing is committed to a problem-solving partnership: dealing
> with crime, disorder, and the quality of life.

The value here is the orientation toward problem solving. In community policing, incidents (such as crime or 911 responses) are viewed
from the perspective of community action, which will seek to resolve the
problem, not simply handle the incident.

> Under community policing, police service delivery is decentralized to the
> neighborhood level.

Community policing holds that policing a city's neighborhoods is
best done at the individual neighborhood level, not by centralized command and control. Since the solutions to most neighborhood problems
are through neighborhood action, the community policing effort concentrates on developing a cohesive neighborhood capability reflecting responsibility, self-help, and co-production of service with the police. The
value of decentralization suggests that every police effort is pushed

down toward the neighborhood level unless there is a specific reason for the effort to be centralized, such as a concern with a citywide problem or issue.

> The highest commitment of the community policing organization is respect for and sensitivity to all citizens and their problems. Community policing values the skills of positive social interaction, rather than simply technical application of procedures to situations, whether dealing with crime, disorder, or other problem solving.

As is the case with several notable private sector companies, community policing's officers have a service orientation. Citizens are supposed to be treated with respect, regardless of the involvement of the citizens in the incident to which the police are responding.

Police officers often find this value difficult to accept. There is a widespread tendency to think of, and describe, street criminals as maggots and other, even less endearing, terms. With a service orientation, such characterizations are avoided, if for no other reason than recognition that the initial police contact may erroneously describe the true nature of the individual.

> The community-oriented police department makes the highest commitment to collaborative problem solving, bringing the neighborhoods into substantive discussions with police personnel to identify ways of dealing with neighborhood problems.

The community-oriented police department recognizes that constructive action by police *and* community is always better than action by the police alone. Before any major action is undertaken, whether a shift in resources or implementation of a new problem-solving approach, the community-oriented police department discusses that change with the appropriate neighborhood. The willingness to discuss publicly priority setting or selection of problem-solving tactics reflects the high value the organization places on bringing the community into the business of policing. It is also recognition that the community is an important source of police authority.

> The community-oriented police department views both the community and the law as the source of the department's authority.

Since police action is not prescribed by the law, the community empowers the police agency to deal with difficult problems of importance to neighborhood residents and accepts the actions taken as long as the police are continually careful to engage the neighborhood in selecting tactics and priorities beyond those set forth under the law. When a police agency has lost its community authority, a range of responses always occurs, from a widespread dissatisfaction with the department to substantial disorder when the police apply the law in the neighborhood.

> The community-oriented police agency is committed to furthering democratic values. Every action of the agency reflects the importance of protecting constitutional rights and ensuring basic personal freedoms of all citizens.

The commitment to democratic values is a cornerstone of community policing. Placement of a high value on the democratic process provides police agencies with the shield they need to ensure that actions proposed by communities do not infringe on others' rights. Embodiment of this value by the organization and its use as a defense against inappropriate neighborhood initiatives will succeed only if the police themselves strictly adhere to the law in all aspects of their work.

Implementing Values.   While a number of police agencies have set forth written statements of their values, few have carefully considered ways of implementing their values so that the actions of agency employees will match the value orientation of the organization.

Police departments that have adopted the community policing philosophy have found it helpful to develop concise value statements that reflect these principles and commitments. The philosophy then can be understood throughout both the department and the community and serve as the basis for the application of discretion within the department.

Written value statements are useful if for no other reason than to force management to reach agreement on the organization's values. Experience in most police agencies indicates that this debate is not an easy task. But written value statements are not sufficient, since the values eventually must be reflected in all aspects of the organization, from training to field operations.

Presenting values through training must involve more than simply handing out value statements, as has occurred in some agencies. Carefully developed case materials, class discussion, tests, and field officer programs must all reflect the official values of the agency. Policy statements not only state the values explicitly but also provide explanations of the reasoning behind the derived policies.

When auditing field operations or investigative performance, the review must include careful consideration of the degree to which the actions follow stated department values. When riding in police cruisers, supervisors and mangers must listen for the "talk of the department" to see if values expressed by police officers reflect those of the department.

Some police administrators will claim that officers will never match the values articulated in their street talk with those of the organization as it pursues excellence. That, of course, is the greatest challenge the police administrator faces; for only when the formal values of the organization match those acted out by the rank and file can the organization be considered "high-performing." Community policing requires that match of values; it provides a structure and orientation that make such a match easier.

Summary. The values of community policing are different from those of previous eras in police history. Equally important, values are no longer hidden, but serve as the basis for citizens' understanding of the police function, judgments of police success, and employee understanding of what the police agency seeks to achieve.

NOTES

1. In describing the characteristics of organizations, Peters and Waterman note that excellent companies "are fantastic centralists around the few core values they hold dear." See Thomas J. Peters and Robert H. Waterman Jr., *In Search of Excellence* (New York: Harper & Row, 1983), p. 15.
2. Thomas J. Watson Jr., the founding father of IBM, authored an early work about how values must be articulated by the successful corporation. See Thomas J. Watson Jr., *A Business and Its Beliefs: The Ideas That Helped Build IBM* (New York: McGraw Hill, 1963).
3. See George L. Kelling, "Police and Communities: The Quiet Revolution," *Perspectives on Policing*, no. 1 (Washington, D.C.: National Institute of Justice and Harvard University, June 1988) and George L. Kelling, Robert Wasserman, and Hubert Williams, "Police Accountability and Community Policing," *Perspectives on Policing*, no. 7 (Washington, D.C.: National Institute of Justice and Harvard University, November 1988) for a discussion of how management through values lessens the need for reliance on strong command and control systems.
4. Wilson published the values to provide both the police and the community with an understanding of why the police department undertook many of its actions. See Orlando W. Wilson, *On This We Stand* (Chicago Police Department, 1983).

ARTICLE 13

THE STRATEGIC MANAGEMENT OF POLICE RESOURCES

David M. Kennedy

Many American police departments feel themselves to be slowly drowning in a rising tide of serious crime and calls for service. Over the last decade, department workloads have risen steadily while their resources have stayed constant or often declined.[1] Police executives generally have responded by striving to enhance the efficiency of police operations and focus police resources on only the more serious calls. Computer-aided dispatching and other information systems have been employed to make the most of the patrol force, and many departments no longer respond at all to nuisance calls or provide services like escorts and house checks that the public once took for granted. Nonetheless, police in many cities find themselves more and more pressed, a problem recently greatly exacerbated—even in smaller communities—by unprecedented increases in drugs and violence.

It is thus understandable that many departments find calls for community policing unrealistic. As most police—and most mayors—understand the concept, community policing means taking on difficult new responsibilities, like fighting fear and solving community problems, using fresh tactics, like foot patrol and community organizing. What room could there possibly be to do new jobs when the department can scarcely do the old ones?

Mayor Bud Clark of Portland, Oregon, was a community policing enthusiast when he took office in 1985, but he saw no place for the new strategy in what both he and the police agreed was a shorthanded, over-

Reprinted from David M. Kennedy, "The Strategic Management of Police Resources," *Perspectives on Policing,* no. 14 (Washington, D.C.: National Institute of Justice, U.S. Department of Justice, and the Program in Criminal Justice Policy and Management, John F. Kennedy School of Government, Harvard University, 1993).

worked department. "Community-oriented policing means less relying on heavy-handed law enforcement and more getting at root causes," said Chuck Duffy, a Clark aide. "But we recognized the fact that you can't do it well unless you have an adequate level of police officers, because you've got to do the community outreach stuff with police on top of your base of patrol officers, and we were having trouble with our base."

Such sentiments are often, and understandably, expressed by police and municipal officials. They are the sum of four widely held beliefs about contemporary policing (until recently, nearly universally held). One is that public demand for police services, particularly 911 rapid-response services, is largely out of police control. The second is that departmental resources are, in the main, already deployed to best advantage, efficiently and effectively. The third is that community policing (like other new policing strategies such as problem-oriented policing) is a discretionary add-on to the core job of policing. Because it is seen as "soft," aimed more at community and public relations than at crime control, it is often delayed and resisted when crime and workloads are on the rise. (In other words, the real job of policing is traditional enforcement, and departments should not be distracted from that mission.) The fourth belief is that police resources, meaning police departments' budgets, are largely static, particularly in the current climate of fiscal constraint. The largest gains a department can hope to make, on this line of thinking, are still small—an improvement in patrol deployment here, a few extra positions there. It is no surprise that the police find large increases in calls for service, or striking new challenges like the crack epidemic and waves of youth violence, very difficult to meet.

Increasingly, however, there is reason to believe that not one of these four beliefs is true. The concrete experiences of numerous innovative police departments—including Portland, which found ways to move into community policing despite resource constraints—are proving otherwise. The police can, in fact, manage public demand and expectations for police services. They can deploy their current resources in new and improved ways. They can use community and problem-solving policing strategies to achieve ambitious crime-control objectives. And they can find and win new resources, budgetary and otherwise, to help them do their various jobs. These are fundamental, not marginal, gains; they hold out the hope of major advances in the struggle to fight crime and improve the quality of life in troubled cities. This paper will take each of these arguments in turn, then turn to a discussion of their combined significance for the future of policing.

CALL MANAGEMENT AND DIFFERENTIAL RESPONSE

No challenge is more immediate, no job more demanding, in many police departments than the crushing burden of answering the public's calls for service. Individual officers in busy cities feel the weight on every shift. "If you drive out there and make yourself available for calls, you wouldn't be available one minute that night for anything else," says

Los Angeles Police Department patrol officer Joe Ciancanelli. "There wouldn't be a dull moment, no time for anything." Patrol forces have, over the last 10 years, increasingly been restricted to answering the tolling of the 911 bell. Fewer and fewer people and less and less time are available for foot patrol, problem solving, crime prevention, or any other important tasks a chief might want the force to perform.

That concern is heightened by a growing sense that for the vast majority of calls for service, rapid response is not—contrary to several generations of police belief and expectations—an appropriate or effective crime-fighting tool. Most dispatched calls—50 to 90 percent, in most jurisdictions—are not about crime. In only a small percentage of those that are about crime—less than 5 percent of all dispatched calls, in most cities—does the officer have a chance to intervene or make an arrest.[2] Nobody doubts that for that crucial 5 percent, the response should be immediate and authoritative. But in the other 95 percent, the scene is cold and the officer can do little more than take a report and soothe the victim. "Most of the time," says Ernest Curtsinger, chief of the St. Petersburg, Florida, Police Department, "irrespective of the call, you get there and the bad guy is gone and the real emergency situation is over." The high hopes once pinned on rapid response and 911 systems have turned, in many police quarters, to a profound concern about their insatiable appetite for resources. "We have created," says one chief, "a monster."

At the same time, many police executives despair of winning public acceptance for any other ways of delivering police services, even approaches like problem solving that might actually improve conditions and cut down on the volume of calls coming into departments. Rapid response, in this view, is a promise that the police have made to the public and that cannot be broken, regardless of its operational shortcomings. "People expect us to come when they call; that's an absolute," says one chief. "Believing anything else is a pipe dream."

Other executives, though, are looking for new ways both to handle calls and to reshape public expectations. Their goal is generally to preserve, and even enhance, their departments' ability to respond immediately to true emergences while finding more efficient, and perhaps more effective, ways to respond to less urgent calls without disappointing the public in the process. Evidence is accumulating that it can be done.

Much of the work being done in this area builds on one core idea: that the public will not insist on immediate responses to nonemergency calls if it is properly prepared for what to expect instead. As long ago as 1976, research showed that public satisfaction with police handling of calls was less influenced by the speed of response than it was by the difference between anticipated and actual response times.[3] The public's expectations, in other words, seemed to be central to their sense of how well the police were performing. Could those expectations be deliberately reshaped?

In the early 1980s, the National Institute of Justice designed its Differential Police Response [DPR] experiments to find out. The DPR research tested public reaction to a range of alternative response strategies for nonemergency calls—walk-in and mail-in reporting, telephone report units, officer response delayed by up to half an hour, officer response by appointment, and the like—in Garden Grove, California; Greensboro, North Carolina; and Toledo, Ohio. Dispatchers were carefully trained in how to rank calls and, when appropriate, inform callers about the new responses. Administrative mechanisms were developed in each department to make sure that what dispatchers promised—for instance, to have an officer arrive to take a report at a particular time—was actually delivered.

The results were striking. More than 90 percent of callers in all three cities who received the alternative response were satisfied with them (with the exception of the write-in option, which proved less popular).[4] Nearly half of all calls could have been so handled (not that many were, because of the experiments' designs).[5] Even with the limited proportion of alternative responses permitted in the experiments, patrol workload was reduced by as much as one-fifth.[6] Instituting and staffing the alternatives turned out to be fairly straightforward and inexpensive; in Toledo, for instance, 4 report-takers in a headquarters telephone unit were worth 10 in the field. Many of the alternatives were, and more could have been, staffed by civilians. The speed and quality of rapid response to priority calls was unaffected. Overall, the NIJ report concluded, "Police departments can achieve a sizable reduction in the number of nonemergency calls for service handled by immediate mobile dispatch without sacrificing citizen satisfaction."[7] Contemporary reports from the field bore them out. Some departments were able to take as many as 45 percent of their reports over the phone.[8]

While that view has gained some currency in policing in recent years, it has generally done so against the grain of police wishes and preferences. Conditions may have made it impossible to answer every call with a dispatched officer, and differential response strategies (particularly telephone reporting units) are no longer as rare as they once were, but there is often a lingering sense that they represent an unfortunate backing away from the ideals of policing. Nor, in most departments, have call management and differential response had much effect on the nature and role of the patrol force. Street officers may be less burdened as a result, but the basic job of patrol and response remains largely as before.

This is beginning to change. Police executives are increasingly undertaking call management and differential response as part of a purposeful shift to new community and problem-solving policing strategies and with the express intent of substantially reshaping patrol (and often other) operations.[9] Chief Darrel Stephens, for instance, relied heavily on a relatively traditional telephone report-taking unit to make room in the Newport News department to do problem-solving policing, which proved successful against a wide variety of crime and order problems.[10] In St. Petersburg, Florida, call management allowed the department to shift significant resources into community policing while simultaneously cutting response times to high-priority calls by more than 20 percent.[11]

The Reno, Nevada, Police Department, a recent convert to community policing, splits its patrol force on a day-to-day basis between special projects and mobile response. Call management is handled through the headquarters dispatching center, which presents callers with a wide variety of service options for nonemergency calls. Where an officer's presence is appropriate or insisted upon, the dispatcher keeps callers apprised of when one should be available. Because mobile response is now handled by perhaps half as many officers as in the pre–community policing department, getting a car to a low-priority scene often takes several hours. But with careful departmental attention to explaining why, citizen satisfaction—tracked by formal polling—has remained high.[12]

There is reason to believe that problem solving can reduce calls for service. Addresses and areas that generate repeat calls for services are easily identified by police from departmental information, and efforts to address these repeat calls often feature in departments' problem-solving efforts. In one now-classic example, a sergeant in the Philadelphia Police Department solved a noise problem caused by a jukebox bar and cut calls for service that had been coming at a rate of a thousand a year down to zero.[13] In Florida, Tampa's QUAD program against street drug dealing appears to have cut citywide calls for service considerably.[14] And, while they generally lack firm proof, officers and supervisors involved in problem solving are invariably convinced that their work lowers their departments' call loads. Difficult though the job may be, making room in departments for proactive, problem-solving policing appears likely to pay substantial returns.

The new strategies' overall emphasis on such things as devolution of police authority, beat integrity, and street-level problem solving is beginning to give rise to new models of call management. One of the most interesting comes from the Houston Police Department, which—as part of its neighborhood-oriented policing philosophy—has planned a high-tech decentralization of call management. Priority one and two calls would still be dispatched from headquarters. Other calls, though, would be patched through via in-car video display terminals to shift sergeants, who would be expected to manage both their officers, via radio, and the callers, via cellular phone. The sergeants' job would be to provide the best mix of police response for their areas, balancing the need to work on community and problem-solving projects against the need to respond to individual callers—and, where necessary, to explain and justify their decisions to the public.[15] The result, if the scheme works, will be call management and police services custom-tailored precinct by precinct, and even shift by shift, to Houston's varied and ever-changing needs.

Two additional important points should be made about community policing and call management. First, community policing itself seems to perform a call management function. Calls in the pioneering Flint, Michigan, foot patrol districts, for instance, dropped 43 percent in the course of that department's formal experiment. Some of the decline was attributable to problem solving, but much of it was due to residents in the districts passing minor complaints directly to the foot patrol officers rather than making formal calls for service. The foot officers then handled them as and when they wished. This was a far more efficient scheme than dispatching officers to every such call and a much more popular one than refusing service for calls that failed to merit a formal dispatch, or promising a rapid response that in fact took hours to materialize.

Second, community policing makes formal call management schemes easier to sell to the public. When call management is used solely to relieve the workload on traditional patrol operations, the public is asked to give up something tangible and immediate—a response—in exchange for an efficiency gain that is usually perceived to benefit only the department. With community policing, the public arguably gets something—more responsive, more effective policing—for its sacrifice. As the Newport News, Reno, and other departments can attest, the public often finds this a welcome trade.

REORGANIZING TO MAKE THE MOST OF DEPARTMENT RESOURCES

Just as departments can reexamine their service preferences and obligations, they can reexamine their allocation and utilization of personnel. The first step is often simply to take a fresh look, with basic principles of good management in mind, at how a department does business. Police agencies, like all organizations, have a tendency to get set in their ways, and a management review, performed internally or by consultants, can often uncover significant room for improvement. For example, the Rivlin Commission on Budget and Financial Priorities of the District of Columbia examined the Washington, D.C., Police Department in 1990. The commission discovered that the department, though an extreme case, had the highest overtime expenses in the country, due chiefly to rigid work rules and hugely inefficient arrangements for the booking and charging of arrestees; the lowest proportion of civilian employees among 13 major departments; no capacity for crime and workload analysis, and therefore none for efficient personnel allocations; and actual assignment practices that bore little relation to formal ones (500 assignments to patrol existed only on paper, while the Youth Division had more than twice its authorized strength).[16] While few departments may be in such dire straits, many could benefit from a similar examination.

Beyond such fundamental attention to rationalization and efficiency, policing is increasingly seeing moves toward a major, sometimes radical, strategic redistribution and reprogramming of departmental resources. One of the most visible is shifting people—and authority—out of headquarters and specialist units back to field commands. When Sir Kenneth Newman took over the London Metropolitan Police Department in 1982, he both "desquadded," returning 10 percent of all headquarters squads and 1,200 additional headquarters posts to the field, and "flattened" the rank structure, entirely eliminating a senior rank that stood between Scotland Yard and its territorial commands. John Avery, commissioner in New South Wales, Australia, shifted much of his detective force to the field and put it under the authority of patrol commanders. Lee Brown put nearly 500 officers back on patrol when he took over in Houston and began a similar but even more ambitious program in New York.[17] The

Reno department effectively eliminated all supervisory ranks between chief and area captain. Such moves are in part efforts to ease the burden of call responses and other field activities. More fundamentally, however, they are intended to promote decentralization, precinct- and street-level problem solving, and responsiveness to the community.

In most departments, headquarters functions have long been valued more highly than precinct functions, and the work of detectives and other specialists more highly than that of patrol. Generations of police chiefs have found creating special squads an attractive response to new problems. It can be done fast; the new unit, consistent with traditional police concern for centralization of command and control, can be easily monitored and supervised from headquarters; and the department has something concrete to point to, demonstrating it has taken the problem seriously. Unfortunately, such units, once established, are difficult to disband and tend to monopolize responsibility for the problem. In this way, they limit opportunities for police officers to learn how to handle such problems and drain strength and creativity from geographic commands and more general functions like patrol.

Many departments now are trying to reverse that tendency by enhancing the authority and discretion of geographic commands. In New South Wales, for instance, detectives probably do not do any more detecting than they did before the shift. However, they worked before according to headquarters' interest in major cases and clearance rates, while now they are guided in part by geographic commands' assessments of the problems and community needs they face. The same is true with shifts of narcotics, juvenile, vice, and other specialists into geographic lines (though care must be taken to preserve the department's capacity to act against highly mobile crime). Not only are more personnel in the field, but the department's overall capacity also is deployed for maximum problem-solving and community-service effectiveness.

This is, in a way, a new version of the very promising but generally short-lived team policing experiments of the 1970s.[18] Those programs often failed because the demands of rapid response and headquarters expectations ran counter to the teams' interest in local problem solving. New strategies, new allocation of resources, and new lines of authority give the new teams a much better chance to succeed.

Less tangible but no less important than these changes, in many innovative departments, is a major development in the philosophy of police administration. Police departments have long been governed by a paramilitary command-and-control approach that puts a premium on close supervision and the prevention of corruption and operational error. The traditional emphasis on discipline and propriety is laudable, but many modern police executives have come to believe that the paramilitary approach won that ground at the cost of organizational flexibility, responsiveness, and innovation. They are actively seeking ways to gain those qualities without at the same time opening the door to police misbehavior.

Beginning to emerge is a managerial and organizational style that looks more toward the best in private-sector and professional organizations than toward policing's own heritage. Modern police executives, no less than the CEOs of innovative high-tech firms, directors of teaching hospitals, or senior partners in architecture firms, are coming to believe that one of their main jobs is forging departments that are tied closely to their clients and in which junior and senior officers alike have the freedom and support to contribute as fully as they are able.[19] This new environment, combined with schemes like call management, resource shifts like enhancing the strength and authority of patrol, and ideas like problem solving, can create significant new police capacities. Traditional policing, with its enforced focus on individual calls for service, gives patrol officers little choice but to handle each incident quickly and with little attention to underlying causes.

The new strategies, by letting officers look at patterns and clusters of calls and complaints, create within the department the capacity to investigate and intervene in situations that previously would have been handled far more superficially. Houston's neighborhood-oriented policing created institutional ground so fertile that one tactical squad sergeant was able to craft a scheme for putting a major open-air drug bazaar out of business, win community and departmental support for it, and see it through not only the elimination of the drug problem but also through the area's commercial redevelopment—all by reprogramming precinct resources and putting them to new use.[20] Such individual successes, if they can be made the rule rather than the exception in policing, would represent not just more efficient, but substantially more effective, use of police resources.[21]

DOING MORE SUCCESSFUL WORK

It increasingly appears that such stories could become policing's norm. In fact, the outlines of a very promising progression now are visible. The beginning came in the 1970s with programs like team policing, the Los Angeles Police Department's senior lead officers, and Flint's foot patrol program, aimed at cultivating officers' contact with the community through innovative use of a relatively small proportion of the force.[22] These programs often showed considerable operational promise, but they also showed insightful police executives that bottom-up, community-focused policing was not easily commensurable with the claims and procedures of a predominantly response-oriented department. Over the course of the next decade came a host of attempts to shift departments wholesale into a new community-policing style, most notably in America by Lee Brown in Houston, but in different ways in a number of other departments as well. This was a time of striking, but frustratingly partial, results. Success stories like Link Valley in Houston; the Community Mobilization Project in Los Angeles; problem-solving policing in Newport News, Virginia; and many others seemed to herald the ability of police to prevent crime and solve problems in league with public and municipal allies. Generally, however, they remained isolated tales, both in the effect they had on cities and in the proportion of police effort they represented even in the most dedicated and experimental departments.[23]

A third phase now appears to be beginning, in which departments more or less familiar with community-policing ideas apply them wholesale to policing cities or to solving major citywide problems. This is happening first, predictably enough, in smaller cities whose forces can shift more readily to the new style. In some of these places, community policing is beginning to deliver on its promises of making a dent in serious crime. In Reno, Nevada, the police credit the new style with ending overt public drug dealing in the city and driving off the Los Angeles–based gangs that were establishing a beachhead in town. In Gainesville, Florida, a problem-solving approach cut convenience-store robberies by 65 percent. Tampa police, whose city was being overrun by crack and crack-related violence, organized a citywide problem-solving and community-policing approach that eliminated street dealing almost entirely and brought overall crime levels down to pre-crack levels. Reported crime was down 12.4 percent in 1989; in some hot spots, reported crime was down more than 20 percent.[24] All of these gains were made without additional resources (at least initially, a point we will return to) simply by employing smarter and more effective policing. One can hope that more cities will soon be able to tell similar stories.

If it is true that new policing strategies can make such striking improvements in police performance, then the most crucial resource management decision facing police executives is a new and extremely fundamental one: how to craft their departments in these new shapes and how to manage the transition from here to there. Facing this task squarely is essential if the new strategies are to succeed. The new strategies are not programmatic add-ons to a police department's traditional organization and functions. Community organizing and problem solving represents a fundamentally different approach to doing the job of policing than do rapid response and retrospective investigation. They represent, in fact, an approach that is in many important ways incompatible with traditional police organization and tactics.

Making patrol officers responsible for problem solving, for example, means granting them a degree of operational discretion and giving them time to think and work that is not easily combined with a centralized dispatching operation devoted to minimizing response time to calls for service. Developing a departmental capacity to respond in a comprehensive fashion to community concerns—be they narcotics, guns, or the homeless—cannot easily be combined with a structure of detectives and other specialist squads operating largely autonomously from patrol and other geographic commands. The creativity, flexibility, and individual initiative that community policing demands cannot easily be combined with the paramilitary hierarchy and often draconian management style common to traditional departments. The list goes on and on; points of conflict are many and severe.

There is, here, both bad news and good news. The bad news is that the job of shifting a department, especially a large department, into the new strategies is a large and probably long one. The good news is that making that transition—not finding new resources—is the fundamental challenge facing a police executive interested in the strategies' potential. *How much money?* and *How many people?*, while clearly still critical, are no longer the central resource questions. The fundamental questions are *Money for what?* and *People for what?* As Houston, Newport News, Reno, and other departments are demonstrating, high workloads and limited resources are not necessarily insurmountable obstacles to moving successfully into community and problem-solving policing. The new ideals, to a considerable degree, open up to reconsideration all departments' traditional resource allocation. Just what can then be done with them the profession is only beginning to discover.

NEW RESOURCES

This is not to say that most police departments would not find more money and other resources very welcome, particularly as they move from traditional policing to more community-oriented, problem-solving policing. During that difficult transition, departments are in some ways in the worst of both worlds: they must invest in the reorganization, training, and technology the new strategy demands and suffer the dislocations and inefficiencies of change without yet realizing many of the new strategy's promised gains. With most departments stretched to their limits already, additional resources would be useful. Fortunately, much is possible on this front. The experience of many departments shows that even cities in serious fiscal trouble often can find ways to offer their police significant new support.

One approach is for departments to raise, or cause to be raised, non-tax revenues. A National Institute of Justice report on supplementing police budgets found the most promising avenues to be donation programs and asset forfeitures.[25] Businesses in Oakland, California, for instance, concerned that declining police budgets would threaten the planned revitalization of the city's commercial areas, raised more than $750,000 for the Oakland Police Department.[26] The Miami Police Department netted $5.5 million over 3 years from seizing and auctioning property used in criminal enterprises.[27] Cash assets seized through drug and money-laundering enforcement have proved important in many jurisdictions. In addition, many departments have experimented with user fees (for instance, for answering private burglar alarms), fee-for-services (for instance, for extra patrol in malls), and in-kind contributions (for instance, management training).

Such efforts can be significant, but they also raise important management and equity issues. Private funding, both of a general nature and for particular details, can create questions of improper access to and control over a public service. Aggressive asset seizure programs can create questions of public authority being deployed for narrow institutional interests. Many departments have managed to avoid any cast of impropriety, but in each instance careful attention to actual and apparent conflicts is essential.

Some special relationships with the private sector, as in programs in which police managers attend corporate training programs, are by their nature much more benign. They can also be extremely important, particularly in departments working to reshape administrative structures and cultures. Kevin Tucker, who took over the Philadelphia Police Department after the disastrous MOVE bombing, made this kind of management training a key part of his strategy to move the department toward more flexible, community-oriented policing.[28] The alliance not only built the kind of capacity in the department that Tucker wanted, it enlisted the cachet of private-sector management ideas in the service of his controversial reforms.

The new policing strategies create fresh and important opportunities for bringing outside resources to bear on police problems. Community and problem-solving police departments have shown over and over again that they can draw heavily on help from outside the department to handle what traditional police departments would have considered entirely police business. This is welcome news. It seems more and more apparent that the police alone cannot solve many crime and order problems, but that in partnership with others who have resources of their own to offer—time, money, expertise, ideas, energy, equipment, and more—perhaps they can. It has become, therefore, the aim, on both theoretical and pragmatic grounds, for innovative police departments to invest a good deal of effort in enlisting the aid of others and to tackle problems by allying police resources and strengths with those of others.

Police give up something when they enter into such partnerships: their claim that responsibility for public safety is theirs and theirs alone. But they gain more than they lose. When public safety becomes a joint police, community, and municipal responsibility, others have to chip in as well. The resulting contributions can be of major importance. When the Houston Police Department, together with a coalition of community organizations, tackled the Link Valley drug market, local people cleaned up the area (a daylong effort by hundreds of volunteers and a large number of corporations), donated technical help with deed and title searches, and made sure that city departments delivered on their obligations to bring property owners into code compliance. When Tampa's police took on the city's crack dealers, they needed—and received—the active help of citizens in identifying, monitoring, and tracking street dealers, and of city departments in cleaning up street-dealing sites, taking down abandoned buildings, and closing down businesses fronting for traffickers.

These cooperative relationships are not always easy. The police and other parties do not always have the same agenda or agree on the merit and propriety of particular ends and means. Police should be sensitive to the possibility, or the perception, that they are demanding too much in the way of public resources or doing so in a way that slights other departments' procedures and priorities.[29] But the proven power of partnerships between the police and the public, and the police and other government agencies, means that with the new strategies, police effectiveness becomes not just a matter of their own resources and operational capacity but [of] their ability to design solutions that capture the support and active aid of others. That ability has only begun to be developed, even in the most innovative departments.

Finally, the new approaches to policing change the nature of the political dialogue about police resources. With the traditional strategy, the political question was basically whether a city wanted to buy more policing: more patrol, more investigation, quicker response. In today's climate, where municipal fiscal crisis and near-crisis are the norm, more of the same can be hard to justify. The new strategies, in important contrast, foster a debate over what kind of policing cities want. Do citizens want foot patrol officers in their neighborhoods? Do they want fear reduction? Do they want a department that both answers emergency calls promptly and has time for attending to neighborhood nuisances? The public is skeptical that simply hiring more people to do traditional police work is worth doing. But hiring more people to do different things is another matter entirely.

There are numerous examples that the public is more willing to pay for a new kind of policing than it is for the old. In 1982, the citizens of financially strapped Flint, Michigan, voted a $3.5 million tax increase specifically to continue the city's innovative foot patrol program (previously grant-funded), a move it repeated twice subsequently.[30] The Reno department shifted to community policing in the explicit hope that it would lead to increased public support. A 1987 study had revealed that 6 of 10 residents thought the police were doing a bad job, and the city had twice voted down a tax override to increase the police budget. Late in 1987, the department switched to community policing, which proved so popular that less than six months later Reno voted for a 40 percent increase in police strength. By the first half of 1989, public satisfaction had increased to nearly 90 percent.[31] Baltimore County, Maryland, and Portland, Oregon, both experienced similar, if less dramatic, increases in tax revenues after undertaking community policing. Portland won its extra money after going through two chiefs in less than 2 years, in considerable part due to intragovernmental feuding over funds. "Their answer to everything was just 'more,'" a Portland official said of the fired chiefs' maneuverings.[32] When a new chief proposed a strategy that was not just more, but different, the city proved more than willing.

CONCLUSION

Policing, then, need not feel that its ability to manage its business and explore innovative strategies is hamstrung by today's admittedly punishing workload. Departments can, experience shows, manage their call burdens; they can deploy their resources in new and more productive ways; they can pursue promising new approaches to policing; and they can, at least sometimes, win substantial new resources, both financial and otherwise. It is not yet clear which techniques, and which combination of techniques, are most effective, though certain tendencies and directions appear to be evident. It is clear, though, that police departments can explore these areas even where call loads are heaviest; that, indeed, exploring them is probably an essential step toward addressing those calls and the crime and disorder that lie behind them.

A warning is in order here regarding expectations and criteria of success. The new strategies carry no guarantee that they will be accompanied by reductions in calls for service, reported crime, or overall police workload. They may well lead to a rise in calls and reported crime, especially in troubled and demoralized parts of cities, as residents come to believe that the police can and will help with their problems. This is no bad thing, but it does mean that departments (and elected officials and newspapers) that look for an automatic reduction in crime statistics and officers' workload can be disappointed and misled when the reduction fails to materialize. Officers' workload likewise may well rise, or at least not fall, since the community organizing, service delivery, and problem solving that the new strategies require all take time. The hope is that, in the long run, they will improve conditions sufficiently that both demands for service and overall workloads will start to decline. Even that cut in workload can be swallowed up, however, if departments take on new responsibilities such as fighting fear (as with COPE in Baltimore County) or coordinating the delivery of municipal services (as community police officers in Los Angeles, Houston, and many other departments tend to do).

This basic fact—that even new strategies of policing that prove effective in traditional terms will not necessarily mean less work for the police—has a major implication for police executives. Policing success will not relieve chiefs of their responsibilities for managing department resources to best effect and may, in fact, add to and complicate them. The new strategies, with their wider range of tactics, new menus of possible responsibilities, and new roles for officers and managers, will require more, not less, in the way of strategic management and hard choices about resource allocation.

NOTES

1. For an account of this pressure in one large urban department, particularly its impact on proactive and community work, see David M. Kennedy, "Neighborhood Policing in Los Angeles," John F. Kennedy School of Government Case Study C16-87-717.0 (Cambridge: Harvard University, 1987).

2. For a nice summary of this research, see John E. Eck and William Spelman, *Problem Solving: Problem-Oriented Policing in Newport News* (Washington, D.C.: Police Executive Research Forum., 1987), pp. 13–14.

3. Tony Pate et al., *Police Response Time: Its Determinants and Effects* (Washington, D.C.: Police Foundation, 1986); Stephen L. Percy, "Response Time and Citizen Evaluation of Police," *Journal of Police Science and Administration* 8, no. 1 (March 1980): 75–86; and James M. Tien et al., *An Alternative Approach in Police Patrol: The Wilmington Split-Force Experiment* (Cambridge, Mass.: Public System Evaluation, Inc., 1977); all cited in J. Thomas McEwen et al., *Evaluation of the Differential Police Response Field Test* (Washington, D.C.: National Institute of Justice, 1986), p. 42.

4. *DPR Field Test,* note above, p. 17.

5. *DPR Field Test,* p. 16.

6. *DPR Field Test,* p. 101.

7. *DPR Field Test,* p. 16.

8. Thomas J. Sweeny, "Managing Time—the Scarce Resource," *Law Enforcement News* (January 11, 1982).

9. For three recent discussion of community and problem-solving policing, see Commissioner Lee P. Brown, *Policing New York City in the 1990s: The Strategy for Community Policing* (New York: City Police Department, January 1991); Herman Goldstein, *Problem-Oriented Policing* (New York: McGraw Hill, 1990); and Malcolm K. Sparrow, Mark H. Moore, and David M. Kennedy, *Beyond 911: A New Era for Policing* (New York: Basic Books, 1990).

10. *Problem Solving,* n. 2 above, p. 40.

11. Chief Ernest Curtsinger, St. Petersburg Police Department, personal communication.

12. Captain Jim Weston, Reno Police Department, personal communication.

13. *Problem-Oriented Policing,* n. 9 above, p. 81.

14. The exact impact is hard to figure, inasmuch as Tampa went to a 911 system for the first time in 1988, just before QUAD was begun. Although it is impossible to ascribe the change with certainty to QUAD after calls had been rising for years, they fell from 606,755 to 549,402 between 1989 and 1990. Against regional and statewide trends, Tampa's crime rate, index crimes per 100,000, and drug-related homicides also fell during the same period. See David M. Kennedy, "Closing the Market: Controlling the Drug Trade in Tampa, Florida" (Washington, D.C.: National Institute of Justice, forthcoming, 1992).

15. Chief Elizabeth Watson, Houston Police Department, personal communication.

16. James F. Fyfe and Patrick V. Murphy, "D.C. Police: Trim the Fat," *Washington Post* (November 27, 1990), p. A21. See also "Financing the Nation's Capital: The Report of the Commission on Budget and Financial Priorities of the District of Columbia" (Washington, D.C., November 1990).

17. Commissioner Lee P. Brown, New York City Police Department, personal communication.

18. See, for instance, Lawrence Sherman et al., *Team Policing: Seven Case Studies* (Washington, D.C.: Police Foundation, 1973).

19. See, for instance, David C. Couper and Sabine H. Lobitz, *Quality Policing: The Madison Experience* (Washington, D.C.: Police Executive Research Forum, 1991) and *Policing New York City in the 1990s,* n. 9 above, pp. 66–72.

20. David M. Kennedy, "Fighting the Drug Trade in Link Valley," John F. Kennedy School of Government Case Study C16-90-935.0 (Cambridge: Harvard University, 1990).

21. For more examples from probably the toughest policing environment of all, New York City, see "CPOP: Community Policing in Practice" (New York: Vera Institute of Justice, October 1988). This paper is included in the excellent James E. McElroy et al., *CPOP: The Research—An Evaluative Study of the New York City Community Patrol Officer Program* (New York: Vera Institute of Justice, 1990).

22. On team policing, see *Team Policing,* n. 18 above. On Los Angeles' senior lead officers, see "Neighborhood Policing in Los Angeles," n. 1. On the Flint foot patrol experiment, see Robert Trojanowicz, *An Evaluation of the Neighborhood Foot Patrol Program in Flint, Michigan* (East Lansing: Michigan State University, 1982).

23. On Link Valley, see "Fighting the Drug Trade in Link Valley," n. 20 above. On Houston and other innovative departments, see *Beyond 911,* n. 9. On Newport News, see *Problem Solving,* n. 2.

24. See n. 14 above.

25. Lindsey D. Stellwagen and Kimberly A. Wylie, *Strategies for Supplementing the Police Budget* (Washington, D.C.: National Institute of Justice, May 1985), p. 2.

26. *Strategies for Police Budget,* note above.

27. *Strategies for Police Budget,* p. 3.

28. *Beyond 911,* n. 9 above, p. 81.

29. For an account of how one local government dealt with these tensions, see David M. Kennedy, "Fighting Fear in Baltimore County," John F. Kennedy School of Government Case Study C16-90-938.0 (Cambridge: Harvard University, 1990), pp. 16–17.

30. Edwin Meese III and Bob Carrico, "Taking Back the Streets: Police Methods That Work," *Policy Review* (fall 1990): 24.

31. Jim Weston, "Community-Oriented Policing: An Approach to Traffic Management" (unpublished paper, November 8, 1990), p. 2.

32. David M. Kennedy, "Patrol Allocation in Portland, Oregon (Part B): PCAM in the City," John F. Kennedy School of Government Case Study C15-88-819.0 (Cambridge: Harvard University, 1988), p. 5. "PCAM" stands for "Patrol Car Allocation Model."

A R T I C L E 14

CORPORATE STRATEGIES FOR POLICING

Mark H. Moore and Robert C. Trojanowicz

Police departments embody a substantial public investment. Each year, the nation spends more than $20 billion to keep police departments on the street and vigilant.[1] More important, each year society puts its freedoms in the hands of the police by empowering them to use force to complete obedience to the nation's laws. That, too, is an investment, for the grant of legitimate authority is a resource granted to police by the citizens. As the Philadelphia Study Task Force explained:

> The police are entrusted with important public resources. The most obvious is money; $230 million a year flows through the police department. Far more important, the public grants the police another resource—the use of force and authority. These are deployed when a citizen is arrested and handcuffed, when an officer fires his weapon at a citizen, or even when an officer claims exclusive use of the streets with his siren.[2]

These resources—money and authority—potentially have great value to society. If wisely deployed, they can substantially reduce the level of criminal victimization. They can restore a sense of security to the nation's neighborhoods. They can guarantee civility and tolerance in ordinary social interactions. They can provide a first-line response to various medical and social emergencies, such as traffic accidents, drunkenness, domestic disputes, and runaway youths.

Reprinted from "Corporate Strategies for Policing," *Perspectives on Policing,* no. 6 (Washington, D.C.: National Institute of Justice, U.S. Department of Justice, and the Program in Criminal Justice Policy and Management, John F. Kennedy School of Government, Harvard University, November 1988).

Stewardship over these resources is entrusted to the nation's police executives. They largely decide how best to use these assets. They make such decisions every time they beef up a narcotics unit or establish priorities for the dispatching of calls or write new policies governing the use of deadly force or the proper use of high-speed auto chases. At such moments, the police executives redeploy the money and authority entrusted to them in hopes that their organizations will produce greater value for society.

Judging how best to use the assets and capabilities of a police department is the principal task of police executives. As Professor Kenneth Andrews of the Harvard Business School says:

> The highest function of the executive is . . . leading the continuous process of determining the nature of the enterprise, and setting, revising, and achieving its goals.[3]

Performing this function well is no trivial task. It requires vision, judgment, and imagination, as well as disciplined analytical capabilities.

In the private sector, executives seek to perform this function through the development of a "corporate strategy." A corporate strategy defines the principal financial and social goals the organization will pursue and the principal products, technologies, and production processes on which it will rely to achieve its goals. It also defines how the organization will relate to its employees and to its other constituencies, such as shareholders, creditors, suppliers, and customers. In short, a corporate strategy seeks to define for the organization how the organization will pursue value and what sort of organization it will be.[4]

A corporate strategy is developed through an iterative process that examines how the organization's capabilities fit the current and future environment. The executive surveys the environment to see what customers want to buy, what competitors are likely to sell, and what investors are willing to stake money on. He analyzes what his own organization is able to do, what new technologies and products are becoming available, and what investments could be made to widen current capabilities. A strategy is defined when the executive discovers the best way to use his organization to meet the challenges or exploit the opportunities in the environment.

In the public sector, executives often consider the question of how best to use their assets much more narrowly. They tend to assume that basic purposes and operating objectives of the organization were set long ago and now remain fixed. Their job is to optimize performance with respect to these objectives, not to consider new challenges, threats, or opportunities, nor to discover new capabilities within their own organizations. They also often assume that in conducting their organization's business, they are restricted to orthodox policies and programs. While public sector executives might field a few innovative programs to deal with special problems, the innovative programs are rarely seen as part of a sustained, staged effort to change the organization's basic strategy.

Recently, some police executives have begun considering different corporate strategies of policing. While these executives see enormous value in the knowledge and skill that have accumulated within police departments over the last 50 years, they are increasingly aware of the limitations of the past conceptions. They are reaching out for new ideas about how police departments should define their basic goals, deploy their assets, and garner support and legitimacy in the communities they now police.

The purpose of this paper is to facilitate the search for a corporate strategy of policing that can deal with the principal problems now besetting urban communities: crime, fear, drugs, and urban decay. The paper first explores the strengths and limitations of the corporate strategy that has guided policing for the last 50 years—a strategy that has been characterized (perhaps caricatured) as "professional crime fighting."[5] It then contrasts this concept with three other concepts that have been discussed, and to some degree developed, within Harvard's Executive Session on Policing. The other concepts are "strategic policing," "problem-solving policing," and "community policing."

THE CONCEPT OF CORPORATE STRATEGY

Defining a corporate strategy helps an organization, its employees, and its executives. An explicit corporate strategy tells outsiders who invest in the organization what the organization proposes to do and how it proposes to do it. It explains to employees what counts as important contributions to the organization. It helps managers maintain a consistent focus in sifting the material that comes through their in-boxes. It directs their attention to the few activities, programs, and investments that are critical to the implementation of the proposed strategy.

For any organization, many possible strategies exist. Three criteria are useful for evaluating and choosing among them. The first is the value of the strategy if successfully implemented. The second test is feasibility—whether the strategy is internally consistent in terms of the products, programs, and administrative arrangements emphasized and whether it is based upon solid information and proven technologies. Feasibility is related to distance from current operating practice; greater distance makes the proposed changes more costly and difficult. The final criterion involves the degree of risk associated with a given strategy. Those strategies that lie close to existing expectations and capabilities involve little risk for the manager to pursue. Those that stretch expectations and capabilities, that are founded on experiments and hunches, involve much greater risk and often depend on substantial investments for their success.

The development of a corporate strategy is a complex matter. Often, however, complex corporate strategies can be captured in relatively simple phrases or slogans. William Ruckelshaus defined the mission of the United States Environmental Protection Agency (EPA) as "pollution abatement."[6] Michael Pertschuk declared that his goal for the Federal

Trade Commission (FTC) was to make it "the largest public interest law firm in the U.S."[7] These apparently simple slogans embodied complex judgments that important changes in the operations of these organizations were both valuable and feasible. "Pollution abatement" focused EPA's efforts on finding sources of pollution and restricting them, not on monitoring levels of pollution or estimating damages. Challenging the FTC to become the "largest public interest law firm" not only raised professional standards in the organization, but also redefined the principal clients of the FTC to be consumers who needed protection from businesses rather than businesses that wanted protection from other businesses.

Simplicity in defining corporate strategies is a virtue for several reasons. First, a simple concept is easy to remember and repeat and therefore more likely to guide discretionary decisions throughout a large organization. Second, a simple concept helps to focus an organization's attention by what it explicitly emphasizes, or implicitly excludes, or the way in which it contrasts with previous strategic concepts. Third, a simple phrase has the virtue of openness. Its very lack of detail allows improvisation, innovation, and evolution in the operations of the organization. Because there is no detailed plan, only general guidance, employees with new ideals can find sanctions for their efforts. And because the corporate strategy sets out purposes in broad language, many outside the organization can find reasons to support the organization's efforts.

LABELS AND CORPORATE STRATEGIES OF POLICING

The simple phrases that came to stand for complex ideas about corporate strategies of policing within the discussions of Harvard's Executive Session on Policing included "professional crime fighting," "strategic policing," "problem-solving policing," and "community policing."[8] At the outset, the discussion treated these concepts as nothing more than labels to be attached to the same elements of a future strategy of policing.

Indeed, many participants thought that the elements emphasized by these new concepts had already been incorporated in contemporary versions of the professional crime-fighting model. Others saw little difference between the concepts of problem-solving policing and community policing. Since there was little substantive difference among these concepts, the only issue in choosing among them appeared to be a marketing question: how powerful were the labels in attracting support from the public, in dignifying the work of the police, and in mobilizing them to action?

In later discussions the words seemed to acquire important substantive significance, reflecting real differences in judgments about such crucial matters as:

- The fundamental purposes of policing
- The scope of their responsibilities
- The range of contributions they could make to society

- The distinctive competence they had to deploy
- The most effective programmatic and technical means for achieving their purposes
- The most suitable administrative arrangements for directing and controlling the activities of a police department
- The proper or most useful way to manage the relationship between the police and the communities for whom they worked

For example, while all the concepts make crime control a central purpose of policing, the concepts of problem-solving policing and community policing accord greater significance to the order-maintenance and fear-reducing functions of the police than they hold in the concept of professional crime fighting.

Similarly, while professional crime fighting encourages the police to maintain their distance from the community to ensure the fair and impartial enforcement of the laws, community policing emphasizes a close embrace with the community to achieve more effective crime control and to ensure that the police respond to the issues that concern the community. Such differences seemed large enough for some participants to advocate adopting one concept and dismissing the others.

Still later, it seemed that the concepts were valuable because each highlighted a different challenge or defined a different frontier for police executives to explore in managing their departments for increased value and effectiveness in deploying the police against the principal problems of the cities. Many departments, for example, are still working at the frontiers defined by professional crime fighting, such as enhanced technical capacities to respond to serious street crimes, greater discipline and skill in the use of force and authority, and greater independence from inappropriate political influences.[9]

Other departments have already realized the value associated with the strategy of professional crime fighting and now face the new challenges defined by these other strategic concepts.[10] Strategic policing highlights the technical challenges of dealing with the most difficult sorts of crimes and offenders: for example, terrorism, narcotics trafficking, political corruption, and sophisticated white-collar crime.[11] Problem-solving policing emphasizes the value of being able to diagnose the continuing problems that lie behind the repeated incidents that are reported to police dispatchers and to design and implement solutions to those problems.[12] Community policing stresses the key role that a working partnership between the police and the community can play in solving crimes, reducing fear, and resolving situations that lead to crimes.[13] According to our Executive Session discussions, these are the challenges that define the frontiers of policing in the next generation.

It is possible that these challenges can all be met simultaneously by a new, integrated corporate strategy of policing. In that case, police executives would not have to choose among competing strategic conceptions. They could meet all the diverse challenges.

Alternatively, it might prove impossible to pursue all the different conceptions simultaneously. The challenges might be sufficiently diverse that, at least in the short run, managerial attention, the public's willingness to invest, and the officers' tolerance for experimentation are too limited to allow simultaneous advances on all fronts. In that case, police executives would have to decide which path to pursue first.

Or it could be that the different strategies are somehow fundamentally incompatible—that the pursuit of one strategy makes it virtually impossible for the police agency to pursue another. This could occur if the different strategies require fundamentally different value orientations or cultures within the organization, too many different kinds of personnel and capabilities, or inconsistent administrative arrangements. In that case, police executives might have to make difficult choices among corporate strategies.

Whether executives must choose among these strategies, or whether some synthesis is possible, remains an important question. This paper seeks to help police executives answer that question. These different conceptions will be developed first as relatively complete, competing corporate strategies of policing. Then, in a concluding section, the paper will consider how, and to what degree, the apparently competing conceptions may be synthesized in an overall corporate strategy of policing.

PROFESSIONAL CRIME FIGHTING

The corporate strategy that guided policing during the last half-century is captured by the phrase professional crime fighting. This strategy achieved a great deal for the police. It carried them from a world of amateurism, lawlessness, and political vulnerability to a world of professionalism, integrity, and political independence.[14] The principal engines of this transformation include:

1. a sharpened focus on crime control as the central mission of the police;
2. a shift in organizational structure from decentralized, geographically defined units to a centralized structure with subordinate units defined by function rather than by geography; and
3. substantial investments in modern technology and training of officers.

The aim of the professional crime-fighting strategy was to create a disciplined, technically sophisticated, quasi-military crime-fighting force. Crime control and crime solving became the dominant goals in policing. Those goals, as well as the common views about the best way to achieve them, are embedded in the current standards of accreditation and form the basic assumptions underlying both the majority of police training and the deployment of police resources throughout the country.

The principal operating technologies of this strategy include (1) patrol forces equipped with cars and radios to create an impression of omnipresence and to respond rapidly to incidents of crime, and (2) investigative units trained in sophisticated methods of criminal investigation, such as automated fingerprint identification and the use of criminal histories.

In addition, this strategy emphasizes accountability to the law by seeking to eliminate police discretion through increased centralization, written policies and procedures, dense supervision, and separation of the police from the corrupting influence of local politicians.

This conception of professional crime-fighting policing embodies powerful values: crime control as an important objective, investment in police training, enhanced status and autonomy for the police, and the elimination of corruption and brutality. With the close connection to all these important values, it is no wonder that the concept of professional crime-fighting policing has been popular and endures as a corporate strategy of policing. There is much that citizens and police can rally around and great value to be claimed in pursuing this ideal.

Still, there are some obvious (and not so obvious) weaknesses of this strategy. The most significant is the limitations of professional policing in controlling crime.[15] Initially, it seemed that patrolling officers and skilled detectives would constitute an effective crime-fighting force. Several decades of operation experience with these basic crime-fighting tactics have revealed some unexpected weaknesses.

One is that the tactics are essentially reactive. They depend on someone noticing a crime and calling the police. That leaves many crimes—those "invisible others" that do not produce victims or witnesses who are willing to mobilize—beyond the reach of the police.[16] Such crimes include consensual crimes (such as drug dealing and bribery, in which the participants do not perceive themselves as victimized), extortionate crimes (such as organized criminal extortion, and often rape, and child and spouse abuse, in which the victims are too afraid to come forward), dispersed crimes (such as embezzlement and fraud, in which victimization is diffused so broadly that people do not know that they have been victimized), and inchoate crimes (such as conspiracies, which do not have victims because the crimes have not yet occurred). Note that this list includes offenses that are committed by sophisticated, determined, and powerful criminal offenders. Thus, there is a gap in police capacities to deal with certain kinds of offenses and certain kinds of offenders.

A second problem with these tactics is that they fail to prevent crimes, except through the mechanisms of deterrence and incapacitation. In the professional strategy of policing, crime prevention is deemphasized in favor of reacting after the fact. Little emphasis is given to mobilizing citizens to defend themselves. Indeed, the help of amateurs is discouraged as inconsistent with the image of a disciplined professional force that can deal with all the problems. Nor is any emphasis placed on analyzing and eliminating the proximate causes of crime. That is viewed as social work rather than crime fighting.

A less obvious weakness of this strategy lies in its discouragement of a close working relationship with the community. The concept of professional policing encourages distance between the police and the community in the interests of ensuring impartiality and avoiding corruption. That distance, useful as it is in pursuing these values, comes at a price.

The police lose their intimate link to the communities. This hurts their crime-fighting capability because it cuts them off from valuable information about the people and conditions that are causing crimes.[17]

Another effect of maintaining professional distance from the community is that the police appear less accessible. Consequently, the police become a less frequent recourse, even for fearful or crime-ridden communities. It is not that the police become unpopular; they remain extremely important to the community.[18] It is just that they seem less present, and therefore, less able to meet the pressing needs and particular worries of citizens.

In some big cities, professional distance became particularly problematic, for just as police departments were seeking to insulate themselves from the communities and set higher professional standards, the cities began to change. In the 1960s, cities absorbed new migrant populations from the rural South, the Caribbean, Mexico, and Asia. Few police came from these immigrant populations, and they had little knowledge of these cultures. The result was that while the police thought of themselves as professionally distanced, the communities began to think of them as unresponsive and indifferent to their concerns. In extreme cases, communities saw the police as an alien occupying army.[19] The political legitimacy of the police began to erode along with their operation value.

Newer conceptions of policing have developed in response to these weaknesses in professional crime fighting, just as professional crime fighting arose in response to the weaknesses of the older political conception of policing. The new conceptions differ from one another in that they respond to different weaknesses and offer different ways to eliminate the weaknesses of professional crime fighting.

STRATEGIC POLICING

The concept of strategic policing seeks to improve on professional crime-fighting policing by adding thoughtfulness and toughness to the basic mission of crime fighting and crime control.[20] In strategic policing the basic goal remains the effective control of crime. The administrative style remains centralized. And the police retain the initiative in defining and acting on the crime problems of the community. In fact, their initiative is enhanced as enforcement capabilities are improved—capabilities that allow them not only to deal more effectively with ordinary street crime but also to confront sophisticated offenders who lie behind the invisible offenses described above.

With respect to ordinary street crime, strategic policing seeks improvements through directed patrols,[21] decoy operations to catch street robbers, and sting operations to disrupt burglary and fencing operations. Strategic policing recognizes that the community can be an important instrument aiding the police. Hence, block watch associations are emphasized, citizens are urged to mark their property, and the police are available to offer advice on security to businesses and private homeowners.[22]

Such programs embody a strategic rather than a reactive approach to street crime.

In addition, strategic policing emphasizes an increased capacity to deal with crimes that are not well controlled by traditional methods. Two kinds of crimes are particularly salient. First are crimes committed by sophisticated, individual offenders, such as career criminals or serial murderers, who operate beyond local boundaries. Second are offenses committed by criminal associations, organized crime families, drug distribution networks, gangs, sophisticated white-collar offenders engaged in computer and credit card frauds, and even corrupt politicians—the so-called superstructure of crime.[23]

To attack the first kind of crime, more sophisticated investigative capabilities are necessary. To attack the second, the police have to employ more intrusive investigative procedures, such as informants, undercover operations, electronic surveillance, and sophisticated intelligence analysis. It is also important that the police gain some independence from their local political base. They need to widen their jurisdiction to attack the sophisticated, multi-jurisdictional criminal offender. They need to separate themselves from the influence of the local political community to be able to attack the superstructure of crime. Unless they can do this, they find themselves subject to its control and thus occasionally hamstrung.

These points have important implications for the administrative arrangements and organizational alignments of police departments. For strategic policing in big-city departments, the need for sophisticated skills and wide jurisdictions necessitates the establishment of specialized, central investigative units. Such units are necessary to develop and sustain the appropriate skills, files, and equipment to carry out complex investigations. Centralized control of these units is also often considered essential to ensure an appropriate degree of supervision over the use of relatively controversial investigative methods.

Strategic policing in suburban and rural areas requires these smaller departments to band together in regional associations. Otherwise, they cannot afford the investment in the required specialized capabilities. Nor do they have a wide enough jurisdiction to deal with offenders operating across community boundaries.

To get out from under the influence of powerful criminal elements, local police departments in both metropolitan and suburban areas form alliances with and establish operational ties to federal enforcement agencies and the judiciary rather than with local politicians. Such alliances enhance investigative sophistication, effectively widen jurisdictions, and ensure that powerful allies are available when locally powerful offenders are the focus of the investigation.

In sum, in strategic policing, the police response to crime becomes broader, more proactive, and more sophisticated. The range of investigative and patrol methods is expanded to include intelligence operations, undercover stings, electronic surveillance, and sophisticated forensic methods. The range of targets is enlarged to include sophisticated offenders and inchoate crimes. The key new investments involve the creation of specialized investigative capabilities and improved criminal intelligence functions. Patrol operations are generally reduced as a share of police operations to make room for the specialized investigative units. The community is seen as an important auxiliary to the police in dealing with crime, but the police retain the initiative in defining and acting upon crime problems. The principal value claimed by strategic policing is improved crime control. The old values of political independence, lawfulness, and technical sophistication are also protected—even promoted—as police departments form alliances with federal law enforcement agencies rather than with local politicians. In an important sense, strategic policing represents the next step along the path marked out by professional crime fighting.

PROBLEM-SOLVING POLICING

Like strategic policing, the concept of problem-solving policing seeks to improve upon the older, professional strategy of policing by adding proactiveness and thoughtfulness. It differs from strategic policing in the focus of the analytic effort.

In professional and strategic policing, the underlying assumption is that crime is successfully controlled by discovering offenses and prosecuting the offenders. Such efforts control crime directly by incapacitating offenders. They also prevent crime by increasing the probability of arrest and successful prosecution (i.e., through general and specific deterrence). Thus, they prescribe tactics that position the police to see offenses and respond to them.

Problem-solving policing takes a different view of crime and its effective control. In problem-solving policing, one does not naturally assume that crimes are caused by predatory offenders. True, in all crimes there will be an offender vulnerable to prosecution under the law. But problem-solving policing makes the assumption that crimes could be caused by particular, continuing problems in a community, such as frustrating relationships or a disorderly milieu.[24] It follows, then, that crimes might be controlled, or even prevented, by actions other than the arrest of particular individuals. For example, the police might be able to resolve a chronic dispute or restore order to a disorderly street. Arrest and prosecution remain crucially important tools of policing. But ideas about the causes of crime and methods for controlling it are substantially widened.

This basic change in perspective requires police departments to widen their repertoire of responses to crime far beyond patrol, investigation, and arrest. For example, the police can use negotiating and conflict-resolution skills to sort out disputes before they become crime problems.[25] Disputes (between parents and children, landlords and tenants, merchants and customers, and between neighbors) might be mediated without waiting for a fight to occur and without immediate recourse to the criminal law, arrests, and prosecutions. Moreover, the police, with a heightened awareness of such underlying problems, might take such corrective action the second time they are called to the scene rather than the sixth or tenth time, thus making substantial savings in the use of police resources.

The police can make use of the civil powers vested in their licensing authority and other municipal ordinances to enhance neighborhood security. Bars can be cautioned on excessive noise,[26] merchants urged to comply with traffic regulations, and children cautioned on curfew violations to reduce occasions in which fear and disputes arise.

Community residents may be mobilized to deal with specific problems. They can replace lights in hallways, clean up playgrounds so that parents and young children no longer feel excluded from the park by teenagers,[27] and accompany the elderly and the vulnerable on errands.

Finally, other government organizations may be mobilized to deal with situations leading to crimes. The Public Housing Authority can be asked to repair fences to prevent incursions by predatory offenders and to seal vacant apartments to eliminate shooting galleries for drug addicts and club houses for juvenile gangs. The Public Works Department can be encouraged to haul away abandoned cars and other debris.

This change in tactics has ramifications for the organizational structure of the police department. To the extent that problem solving depends on the initiative and skill of officers in defining problems and devising solutions, the administrative style of the organization must change. Since much more depends on individual initiative, the department must become more decentralized. Otherwise, the advantages of local knowledge and adaptiveness are lost. A further implication is that generalist patrol officers, knowledgeable about the communities they serve, become the new heroes of the organization (traditionally, the heroes have been the specialist investigators).

The focus of police action is widened in a different way from that of strategic policing. Strategic policing challenges the police to deal with sophisticated crimes and powerful offenders in addition to the street crimes, such as robbery, rape, and burglary, that are the main focus of professional crime fighting. Problem-solving policing challenges the police to deal with the disputes and conditions that make life feel disorderly and frightening to citizens and therefore breed crime and underlie later demands on the police department.

In sum, like strategic policing, problem-solving policing seeks enhanced crime control. The means, however, are quite different. They include diagnosing underlying problems that give rise to crime (rather than identifying offenders) and mobilizing the community and government agencies to act on the problems (rather than arresting and prosecuting offenders). Reliance on these means naturally encourages geographic decentralization and dependence on resourceful generalist patrol officers rather than on the centralized functional specialist units. The problem-solving approach also draws the police into a different relationship with the communities—one in which the communities and other government agencies help the police work on underlying problems. Because many of those problems are not, strictly speaking, problems of crime and criminal victimization, a police department pursuing a strategy of problem solving will end up pursuing a broader set of objectives than the effective control of street crime. It will pursue order maintenance and fear reduction objectives as well as crime control.

Community Policing

The third new concept, community policing, goes even further in its efforts to improve the crime control capacities of the police. To achieve that goal, it emphasizes the creation of an effective working partnership between the community and the police.

Many of the participants in the Executive Session see little difference between the strategy of problem-solving policing and community policing. They think of problem solving as a technique to be used in community policing rather than a different corporate strategy for policing. If there is a difference between the strategy of problem solving and the strategy of community policing, however, it lies in a different view of the status and role of the community institutions and in the organizational arrangements constructed to enhance community involvement.

In community policing, community institutions, such as families, schools, neighborhood associations, and merchant groups, are seen as key partners to the police in the creation of safe, secure communities. The success of the police depends not only on the development of their own skills and capabilities but also on the creation of competent communities. Community policing acknowledges that police cannot succeed in achieving their basic goals without both the operational assistance and political support of the community. Conversely, the community cannot succeed in constructing decent, open, and orderly communities without a professional and responsive police force.

To construct the working partnership and build competent communities, a police agency must view the community institutions as more than useful political allies and operational partners in the pursuit of police-defined objectives. They must see the development and protection of the institutions as partly an end as well as a means. Moreover, the police must recognize that they work for the community, as well as for the law and their professional development.

Partly to recognize the status of the community institutions and partly to develop the working partnership, police agencies pursuing the strategy of community policing must become more open to community definitions and priorities of problems to be solved. In problem-solving policing, the police retain much of the initiative in identifying problems and proposing solutions to the community. They are the experts. They know what crimes are being committed. They know what citizens have been calling to complain about. They know how police resources can be deployed to deal with the problem. In community policing, the community's views have a greater status. Their views about what constitutes a serious problem count. So do their views about what would be an appropriate police response. In short, the police seek a wider consultation and more information from the community.

Consistent with that philosophy, a police agency pursuing a strategy of community policing relies on many different organizational devices to open the department to the community. Police executives direct their officers to make face-to-face contact with citizens in their area of responsibility.[28] Where feasible, police executives establish foot patrols to enhance the citizens' sense of access to the department.[29] The executives restructure the organization in decentralized, geographic commands, symbolized by neighborhood police stations.[30] Community consultative groups are established and their views about police priorities are taken seriously. Community surveys, as well as crime statistics, are incorporated in evaluating the overall effectiveness of the police.

Opening police departments to community concerns inevitably changes their operational focus, at least to some degree. As in problem-solving policing, the focus widens beyond incidents of criminal victimization to include lesser disorders that stimulate fears and conditions that suggest a general deterioration of community standards; for it is these things that are often of greatest concern to citizens. The inevitable police involvement in social and medical emergences is also viewed differently in community policing. While the police role in handling domestic disputes, runaway children, and traffic accidents is viewed as a dangerous distraction in professional crime fighting, these activities are viewed more positively in the strategy of community policing, since they provide a basis for developing the working relationship with the community. With community policing, a police executive might see value in deploying police resources for such activities as school-based drug education programs, programs to punish and educate drunk drivers, or a joint program with schools and the juvenile justice system to stop school violence and reduce truancy.[31]

The close relationship with the community also raises important questions about political interference that must be resolved with new understandings of police accountability.[32] From one perspective, creating close links with local communities increases the risk that the police will be unduly influenced by illegitimate political demands. The police might be used by powerful local interests to undermine the interests and rights of less powerful citizen groups.

From another perspective, however, the relationship enhances police accountability by making the police more responsive to community concerns as expressed in meetings, surveys, and face-to-face and telephone contacts. The issue here is whether the police are accountable to the law and its impartial enforcement or to the community and its representatives who pass the laws and consent to be policed in a particular way.

This tension between legal impartiality and political responsiveness as the basis of police legitimacy can be theoretically resolved by saying that the police are strictly accountable to the law except where discretion exists. In those areas for discretion, the police may properly be guided by the desire to be responsive to legitimate expressions of neighborhood concerns. What this theoretical perspective leaves unacknowledged is that many of the most important questions facing police executives remain unanswered by the law. The criminal law simply distributes a set of liabilities through the society, which the police are duty bound to act on if requested by a citizen. It does not tell police executives how they ought to deploy their resources in response to citizen complaints, nor what offenses they should emphasize as enforcement targets, nor the extent to which the police should feel responsible for preventing crime, reducing fears, or offering emergency services as well as enforcing the law.

As a practical matter, what the police must take from their legal foundation is the obligation to say no to the community when the community asks them to do something that is unfair, discriminatory, or illegal. In the end, although it is valuable for the police to seek a close working relationship with the community by being responsive to community concerns, the police must also stand for the values of fairness, lawfulness, and the protection of constitutional rights. Indeed, they must defend those interests from the interests of the politically powerful. That crucial lesson is the hard-won legacy of the strategy of professional crime fighting.

Overall, under the community policing concept, the ends, means, administrative style, and relationship with the community all change. The ends expand beyond crime fighting to include fear reduction, order maintenance, and some kinds of emergency social and medical services. The means incorporate all of the wisdom developed in problem-solving approaches to situations that stimulate calls to the police. The administrative style shifts from centralized and specialized to decentralized and generalized. The role of the community is not merely to alert the police to crimes and other problems but to help control crime and keep communities secure. While the department remains confident in its professional expertise and committed to the fair application of the law, it is more open to discussions with local communities about its priorities, its operating procedures, and its past performances.

EXCELLENCE IN POLICING: A SYNTHESIS

The frontiers marked out for development by these different strategies of policing add up to a major challenge for police executives. If pursued simultaneously and aggressively, the different strategies would require significant changes in the mission, primary programs and technologies, and basic administrative arrangements of police departments. They would also require important changes in the relationship with the community. In some cases, the cumulative challenges merely stretch the organization to incorporate new capabilities. In other cases, however, the different challenges seem to twist the organization in opposite directions.

With respect to the mission of policing, the cumulative impact of these corporate strategies is to broaden more than to twist. The mission is no longer limited to the effective control of street crime. It also includes (1) a strengthened attack on dangerous offenders, organized criminal groups, and white-collar offenders; (2) a more determined effort to resolve the problems that underlie incidents reported to police dispatchers; and (3) a heightened concern for fear, disorder, and other problems that communities designate as high-priority issues or that the police choose to handle as the basis for forming a more effective partnership with the community. The mission might even widen to include police action on community problems such as drugs in schools, drunk driving, public drunkenness, unsupervised children, and other medical and social crises. While it is by no means easy for an executive to create an organization that can accommodate these diverse purposes, there does not seem to be any fundamental tension among these missions. Indeed, most police departments are already pursuing these diverse missions with reasonable degrees of success.

With respect to the principal programs and technologies, the cumulative impact of the challenges is once again primarily to stretch and widen, not to twist. To deal with the broader mission, new functions and programs must be created. Strategic policing demands much more effective intelligence and investigative techniques than are commonly used in professional crime fighting. Problem-solving policing demands greater diagnostic skills and a far broader repertoire of responses to problems than arrest and prosecution. Community policing demands a more varied set of interactions with individuals and groups within the community, as well as the development of new capacities to deal with community-designated problems such as teenage drug use, violence in schools, or public drunkenness.

With respect to the administrative organization of the police department, the combined set of challenges twists police organizations in opposite directions. Strategic policing requires (1) centralization (to ensure tight administrative control over sensitive intelligence and investigative functions); (2) the establishment of specialized functional units (to ensure the development and maintenance of expertise in key areas); and (3) independence from local communities (to ensure a platform from which to attack powerful local interests if they are committing crimes). Problem-solving and community policing, however, require (1) decentralization (to encourage officer initiative and the effective use of local knowledge); (2) geographically defined rather than functionally defined subordinate units (to encourage the development of local knowledge); and (3) close interactions with local communities (to facilitate responsiveness to and cooperation with the community).

Perhaps the greatest torque created by the cumulative weight of these challenges exists in the domain of community relations. It is a deep philosophical divide as well as an administrative issue. In strategic policing, the community is seen as a potential threat insofar as it conceals, even nourishes, the superstructure of crime. In community policing, the community is seen as a crucial aid in dealing with crime and fear. In strategic policing, the community is to be held at arm's length and worked on by the police department. In community policing, the community is to be embraced and worked with.

These contradictions may be more apparent than real: a product of the stylized way in which the alternative strategies are presented. But as police executives contemplate the demanding challenges envisioned in these strategies, two important conclusions emerge.

First, if police departments are to stake out the frontiers marked for exploration by these different corporate strategies, they will have to become more capacious, flexible, and innovative than they now commonly are. They will have to contain within the organization a wider and more complicated set of functional capabilities than now exists. For example, they will need:

- Sophisticated answering and call-screening capabilities to preserve time for activities other than responding to calls for service
- Generalist patrol officers who are as comfortable outside their cars as in, and as capable of organizing meetings and mediating disputes as of making arrests
- Analytical and intelligence capabilities that can discern both nagging community problems and activities of dangerous, sophisticated offenders
- Sufficient flexibility in deployment and capability to deal with different sizes and kinds of problems

Indeed, police departments might well have to shift from a relatively inflexible organizational structure based on stable, fixed chains of command to a structure based on projects and programs of different sizes and duration led by people of many different ranks. That will cut deeply into traditional organizational structures and command relationships.

Second, if police organizations of the future are to respond to the various challenges posed by the different strategic concepts, police executives must face up to the apparent contradictions and be able to resolve them. In some cases, this will not be hard. It seems relatively simple, for example, to resolve the question of whether the police will seek to deal with street crime, sophisticated crimes, problems giving rise to incidents that trigger calls, or community-designated priorities. They have to deal with all of them. None can safely be neglected. The only thing necessary to incorporate all of these within the mission of policing is to keep reminding the officers and others that the mission properly includes all of these features. No single front represents "real police work."

It also seems relatively easy to resolve the question of whether the police are responsible for managing fear and disorder as well as serious criminal victimization. The answer is clearly yes; certainly no other government agency regards itself as specifically responsible for it. Without doubt, the police are responsible for these matters not only as an important approach to crime prevention but also as important value-creating activities in their own right.

It is a bit more difficult to resolve the apparent tension between the further development of sophisticated investigative techniques to deal with complex offenses and powerful offenders on the one hand, and, on the other, the development of the diagnostic capabilities and working community partnership that can solve nagging community problems. There seems to be a cultural stumbling block in confronting these challenges. The crucial difference seems to be that professional crime fighting and strategic policing focus on "serious crime," view the cause of such crimes as the bad motivations of offenders, and seek to deal with the problem by arresting and prosecuting offenders. Problem-solving policing and community policing, on the other hand, focus on anything that is named as a community problem and seek to handle the problem with any means available—not simply arrest and prosecutions.

Part of the reason that these directions strike a sensitive nerve in police departments is that the differences are enshrined in an organizational distinction between detectives and investigative units on the one hand and patrol officers and community relations units on the other hand. The long ignored reality, however, is that these apparently diverse functions have a great deal in common. Both depend on being able to see behind the surface manifestations of a problem. The attack on sophisticated crimes and dangerous offenders requires an ability to discern a common mechanism behind apparently unrelated incidents. The attack on community problems similarly requires the officers to see behind sets of incident-driven calls, widespread community fears, or persistent crime problems and to understand and deal with the deeper causes.

Both also require a great deal of imagination and initiative on the part of the officer in devising and executing a solution to the operational problems they encounter. In both countering sophisticated crimes and problem solving in the community, the investigative approaches must be invented and tailored to individual cases.

In short, the investigative-detective style of operating needs to be applied to a wider range of problems than investigators now handle. It is therefore important that the investigative style (without the narrow focus on crimes and offenders) seep into the rest of the organization. The manager has to be aware that the same imagination and resourcefulness which is invoked in combating high-tech crime can also be profitably spent on more common and more nagging problems facing the community.

Perhaps the most difficult contradictions to resolve are those related to organizational structure and to the relationship between the department and the community. These are firmly linked because the structure of organization has strong implications for whether and how community institutions can have access to the police. Centralized structures tend to make midlevel managers responsive to the administrative demands of headquarters rather than to the interests of local communities. Decentralized structures do the opposite. A functional organization (in which the subordinate units are based on technical specialities) tends to be unresponsive to local demands; a geographic organization (in which technical specialities are lumped together in units that are coterminous with organized communities) is much more responsive to local concerns.

Initially, the tensions between the centralized, functional structures suited to professional crime-fighting policing and strategic policing, and the decentralized, geographic structures suited to problem-solving and community policing seem irreconcilable. Professional crime-fighting policing needs the tight discipline and control that centralization seems to promise. Strategic policing requires the development of specialized skills that can be produced only by committing a portion of the force to the development of those skills and by protecting it from ordinary demands. Problem-solving and community policing, on the other hand, need decentralization to encourage the initiative of the officers. They require geographically based units to encourage the creation of working partnerships. And they need generalists to ensure that diverse skills can be combined to produce solutions to community problems.

One possible resolution of this conflict is to create specialist units but to keep them small and use them as consultants to the generalist units rather than rely on them for all operations within their sphere of competence. For example, one could create a narcotics squad to develop specialists who would be knowledgeable about drug problems and the complex investigative techniques they require. But they would not be responsible for all narcotics operations. Their principal assignments would be to equip and assist the generalist units as narcotics problems arose. They might also function as program managers for narcotics enforcement throughout the department as a whole. The program would not be executed by the narcotics unit alone but instead by many officers outside the unit's command.

An alternative would be to organize primarily around geographic commands, which would include officers qualified by training and experience in specialized functions. Assignments of officers would be created from projects and programs that varied in terms of scale and longevity. When a problem arises that requires the services of an officer skilled in, say, juvenile matters, officers would be drawn from the geographic commands to resolve the problem. When a citywide program in narcotics enforcement is needed, officers skilled in narcotics enforcement would be called on to work on the problem.

In short, instead of organizing by relatively large, durable commands, police departments would organize (and frequently reorganize) on the basis of specific problems and programs that are identified as being important. These would vary in terms of scale and longevity. This would require the police to shift from managing through specialized operational commands to managing through a combination of program managers and general geographic commands—a change that challenges traditional conceptions of responsible police management.

Even harder than creating flexible responses to specific problems is the issue of how to properly structure community relations. In professional crime fighting, the community is operationally important as an aid to solving crimes. Calls from individual citizens alert the police to crime being committed. Victims and witnesses supply the evidence necessary to convict offenders. Thus, the community is a key operational component of professional crime fighting. But a key imperative of professional crime fighting is separation from community demands lest law enforcement integrity be compromised.

Strategic policing goes even further in seeking police independence as it tries to find a secure platform from which to launch attacks on powerful offenders. Problem-solving and community policing, on the other hand, seek a closer embrace with the community. In the interests of building effective working partnerships, both problem-solving policing and community policing reach out for a close relationship and respond to community concerns.

The resolution of this paradox is conceptually simple but exceedingly difficult to implement and to explain to outsiders. The police must remain loyal to the values that they have pursued for so long in professional policing: a commitment to the fair and impartial enforcement of the law; a capacity to use force and authority economically and fairly; a determination to defend constitutional rights, particularly those of minorities; a kind of discipline that allows them to resist the desires of powerful people to use the powers of the office for expressing their own angers, fears, and prejudices; etc. At the same time, they must recognize that while these values might be tested in seeking a close connection with the community, they need not be compromised.

Indeed, to assume that the only way these values can be protected is by separating the police from the community is to give too little credit to the achievements that have been made in professionalizing the police. A true professional is one who can hold to his values (and exercise his skills) when they are tested in use. In practical terms, this means constant affirmation of these professional values throughout the organization, especially as members of the force at all levels are urged to do more to respond to the public's concerns.

These conclusions suggest the shape of a future corporate strategy of policing. It might be called "professional, strategic, community, problem-solving policing." It is a challenging task for police executives to realize such a vision. They must overcome the powerful claims of tradition in articulating the mission and organizing their departments. They must override the desires and expectations of many of their employees who have different visions of policing. They must cope with powerful external pressures to produce the illusion of accountability through rigid, centralized management. And, most important, they must cope with their own uncertainties about the best way to use the assets of their organization to produce decent, civil, tolerant communities. It is up to today's police executives to find the solution.

NOTES

1. Katherine M. Jamieson and Timothy J. Flanagan, eds., *Sourcebook of Criminal Justice Statistics—1986* (Washington, D.C.: Bureau of Justice Statistics, 1987), p. 2.
2. *Philadelphia and Its Police: Toward a New Partnership,* a report by the Philadelphia Police Study Task Force (March 1987), p. 129.
3. Kenneth R. Andrews, *The Concept of Corporate Strategy* (Homewood, Illinois: Richard D. Irwin, 1980), p. iii.
4. *Ibid.,* p. 18.
5. March H. Moore and George L. Kelling, "To Serve and Protect: Learning from Police History," *The Public Interest* 7 (winter 1983).
6. "William Ruckelshaus and the Environment Protection Agency," John F. Kennedy School of Government Case Program #C16-74-027 (1974).
7. "Mike Pertschuk and the Federal Trade Commission," John F. Kennedy School of Government Case Program #C16-81-387.0 (1982), p. 5.

256   *Organization and Management*

8. The Executive Session on Policing at Harvard University's John F. Kennedy School of Government, Program in Criminal Justice Policy and Management, 1985–88.

9. *Philadelphia and Its Police: Toward a New Partnership.*

10. David Kennedy, "Neighborhood Policing: The London Metropolitan Police Force," John F. Kennedy School of Government Case Program #15-87-770 (1987); David Kennedy, "Neighborhood Policing in Los Angeles," John F. Kennedy School of Government Case Program #C15-86-717 (1986).

11. This idea was most thoughtfully articulated in the Executive Session on Policing by Edwin Meese III, former Attorney General of the United States; Sir Kenneth Newman, former Commissioner of Scotland Yard; and James K. Stewart, Director, National Institute of Justice.

12. John E. Eck and William Spelman, "Solving Problems: Problem-Oriented Policing in Newport News" (Washington, D.C.: Police Executive Research Forum, January 1987); Herman Goldstein, "Improving Policing: A Problem-Oriented Approach," *Crime and Delinquency* (April 1979): 236–58.

13. Susan Michaelson, George L. Kelling, and Robert Wasserman, "Toward a Working Definition of Community Policing," Working Paper No. 88-08-09, Project in Criminal Justice Policy and Management, John F. Kennedy School of Government, Harvard University, January 1988.

14. George L. Kelling and Mark H. Moore, "The Evolving Strategy of Policing," *Perspectives on Policing,* no. 4 (Washington, D.C.: National Institute of Justice and Harvard University, June 1988).

15. Mark H. Moore, Robert C. Trojanowicz, and George L. Kelling, "Crime and Policing," *Perspectives on Policing,* no. 2 (Washington, D.C.: National Institute of Justice and Harvard University, June 1988).

16. Mark H. Moore, "Invisible Offenses: A Challenge to Minimally Intrusive Law Enforcement," in *Abscam Ethics,* ed. Gerald M. Caplan (Washington, D.C.: Police Foundation, 1983).

17. Wesley G. Skogan and George E. Antunes, "Information, Apprehension, and Deterrence: Exploring the Limits of Police Productivity," *Journal of Criminal Justice* 7 (1979): 217–42.

18. Edmund F. McGarrel and Timothy J. Flanagan, eds. *Sourcebook of Criminal Justice Statistics—1984* (Washington, D.C.: Bureau of Justice Statistics, 1985), p. 215.

19. *United States Kerner Commission Supplemental Studies for the National Advisory Commission on Civil Disorders* (New York: Praeger, 1968).

20. This idea emerged from the Executive Session on Policing at Harvard University's Kennedy School of Government, 1985–88.

21. *Integrated Criminal Apprehension Program Review of Patrol Operations Analysis: Selected Readings from IACP Cities* (Washington, D.C.: Law Enforcement Assistance Administration, 1978).

22. Robert Trojanowicz et al., *Community Policing Programs: A Twenty-Year View* (East Lansing: Michigan State University, The National Neighborhood Foot Patrol Center, 1986), p. 36.

23. This idea was presented by Sir Kenneth Newman, former Commissioner of Scotland Yard, at the Executive Session on Policing.

24. Eck and Spelman, "Solving Problems: Problem-Oriented Policing in Newport News"; Goldstein, "Improving Policing: A Problem-Oriented Approach."

25. Daniel McGillis, "Community Dispute Resolution Programs and Public Policy" (Washington, D.C.: U.S. Department of Justice, December 1986).

26. *Philadelphia and Its Police: Toward a New Partnership.*

27. Eck and Spelman, "Solving Problems: Problem-Oriented Policing in Newport News"; Goldstein, "Improving Policing: A Problem-Oriented Approach."
28. Antony Pate et al., *Reducing Fear of Crime in Houston and Newark: A Summary Report* (Washington, D.C.: Police Foundation, 1986).
29. *Ibid.*
30. *Ibid.*
31. William DeJong, "Arresting the Demand for Drugs: Police and School Partnerships to Prevent Drug Abuse" (Washington, D.C.: U.S. Department of Justice, November 1987).
32. George L. Kelling and Mark H. Moore, "Observations on the Police Industry," Working Paper #85-05-03, Program in Criminal Justice Policy and Management, John F. Kennedy School of Government, Harvard University, Cambridge, 1987.

IMPLEMENTING COMMUNITY POLICING: THE ADMINISTRATIVE PROBLEM

George L. Kelling and William J. Bratton

The current generation of police leadership, tuned to changes in American society, technology, and economics, is revising the strategy of municipal policing. Whether identified as community or problem-oriented policing, the current changes represent nothing less than a strategic shift in the basic "business" of policing. As dedicated as they are, as supported by research, as responsive to neighborhood demands for change, this generation of reformers finds regeneration and strategic repositioning as difficult as has any other. Why is it that innovators of every generation have so much difficulty shifting the strategies of their organizations and professions?

For police executives, three sources of resistance seem to be foremost in their minds and conversations: unions, detectives, and mid-management. This paper will deal with mid-management. We have repeatedly heard top police executives say with frustration, "If only it wasn't for mid-management," or "If only I could wipe out lieutenants, I could really change this department." The experience with team policing during the 1970s seemed to confirm this impression empirically. Sherman et al. conclude in their case studies of team policing: "Mid-management of the departments [studied], seeing team policing as a threat to their power, subverted and, in some cases, actively sabotaged the plans."[1]

Yet there are problems with this formulation. Review of the literature on mid-management presents a more complicated picture. On the one hand, many articles, especially those in journals of a semipopular

Reprinted from George L. Kelling and William J. Bratton, "Implementing Community Policing: The Administrative Problem," *Perspectives on Policing*, no. 17 (Washington, D.C.: National Institute of Justice, U.S. Department of Justice, and the Program in Criminal Justice Policy and Management, John F. Kennedy School of Government, Harvard University, 1993).

nature, portray mid-managers as a dying breed in organizations, especially in those organizations that are being downsized or in which their services or products are information-based. Certainly, many organizations are portrayed as top-heavy, especially at mid-managerial levels. This is not just a "pop" view; Peter Drucker states it strongly.

> Middle managements today tend to be overstaffed to the point of obesity. . . . This slows the decision process to a crawl and makes the organization increasingly incapable of adapting to change. Far too few people, even in high positions with imposing titles, are exposed to the challenge of producing results.[2]

Mid-management ranks are bloated in many departments: some have many captains and lieutenants without commands but serving as aides, often doing relatively menial work that could be carried out by a secretary or administrative assistant.

It does not follow from this, however, that mid-managers—captains and lieutenants—are a hindrance to innovation per se. Having too many mid-managers is a different issue from suggesting that mid-managers are inherently resistant to change. Indeed, many people who study organizations, especially in the private sector, identify the locus of innovation precisely in mid-management. Probably the work of Rosabeth Moss Kanter is most noteworthy in this regard. She argues that middle managers are essential to the process of innovation, and argues even more strongly that creativity can originate only in middle management.[3] Perhaps the experience of mid-management in organizational change in the private sector is instructive as we consider the current changes in policing. The role of mid-management in change—which for reasons that will become apparent, we call the *administrative problem*—is a generic issue in innovation and the strategic repositioning of organizations.

DEFINING THE ADMINISTRATIVE PROBLEM

Considering the circumstances within which early 20th-century police reformers like August Vollmer and O. W. Wilson found themselves, the law enforcement strategy they constructed had much to commend it. Those circumstances included extensive political corruption of police agencies, widespread financial corruption of police officers and departments, extensive police abuses of their authority, and large-scale inefficiencies. To counter these circumstances, reformers redefined the basic strategy of American policing. They narrowed police functioning to criminal law enforcement. They centralized police organizations, standardized and routinized the official functioning of police, and measured their success by arrests and clearances and the newly created Uniform Crime Reports.

Over time, this strategy became consistent, coherent, integrated, marketable, and dominated the police field. This strategy has shaped both how police are thought about and how they think about themselves. It has been so potent that for a generation, questioning it was tantamount to uttering "fighting words." To suggest that the police role was more complex was heard as tantamount to demeaning police, reinviting political meddling and financial corruption into policing, suggesting that police were social workers, and pandering to criminals.[4] Real policing was law enforcement, crime fighting.

The business of policing in this strategy had two elements. The first element, crime fighting, was conducted through preventive patrol, interception patrol, rapid response to calls for service, and criminal investigations. The intent of preventive patrol was to create a feeling of police omnipresence in a community; the intent of interception patrol and rapid response was to intercept crimes in progress; and the intent of criminal investigation was to investigate crimes. In each of the latter two activities, the goal was to arrest offenders and feed them into the criminal justice system.

Controlling officers was the second element of the strategy. At first, this assertion seems strange—control of officers should be a means of improving police performance, not an end in itself. Yet one has to put oneself in the position of the reformers. For them, political meddling, corruption, and abuse were so rampant in policing that it was impossible to direct effectively efforts to any desired goal; therefore, control was in the forefront of all their innovations.[5] Concern for means overshadowed ends. Control became the strategy. Thus, it is no surprise that even as recently as the 1970s in New York City, patrol officers were constrained from making low-level drug arrests because administrators feared they would be corrupted. As Herman Goldstein observes: "It is a sad commentary on the state of policing in this country that the need to control corrupt practices stands in the way of more effective policing."[6]

Much could be written about the fact that control of officers was central to the reform strategy: its wisdom, its efficacy, the extent to which it interfered with good policing activity, how the public came to judge police departments as it does, and other issues. Our purpose here, however, is simply to argue that the basic business of police organizations was two-fold: law enforcement and control of officers.

Early reformers confronted three sets of problems as they attempted to shift the strategy of policing to law enforcement: entrepreneurial, tactical, and administrative.[7] In this respect, they were similar to entrepreneurs and owners/executives in commerce. They had to define their *core services* in a changing environment, the *engineering services* required to produce their services, and the *administrative mechanisms* to ensure production. For police reformers:

1. entrepreneurial problems included redefining core police services and ensuring that an adequate market or demand for such services existed;
2. engineering problems included devising the tactics and technologies that were required to provide those services; and

3. administrative problems included creating the organizational structure and managerial processes required to develop, maintain, and monitor the organization's activities.

For each of these problems, police reformers such as Vollmer and Wilson devised solutions.

The Entrepreneurial Solution

The entrepreneurial solution was discussed above. The reformers emphasized crime fighting and control of officers as their core services and systematically marketed them as their core competencies. Allying themselves with progressive reformers, police leaders adroitly steered public attention towards what they perceived as a major crime wave, police corruption, and political interference. They accomplished this reorientation of the public to the new business of policing through advertising, public relations, public education, local and national commissions (e.g., Wickersham[8]), and police surveys (assessments of local police departments by recognized experts like Vollmer and Bruce Smith).[9]

The Tactical Solution

The tactical solutions of the reformers initially centered on patrol and criminal investigation. At first, patrol was modified by the rather simple move of abandoning foot patrol for cars (during the 1930s and 1940s). Primary justification for putting police into automobiles were to match the speed and mobility of criminals in cars and to increase the sense of the prowess of the officer, equipped as the officer would be with a powerful car. Later, reformers developed the more sophisticated tactics of preventive patrol, rapid response to calls for service, and interception patrol.

Additionally, criminal investigation came into its own during the reform era. Previously, criminal investigation units and detectives had unsavory reputations. Recruited from the private sector until the early 20th century, detectives and detective units and agencies (the Bureau of Investigation—the predecessor of the FBI) were noted for corruption and unprofessional behavior. J. Edgar Hoover's strategy for eradicating corruption from the Bureau of Investigation and converting it into a highly respected and professional FBI became the model for local police chiefs and helped reshape the public view of local police department detectives as well.

Detectives began to look and act like professionals. They worked regular hours, controlled their own schedules, saw people by appointment, "took over" crime scenes, controlled esoteric information, and in other ways operated with professional prerogatives. Additionally, detectives became the "stuff" of movies, radio, and later, television. As a consequence, they became the leading edge in the law enforcement strategy. Their prestige and external and internal clout soared. The successful cop? A detective. The failed cop? An unpromoted patrol officer.

The Administrative Solution

The administrative problem for the reformers consisted of the need to establish the structural and administrative mechanisms required to produce the desired services. The administrative solution was large-scale adoption of the ideas of Frederick Taylor, the renowned early 20th-century organizational theorist. Known as scientific (or classical) management, Taylor's work focused on improving productivity by rationalizing both production efforts (human work) and management. His concepts and practices have become well known. They include time and motion studies; routinization and simplification of work tasks; division of work tasks; and administrative control mechanisms, which include unity of command, layers of command, close supervision, span of control, and linking productivity to reward systems.

The undertakings of reformers to rationalize the productive work (tactics and technologies) of patrol officers are now well known: narrowing the official responsibility of patrol to law enforcement; reducing, even attempting to eliminate, patrol officer discretion; and developing routinized patrol tactics (preventive patrol and rapid response to calls).

The reformers' rationalization of administration—their attempts to solve the administrative problem—as well as the attempt by the current generation of reformers are the central concerns of this paper. Consider the situation of a chief of police during the early decades of this century. Generally a political appointee, the chief served at the pleasure of the mayor. Tenure or contracts for chiefs were unheard of. Police districts were contiguous with wards, and ward leaders made most of the police appointments, administrative and operational. The link between ward leaders and police were so close during the political era of policing that historians like Fogelson have dubbed police "adjuncts" of urban political parties (machines).[10]

In these circumstances, police reformers needed to accomplish two things to gain control over their departments. The first was to sever *all levels* within police departments from undue external influences. This was accomplished largely by adopting the political agenda of progressive reformers: centralization of urban services (taking control away from ward leaders); election of councilpersons-at-large (weakening neighborhood-based ward politicians); strengthening mayors and creating city management forms of government; creating civil service (hiring, retaining, promoting, and terminating personnel on the basis of merit); removing control of police chiefs from politicians; and developing mechanisms to protect the tenure of police chiefs. Elements of this agenda were achieved with varying degrees of success; however, the overall results were so successful that by 1977, Herman Goldstein appropriately pointed out that many, if not most, police departments had achieved such degrees of autonomy that they were virtually unaccountable to local government.[11]

The second task for police reformers was to extend the reach of police chiefs into the department itself. That is, police executives had to implement and maintain over time their strategy by socializing and managing personnel; devising a range of specialized tactical functions; establishing new relations to the external environment; maintaining equipment, including a fleet of automobiles and later telephone, radio, and computer equipment; controlling financial functions, including record-keeping, allocating resources, and reporting; and developing the means of reporting on the achievements of their new strategy.

In some respects, their responsibility was akin to that of late 19th-century owner-managers in industry who, confronted with the need to extend their reach into their increasingly large enterprises, "literally invented the methods and systems of administrative coordination and, in the process, gave definition to a wide range of functions such as finance, collection, service, marketing, distribution, pricing, sales, training, and labor management."[12] That is, police reformers, like owner-managers of burgeoning industrial enterprises some decades earlier, created a mid-management infrastructure, the purpose of which was to ensure the implementation and maintenance of the reform strategy. Creating functional organizations, as opposed to the geographically based organizations of early policing, chiefs delegated to a mid-managerial group specific authority over functions that included training, analyzing and planning, accounting, reporting, allocating personnel, scheduling, and other functions. Over time, the skills required to manage these functions became increasingly complex, resulting in a management group that had many of the skills of professional managers in the corporate world: planning, fiscal and budgeting analysis, marketing, research, and education.

Police chiefs extracted from their own executive functions, authority, and skill the elements that could be rationalized. Chiefs delegated these functions to mid-managers—captains and lieutenants who oversaw administrative units and patrol operations on a day-to-day and shift-to-shift basis. Administratively, captains generally head departments and units such as planning and the police academy.

In operations, captains serve usually as district/precinct/area commanders and commanders of special units. Responsible to inspectors/assistant chiefs/majors, captains in patrol direct activities in a geographic area. Responsibilities of these captains include the establishment of district priorities; supervision of operations; relations with community and neighborhood groups; coordination with other patrol districts and police units; direction of assignments, scheduling, instructions, procedures, and the preliminary handling of citizen complaints against officers. Generally, captains work business hours and days. In special units, captains have similar duties but usually have citywide responsibility for a function, such as handling juveniles, rather than for a geographic area.

Lieutenants work directly under captains. Often designated as "desk officers" in patrol units, lieutenants are responsible for the shift-to-shift operation of a district or function. As such, most lieutenants work shifts. During shifts, lieutenants are responsible for equipment, proper preparation of all reports, review of field investigations, maintenance of logs, transmission of all orders, supervision of sergeants, investigation of complaints, and other administrative duties. Typically, lieutenants "sign off" on all reports and district records. As such, they are the guarantors of line performance. But under the reformers, captains and lieutenants also gained control of the *practice, knowledge, and skill base* of the occupation. This requires some explanation.

As part of the law enforcement strategy, reformers moved to simplify and routinize the work of patrol officers, the service base of the occupation. This was accomplished in policing, as it was in industry, by attempting to reduce the discretion of line personnel, those providing the service of the organization. To accomplish this, the essence or the craft of the work had to be understood and then distilled by engineers and planners (mid-managers). Once understood and distilled, the productive efforts of workers could be reduced to relatively simple and repetitive tasks. In this way, both skill and knowledge about productivity were concentrated in the managerial domain.[13] Sparrow et al. captures this:

> Police officers, for all their field's talk about professionalism, are treated not like professionals but like factory workers. The duties and methods of their job are presumed to have been well worked out. Someone else has already done the thinking; only their faithful adherence to procedure and their willingness to show up for work are required. Their superiors, for the most part, merely supervise and discipline.[14]

The concentration of expertise, the practice skill, was located in the leadership of line operating units (patrol and special units) and staff units like planning and the training academy. Mid-managers would thus define the problems that police would address and the methods that police would use to manage them.

The task of police officers was simply nondiscretionary law enforcement. If someone breaks the law, he or she is arrested. If laws are not broken, nobody need fear the police. Some training in procedure was required, but as Bittner has noted, all a police officer really needed in this view of police work was a little common sense and the "manly virtue" of being able to overcome resistance.[15]

Thus, the solution to the administrative problem in police departments was the establishment of a powerful mid-management group that (1) extended the reach of chiefs throughout the police department and (2) became the locus of the practice and skill base of the occupation. As such, mid-managers became the *leading edge in the establishment of centralized control over police departments' internal environment and organizational operations.*

CONCLUSION: THE ADMINISTRATIVE SOLUTION

This paper began by examining the role of mid-management, especially captains and lieutenants, in policing during the past 50 years. Largely that role has been to extend the reach of management into the day-to-day operations of police departments by standardizing and controlling both organizational procedures and officer performance. As such, captains and lieutenants have been the leading edge of the control functions of police departments. They, especially lieutenants, are the guarantors of quality—the buck stops with them. They sign off on shift reports.

Discussion of the role of middle managers in strategic innovation of police departments, at least at a casual level, has tended to focus on its resistance to change. We have seen, however, that whether one considers project or strategic innovation, abundant examples of mid-management creativity exist. Abundant examples of mid-management resistance to change exist as well, whether one thinks of the Police Foundation efforts of the 1970s or of current examples.

Perhaps such resistance to change should not be surprising if we recall that in the past, one of the basic functions of captains and lieutenants—their raison d'être—has been to forestall creativity and innovation.

Consider the situation of lieutenants. They are responsible for the activities of patrol officers during a shift. Departmental procedures are in place for responding to calls for service, filing forms, receiving complaints. In the name of new models of policing (formerly called team policing, now called community or problem-oriented policing), officers respond differently to calls, modify reporting procedures, alter practices, and establish new priorities. Officers are encouraged to innovate, to be risk takers, to be creative.

Yet lieutenants still perceive themselves as accountable to captains for the maintenance of patrol priorities; to detectives and ultimately to the prosecuting attorney for offense reports; and to communications for the proper response of officers to calls for service. Lieutenants, in the past, were on the leading edge of a prime mid-management responsibility: maintaining control and ensuring that operations functioned according to the book. Now lieutenants, attempting to maintain the standards that have been their reason for being, find themselves cast as the *lagging edge:* a major source of resistance to innovation. Such a characterization of mid-managers in policing is not surprising, given their basic function.

This conflict is not of their own making; mid-managers are victims more than culprits in a process that catches them between conflicting role demands (control your officers so that all former expectations can be met versus encourage your officers to be creative and self-initiating). Focusing on mid-managers as a source of resistance may be exactly the wrong approach.

As Drucker points out:

> To focus on resistance to change is to misdefine the problem in a way that makes it less, rather than more, tractable. The right way to define the problem so as to make it capable of resolution is as a challenge to create, build, and maintain the innovative organization, the organization for which change is norm rather than exception, and opportunity rather than threat.[16]

This conceptualization appropriately shifts the focus from the resistance of mid-managers to the responsibilities of top management—CEOs, chiefs. The question becomes: how should top management behave to ensure that those in the organization who have been the organization's champions for standardization and control—captains and lieutenants—become its leading edge for creativity and innovation? We believe some principles emerge from police experience in innovation to date.

First, the experiences in Kansas City, Cincinnati, Madison, Reno, and Houston suggest that when mid-managers are involved in the process of planning innovations, they are capable of providing instrumental leadership regardless of whether the innovations are programmatic or strategic. Alternatively, whenever mid-managers are kept out of planning or perceived as a source of resistance, they *are* a potentially strong source of resistance. Mid-managers must be included in the planning process.

Second, chiefs have to acknowledge that mid-managers have legitimate vested self-interest that must be served if commitment to change is to be secured. Middle managers have legitimate professional goals. When innovation threatens mid-managers' achievement records and performance indicators, it should be expected that they will be less than enthusiastic about change. If goals have been predicated on successful control, they must be replaced with goals predicated on creativity. Experiences make this abundantly clear. It is the function of the CEO to shape the new goals and to tie professional rewards to them.

Third, when CEOs (chiefs) create a strong vision of the business of the organization, mid-managers (captains and lieutenants) are prepared to pick up the mantle and provide leadership in innovation. The experiences in Madison, Baltimore County, Houston, and Reno and the Transit Police attest to mid-management leadership when a relatively clear mandate is given by the chief, preparatory experiments or efforts are conducted, clear authority to implement is granted, and rewards are linked to performance. [There are many] examples of the innovativeness of mid-managers when values and strategy are articulated clearly and when mid-managers are given the space and freedom to innovate within their context. Rosabeth Moss Kanter's work gives similar examples from the private sector.[17]

Fourth, mid-managers must believe that they can succeed.[18] The vision or new direction of the CEO must be clearly articulated, bolstered unwaveringly, tied to organizational "winners," and supported through resource allocation, administrative action, and emergent policies and procedures. Early milestones of success must be clearly identified, and management must provide feedback about successes and failures.

Fifth, organizations must develop tolerance for failure. This is difficult in the public sector, in which rewards for success are rare but penalties for failure are potentially severe.[19] Nevertheless, if managers are to be risk-takers, they must be buoyed by their sense of mission and their commitment to improve service. Respect and rewards should be given for acknowledging failure and backtracking; covering up or perpetuating failures must be perceived as a serious breach of responsibility. Finishes, whether efforts are successful or not, must be valued as starts.

Finally, given the importance of attempting to develop a system in which innovation and renewal are to be valued, mid-managers will need to add skills not necessarily in their current repertoire, dominated as police organizations have been by the need to control. We will mention just two here.

First, managers must develop team-building skills. Building coalitions, managing task forces, establishing linkages between departments and other units of the organization, and building relationships with consumers of police services will require extraordinary team-building skills. Such skills must be basic in mid-managers.

Second, mid-managers must be real managers, not overseers. The focus of overseers is control. Overseers know best and their purpose is to ensure that their instructions are followed. Managers view their responsibilities differently. Their task is, or ought to be, to develop personnel who will be free to innovate and adapt—break the rules if necessary on behalf of the values of the organization. Thus, the core competency of managers is to make long-term investments in people, their staff. They teach and create an organizational climate in which persons can experiment; but primarily they present themselves as models for persons in their charge. That is, they coach, lead, protect, inspire, understand mistakes, and tolerate failure.

The idea that mid-managers are spoilers, that they thwart project or strategic innovation, has some basis in fact. Mid-managers improperly directed can significantly impede innovation. Yet ample evidence exists that when a clear vision of the business of the organization—its purpose or objective—is put forward, when mid-managers are included in planning, when their legitimate self-interests are acknowledged, and when they are properly trained, mid-managers can be the leading edge of innovation and creativity.

NOTES

1. Lawrence W. Sherman, *Team Policing: Seven Case Studies* (Washington, D.C.: Police Foundation, 1973), p. 107.

2. Peter Drucker, *The Frontiers of Management* (New York: Truman Talley Books, 1986), p. 200.

3. Rosabeth Moss Kanter, "The Middle Manger as Innovator," *Harvard Business Review* (July–August 1982): 95–105.

4. For a detailed discussion of these issues, see George L. Kelling and Mark H. Moore, "The Evolving Strategy of Policing," *Perspectives on Policing*, no. 4 (Washington, D.C.: National Institute of Justice and Harvard University, November 1988).

5. See, for example, George L. Kelling and James K. Stewart, "The Evolution of Contemporary Policing," In *Local Government Police Management*, William A. Geller, ed. (Washington, D.C.: International City Management Association, 1991), pp. 5–6.

6. Herman Goldstein, "Toward Community-Oriented Policing: Potential, Basic Requirements, and Threshold Questions," *Crime and Delinquency* 33, no. 1 (1987): 21.

7. This categorization is based on Raymond E. Miles and Charles C. Snow, *Organizational Strategy, Structure, and Process* (New York: McGraw Hill, 1978).

8. The National Commission on Law Observance and Enforcement, established by President Hoover in 1929, was usually called "The Wickersham Commission" after its chairman, former Attorney General George W. Wickersham.

9. See Kelling and Stewart, n. 5 above, at p. 8 for a discussion of reformers' use of these techniques.

10. Robert M. Fogelson, *Big-City Police* (Cambridge: Harvard University Press, 1977).

11. Herman Goldstein, *Policing a Free Society* (Cambridge, Mass.: Ballinger, 1977), pp. 134–136.

12. Shashana Zuboff, *In the Age of the Smart Machine: The Future of Work and Power* (New York: Basic Books, 1988), p. 108.

13. Zuboff, n. 12, p. 69.

14. Malcolm K. Sparrow, Mark H. Moore, and David M. Kennedy, *Beyond 911: A New Era for Policing* (New York: Basic Books, 1990), p. 120.

15. Egon Bittner, "Introduction," *Aspects of Police Work* (Boston: Northeastern University Press, 1990), p. 6.

16. Peter Drucker, *Management: Tasks, Responsibilities, Practices* (New York: Harper and Row, 1974), p. 797.

17. Kanter, "Middle Manager . . ." n. 3 above.

18. William D. Guth and Ian C. MacMillan, "Strategy Implementation Versus Middle Management Self-Interest," *Strategic Management Journal* 7 (1986): 313–327.

19. Alan Altshuler and March Zegans, "Innovation and Creativity: Comparisons Between Public Management and Private Enterprise," *Cities* (February 1990): 16–24.

A R T I C L E 16

POLICE ACCOUNTABILITY AND COMMUNITY POLICING

George L. Kelling, Robert Wasserman,
and Hubert Williams

The accountability of individual police officers is a fundamental issue for police executives. This is fitting: police officers are the public officials society has authorized, even obliged, to use force. Ensuring that police officers use that warrant equitably, legally, and economically on behalf of citizens is at the core of police administration. The enduring concern of police executives to ensure accountability in American policing is a reflection of their professional commitment.

Not only is it fitting that a police executive give high priority to ensuring the accountability of police officers, it is essential to surviving as the leader of a police department. Police chiefs continually worry about abuse of authority: brutality, misuse of force, bribery, manufacture of evidence in the name of efficiency or success, failure to apply the law because of personal interests, and discrimination against particular individuals or groups. These issues are grist for the mill of persistent and influential watchdog groups concerned about impartial enforcement under the law—the media, civil rights groups, and lawyers. Rising crime or fear of crime may be problematic for police administrators, but rarely does either threaten their survival. Scandal associated with abuse of authority, however, does jeopardize organizational stability and continuity of leadership.

As a consequence, it is not surprising that police leaders have developed organizational mechanisms of control that seek to ensure police

Reprinted from George L. Kelling, Robert Wasserman, and Hubert Williams, "Police Accountability and Community Policing," *Perspectives on Policing,* no. 7 (Washington, D.C.: National Institute of Justice, U.S. Department of Justice, and the Program in Criminal Justice Policy and Management, John F. Kennedy School of Government, Harvard University, 1988).

accountability to both the law and the policies and procedures of police departments. This paper reviews the ways police administrators try to control the accountability of individual police officers and examines the relationship between accountability procedures and community policing.

The paper's focus on accountability and community policing results from the concerns of many police executives and policymakers that certain characteristics of community policing threaten police officer accountability. These characteristics of community policing include organizational decentralization, increased intimacy between police officers and citizens and neighborhoods, receipt and interpretation of citizen demand for service by individual patrol officers, and development of patrol and policing tactics (problem solving, for example) by patrol officers at a neighborhood or community level. All of these characteristics require increased officer use of discretion and empowerment of patrol officers. Advocates of community policing who call for empowerment of officers should be extraordinarily scrupulous about ensuring that officers are held accountable for their actions.

Police organizations, like all organizations, rely on distinctive structural forms and management processes to maintain accountability. Characteristically, their structures are centralized with functionally defined bureaus, and their management processes emphasize preservice training and elaborate command and control mechanisms. In many respects, police organizations have typified the classical command and control organization that emphasizes top-level decision making: flow of orders from executives down to line personnel, flow of information up from line personnel to executives, layers of dense supervision, unity of command, elaborate rules and regulations, elimination of discretion, and simplification of work tasks.

Command and control management has met two sets of needs in American policing. First, command and control systems have strengthened the ability of police to respond to civil disturbances, riots, labor disputes, and other problems for which coordinating large numbers of police was required.

Second, command and control systems have resolved many of the inherent tensions of policing—tension, for example, between constraints imposed on police by law and the opportunities for effectiveness provided by their warrant to use force. There are other tensions as well—tensions between efficient processing of offenders and protection of their constitutional guarantees, between conflicting definitions of morality in communities and neighborhoods, between competing political interests.

Command and control systems have appeared to resolve these tensions by (1) instituting rules that prescribe the behavior of officers, (2) creating dense patterns of command and supervision to enforce these rules, (3) establishing the principle of unity of command to eliminate ambiguity in the chain of authority, and (4) routinizing the job of police officers by defining it as law enforcement.

This strategy has its successes. These successes include reduced political control of officers; reduced corruption; improvements in qualifications and training of police officers; constraints on police officer use of force, especially deadly force; production of more equitable police service; and arguably, enhancement of the tenure of police chiefs. Additionally, command and control management has improved the capacity of police to respond to riots and other disturbances that require coordinated group responses.

But there are strains in this strategy as well. As logically appealing as the command and control organization seems, many aspects of police work are not compatible with classical command and control organizations. First, patrol work is not amenable to attempts to simplify or routinize it. The types and multiplicity of problems with which police deal preclude the simplification or routinization of patrol work.[1] The metaphor of the assembly line, basic to classical management theories, has proved to be inapplicable to the realities of patrol. Second, police officers, unlike assembly line workers or military troops, do not work under the direct scrutiny of supervisors. Even when sergeants are in the field, the unpredictable timing and location of police activities thwart ordinary supervision of performance. Consequently, although serious attempts have been made to eliminate or structure discretion, it has remained an integral and pervasive feature of police work,[2] especially at the level of patrol officer.

This strain between the realities of police work and the command and control systems of departments creates problems for administrators. First, the mechanisms of command and control are elaborate and expensive to maintain; layers of command, extensive training, and the maintenance of multitudinous rules and procedures obligate time, personnel, and money. Second, the discontinuities between organizational prescriptions and work realities are not lost on police officers. The results? At least two: (1) considerable role strain on officers who are portrayed as professionals on one hand but treated as recalcitrant semi-skilled workers on the other and (2) the rise of the union movement, which, at times, fosters acrid labor–management relationships.

Further, there are additional, more subtle costs to police departments. First, use of individual discretion has been driven underground; creativity and productive adaptations go unrecognized and unrewarded. Second, police departments often fail to tap the potential abilities of their officers. An ethos of "stay out of trouble," which has developed in many departments, stifles officers who are otherwise resourceful and abets officers who "perch" in their positions. Finally, a police culture has developed that maintains values that are alien to both police departments and communities. This police culture is characterized by suspiciousness, perceptions of greater danger, isolation from citizens, and internal solidarity (the "blue curtain").

MANAGING THE CULTURE

Are there alternatives to command and control for managing police culture and improving accountability?

It is generally acknowledged that a primary determinant of police officer behavior is the culture within which officers find themselves. This
is true not only in policing, but also in most other types of organizations.
Good management is often described as the management of organizational culture.[3]

The tendency in policing, however, is to emphasize the importance
of the formal elements of the organization and ignore the informal elements (organizational myths, the norms and mores of the organization,
etc.). The point, however, is not whether culture is influenced, but who
influences it. To the extent that management has not worked to shape
police culture, other forces have.

Often, management's attempt to manage culture through command
and control merely fosters suspicion, isolation, insularity, demeaning
perception of citizens, grumpiness, the "blue curtain," and cynicism.[4]
The result is an attitude on the part of police officers that says: "Management, leave me alone—let me do my work." In the worst of circumstances, police culture implies: "I am being paid for being a police officer. Beyond staying out of trouble, if you want me to do anything, bring
me in on overtime."

The traditional approach has been to work against culture through
the use of command and control. That workers do not like work and
have little to contribute to its substance or conduct are basic tenets of
classical organizational theory. Alternate managerial approaches recognize the importance of informal leadership and peer influences, assume
that workers do care about the substance of their work, and strive to use
informal leadership and peer influences on behalf of the mission of the
organization. We believe that successful management of culture is
achieved in three ways:

- Leadership through values
- Accountability to the community
- Administrative mechanisms of control

LEADERSHIP THROUGH VALUES

All organizations have values. They are implicit in every action of organizational incumbents. When explicit, statements of values attempt to set
forth the beliefs of an organization, the standards that are to be maintained by its members, and the broader mission expected to be achieved
through their activities. Most often, values operate at several levels of individual and organizational awareness. At times, workers make decisions by considering and selecting from alternatives—well aware of their
value implications. At other times, workers make decisions without conscious recourse to their value dimensions. Often the values that under-
gird routine decisions and practices are so deeply ingrained as to make
them automatic.[5]

Values, even those we consider positive, can conflict. For example,
loyalty to peers can conflict with the maintenance of high standards of

professional practice. When police officers decide to close their eyes to the incompetence or corruption of colleagues and draw the "blue curtain" around them, they choose the value of loyalty to peers over other values, such as quality service to the community. In many police departments, other values, some explicit and others implicit, can be identified that shape and drive police performance: "stay out of trouble," "we are the finest," "machismo," "serve and protect," and many others.

The responsibility of police managers is to (1) identify values that flow from the law and the Constitution, that represent the highest norms of the profession, and that are consistent with the ideals of communities and neighborhoods, and (2) enunciate them persuasively and unambiguously.

How are a department's values properly enunciated? First, many departments make their values explicit through the development of concise value statements. Such practices are not new in policing: O. W. Wilson developed visionary value statements both in Wichita and Chicago; the Los Angeles Police Department's statement of values had its origins in the administration of Chief Ed Davis. More recently, such statements have been developed in departments in Houston, Texas; Madison, Wisconsin; Dayton, Ohio; and many others.

Second, statements of policy, on issues such as use of deadly force, for example, are derived from departmental values and inform and guide police officers and citizens—whether the department maintains a clear-cut value statement or not—about values of the department. Equally important, the absence of policy statements in crucial areas, such as use of deadly force, expresses values and creates policy as well through administrative inaction.[6] In turn, procedures (methods of performance that direct action in distinct situations) and rules (specific prohibitions or requirements stated to prevent deviance) are derived from value-based policies.[7]

Without rejecting all procedures and rules, the primary focus in value-based administration and leadership is not on prohibitions constraining officers but rather on encouraging police officers to weigh their actions constantly in light of departmental values. This switch in emphasis from rule conformity alone to quality action and outcome empowers officers to select appropriate courses of action from within a range of options rather than in the rote fashion too often prescribed by advocates of command and control. Leadership by values addresses the issue of accountability by attempting to link the nature of police work (application of discretionary judgments to a wide range of problems) with mechanisms of control that emphasize professional self-regulation rather than mere obligatory accommodation to rules.

ACCOUNTABILITY TO THE COMMUNITY

Two familiar forms of police accountability to communities are community relations units and civilian review boards. Community relations units are supposed to carry the message of police departments to communities but have proven to be insufficiently responsive to community definitions of problems and solutions. In the few places where they exist, civilian review boards focus primarily on the performance of individual officers, particularly on mistakes and incompetence.

The difference between the role of citizens in community policing and in civilian review boards is that civilian review boards concentrate on perceived or real abuses while community policing focuses on the substantive issues of problems, crime, and quality of life in neighborhoods. Citizens bring to the relationship their sense of community, knowledge about the problems in their neighborhoods, their own capacities to solve problems, and the potential to support or authorize police action. Police bring to communities concerns not only for their welfare but for the constitutional rights and the welfare of all individuals and the community-at-large—thus countervailing the tendencies of neighborhood residents to be overly parochial or opposed to the legitimate interests of strangers or particular subgroups.

To us, accountability to the community means something different. It implies a new relationship to the community in which police departments establish an understanding with communities. This can take several forms. One form is for the community to be brought into policy-setting procedures—a practice pioneered during the 1960s by Chief Robert Igleburger of Dayton, Ohio. A second form of new relationship to the community, but not necessarily exclusive of the first, is for both police and citizens to nominate the problems with which police and citizens will deal, the tactics that each will use to address those problems, and the outcomes that are desired.

The understanding between police and community, more or less explicit, establishes a mutual accountability. It provides measures against which each can evaluate the other. This understanding does not abrogate police officers' responsibility for their professional knowledge, skills, or values. Likewise, it does not free citizens from their responsibility for their own safety. To use a medical analogy, it makes physician and patient accountable to each other.

ADMINISTRATIVE MECHANISMS OF CONTROL

The list of administrative mechanisms of control that are available to managers is conventional: education, training, rewards, discipline, peer influence, direction, supervision, recognition, and career opportunities. Use of, and emphasis on, these mechanisms varies across occupations. Police in the past, using classical organizational principles, have emphasized direction, supervision, discipline, and preservice training. (This does not mean that other mechanisms were not used as well. The primary mechanisms, however, were those we identified.) These mechanisms can be adapted by police to improve accountability, just as they have been adapted by many other professional and private sector organizations. In the section that follows we shall briefly discuss the adaptation of control mechanisms to contemporary policing: supervision, training, program auditing, discipline, reward, and peer control.

Supervision

Supervision of police is essential to improving the quality of police services. Typically, police administration portrays supervisors as directors who oversee workers who perform specific activities laid out in advance by management. Given the conditions of police activity, however—officers work alone, events occur in locations and at times that make them unavailable for direct oversight, the problems citizens present to police require novel solutions—different forms of supervision are required. These forms of supervision are more akin to coaching than directing. They include teaching, reviewing, considering alternatives, training, and other similar techniques.

A special function of supervisors is to empower officers. By empower we mean providing officers with the authority to use their knowledge, skill, and values to identify problems and work toward their solution. Empowerment of officers is the opposite of encouraging them to "stay out of trouble" or "not bother" their sergeants. Confronted with ambiguous problems not responsive to standard solutions, police officers can be empowered by sergeants to search for creative solutions to problems rather than respond in some rote fashion. Organizational policies should be sufficiently pliable to accommodate the breadth of discretion that officers will be expected to exercise under this arrangement.

It is our contention that as departments shift away from the authoritarian model of policing to a more flexible community-oriented approach, a re-examination of the structure of the bureaucracy will be essential to the efficient performance of the officer on the beat as well as the effectiveness of the department's operations.

We recognize that the complexity of this issue mandates far more thought and consideration than can be given in this paper. Departments cannot expect to eliminate an entire structure one day and begin with a new one the next. But they must begin to address the question of whether or not the existing rank structure and its functioning lend themselves to the type of police performance required to meet the needs and expectations of the communities served by the department.

This is particularly true in cities with a diverse ethnic and cultural mix. In these jurisdictions, the varying interests and demands of neighborhoods necessitate flexibility at the point of contact through which the department provides the services. This means that patrol officers need greater discretion and flexibility and less rigid adherence to monolithic rules and procedures. Thus, it might be possible to eliminate some of the tiers of authority within the bureaucracy while at the same time being more cost-effective.

We should begin with the establishment of a career track for patrol officers that would provide incentives for meeting specialized goals. Many of these goals could be the result of an accord between neighborhoods and department representatives in which the line officer is an active participant, provided with sufficient authority to draw upon required departmental resources to achieve objectives. This requires more functional supervision than direct line authority over the officer. Therefore, it would be possible under this configuration to reduce the number of sergeants and increase the opportunities for advancement within the patrol officers' line. Thus, promotions based upon abstract examinations could be replaced by a more practical system of performance measures that link community needs with departmental objectives.

Training

Police recruit training is organizationally based, preservice training that emphasizes law, rules and procedures, and officer discipline.[8] This is consistent with the thrust of earlier reform to enhance the lawfulness and eliminate the discretion of police officers. It can be argued that this training serves its purpose very well, at least as far as it goes. It does emphasize important values: adherence to law and discipline.

The difficulty with training that concentrates primarily on law and discipline is that is fails to take into account the workaday circumstances of police officer activity: dealing with unpredictable events, most often when alone and without available supervision. Knowledge of law in such circumstances is important, but insufficient. More often than not it tells officers what they cannot do rather than what they can or should do. Military discipline is almost irrelevant under conditions in which a police officer confronts a situation alone, diagnoses it, selects one set of responses from a range of alternatives, and develops follow-up plans.

For routine circumstances, officers require basic knowledge about the kinds of events they encounter, skills that are applicable in such encounters, and values that inspire and constrain officers in their practice.[9] Moreover, the knowledge, skills, and values that are required to shape officer discretion in the handling of events must be internalized into the professional self of each officer. This can come about only through prolonged socialization that emphasizes discretionary application of a range of skills to a variety of real-world circumstances. Yet, academy training is notoriously deficient in the provision of such training.

There are models from other disciplines for the acquisition of such knowledge, skills, and values: engineering, education, and others. They offer possibilities for police leaders for the future.

Audit Mechanisms

No matter how good the training, how instrumental management has been in shaping the culture, and how positive supervision has been, the circumstances of police work will continue to allow for corruption, malfeasance, and incompetence. Policing is not unique in this respect, but stakes are higher when lethal governmental power is involved. There are reasons to believe that skillful administration will reduce such problems. Even so, managers will have to be ever vigilant.

One form of vigilance is auditing. An analogy is found in a financial audit of a business. It is conceded that a financial audit cannot be universal; indeed, attempts to audit everything may result in auditing nothing. Audits, instead, sample a representative number of transactions (events) from the relevant universe. There is nothing to prevent police from adopting similar schemes. An example: undercover decoy squads are often valuable anticrime units. They can be problematic, however. It is not uncommon for enthusiasm to become zealotry. Auditing a given sample of arrests by interviewing witnesses, defendants, and other interested parties is one way of maintaining control of such units. Another example is found in departments that routinely send postcards to a sample of "customers" to determine how satisfied they were with police service. Other departments routinely monitor samples of citizens complaints to determine whether they are being properly handled.

Three additional points should be made about audits. Typically, audits tend to become inspections of production quantity rather than quality. We are concerned about quality over quantity. It is well known that the number of arrests is a measurable subject to enormous manipulation if not carefully monitored to ensure that the arrests are legitimate, properly conducted, appropriate, and fair. If arrests are to be a measure of individual or unit effectiveness, the only systematic means of ensuring their quality is through careful auditing of each step of the process that led to the arrest.

Second, audits are a form of after-the-fact accountability. They are no substitute for other mechanisms of administrative control, like leadership, education, and training, that attempt to ensure quality performance in advance rather than discover mistakes after they occur.

Finally, audits can be administered in a variety of ways. They can be carried out by high-level inspectors as well as by sergeants who are responsible for units. In some circumstances, they can be carried out by specially charged task forces comprised of officers of varying ranks, including patrol.

Discipline

Discipline will always be an important mechanism to ensure officer accountability: every organization, no matter how well managed, will have a small number of officers who perform irresponsibly or incompetently. Because the stakes are so high in policing, strong messages must be given to officers at all levels that incompetent performance—brutality and corruption, for example—is intolerable. We believe that if supervision and audits are well performed and documented, discipline can be exercised in ways that are both fair and perceived as fair.

One caveat, however. Line officers are understandably sensitive about how discipline is exercised in many departments. In a world in which staying out of trouble is a primary measure of officer adequacy, it should be no wonder that discipline is seen as arbitrary and unjust. Too often discipline follows the commission of mistakes, rather than officer incompetence or irresponsibility. Mistakes, incompetence, and irresponsibility are different issues. Mistakes, which are bound to occur in all work, should routinely evoke coaching, consideration of options, training, and other such control options. Incompetence and irresponsibility should result in discipline. Managers cannot have it both ways. They cannot ask officers to be risk-takers and then discipline them when occasional mistakes occur. Those who take risks on behalf of an organization—if they use methods and have goals that are within the values of the organization—and then make mistakes, need support and assistance, not discipline.

Rewards

Rewards continue to be powerful motivators for workers. Rewards can take the form of increased pay, job perks, promotion, special assignments, recognition, and other forms. Police agencies have used every conceivable form. The questions that arise in policing about rewards are not whether they are used fairly and appropriately. Questions about the fairness and propriety of police reward systems are based on the concern that only a small range of police officer activities is reflected in current measures of police performance. A good many areas—dispute resolution, crime prevention, problem solving, and order maintenance, for example—are rarely reflected in the data collected about officer performance. Given the importance of these activities in community policing, ways of evaluating the quality with which officers perform these functions and then linking these evaluative measures to rewards will have to be developed.

Two innovative ways of recognizing and rewarding officers, methods compatible with other elements of community policing, would be peer review of performance and performance contracts. Peer review of performance is discussed below. Performance contracts, a method of supervision in which a supervisor or colleagues negotiate a set of performance goals over a distinct period of time, are now being experimented with in Madison, Wisconsin. There, in an experiment in community policing and organizational decentralization, officers and their supervisors are negotiating personal performance contracts for the purpose of evaluating performance of patrol officers.

Peer Control

Peer control is an important means of achieving accountability. Although heavy reliance on peer control has been traditional in the professions of medicine, law, and science, it has not always ensured the desired quality of performance. However, when combined with other mechanisms of control, it will continue to be an important means of maintaining the standards of professional performance for police.

Despite the potential of peer review, police administrators have been reluctant to use methods of control that exploit opportunities for collegial or peer review. There have been exceptions to this generalization: the Peer Review Project in Kansas City during the mid-1970s (which focused on excessive use of force) and stress and alcohol-abuse programs in other departments. Other exceptions that come to mind are the Home Beat Officer program in the London Metropolitan Police, the Senior Lead Officer program in the Los Angeles Police Department, and the current experiment in decentralization in Madison, where officers have elected their own lieutenants. For the most part, however, collegial review of basic police practice has been extremely limited.

CONCLUSION

The concern of this paper is not the reduction of police accountability but rather its increase and strengthening. In a sense, there is a paradox. Those mechanisms that have seemed most certain to ensure control (command and control systems) have created the illusion of control, but often little more than that. Other mechanisms of control recognize and promote the use of discretion by police officers. These mechanisms, such as auditing, rewards, and peer control, offer significant opportunities for increasing officer accountability.

From this brief discussion of managing police culture and accountability, it is clear that we do not believe that community policing threatens police accountability. Rather, the proper management of community policing adds additional opportunities for the maintenance of accountability in police organizations.

NOTES

1. Mary Ann Wycoff, *The Role of Municipal Police: Research as Prelude to Changing It* (Washington, D.C.: Police Foundation, 1982).
2. Herman Goldstein, *Policing a Free Society* (Cambridge, Mass.: Ballinger, 1977).
3. See, for example, Edgar H. Schein, *Organizational Culture and Leadership* (San Francisco: Jossey-Bass, 1985).
4. For a discussion of police culture see, for example, Peter K. Manning, *Police Work* (Cambridge: MIT Press, 1979).
5. For an extended discussion of values in police departments, see "Values in Policing" by Robert Wasserman in this same series.
6. See, for example, City of Canton, Ohio v. Geraldine Harris, Willie G. Harris, Bernadette Harris, Amicus Curriae Brief of the American Civil Liberties Union and ACLU of Ohio in Support of Respondents in the Supreme Court of the United States, October term, 1987.
7. The authors thank Los Angeles Chief of Police Daryl Gates for helping us think through the relationship between values, policies, procedures, and rules, although he is in no way responsible for our conclusions.
8. For a discussion of recruit training and socialization, see John Van Maanen, "Observations on the Making of Policemen," *Human Organization* 32, no. 4 (winter 1973): 407–418.
9. An extreme example of the role of values is found in police use of deadly force. As important as rules and procedures may be, no set of rules about its use will ever be able to take into account all of the exigencies that occur in real-world circumstances; use of deadly force will always be discretionary, guided, at best, by values expressed through departmental policies.

PART 5

THE ACTORS

This section deals with the fact that there are various actors involved in the community policing concept. It is not a "police-only" program but a method that attempts to involve the community as well. The most difficult aspect of this statement, however, is generally found in defining "community." For the purposes of community policing, this has been debated in and of itself, but barring the details of the debate, community should, in a sense, mean everyone. It should include residential neighbors, business owners, other government employees, school children, homeless persons, citizen groups, and, of course, the police. Although there could be a number of articles focusing on each one of these groups, the intent of this section is to look at the police and the community for some early understanding of their roles under community policing.

The first article in this section is written by George L. Kelling and James K. Stewart. The article is very explicit in stating that neighborhoods can and should act as a polity and hence should be responsible for defending themselves. The police do play a role in assisting neighborhoods deal with crime, disorder, and fear, but they cannot be solely or even primarily responsible for neighborhood safety. Recognizing this fact, the authors articulate how the police and community should relate to one another under the community policing philosophy.

The second article in this section is written by Edwin Meese III, the former Attorney General of the United States under the Reagan administration. In this article, he discusses the historical background of police officers' movement toward crime fighting and professionalization and then provides a very clear understanding of how the community policing officer differs from this traditional approach. This article essentially defines what it means to be a community policing officer.

The final article is this section is written by Stephen Mastrofski, an academic professional who has become instrumental in evaluating the community policing movement. This is an article that is very short but often cited and reprinted. It details in simple, pragmatic terms what it means to be a community policing officer and what the job may look like in comparison to the traditional approach to policing.

ARTICLE 17

NEIGHBORHOODS AND POLICE: THE MAINTENANCE OF CIVIL AUTHORITY

George L. Kelling and James K. Stewart

A cardinal tenet of community policing is that a new relationship between police and neighborhoods is required if the quality of residential and commercial life is to be protected or improved in cities. This assertion raises several questions. What are neighborhoods? Do they exist, or are they largely a concoction of nostalgic policy makers, police reformers, and revisionists who perpetuate ideals that may or may not have existed in the past, but certainly are outside of current urban experience? Assuming that neighborhoods exist, what should their relationship be with police? What opportunities are offered both to neighborhoods and to police by restructuring their relationship? How should police resolve the potential conflict between the rule of law and neighborhood standards of conduct that they might be asked to uphold?

This paper addresses these questions by focusing on three aspects of neighborhoods: (1) the neighborhood as polity; (2) the ability of neighborhood to defend itself against crime and disorder without eliminating civility and justice from social relations there; and (3) alternate visions of the role of municipal police in neighborhoods.

NEIGHBORHOOD AS POLITY

At a minimum, neighborhoods are places in which people live or work near each other, recognize their recurring proximity, and signal this

Reprinted from George L. Kelling and James K. Stewart, "Neighborhoods and Police: The Maintenance of Civil Authority," *Perspectives on Policing,* no. 10 (Washington, D.C.: National Institute of Justice, U.S. Department of Justice and the Program in Criminal Justice Policy and Management, John F. Kennedy School of Government, Harvard University, 1989).

recognition to each other.[1] As Suttles[2] notes, residents of cities construct "cognitive maps" in which they allocate distinctive places as "theirs"— their neighborhood. Moreover, neighbors are not just the residents of a special geographical area but also include shopkeepers and their employees, other workers who frequent areas regularly (postal workers, for example), and even the homeless.[3]

The *intensity* of neighboring relationships depends on many factors, including geographical and physical characteristics of the community, ethnic and kinship networks, affective attachment of residents to the neighborhood, home and business ownership, building construction features, local facility usage, pedestrian and automotive traffic patterns, the amount of time neighbors spend in the area, as well as demographic patterns (e.g., the number of children, nonworking adults, and aged who live in a community). The *content* of neighboring can range from curt nods of the head ("good fences make good neighbors") to regularly scheduled neighborhood meetings ("strength through units").[4]

Periodicity characterizes both the intensity and content of neighboring. Citizens live in time, as well as area, zones. Periodicity has two sets of implications.

First, many residents abandon their neighborhoods during the day: workers may commute to their workplaces and children may be bused to schools outside their immediate neighborhood. Other people use neighborhoods during particular times: merchants arrive for the opening of their shops and depart after closing; shoppers arrive and depart; postal workers move through a neighborhood on a relatively predictable schedule. During particular times, the homeless can comprise the residents of a neighborhood. Traffic on major thoroughfares ebbs and flows daily. Bars open and close.

Second, citizen perception about areas changes depending on the time of the day or day of the week. During rush hour, while awaiting transportation, citizens can view a neighborhood as being theirs, in a sense, and as a comfortable place in which to be. The same area at another time of day or week (midnight or Saturday) may be perceived as extraordinarily alien and threatening.

Citizen participation in neighborhood activities and governance has long been perceived in this country as central to the formation of an individual's character, the inculcation of traditional values, and the maintenance of freedom. Integral parts of this participation have been self-help and self-governance. Despite this political philosophy, the aim or the consequence of American urban *policy* during the last hundred years has been to decrease the influence of neighborhoods in American life. What factors have contributed to this decline?

First, the progressive reform movements that centralized city government have contributed to a decline in neighborhood influence. As Glazer notes:

> All during the twentieth century, indeed until the mid-1960s, the proposals for city reform generally followed . . . progressive tradition: make the mayor or the board of supervisors stronger.[5]

The consequence of strengthening centralized city government has been the reduction of the political strength and capacity for self-help of neighborhoods.

Second, congruent with the centralization of political power were the professionalization and bureaucratization of services, especially social and police services. Problem solving and the provision of services not only came under the political and administrative control of executives, but also were provided by newly developing bureaucracies with full-time staff recruited and promoted on the basis of achieved qualifications, professional or otherwise.[6] Within neighborhoods, self-help in many areas, such as education, was eliminated or, in the case of police, denigrated and discouraged.

Third, during the 1950s and 1960s, urban renewal policies decimated many neighborhoods in the name of eliminating slums, improving the urban housing stock, and integrating ethnic groups into America's "melting pot." It seems ironic that many neighborhood self-help groups organized in resistance to the implementation of such policies in their immediate locales.

Fourth, low-income housing developments concentrated on the construction of high-rise apartments rather than on low-rise or single-dwelling residences. Jane Jacobs and Oscar Newman have written persuasively about the largely negative consequences of such building practices on neighborhoods and cities.[7]

Fifth, transportation policies concentrated on facilitating the movement of automobiles into and out of cities, at the expense of the public building, improvement, or even maintenance of transportation into and within cities. Such policies encouraged the abandonment of cities for suburbs and left isolated those citizens who did remain in urban neighborhoods.[8]

Sixth, during the twentieth century, public spaces have been redefined. The street traditionally was a diversified place enjoyed and used for its own sake—a place to congregate, meet others, enjoy human-scaled architecture. But during the midcentury the tower-block—high-rise buildings surrounded by open spaces—came to symbolize the new use of public space: segregated by purpose, with the street serving primarily as a means of transportation between facilities. Thus, streets became public areas through which people pass to gain easy access to specific facilities: quasi-public and quasi-private shopping, recreational, residential, and work areas in which internal control is privatized.[9]

Finally, for good or ill, social policies that relied on busing to ensure equality of educational opportunity eroded the strengths of neighborhoods.

To be sure, these trends did not operate uniformly across cities. Moreover, these forces notwithstanding, destruction of neighborhood life and polity has not been uniform within individual cities or throughout the country. In some cities, such as Chicago, at least through the administration of the late Mayor Daley, neighborhoods and wards retained considerable power over the provision of city services and the allocation of political goods and services. Likewise, in Boston for example, some neighborhoods have considerably more power and access to goods and services than others.[10] One neighborhood, for example, not only garnered its own foot patrol officer who patrolled the area regularly at a time when neither foot patrol nor regular beat assignments characterized police tactics, but successfully lobbied to restrict the types of off-duty assignments police could accept.[11] These variations in neighborhoods are explained by factors such as the political culture of the city, the form of city government, the demographic composition of the given neighborhood, and the extent to which neighbors feel threatened and have been able to mobilize.

Moreover, contemporary trends rejected the centralization of governmental power. During the 1960s, dissatisfaction with centralization had its inchoate beginnings.

> At the local level, in the 1960s, for the first time the intellectual elite and the liberal national media abandoned the argument of progressive reformers and supported demands for decentralization of city functions.[12]

Although support of decentralization was initiated by advocates from the political left, by the late 1970s it had become as popular with the political right.[13]

Today the call for devolution of power and control over services—indeed, the call for a self-help approach to problem solving—has spread from the intellectual and political elite to residents within communities and neighborhoods. No longer are citizens in many communities willing to hear from remote politicians what government *cannot* do and citizens *should not* do; citizens are demanding new kinds of accountability and responsibility; and neighborhoods are becoming sources of polity rather than mere locales in which people live and work.

Yet there is one important dimension in which neighborhoods, even those that actually functioned as political units, do not operate as a true political system: the exercise of lawful coercive force. Neighborhoods can serve as a polity, whose citizens lobby, unofficially govern in many dimensions, indeed, even patrol streets and parks. But the exercise of official coercive force is reserved for city hall, for government. This is not to say that neighborhoods do not use coercion. Most often it takes the form of social persuasion, threats, and informal means of approval and disapproval. Sometimes, however, illegal force is used in neighborhoods by criminal gangs, for example, who may use threats, vandalism, extortion, and other forms of coercion.[14] Regardless, "official" government largely maintains a monopoly on legitimate use of force, primarily through its police departments.[15]

NEIGHBORHOODS DEFENDING THEMSELVES

Six factors in neighborhoods may contribute to the defense of a neighborhood against crime and disorder:

1. *Individual citizens in association with police and criminal justice agencies.* Individuals may act on their own to notify police of something untoward in their neighborhood or elsewhere. Moreover, citizens can become involved in other elements of the criminal justice system in other ways, for example as witnesses in court hearings.

2. *Individual citizens acting alone.* Individuals may act on their own to protect themselves, others, and their neighborhood from crime, disorder, and fear. These actions include: buying locks, weapons, alarm systems, and other hardware; avoiding certain locations; restricting activities; assisting, or not assisting, other persons who have difficulty; moving out of the neighborhood; and hiring protection from private security firms.

3. *Private groups.* Groups of citizens may act on their own behalf to protect the neighborhood, its residents, and users. Their actions [can] include holding meetings; organizing neighborhood watch groups; patrolling; lobbying; creating telephone trees and "safe houses" for children; and monitoring courts. Further, they may purchase private security to protect their homes, streets, entrance-ways, or lobbies.

4. *Formal private organizations.* Organizations such as funded community activist and community development organizations implement and maintain neighborhood programs that may include recreation for youth, victim assistance, gang and other forms of youth work, and community organization. (These organizations are different from traditional social agencies that operate city-wide.)

5. *Commercial firms.* Small shopkeepers and large corporations, such as hospitals, universities, shopping malls, and other institutions, may purchase, or in some cases provide their own, proprietary protective services.

6. *Public criminal justice agencies.* Police, as well as the other elements of the criminal justice system, may operate on their own to defend the safety of neighborhoods.

Several observations can be made about these elements of a community's self-defense capacity. First, in the Anglo-Saxon tradition, crime control was a private, community responsibility. Most public organizations of social control are barely 150 years old.[16] Moreover, American political ideology still holds that private solutions to problems, whether the problems are related to health, education, welfare, or crime and disorder, are preferable to public solutions. Just as neighborhoods provide the informal political infrastructure that keeps urban government afloat,[17] neighborhoods and private social control provide the underpinnings on which public institutions of control build.

Second, the impact of the elements of neighborhood social control is not necessarily cumulative. The forms that neighborhood defense take can not only increase or decrease the capacity of neighborhoods to defend themselves, but also can influence the quality of neighborhood life in other ways. Purchasing guns and locks does little or nothing to create or sustain community relationships; they might even interfere with their development and maintenance. Similarly, calling police to deal with incidents does little to create relationships within neighborhoods. Citizens patrols, neighborhood watch, neighborhood meetings with police to discuss problems, on the other hand, all foster the development of neighborhood relationships and sense of community.

There are legitimate reasons to be concerned about fairness and equity in the supply of resources for community defense. The poor are in need of as much protection as the rich—at times, more. Moreover, there are reasons to fear that the actions of the well-to-do to defend themselves might increase the jeopardy of the less well-off. Thus, we are concerned about the public quality of individual and organizational responses to crime, disorder, and fear. Guns and locks might protect individuals but do nothing for neighborhood security. Walling off corporations from communities by architectural and security measures can secure those organizations but further erode community bonds and safety.[18]

Also, ensuring the rights of those who have a different sense of public morality and the rights of offenders is an important part of the public quality of a community's self-defense efforts. We will discuss these issues in some detail later.

In sum, although we are developing some knowledge about the ecology of crime in cities and neighborhoods,[19] we know practically nothing about the ecology of neighborhood or city self-defense. Depending on circumstances, elements of control (1) complement each other and thereby improve overall neighborhood self-defense; (2) neutralize each other and cancel out their impact; or (3) interact to make problems worse. We simply do not know how to take the different circumstances into account.

Both critics and supporters of the idea of neighborhood primacy in efforts to control crime, fear, and disorder have been troubled by the limited evidence of the success of community crime control efforts and by the limited number of citizens who participate in such efforts. Although we hope that such efforts will meet with success (and believe that over the long term they will) and wish that many more citizens would involve themselves in such efforts, we do not share the concerns mentioned above.

Regarding the issue of effectiveness, we agree with Nathan Glazer:

> Whatever the failures of community control and community participation, whatever the modification of the new procedures built on the slogan of more power to the people, the thesis that had characterized the old progressivism, with its enthronement of the strong mayor, the single powerful board, the strong federal government, and the wisdom of the experts they selected, a thesis that had been dominant for sixty years or more among liberal experts on government, never returned. Community control and participation may not have been a great success, but it led to no desire to return to a situation that was seen as even less desirable.[20]

Given the continuing intolerably high levels of crime, fear, and disorder, and the inability of police and other criminal justice agencies to manage it effectively, this is as true in community self-defense as in other areas Glazer may have in mind.

Moreover, we do not despair at the number of citizens who actively participate in neighborhood governance. Elsewhere, one of the authors (Kelling) has discussed this issue and noted that many neighborhoods appear to be in the hands of "caretakers"—persons who meet regularly, note neighborhood conditions, schedule a few annual events, maintain liaison with other neighborhood groups and "official government," and rally neighborhood forces in the face of some threat.[21] Their numbers may not be large (often six to ten persons), but their influence and potential are. Suttles describes a similar situation:

> Protest groups, conservation committees, landowners' groups, and realty associations spring into existence, thrive, and then decline, as the issue which brought them into existence waxes and wanes. All this tends to give the defended neighborhood an ephemeral and transient appearance, as if it were a social artifact. But these social forms are real enough, and they leave at least a residue of a formula for subsequent cohesion.[22]

What is clear is that just as neighborhoods vary in their ability to obtain goods and services, they also vary in their competence to defend themselves against predators. Defining neighborhood competence, however, is difficult. Peter Hunt, a member of the Executive Session on Community Policing and former executive director of the Chicago Area Project, uses such phrases as "problem-solving community," "self-regulating," "organized," and "able to exert power on behalf of its interests" to describe neighborhood competence.[23] Crenson[24] would add others: "rich in civility," "able to respond to crises," and "well governed." Suttles[25] identifies strong communities as places in which "communion" of personal thoughts and feelings can take place among others with whom one has chosen to live or work.

The issue of neighborhood competence is of enormous significance. Current discussions of extraordinarily troubled neighborhood areas, such as the Robert Taylor Homes in Chicago, raise basic issues of the competence of neighborhoods to defend themselves.[26] Stripped of working- and middle-class residents—the skills they possess, the values they represent, and the institutions they support—such neighborhoods and their residents experience massive problems. As Wilson notes:

> . . . the communities of the underclass are plagued by massive joblessness, flagrant and open lawlessness, and low-achieving schools, and therefore tend to be avoided by outsiders. Consequently, the residents of these areas, whether women and children of welfare families or aggressive street criminals, have increasingly been socially isolated from mainstream patterns of behaviors.[27]

It is widely believed that a key element of the vitality, or competence, of neighborhoods is commerce, especially small shops that appear to have a substantial stake in the civil functioning of neighborhoods. Yet little is known, beyond narrative discussion, about the contribution of commerce to neighborhoods, especially commerce's contribution to the capacity of a neighborhood to defend itself against crime, fear, and disorder.[28, 29] However, as one of the authors of this paper points out:

> Reducing crime and its disruptive effects on community ties eliminates the largest and most devastating obstacle to development in many poor neighborhoods. And where business can develop, they encourage further growth and help create a community's cohesiveness and identity.[30]

Neighborhoods and their self-help activities also have their dark side. By their very nature, cities, and neighborhoods within them, are pluralistic places in which strangers routinely meet. These characteristics, pluralism and the interaction among strangers, present latitude for civil and more injustices.

Pluralism characterizes neighborhoods in two dimensions: the relationship of different groups (often ethnic or racial) *between* neighborhoods, and the relationship of difference groups *within* neighborhoods. Interneighborhood pluralism needs little discussion—it is widely accepted as descriptive of cities. Intraneighborhood pluralism, however, has not been as readily apparent.

The ethnic, racial, and cultural homogeneity of neighborhoods has been emphasized in popular images of neighborhoods as well as in scholarly work.[31] Yet, contemporary research has demonstrated that neighborhoods, even those that appear to be homogenous on some basis, are characterized by considerable heterogeneity. A particular group might culturally *dominate* an area; yet as Suttles[32] and Merry[33] have demonstrated, neighborhoods are characterized by extensive internal diversity—individuals and groups move into and out of neighborhoods, differing groups share space, and boundaries (cognitive, as well as physical) shift over time.

Intraneighborhood and interneighborhood pluralism and the use of neighborhoods by strangers create the possibility for conflict between groups and individuals who maintain different lifestyles, define neighborhood civility in different ways, or wish to impose their standards on others—either in terms of how they behave or how they wish others to behave.

Most transactions between members of different groups or strangers occur with little difficulty. Goffman[34] demonstrates clearly that even strangers meet in patterned uncommitted interactions. That is, a traffic relationship is maintained, the purpose of which is to avoid untoward physical contact, achieve satisfactory spatial distance, avoid eye contact, and manage civilly the numerous contacts that occur as strangers negotiate cities.

Within or between neighborhoods, problems develop when individuals, groups, or residents of a neighborhood either take or give offense.[35, 36] When an offense occurs between strangers, the incident itself and the behaviors signifying offense are generally minor—part of the cost of living a cosmopolitan life. Feelings may be ruffled, demeanor turned grumpy, but all of meager consequences.

When, however, the offense is major (prostitutes haranguing pedestrian and automotive traffic) or neighbors become aggrieved too easily (neighborhood residents resenting minorities passing through their neighborhood), civility is shattered and the possibility of serious conflict erupting is created. In the case of prostitutes haranguing citizens, almost everyone in the neighborhood would agree that something should be done, if necessary, by police.

The case of minorities in neighborhoods, however, is an example of the potential tyranny of neighborhoods, indeed, the potential tyranny of democracy—the suppression of persons who for one reason or another are considered objectionable.[37] This is the dark side of intimate neighborhoods; just as neighborhoods can be places of congeniality, sociability, and safety, they can also be places of smallness, meanness, and tyranny.

THE ROLE OF POLICE IN NEIGHBORHOODS

Police have been depicted as a community's bastion against crime, disorder, and fear: the "thin blue line" fortifying a community against predators and wrongdoers.[38] This notion, if not promulgated by the current generation of police leaders, at least has not been denied by most police. In this view, police are a city's professional defense against crime and disorder; the responsibility of citizens is to report crimes quickly to police via 911 systems, provide information to police about criminal events, and to cooperate with prosecutors and courts in the adjudication of offenders.

This is a troubling and deeply mistaken metaphor for police. First, it suggests police are out there alone fighting evil misdoers. This is specious. We know that citizens, groups, and organizations are deeply involved in dealing with community problems. Second, the imagery of the thin blue line misrepresents the origins of crime and disorder. True, some predators do enter neighborhoods from outside, but a significant portion of neighborhood problems, even serious crime problems such as assault, child abuse, burglary, date rape, and others, have their origins within a neighborhood as well as from without. Third, it misrepresents the objectives of the majority of police work. The imagery suggests isolating persons who are dangerous from the good people of the community. This might be true for some serious and repeat offenders. If, however, we believe that the origins of many problems are within neighborhoods and involve disputes, disorder, and conflicts, as well as serious crime, a more proper representation of police is that of problem identifiers, dispute resolvers, and managers of relations—not merely persons authorized to arrest criminals.[39]

The metaphor of the thin blue line is deeply mistaken not just because it misrepresents police business, but because it has largely determined how police have shaped their relationship to neighborhoods and communities in the past. Moreover, it has often put them in conflict with neighborhoods.

Police are starting to modify their positions, however, and in doing so have begun to change the nature of their relationship to communities.[40] We believe that the following principles are now shaping the relationship between police and neighborhoods in many cities and should shape the position of police in most communities.

1. Community self-defense against crime and disorder is primarily a matter of private social control supported, but never supplanted, by public police.
2. Because neighborhoods vary in the nature of their problems and in their capacity for self-help (their ecology of self-defense), police tactics must be tailored to specific neighborhoods.
3. Tailoring tactics to neighborhoods will require decentralization of police authority and tactical decision making to lower levels of the organization and the empowerment of sergeants and patrol officers to make decisions about the types of problems with which they will deal and the tactics they will employ to deal with them.
4. Precinct and beat configurations must be changed to reflect community and neighborhood form.
5. In the most troubled neighborhoods, especially those now being ravaged by the problems associated with drugs, police must at least seek authority from residents to act on their behalf. In neighborhoods that are most bereft of self-help capacities, in inner-city underclass areas, and in neighborhoods most plagued by lawlessness, it is tempting for police to operate independently and without consultations. The problems are so acute and resources so meager that consultations may appear inefficient and needlessly time-consuming. This serves neither police nor residents well. Deprived of community authorization, police are vulnerable to charges of both neglect and abuse. Moreover, the willingness of police to fill in the gap and "do it themselves" deprives citizens of the very kinds of experiences that American political philosophy suggests will lead them to "acquire a taste for order" and develop their capacities as citizens.
6. If it is believed that the function of police is to support and increase the inherent strength and self-governing capacities of neighborhoods that enable them to defend themselves against crime and disorder, it follows that a priority of police in bereft neighborhoods is not only to gain authorization for police action but also to help develop capacities for community self-defense. Given the desperate circumstances of some inner-city neighborhoods, this will be an extremely difficult task. It will, at times, be extraordinarily risky for citizens to attempt to defend their neighborhoods. The risk can be justified only if police commit them-

selves to pervasive presence for long durations of time. Such presence must always support and encourage self-help.
7. In neighborhoods that are capable of self-help and governance, police activities should be designed and implemented for the purpose of strengthening neighborhoods. Police, like other agencies of government, should not do for citizens what citizens can do for themselves. There are reasons to believe that when government does supplant self-help, the capacity of citizens for self-help diminishes.
8. Because different neighborhoods have different interests, interests that at times conflict with each other, police will have to manage interneighborhood, as well as intraneighborhood, relations. Neighborhoods require free commerce and penetration by strangers and other groups if they are to thrive.
9. Police must understand that just as their task is to support the self-help capacities of neighborhoods when those capacities are used for appropriate ends, they must thwart self-help capacities of neighborhoods when they turn petty, mean, and tyrannical. Police are well-equipped for this. During the past two decades, "constitutional policing," at first resisted by many police but later embraced and incorporated by the great chiefs and police leaders of the era, has empowered police to withstand parochial pressure.[41] This does not mean that police will not have to be vigilant in resisting inappropriate pressure; it means that police executives have moved to instill the values and policies that will help them maintain constitutional practice. Justice is as important as security in policing.

CONCLUSION

Police are now adapting to changes taking place in American society. One of those changes is the reversal in the trend to centralization in government and the reemergence of neighborhoods as a source of governance. This change raises a hot issue for police. Are they agents or servants of neighborhoods?

While we have emphasized restructuring police and increasing their accountability to neighborhoods, we do not see them as servants of neighborhoods. Police protect other values, as well as neighborhood values. What are those values? [There are] at least three.

First, public police must be distributed fairly across cities on the basis of neighborhood need, not neighborhood political clout.

Second, police must be able to maintain organizational integrity. Police departments must have the right to develop and maintain their own personnel, administrative, and technological capacities without political interference.

Finally, they must defend minority interests and civil rights against the more parochial interests of some neighborhoods.

Neighborhoods need police for assistance in the control of crime, fear, and disorder. Some neighborhoods need police only rarely; in other neighborhoods pervasive police presence is required to assure the simplest of rights—shopping, keeping one's property, and even keeping one's life or physical well-being. Regardless of the severity of neighborhood problems or the competence of neighborhoods in dealing with them, the police monopoly over legitimate use of force requires that police assist neighborhoods when force might be required to settle neighborhood problems.

To respond appropriately, police must view their role in neighborhoods as a means of reestablishing the neighboring relationship and strengthening the institutions that make a community competent and able to deal with its problems. Zachary Tumin has summarized the role of a police officer in carrying through such a function:

> The role of the professional police officer as a professional is therefore to know the status of his local institutions; to understand how, when, and why they work; to understand their strengths and their vulnerabilities; to know their members or users; that is, to know the people whose relationships comprise the institutions, and why they participate or don't.[42]

Police are now attempting to create a world in which they are more responsive to neighborhoods and communities. Their task is not just to serve; it is also to lead by helping to foster wider tolerance of strangers, minorities, and differing definitions of morality. How will this be accomplished? Many tactics will be used. But, at a minimum, it will require setting firm control over their own conduct and embodying a civil approach.

NOTES

1. Ulf Hannerz, *Exploring the City* (New York: Columbia University Press, 1980).
2. Gerald D. Suttles, *The Social Construction of Communities* (Chicago: University of Chicago Press, 1972), p. 22.
3. In a Boston neighborhood observed by one of this paper's authors, George Kelling, residents who organized a community anti-crime effort that included both regular meetings and citizen patrol invited a homeless woman who lived in a corner park to a special meeting on rape prevention. She not only attended the meeting, she recounted her own rape. Subsequent citizen patrols always checked the park to ensure her safety. In fact, it could be argued that there are times in some areas of cities when the homeless comprise the residency of the neighborhood—downtown areas, for example, which other citizens abandon during the evenings for their own residential neighborhoods.
4. See, for example, Stephanie W. Greenberg, William M. Rohe, and Jay R. Williams, *Informal Citizen Action and Crime Prevention at the Neighborhood Level: Synthesis and Assessment of the Research* (Research Triangle Park, N.C: Research Triangle Institute, March 1984); and Hannerz, *Exploring the City.*

5. Nathan Glazer, *The Limits of Social Policy* (Cambridge, Mass.: Harvard University Press, 1988), p. 120.

6. Andrew J. Polsky, "Welfare Policy: Why the Past Has No Future," *Democracy* 3, no. 1 (winter 1983): 21–33.

7. Jane Jacobs, *The Death and Life of Great American Cities* (New York: Random House, 1961); and Oscar Newman, *Defensible Space: Crime Prevention through Urban Design* (New York: Macmillan, 1972).

8. Glenn Yago, "Sick Transit," *Democracy* 3, no. 1 (winter 1983): 43–55.

9. Marcus Felson, "Routine Activities and Crime Prevention in the Developing Metropolis," *Criminology* 25, no. 4 (1987).

10. Research on neighborhood groups recounted in this paper was conducted during 1982 and 1983 and reported in George L. Kelling, "Neighborhoods and Police," Occasional Paper, Program in Criminal Justice Policy and Management, John F. Kennedy School of Government, Harvard University, Cambridge, Mass., August 1985.

11. This neighborhood was laced with many nightclubs and bars. Police were employed off-duty as security personnel. When conflicts arose between establishment owners and residents, over the noise at bar-closing time, residents believed that public police employed off-duty by owners took the side of owners against residents.

12. Glazer, *Limits of Social Policy,* p. 121.

13. *Ibid.,* p. 122.

14. An interesting account of a neighborhood using physical force was recounted in the *New York Times,* October 8, 1988. Two citizens in a Detroit neighborhood burned down a building alleged to be used by drug dealers, admitted it, and blamed their need to do it on the failure of city and police officials to heed their requests for assistance. Tried, the two were found innocent by their peers. The jury foreman was quoted: "I imagine the verdict does [send] out a message in two directions—to the Mayor and the Chief of Police that more has to be done about crack houses." Another juror said he would have done the same thing, but then added: "No. I would have been more violent." The Wayne County Prosecutor said after the verdict: "Vigilantism simply will not be tolerated."

15. Egon Bittner, *The Function of Police in Modern Society* (Washington, D.C.: U.S. Govt. Printing Office, 1970).

16. See, for example, Leon Radzinowicz, *A History of English Criminal Law,* vol. 2, *The Enforcement of the Law* (London, Stevens & Sons, 1956).

17. Matthew B. Crenson, *Neighborhood Politics* (Cambridge, Mass.: Harvard University, 1982), p. 19.

18. See, for example, James K. Stewart, "The Urban Strangler: How Crime Causes Poverty in the Inner City," *Policy Review* 37 (summer 1986), for examples of corporations that have done just the opposite and contributed to community life through the forms that their security efforts took.

19. See, for example, Lawrence E. Cohen and Marcus Felson, "Social Change and Crime Rate Trends: A Routine Activity Approach," *American Sociological Review* 44 (1979): 588–608.

20. Glazer, *Limits of Social Policy,* p. 123.

21. Kelling, "Neighborhoods and Police."

22. Suttles, *Social Construction of Communities,* p. 36.

23. Peter Hunt, "Community Development—Should It be Included as Part of the Police Mission?", note drafted for Executive Session on Community Policing, Program in Criminal Justice Police and Management, John F. Kennedy School of Government, Harvard University, Cambridge, Mass., 1987.

24. Crenson, *Neighborhood Politics,* p. 18.

25. Suttles, *Social Construction of Communities,* p. 265.

26. See, for example, Gerald D. Suttles, *The Social Order of the Slum* (Chicago: University of Chicago Press, 1968); William Julius Wilson, *The Truly Disadvantaged: The Inner City, the Underclass, and Public Policy* (Chicago: University of Chicago Press, 1987).

27. W. J. Wilson, *Truly Disadvantaged,* p. 58.

28. See, for example, Jane Jacobs, *Death and Life of . . . Cities,* for a discussion of the importance of local commerce in the maintenance of neighborhood safety.

29. Ulf Hannerz notes both the importance and lack of research about the role of commerce in neighborhoods. "One also finds neighborhoods more or less wholly recruited on a work basis, such as shopping streets with shopkeepers and their employees as daytime neighbors. Of this kind of neighboring there is hardly any ethnography." *Exploring the City,* p. 264.

30. Stewart, "Urban Strangler," p. 6.

31. See, for example, Robert E. Park, Ernest W. Burgess, and Robert D. McKenzie, *The City,* 4th ed. (Chicago: University of Chicago Press, 1967).

32. Suttles, *Social Construction of Communities,* p. 25.

33. Sally Engle Merry, *Urban Danger: Life in a Neighborhood of Strangers* (Philadelphia: Temple University Press, 1981), pp. 93–124.

34. Erving Goffman, *Relations in Public* (New York: Basic Books, 1971).

35. This is based on Mark H. Moore's definition of civility: "Neither to give nor take offense easily." Personal conversation.

36. Marcus Felson suggests that the problem of dealing with strangers is becoming even more complicated in contemporary American cities, characterized as they are by large numbers of highly mobile untended youths (the source of the majority of the problems of crime, disorder, and fear) and untended neighborhoods (two-career marriages). See n. 9, "Routine Activities and Crime Prevention in the Developing Metropolis."

37. This fear was expressed early in America's history by Alexis de Tocqueville, *Democracy in America,* vol. 1 [1833] (New York: Vintage Books, 1954).

38. See, for example, Anthony V. Bouza, "Police Unions: Paper Tigers or Roaring Lions?" in William A. Geller, ed., *Police Leadership in America: Crisis and Opportunity* (New York, Praeger, 1985).

39. For a discussion of the erosion of this belief, see George L. Kelling, "Police and Community: The Quiet Revolution," *Perspectives on Policing,* no. 1 (National Institute of Justice and Harvard University, Washington D.C., February 1988).

40. For a discussion of the reason behind this change, see Kelling, "Police and Communities: The Quiet Revolution."

41. James K. Stewart, one of this paper's authors, has pointed out that the period 1960 to 1980 is likely to be remembered as the "constitutional era"—the era when chiefs of police Patrick V. Murphy, Clarence Kelley, Robert Igleburger, and many others embraced, rather than resisted, many of the major constitutional and legal decisions that affected police practices (*Miranda,* the exclusionary rule, etc.).

42. Zachary Tumin, "Managing Relations with the Community," Working Paper #86-05-06, Program in Criminal Justice Policy and Management, John F. Kennedy School of Government, Harvard University, Cambridge, Mass., November 1986, final page.

ARTICLE 18

COMMUNITY POLICING AND THE POLICE OFFICER

Edwin Meese III

Alvin Toffler, the author of *Future Shock,* and Heidi Toffler have stated that ". . . almost all the major systems on which our society depends . . . are in simultaneous crisis" and the "failure to prepare in advance for the turbulent [nineties] could produce a grave breakdown in public security."[1] For almost a decade, many farsighted law enforcement executives and public safety scholars have been responding to this challenge in what has been described as "a quiet revolution" that is reshaping American policing.[2]

Under a variety of names—strategic policing, problem-solving policing, neighborhood-oriented policing, community policing, and others-police agencies are developing new concepts to better satisfy the demands and needs of the citizens they serve. In the course of the self-examination and creative thinking that are taking place, fundamental questions have been raised about the basic purpose and responsibilities of the police, the capabilities they possess, the types of contributions they can make to society, the optimum methods of their organization and deployment, and the relationship that they have with the communities that employ them. In contrast to a philosophy of "business as usual," police executives sense the need to "redeploy the money and authority entrusted to them in hopes that their organizations will produce greater value for society."[3]

Much has been written about the potential effects of these innovative changes in policing on community involvement, city government, and the police department itself.[4] This paper examines the impact of creative

Reprinted from Edwin Meese III, "Community Policing and the Police Officer," *Perspectives on Policing,* no. 15 (Washington, D.C.: National Institute of Justice, U.S. Department of Justice and the Program in Criminal Justice Policy and Management, John F. Kennedy School of Government, Harvard University, January 1993).

forms of policing on the ultimate key to their success—the individual police officer.

As the emphasis and methods of policing change, the position of the police officer in the organization changes also. Instead of reacting to specific situations, limited by rigid guidelines and regulations, the officer becomes a thinking professional, utilizing imagination and creativity to identify and solve problems. Instead of being locked in an organizational straitjacket, the police officer is encouraged to develop cooperative relationships in the community, guided by values and purposes, rather than constrained by rules and excessive supervision. To make this possible, much thought must be given to designing the structure of police organizations and to recruiting, selecting, training, and supporting officers in the field. Changes must be made in all of these areas to create a new police professionalism.

NEW STRATEGIES REQUIRE NEW ROLES

This new philosophy of police work has been called "community policing," a term intended here to include problem-solving techniques, strategic utilization of resources, and increasingly sophisticated investigative capabilities. But these attributes must be understood in the context of a different view of the status and role of community institutions in guiding and assisting police operations. As Moore and Trojanowicz note:

> "In community policing, community institutions such as families, schools, neighborhood associations, and merchant groups are seen as key partners to the police in the creation of safe, secure communities. The success of the police depends not only on the development of their own skills and capabilities, but also on the creation of competent communities. Community policing acknowledges that police cannot succeed in achieving their basic goals without both the operational assistance and political support of the community. Conversely, the community cannot succeed in constructing decent, open, and orderly communities without a professional and responsive police force."[5]

The police, then, must be more than a reactive force that responds to crimes already committed. They must develop into a proactive entity that deals with a broad variety of conditions that tend to disrupt the community peace or adversely affect the quality of life.

This description of the police task and the citizen relationships that are required to fulfill it is different from the popular concept of a crime-fighter in blue, whose position is reminiscent of the pistol-toting marshal of the Old West. Indeed, the success of new policing strategies depends on the ability of a police agency to recruit, develop, and field a group of officers who not only understand their role as highly visible representatives of governmental authority, but also recognize that their responsibility for community service and peacekeeping is of equal importance to law enforcement and crime suppression. These requirements give new meaning to the notion of a professional police officer in the modern era.

The conflicts that some perceive in the various roles of peacekeeping, community service, and crime fighting are not a new problem. A report to the National Commission on the Causes and Prevention of Violence, published in 1970, states, "Perhaps the most important source of police frustration . . . is the conflicting roles and demands involved in the order-maintenance, community service, and crime-fighting responsibilities of the police."[6] Too often officers feel that their efforts are not appreciated or deemed important by either their supervisors or the public.[7] One police executive has even suggested that the police function should be divided into two separate agencies under one department: one agency for law enforcement, the other for community service.[8]

A more sophisticated view of the police function, which is inherent in the concept of community policing, is that community service, peacekeeping, and crime fighting are complementary, not conflicting, activities. Historically, the "patrolman on the beat," maintaining order and communicating with the citizenry, was carrying out a major police priority.[9] In addition, the information obtained though expanded direct contact with citizens, generally on a routine and informal basis, helps to solve crimes and apprehend offenders.[10]

As one police department notes, neighborhood disorder and crime are viewed more and more as slightly different aspects of the same problem. When police officers deal with the symbols of urban decay—abandoned buildings, accumulated rubbish, panhandlers roaming the streets—they mitigate the conditions under which crime and disorder flourish. The result is lessened fear of crime and greater satisfaction with the police among members of the community.[11] The attention of the police to such matters, combined with increased communication between officers and the public, can stimulate community pride and provide the basis for police-citizen cooperation in building safer neighborhoods and an improved quality of life.

A NEW PROFESSIONALISM

The changed strategy of policing alters in important ways the content of the police officer's job. Police responsibilities expand beyond attempting to control criminal activity—to preventing crime, promoting order, resolving disputes, and providing emergency assistance in social crises. The officer's methods and resources extend beyond arrests and citations. They now include mediation and negotiation, referrals to other municipal agencies, and community mobilization. As police activity focuses on the neighborhood, the demands on the basic police officer increase, as do the scope of responsibility and the skills required.

More fundamental than the change in skills, however, is the change in the basic position of the police officer. Instead of primarily reacting to incidents, the officer analyzes, plans, and takes the initiative. Instead of constantly looking up the bureaucratic chain of command for guidance and assistance, the community police officer looks out toward the problems to be solved, and toward the community's interests in helping to solve them. In community policing, the de facto discretion that always existed (and that often was used well by police officers) is recognized and developed, rather than limited or discouraged.

In both the complexity of the skills and the initiative required of the officers lies a new version of police professionalism. James Q. Wilson has stated that the characteristics of a professional include the exercise of "wide discretion alone and with respect to matters of the greater importance" and that this is based on a status "conferred by an organized profession" that "certifies that the member has acquired by education certain information and by apprenticeship certain arts and skills that render him competent" to "handle emergency situations, to be privy to 'guilty information' and to make decisions involving questions of life and death or honor and dishonor." He goes on to say that a professional "is willing to subject himself to the code of ethics and sense of duty of his colleagues."[12]

Professionalism has been the goal of modern policing for several decades and is indeed a worthy objective. Police have pursued it by trying to develop their technical skills through discipline, training, and apprenticeship,[13] and by the use of increasingly sophisticated methods and equipment. While that is an important part of professionalism, it is only a part.

Another aspect of professionalism, which requires extensive development if community policing is to be successful, focuses on the values that the profession must adopt, the position of the officer in the organization and the community, and the manner in which the police are held accountable for their professional performance. It is a matter of both self-image and community perception. The commitment to constitutional and legal values, to mutual respect, and to service to the community, combined with self-reliance and self-motivation, are the hallmarks of the new police professional.

THE MILITARY MODEL AND PROFESSIONALISM

Ironically, one of the principal factors preventing the development of a strong sense of professionalism among police officers—not only in their own eyes, but in the eyes of the public—may be the military form of organization that the police have adopted from their earliest days.[14] The military system, with its rigid organizational structure and authoritarian management style, increasingly has been called into question as a proper model for modern policing.[15]

In some respects, the military form has served the police well, at least for traditional policing. It has created a structure of discipline within which ordinary people, hired for an exacting job, can be trained, equipped, and motivated to function effectively. It has provided a means of controlling the behavior of "working-level" employees. It has been useful for coordinating large numbers of officers in operations such as crowd control, riot suppression, and investigative searches. And it has enhanced the stature of police as a whole by presenting an attractive image of discipline, skill, and service.

Yet, it has not often been acknowledged that the military model, as it traditionally has been applied by police organizations, inadvertently downgrades the position of the primary figure in police service: the individual officer. Too often the basic police officer is viewed as comparable to a private in the army, the lowest ranking military person, who has virtually no individual authority. Such a perception is understandable when several police officers report to a sergeant who, in turn, reports to a lieutenant, and so on up the chain of command. Sometimes, police officers are described as constituting a "squad," again a reference to those holding the lowest military rank. In some departments, the rank of corporal further reinforces the enlisted person versus commissioned officer stereotype. It is little wonder, then, that those holding the rank of police officer often are regarded as something less than professionals and that they are denied individual authority, the presumption of expertise, and the discretion that normally would accompany professional status.

Nevertheless, there are ways in which certain constructive aspects of the military style could be retained, while still affording the basic police officer the professional standing that modern policing strategies require. Rather than being considered as the equivalent of an army private, the police officer should be given the distinction of an aviator in the military services. Aircraft pilots initially are appointed as lieutenants in the Air Force or ensigns in the Navy,[16] not because of the number of personnel reporting to them (which is usually small or nonexistent), but because of the great responsibility entrusted to them when they are given charge of an expensive and potentially dangerous aircraft. Just as military pilots must exercise considerable judgment on their own and accept that their individual actions may have grave consequences, so police officers on the street should be considered the equivalent of commissioned officers, with concomitant respect, authority, and discretion.

This change in the perceptions of a police officer—on his or her own part and on the part of police superiors and the public—may be a difficult task in most places, but it is crucial to properly defining the individual officer's role in community policing. Several federal law enforcement agencies already have moved away from the military model in their organization and rank structure. The Federal Bureau of Investigation and the U.S. Secret Service classify their basic officers as special agents, a term used for all nonsupervisory positions from entry level through veteran member. All required to be college graduates, special agents are regarded as, and expected to perform as, professionals.

REDUCING HIERARCHY AND ENRICHING SKILLS

Organizations of professionals are distinguished by extensive and continuing professional training, by shared understanding of and commitment to the values of the profession, by extensive lateral communication, and—perhaps most important—by the absence of elaborate and complex hierarchies. Organizational structures are relatively flat, but often deep and differentiated in types and levels of skills. How to create such arrangements for policing has been the subject of attention for many years. In 1967, for example, the President's Commission on Law Enforcement and Administration of Justice recommended changes in personnel practices that would improve the quality and professionalism of the police service.

One such proposal, designed to "attract better personnel, to utilize them more effectively in controlling crime, and to gain greater understanding of community problems," suggested that police candidates enter departments at three levels of qualifications, competence, responsibility, and pay: community service officer, police officer, and police agent. The community service officer would be essentially an apprentice working on the street under close supervision, unarmed and without full law enforcement authority. The police officer would carry out regular police functions, such as response to calls for service, routine patrol, traffic enforcement, and accident investigation. The police agent would handle the basic police tasks that are the most complicated, sensitive, and demanding. Under this scheme, an individual could enter the police department at any one of the three levels, depending upon prior education and experience, and could advance through the various levels and attain the position of police agent without having to compete for the limited number of supervisory positions available in a traditional hierarchy.[17] Thus, an officer who was good at street policing or investigation could continue performing those types of duties throughout his or her career without having to become an administrator.

Although various aspects of the Commission's recommendations were tried by a number of departments throughout the nation, the proposal never caught on, and very few police agencies utilize either the concept or the nomenclature today. One defect of the proposal, particularly in the context of the community policing philosophy, is the creation of a structure that relegates community service to the lowest level of the pyramid.

One way to eliminate the view of the police officer as a nonprofessional army private is to revise the police rank system, utilizing nonmilitary titles for some or all personnel grades. Such a revolutionary change may be difficult to achieve, since law enforcement agencies typically are resistant to major changes and may be more comfortable with the rank nomenclature that traditionally has been used.[18] Nevertheless, such a change in titles could be used skillfully by enterprising departments as part of their implementation of new policing strategies.

A more limited change in the grade structure would be to substitute another title for the rank of sergeant, to eliminate the noncommissioned officer connotation. Terms such as supervising police officer, master police officer, or inspector (a title historically used in many parts of the country to depict a rank just below lieutenant[19]) could be used for the first level of supervision. This would retain the existing management position while encouraging the view of the basic police officer as professional.

One major problem of current rank systems is that promotional opportunities and the accompanying financial reward and rise in professional stature are relatively few. They could become even fewer if police organizational structures are simplified as suggested below. It is desirable, therefore, to expand the array of nonsupervisory positions to make a graduated series of opportunities available to most career police officers. The Los Angeles Police Department has done this by creating four grades of police officer and three grades of detective. An officer in that department can earn more than $50,000 per year without having to attain an administrative position.[20] A system that provides sufficient incentives for the successful police officer throughout a career of basic police work properly recognizes the professional status of the person who is on the street and in the neighborhood, working directly with the public.

ORGANIZING FOR EMPOWERMENT

Changing titles and rank structure, however, is not enough to elevate the professional standing of the basic police officer. Police organizational structures should be revised to decrease the number of levels of authority, particularly at the bottom of the hierarchy. Community policing envisions the empowerment of officers to take independent action to solve problems, work with community leaders, and improve the social environment of the neighborhoods they serve. Such a vision, however, is a far cry from the experience of most officers today. The average police officer spends an eight- or ten-hour tour of duty sitting in a police car, responding to calls when directed by a dispatcher, and complying with the rigid structure of detailed rules and regulations that will keep the officer from being criticized or penalized by superiors.

As Herman Goldstein notes:

> "The dominant form of policing today continues to view police officers as automatons. Despite an awareness that they exercise broad discretion, they are held to strict account in their daily work—for what they do and how they do it . . . Especially in procedural matters, they are required to adhere to detailed regulations. In large police agencies, rank-and-file police officers are often treated impersonally and kept in the dark regarding policy matters. Officers quickly learn, under these conditions, that the rewards go to those who conform to expectations—that nonthinking compliance is valued."[21]

These rigid prescriptions for police conduct and limitations on creativity are caused by the desire of both supervisory and command officers to avoid wrongdoing by police officers and to ensure that the activities of subordinates will not result in criticism of or embarrassment to their superiors. Obviously, the successful implementation of community policing requires a major change in attitudes and methods of supervision by managers. The new philosophy requires that officers perform their responsibilities on the basis of shared values and personal commitment to professionalism, rather than by constant supervision and limitations of their authority.

As more discretion and decision making authority are shifted to individual officers, many police executives recognize that the rigid, hierarchical model of organization is obsolete. New structural arrangements,
emphasizing streamlined administration and fewer layers of management, are being employed. This has facilitated rapid decision making,
more relevant policy guidance, and overall improvement in communications among all ranks.

Community policing has a variety of organizational styles in the
United States, Canada, and the United Kingdom. They range from home-
beat officers in outlying areas of London, to basic car units in Los Angeles, to crime control teams composed of both patrol officers and detectives, to officers patrolling in pairs on fixed neighborhood beats, as well
as numerous other structural combinations. An important ingredient of
all organizational patterns, however, is the decentralization of authority
to the lowest operational level—to the officers in direct contact with citizens and the community. No longer is the individual police officer
merely a report taker who must pass along information about a problem
to superiors, who then make the decisions and take the actions for solving the problem. Instead, the patrol officer becomes a decision maker,
solving the problem if possible or at least participating in decisions
about the ultimate response.

In England, for example, the chief superintendent commanding a division in London (an organizational element roughly equivalent to a
precinct in a U.S. police department) divided the area of his command
into four quarters. He then placed an inspector (the equivalent of a U.S.
police lieutenant) in charge of each quadrant. He gave that middle management officer full authority to act as a "mini-chief" in implementing
community policing. Specifically, the local inspector was given great
flexibility in deploying the sergeants and constables assigned to that area
in order to meet the particular needs of the community.[22]

The purpose of changes in the management structure is to create a
supportive organizational environment for community policing and to
revise the relationship between the police leaders and rank-and-file officers. One caveat should be mentioned: new organizational changes imposed by police executives often look good on paper, but the test must
be whether they do in fact improve communication and expedite action.
For this reason, it is important that feedback be obtained from line officers at each stage of implementation, to determine whether the new
structure is providing the intended benefits. Tables of organization and
channels of communication should be regarded as provisional, not im-
mutable, until they have been proved in practice. Even then, changes in
conditions may require further changes in organizational arrangements.

Whatever the organizational model, it must facilitate maximum participation by the line officer who is in direct contact with citizens of the
community. As Herman Goldstein has written:

> "[by] . . . making it legitimate for rank-and-file officers to think and be
> creative in their daily work . . . the potential benefits are of two kinds. The
> most important is the improvement that this could produce in the quality of

responses that the police make to oft-recurring problems. In addition, such a change would be directly responsive to some critical needs in the police organization—the need to treat rank-and-file police officers as mature men and women; to demonstrate more trust and confidence in them; to give them more responsibility and a stake in the outcome of their efforts; and to give them a greater sense of fulfillment and job satisfaction."[23]

SELECTING AND DEVELOPING THE NEW PROFESSIONAL

Changes in titles and organization can provide the conditions for improved professionalism, but only human beings can fulfill the potential of the new strategies for police work. Community policing is said to rest "on the belief that no technology can surpass what creative human beings can achieve together." Police departments must deploy the most innovative, self-disciplined, and self-motivated officers directly into the community as outreach specialists and community problem solvers.[24] Furthermore, commanders and supervisors will be supportive of the new philosophy and the accompanying modifications of managerial style only if, in the long run, the people under their supervision justify the increased freedom and greater discretion that are inherent in successful community policing. It must be remembered that the individuals who work most directly with the public and who are perceived as the primary representatives of the police department are patrol officers who occupy the lower ranks in the police agency and who will probably serve out their careers in those positions.[25]

Considerable attention must be given, therefore, to the type of individual who is encouraged to join a police department that emphasizes community policing. Qualities that traditionally have been associated with the higher ranks, such as leadership, communication skills, and the ability to persuade and motivate others, must now be required of all officers. Recruiters must look for self-starters who possess initiative and imagination, rather than "plodders" who will unquestioningly follow directions and will be comfortable merely by complying with explicit regulations. Indeed, as one of America's foremost law enforcement leaders has stated, "the officer in a modern department today must possess many skills, including those of information processor, community organizer, crime analyst, counselor, street corner politician, arresting officer, school liaison, and community leader."[26]

IS COLLEGE NECESSARY?

An immediate question arises about the selection of the "new" police officer: should a college education be required? This has been a subject of great debate over the years, with advocates on both sides of the question. An argument for college-educated officers is that the department would be composed of people from the general population "who have certain qualities (motivation, self-discipline, general intelligence) that are probably quite useful in a police career and, second, it inculcates certain characteristics (civility, urbanity, self-control) that might be especially desired in an officer."[27]

On the other hand, it also has been argued that college-educated people may not understand the problems and attitudes of lower and working-class persons with whom police officers must deal; that a police career often is unattractive for the college graduate because it is "routine, sometimes dull, frequently unpleasant, and occasionally dangerous"; and that advanced education may produce a higher level of cynicism than would be present among those with less schooling.[28]

Another concern is that the requirement of a college degree might decrease the number of minority citizens available for recruitment into police work. This is a matter of great concern to many city governments that are seeking to have the police department reflect the demographic composition of the citizenry.

Most recent studies and commentators, however, have concluded that a college education is necessary, or at least desirable, in contemporary policing. One factor has been a change in society itself. As more of the general public has attended higher education institutions, and as the educational level of the community at large has increased, it is necessary that the educational level of the police also be raised.[29] In addition, a college-educated police force makes a difference in the agency itself. As Patrick Murphy has stated:

> "In general, a police department that has had a four-year college degree as an entry requirement for ten years or more can be quite a different organization from one requiring only a high school diploma. More responsibility can be placed on the officers, and a more collegial style of management can be utilized. The college-educated force sets higher professional standards and goals, which in turn, command public respect and help shape public opinion. Finally, a college-educated police force has the potential to proactively, rather than just reactively, address the crime and drug problems that plague society today."[30]

It is notable that the educational level of police officers has risen considerably during the past 20 years. In 1967, the average educational level for police was 12.4 years, just beyond a high school diploma. The most recent survey indicated that the current average educational level among law enforcement officers was 13.6 years, more than halfway through the second year of college. The study found that 65.2 percent of officers in the responding agencies had one or more years of college, 22.6 percent had earned at least a baccalaureate degree, and 3.7 percent had a graduate degree.[31]

There are various approaches to achieving a college-educated police department, several of which address the matter of attracting minority applicants. Many police executives do not believe that lack of a college degree should absolutely disqualify an individual from entering a department, if the person is willing to seek higher education during his or her career. Many departments help the individual attend college, some by arranging work schedules to permit class attendance, others by providing financial support. One department, for instance, pays half the college tuition of any officer working toward a bachelors' degree. Another pays all the costs of books and tuition for its officers. Some departments require one or two years of college as an entry requirement, while many provide premium pay for those who have attained a bachelor's or master's degree.[32]

Another approach that has been suggested is to use federal funds already available:

> The U.S. Department of Education now distributes a large amount of public funds in grants and loans for higher education, most of which require no obligation of public service. A portion of these grants and loans should be allocated to young men and women willing to enter the police service, or to those already serving in police departments, who seek higher education. Loan funds could be disbursed with the understanding that repayment would be forgiven if the individual serves two years in the police service for each year of college education. Grants and loans should also be available for veteran officers to pursue advanced degrees, with a requirement of three additional years of service for each year of graduate education.[33]

A variation of this idea is the creation of a Police Corps, which already has been proposed through legislation introduced in Congress. Like the military Reserve Officer Training Corps, the Police Corps would provide educational funding for college students, provided they serve a period of several years in a police agency after graduation. Also, these types of programs that provide higher education benefits for both preservice and inservice police officers could increase the opportunities for minority citizens to attend college and thus expand the pool of qualified applicants for police service.

While the specific selection criteria, types of individuals recruited, and educational background required may vary from department to department, it is clear that "if the new mode of policing is to realize its full potential in crime control and community service, police departments must attract highly educated persons with broad life experience and an expanded perspective on their position of public service."[34]

EXPANDED TRAINING PROGRAMS

If the concept of community policing is to be the guiding strategy for a police department, it must be reflected not only in recruiting, but throughout the training program as well. This includes both the basic training for new recruits, who presumably have been selected for their potential capabilities to carry out community policing, as well as veterans of the department who essentially have to be retrained in the new philosophy and practices. The revisions that must be made in the curriculum of traditional police academies reflect the range of changes that must be made in the department as a whole. It usually will involve expanding the entire program, lengthening the number of weeks of recruit training, and adding additional periods of inservice training for veteran officers.

Most important is the approach or "tone" inherent in the revised training. Community policing cannot be imposed from "on high," but must become a part of the culture of the department, and thus be reflected in significant attitude changes. As one law enforcement agency phrased it, such attitude changes cannot be mandated through policy, but must come about "through a long series of environmental changes that foster behavior modification which consequently alters attitudes."[35] Officers must understand that community policing helps them to be more effective, that it gives them a greater participation in fashioning their own work environment, and that they, as well as the community, will benefit from the new policing strategy.

The content of training programs must provide recruits with an ample understanding of police tasks. It should provide information on the history of law enforcement, the role of police in modern society, and the need for discretion in law enforcement. Rather than preparing officers to perform police work mechanically, is should help them to understand their communities, the police role, and even the imperfections of the criminal justice system.[36] In addition, the following specific skills—which have not necessarily been a part of traditional police training curriculums—must be taught:

1. Communication skills: the ability to talk effectively with all types of citizens, from community leaders to ordinary residents, as well as the ability to listen and learn effectively.
2. Public speaking: the ability to articulate ideas and motivate others, as well as the art of leading meetings in ways to draw out the thoughts and ideas of the participants.
3. Problem-solving techniques: how to identify and analyze problems, as well as how to develop effective responses and solutions.
4. Conflict resolution and negotiating: how to help citizens resolve disputes within the community, rather than resorting to violence or "self-help" or engaging formal legal mechanisms.

In addition, two bases of knowledge about the community should be taught:

1. Social, economic, and demographic conditions of the community.
2. Supporting agencies in the community: the existence of city departments, social agencies, and other resources that can be used for referral of citizens and support for officers in their work.

Two other specialized skills should be included in the training curriculum. One is the ability to type, since more and more police work will involve the use of computer keyboards, whether on mobile digital terminals in police cars or laptop computers. Being able to type quickly and accurately will save a great deal of time during an officer's career. The other specialized skill, which would be adapted to particular community conditions, is language capability. The ability of an officer to converse, or at least understand, the languages spoken in his or her patrol area is not only a valuable attribute but may be necessary for the officer's safety.

Field training, under the specific leadership of qualified field training officers (FTOs), has become a regular part of most recruit training programs. A variation of the traditional training sequence, in which recruits complete the academy phase and then go on the street for training under the FTOs, might better relate the two types of training, however. For example, the initial training of the recruits should be in the academy, where they would learn the history and role of policing, as well as specific skills and techniques, such as use of firearms, laws of arrest, police procedures, defensive combat, and others. Then officers might go on the street for field training for several weeks, where they would observe conditions in the community. They could then return to the academy for more advanced training in communication skills, community conditions, techniques of community policing, and other subjects related to their work as members of a community policing team. The street experience between the phases of academy training will make them more knowledgeable about the community they will serve and thus more receptive to learning the police role in dealing with neighborhood problems.

Training in the concepts of community policing is as important for those already in police service as it is for recruits. The way in which new ideas are presented is critical, since the revised orientation will require many officers to change the manner in which they perform their duties. Again, the emphasis on benefit to the officer and increased participation in decisonmaking should be stressed. The formal training in community policing, particularly in the subjects described above, should be continually reinforced by informal discussions at all levels of command. Two-way communication and the opportunity for effective dialog is a vital part of a truly professional organization.

QUALITY SUPERVISION

The most careful recruiting and selection, accompanied by an enlightened and motivating training program, nevertheless can be nullified by poor supervision on the street. If the new officers find that the values they were taught in the police academy are not respected by their superiors under actual working conditions, or that their own participation is reduced to mindlessly obeying orders and regulations, the idealism and initiative fostered during the training period will be neutralized, if not destroyed. The climate of the officer's working environment is established to a great extent by the immediate supervisor. As Goldstein has stated, "However strongly the head of an agency may elicit a different style of policing, the quality of an officer's daily life is heavily dependent on how well the officer satisfied the expectations and demands of his or her immediate supervisor."[37]

Changing the supervisory style to reflect the values and techniques of community policing is therefore of critical importance. Supervisors must demonstrate that the objectives and expectations developed in the police academy are carried out in practice. The emphasis on relating to the community, on problem solving, and on the use of creativity and imagination must be fostered by the daily contacts that an officer has with the supervisor. Leaders on the street must learn to develop the talents and capabilities of each of their subordinates to the maximum, and must provide guidance rather than simply issuing orders. Since the individual officer has more discretion and is being urged to utilize his or her own skills and judgment to a greater extent, the supervisor's function as a coach and role model becomes even more significant. The new requirement includes being a facilitator, to increase the effectiveness of those who serve under his or her leadership.

Teamwork, flexibility, mutual participation in decisionmaking, and citizen satisfaction are concepts that initially may threaten the supervisor who is more comfortable with the authoritarian role and routinized operations inherent in traditional policing. Thus, the education of supervisors in new styles of leadership and management must be given a high priority if they are to carry out their responsibility for the success of community policing.

This establishment of a new philosophy must go beyond management training. Commanders and supervisors must not only be knowledgeable, but must be committed to the new form of leadership. The values that underlie the culture of the department must be modified and reflected in appropriate statements of policy by the departmental command group. Furthermore, rules and regulations must be streamlined and, generally, reduced in number, so that the flexibility needed by both supervisors and line officers will be possible. Just as the new policing style requires more communication and guidance between supervisors and officer, it also requires continuous dialog and sharing of information between the police chief and command officers and those involved in direct supervision. It is unlikely that improved communication will occur between police officers and citizens if effective communication within the department has not been established first.

MAXIMIZED PARTICIPATION IN DECISION MAKING

Since the 1970s, police executives have been following the example of private sector business and industrial firms in developing new mechanisms for participatory management. The Newport News, Virginia, Police Department utilized a variety of task forces and committees to implement its problem-oriented policing project. A management committee, comprising bureau heads and unit commanders, participated in all major patrol decisions. An operations advisory committee, composed of patrol officers and detectives, met regularly with the chief to discuss their concerns. These groups dealt with a variety of issues, from police development and flexible deployment of officers on patrol beats, to shift scheduling and equipment purchases.[38]

In the London Metropolitan Police, the division chief superintendent held a meeting of all his officers, from constables up through command officers, every five weeks to identify and analyze problems in his area and to obtain suggestions from officers as to their solutions. This opportunity to participate in important decisions on police activities not only gave officers of all grades the opportunity to demonstrate their creativity, but by being part of the process they also were more committed to the results. A further extension of this method that was being contemplated was to include citizens of the community in such meetings to broaden the input into police decision making.[39]

The Sheriff's Department of Los Angeles County, California, instituted a new effort called "service-oriented policing." To move the department and its personnel toward a more service-oriented posture, the sheriff established an SOP committee composed of representatives from all elements of the department: command officers, middle managers, supervisors, line deputies, and civilian employees. The committee's task included examination of the department's organization and culture; the expectations, rights, and needs of the service recipients (citizens) and the service deliverers (departmental personnel); and the services that were being provided, as well as how they might be enhanced or expanded. The SOP committee also sought the ideas and responses of the more than 11,000 members of the department.[40]

SUPPORTING OFFICERS IN THE COMMUNITY

Community policing officers are expected to be on the street during most of their time on duty, communicating with citizens, patrolling neighborhoods and business districts, attending meetings of residents, and conducting other police activities. It is important, therefore that they have technical and logistic backup in the form of field support units (FSUs). Organizationally placed at precinct or headquarters level, according to the size of the city, the FSUs are a valuable staff counterpart to the officers in the field. They should include crime prevention specialists, who can provide presentations at meetings and technical assistance on specific crime problems. The FSU can provide publications and materials for neighborhood meetings, as well as specialized equipment such as videocassette recorders and viewgraphs. In addition, it can handle the printing and duplicating of notices and other documents that are needed by community officers for distribution to citizens. The FSU also can serve as a message center for officers in the field, facilitating rapid callback responses to citizens. The leader of the FSU (a sergeant or lieutenant) also can be available to provide advice and technical assistance to the community policing team leaders and officers, incorporating the experiences and lessons learned of other policing teams.

An important responsibility of the field support units is to provide liaison and followup activity with other elements of the police department as well as the various city departments whose services are needed to resolve community problems. The Los Angeles Police Department has developed a "community enhancement request" form that enables an officer to request specific services from city agencies to handle conditions that may result in crime or community decay. When such a request is turned in by a local officer, the FSU forwards it to the appropriate city department or other unit of the police department, then maintains a suspense file on the item until a response has been received and the problem alleviated. If no response occurs within a reasonable time, the FSU itself can stimulate the necessary action. It also can furnish continuing feedback to the officer on the street.

The FSU function is critical to the community policing officer. He or she is on the line with the citizens, responding to their needs and requests. The ability to make something happen when citizens complain directly affects the officer's credibility and ultimate success, as well as that of the police department. The responsiveness of city government, or lack thereof, can result in either personal frustration or a sense of accomplishment for the individual officer. The line officer's effectiveness, therefore, is directly proportional to the followup work of the FSU. To perform several of these field support functions, the Los Angeles Police Department has established a community relations officer/crime prevention unit, under a sergeant, in each area's headquarters.[41]

Another type of specialized support needed by the community policing officer involves crime analysis and information about ongoing criminal activities in his or her territory. To fill this need, the London Metropolitan Police have established a Division Intelligence and Information Unit (DIIU) in each precinct-level command. Composed of detectives and support personnel, the DIIU collects, analyzes, and disseminates to local police officers information about criminals and crimes located within their area. This information can be used not only to apprehend specific offenders, but also to develop crime prevention strategies.

Information support for the officer in the community must go beyond crime analyses. The full resources of the police agency's records and identification facilities must be available quickly and conveniently. Computer equipment in the field, such as mobile digital terminals in patrol cars and laptop units equipped with telephone connections, can save valuable time in preparing reports and can provide immediate access to essential data. In addition, officers should receive timely information on municipal government actions (such as ordinances or regulation changes affecting neighborhood residents and businesses), as well as facts about public and private health, welfare, and education resources that might be used for referral or assistance.

RELATIONSHIPS WITHIN THE POLICE DEPARTMENT

An important part of the community policing officer's success and personal satisfaction is the relationship that he or she has with the rest of the police department. Particularly important is the working relationship between patrol officer and detectives. The function of report taking, information collecting, crime investigation, and apprehending criminals become more integrated under community policing, and the distinction between patrol and detective operations should diminish considerably. In some agencies, detectives are part of the neighborhood crime control teams.

The officer in the community is able to obtain valuable information, both from citizen input and his or her own observations, about crime conditions, particular offenses, and criminal suspects. The officer can use neighborhood-based information for followup investigations within the local community, including the arrest of perpetrators found there. Information also can be passed on to detectives investigating crimes over a broader geographical area. When an officer's information has assisted in the identification and apprehension of a suspect and in a conviction, feedback should be given to the patrol officer to validate the value of those efforts and to motivate the officer to continue to provide such information. Similarly, by continual communication with street officers, detectives can alert them to crimes committed, information needed, and suspects to be sought.

Through this exchange of information, the solution to many crimes and the arrest of criminals increasingly can be accomplished by officers working in neighborhoods. Centralized detective activities then can focus more on problem solving—identifying the nature of criminal activity in the community and designing crime reduction strategies that will affect different types of crimes.

The police officer working in a particular neighborhood should be supported by other specialized elements of the police department. As conditions require, special investigative units such as narcotics, juvenile, and gang units should be available for specific crime problems. The officer should be able to call upon staff units such as criminal intelligence, crime laboratory, and records and identification for their expertise. The planning and research staff should assist the community policing effort as a whole, through citywide operational research and evaluation programs to improve the effectiveness of the agency in handling the problems of the community, as well as through assistance to individual field officers in solving specific problems in the neighborhoods they patrol.

Assistant Chief Robert Vernon, Director of Operations for the Los Angeles Police Department, has described this relationship between specialized units of a police agency and the field officers responsible for community policing in terms of a medical model: the patrol officer in a specific neighborhood or beat area is like a general practitioner physician who has the principal interface with the individual citizen. Surrounding and supporting the police general practitioner is a series of specialists— detectives, juvenile investigators, narcotics officers, headquarters staff units, and others—who are available for consultation or referral of the case.[42]

QUALITY ASSURANCE

Under the traditional style of policing, with a quasi-military environment and rigid set of rules and regulations, inspection and control are relatively easy functions to perform. Regular inspections and audits are conducted to determine whether officers are complying with regulations. The more mechanically the individual adheres to the letter of the rules, the less likely he or she will get into trouble. Displaying unusual creativity, going beyond minimal requirements of the job, or exercising individual judgment are at odds with the rule-compliance mode. It is easy to see, then, that community policing—with its emphasis on self-motivation and individual initiative—requires a new approach to the inspection function.

Nevertheless, the importance of that function—maintaining the quality and integrity of the police force—is in no way minimized by the new concepts of policing. Indeed, the greater freedom of action afforded the individual officer places greater reliance on effective systems for monitoring, evaluating, and, when necessary, disciplining police conduct. If the community is to sustain satisfaction with and confidence in the police department, executives must insure that internal wrongdoing is prevented and that sufficient safeguards are established to preserve the integrity, efficiency, and effectiveness of the force.

The philosophy of community policing, in recognizing the professionalism of the police officer and emphasizing greater opportunities for job satisfaction, is ideal for making a commitment to essential values the basis for maintaining necessary standards of conduct. Such value orientation is an essential component of achieving professional responsibility within the force.[43]

Beyond the delineation and promotion of values, mechanisms for quality control—monitoring of performance and investigation of complaints—must be part of overall management controls. In a professional organization, the model should be the "quality assurance" programs of modern business and industrial institutions, where the emphasis is less on rigid compliance with rules than on successful results. Techniques such as self-evaluation by individuals and patrol teams, citizen surveys, and performance audits should be used to stimulate analysis and improvement, rather than as negative instruments of penalization.

At the same time, investigation and resolution of complaints or indications of misconduct should be prompt, thorough, and decisive. A professional police organization cannot tolerate betrayal of its values or breaches of integrity. When such incidents occur, the factual situation should be analyzed carefully so that candid information about the matter can be incorporated into future training sessions to prevent other officers from becoming enmeshed in wrongdoing.

CONCLUSION

Community policing is now an established concept of modern law enforcement doctrine. While much experimentation and innovation continues to occur, the benefits of this strategy are being proclaimed by more and more cities throughout the nation. But "making the transition from a traditional reactive, incident-driven style of policing to a more contemporary proactive, problem-directed style of community-oriented policing requires a comprehensive strategy that is based on long-term institutional change."[44]

The practice of community policing, and the implementation planning that inaugurates it, must recognize the pivotal role of the individual officer. As an article in *Footprints: The Community Policing Newsletter* states, "we must always remember that it is the Community Policing Officers themselves who make the system work . . . All the theories, strategies, and tactics associated with Community Policing that the experts discuss ultimately boil down to a single officer on the street, intervening one-on-one in efforts to . . . make the community safer."[45]

By lifting some of the constraints under which police officers in the field now operate, and by giving them the freedom to make decisions, innovate, and be problem solvers, community policing promises great benefits for the community in terms of quality of life and for the officers in terms of job satisfaction. By focusing on the person in the front lines of police service—the individual patrol officer—the community policing strategy will be built on a solid foundation.

NOTES

1. Alvin and Heidi Toffler, "The Future of Law Enforcement: Dangerous and Different," *FBI Law Enforcement Bulletin* (January 1990): 2–5.
2. George L. Kelling, "Police and Communities: The Quiet Revolution," *Perspectives on Policing,* no. 1 (Washington, D.C.: National Institute of Justice and Harvard University, June 1988), p. 1.
3. Mark H. Moore and Robert C. Trojanowicz, "Corporate Strategies for Policing," *Perspectives on Policing,* no. 6 (Washington, D.C.: National Institute of Justice and Harvard University, November 1988), p. 2.
4. See *Perspectives on Policing* nos. 1–11 (Washington, D.C.: National Institute of Justice and Harvard University, June 1988–September 1989); *Footprints: The Community Policing Newsletter* (National Center for Community Policing, Michigan State University).
5. Moore and Trojanowicz, "Corporate Strategies," p. 9.
6. James S. Campbell et al., *Law and Order Reconsidered,* Report of the Task Force on Law and Law Enforcement to the National Commission on the Causes and Prevention of Violence (New York: Bantam Books, 1970), p. 286.
7. See Jesse Rubin, "Police Identity and the Police Role," in *The Police and the Community,* ed. Robert F. Steadman (Baltimore, John Hopkins University Press, 1972), p. 26.
8. Bernard L. Garmire, "The Police Role in an Urban Society," in *The Police and the Community,* p. 6.
9. See James Q. Wilson and George L. Kelling, "Police and Neighborhood Safety: Broken Windows," *The Atlantic Monthly* (March 1982): 29–38.
10. Tony Pate et al., *Three Approaches to Criminal Apprehension in Kansas City: An Evaluation Report* (Washington, D.C.: Police Foundation, 1976).
11. William Medina, "Neighborhood-Based Policing," unpublished paper (Los Angeles Police Department, 1987).
12. James Q. Wilson, *Varieties of Police Behavior: The Management of Law and Order in Eight Communities* (Cambridge: Harvard University Press, 1968), pp. 29–30.
13. Rubin, "Police Identity," p. 22.

14. Note that while in the early days of an organized police in England, ranks such as inspector and superintendent were substituted for the military ranks of lieutenant, captain, etc., the same basic hierarchical structure of command was retained with the position of sergeant as the first level of supervision.

15. William L. Tafoya, "The Future of Policing," *FBI Law Enforcement Bulletin* (January 1990): 15.

16. In the Army, a helicopter pilot usually is appointed as a warrant officer, a professional rank just below second lieutenant, but pay and career status rise in parallel to officer ranks.

17. *The Challenge of Crime in a Free Society,* Report of the President's Commission on Law Enforcement and Administration of Justice (Washington, D.C.: U.S. Govt. Printing Office, 1967), pp. 107–109.

18. See Dorthy Guyot, "Bending Granite: Attempts to Change the Rank Structure of American Police Departments," *Journal of Police Science and Administration* (September 1979): 253–284.

19. The rank of inspector has had several different usages in the United States. In many police departments, particularly in the West, it was the title assigned to detectives, placing them between sergeants and lieutenants in the hierarchy. In other departments, it was an executive rank above captain. Because of this confusion, the term has fallen into disuse in many parts of the country, but still is common as a command rank in the Northeast.

20. "Promotional/Advanced Paygrades," memorandum provided to the author by the Los Angeles Police Department, March 1990.

21. Herman Goldstein, *Problem-Oriented Policing* (New York: McGraw Hill, 1990), p. 27.

22. Author's interview of Commander D. Monk, Metropolitan Police of London, February 1990.

23. *Problem-Oriented Policing,* p. 27.

24. Robert C. Trojanowicz and David L. Carter, "The Changing Face of America," *FBI Law Enforcement Bulletin* (January 1990): 9.

25. *Problem-Oriented Policing,* p. 28.

26. Patrick Murphy, foreword to *The State of Police Education: Police Direction for the 21st Century* by David L. Carter, Allen D. Sapp, and Darrel W. Stephens (Washington, D.C.: Police Executive Research Forum, 1989), p. iii.

27. James Q. Wilson, "The Police in the Ghetto," in *The Police and the Community,* p. 73.

28. *Ibid.,* pp. 73–74.

29. Carter et al, *The State of Police Education,* p. 157.

30. Murphy, foreword to Carter et al, p. iv.

31. *The State of Police Education,* p. 38.

32. Andrew H. Malcolm, "Police Chiefs' Objective: Greater Responsiveness," *New York Times,* April 23, 1990.

33. Edwin Meese III, "Criminal Justice—A Public Police Imperative," in *Thinking about America: the United States in the 1990s,* ed. Annelise Anderson and Dennis L. Bark (Palo Alto, Calif.: Hoover Institution, 1988), p. 434.

34. *Ibid.*

35. Los Angeles County Sheriff's Department, *Star News* (March 1990): 6.

36. President's Commission on Law Enforcement and the Administration of Justice, *Task Force Report: The Police* (Washington, D.C.: U.S. Govt. Printing Office, 1967, p. 138.

37. *Problem-Oriented Policing,* p. 157.

38. See John E. Eck and William Spelman, *Problem-Solving: Problem-Oriented Policing in Newport News* (Washington, D.C.: Police Executive Research Forum, 1987).

39. Author's interview of Commander Monk.
40. Los Angeles County Sheriff's Department, p. 6.
41. Los Angeles Police Department, unpublished briefing paper on community policing provided to author, March 14, 1990.
42. Author's interview of Assistant Chief Robert L. Vernon, Los Angeles Police Department, March 14, 1990.
43. Robert Wasserman and Mark H. Moore, "Values in Policing," *Perspectives on Policing,* no. 8 (Washington, D.C.: National Institute of Justice and Harvard University, November 1988).
44. National Law Enforcement Leadership Institute Bulletin on "Community-Oriented Policing Implementation Strategy Session," August 1990.
45. "Community Policing: The Line Officer's Perspective," *Footprints: The Community Policing Newsletter* 3, no. 2 (summer 1990): 5.

A R T I C L E 19

WHAT DOES COMMUNITY POLICING MEAN FOR DAILY POLICE WORK?

Stephen D. Mastrofski

Although interest in community policing has grown rapidly in the last decade, we know remarkably little about what it means to the work of the street-level officer. The term has been used to describe aggressive order maintenance, community crime prevention, problem-solving, and a host of police-community relations strategies.

This article is not so much concerned with defining community policing as with identifying how community policing—whether a state of mind, or program—affects police officers' daily work, including how they spend their time, with whom, and for how long.

Most evaluations of community policing to date have focused on describing some program and its impact on crime or victimization rates, on crime or victimization rates, citizen satisfaction, fear of crime, or other quality-of-life indicators. Reports resulting from these evaluations have described program goals, methods, and activities. Some include anecdotal accounts of the experiences of police and citizens in carrying out the program, but these are selective and fail to provide a larger context for understanding what community policing means for the everyday work of the men and women who engage in it. If the driving force of community policing reform is to change the way that police do their work, we must know what the police do when they do community policing. Only then will we know how to interpret the findings of even the rigorous impact evaluations.

Accordingly, the National Institute of Justice [NIJ] is sponsoring a new study that will develop new information on the specific activities police engage in when they take on community policing responsibilities,

Reprinted from Stephen D. Mastrofski, "What Does Community Policing Mean for Daily Police Work?" *National Institute of Justice Journal* (Washington, D.C.: National Institute of Justice, August 1992), pp. 23–27.

who determines the activities, and what proportion of time officers spend on them.

The new study builds on previous NIJ research, most of it concentrated on a well-established tactic of community policing—foot patrol.

FOOT PATROL STUDIES

Some researchers have concluded from foot patrol research that this form of community policing can reduce fear of crime, increase citizen satisfaction, and perhaps even reduce crime itself. Others point to mixed results. From the researcher's perspective, studies of foot patrol offer a striking example of the need to learn more about what happens at the officer level.

Newark.   One of the first foot patrol studies to offer encouraging conclusions was one conducted by the Police Foundation for the National Institute of Justice in the late 1970s.[1] Although the researchers in Newark found that foot patrol had no impact on reported crime and victimization, they concluded it did have a positive effect on citizen perceptions about crime and police services. The thrust of the study, however, was not so much on the actions of the foot patrol officers as on the impact of the strategy on crime and the fear of crime. Efforts were made to verify that foot officers were indeed on their assigned beats, but there was no analysis to indicate how foot patrol activities differed from motorized patrol activities.

A second study of foot patrol in Newark[2] did obtain foot officers' activity reports. Foot patrol was one of several strategies designed to intensify enforcement of laws regulating conduct in public places.

Foot officers were expected to engage in a wide variety of nonenforcement as well as enforcement activities. It appears that relatively little of their effort was given to enforcement, judging from patrol officers' activity statistics. Officers engaged only about 1.5 enforcement activities per eight person-hours (or three activities per shift for each two-officer team). About half of these actions were summonses.

Flint.   A study of foot patrol was also conducted in Flint, Michigan, at about the same time as the first Newark study.[3] Although some of the study's conclusions are in dispute, the study did attempt to document systematically what police did on foot patrol and how that differed from motorized patrol.

Looking at the department's daily report forms, the researchers found that foot officers reported many more self-initiated activities—such as home and business visits and security checks—than police in cars. Officers on foot averaged much higher levels of productivity across most of the standard performance measures: arrests, investigations, stopping of suspicious persons, parking citations, and value of recovered property. The only category in which motor patrol officers clearly outproduced their foot patrol counterparts was in providing miscellaneous services to citizens. Of course, foot patrol and motor patrol officers had different responsibilities and were monitored for different forms of activity. For instance, motor patrol officers had exclusive responsibility for dealing with traffic violations and accidents. Foot patrol officers were the only ones monitored for a wide range of police-public contacts: meetings and speaking engagements, business and home visits, and security checks. Not surprisingly, foot patrol officers had a much higher rate of nonadversarial public contact and a much lower rate of adversarial public contact than motorized patrol officers. They spend more time on training, roll call, office and administrative time, and meetings with the public and much less time on complaints than their motorized counterparts.

Edmonton.   A 1988 time budget study of foot and motorized constables in Edmonton, Alberta, provides an instructive counterpoint to the Flint study.[4] Some findings were comparable with Flint's. Foot constables handled many fewer calls for service than motor officers. They spent much less time on the street and in family residences and more time in schools and police offices. They also spent much less time with complainants and victims and more time with other constables, professionals, business people, and the general citizenry. This may be because they were oriented to solving rather than only responding to problems.

Some Edmonton findings were different from Flint's. Foot constables were more likely than motor constables to have contact with white-collar workers. This runs counter to the speculation of the Flint researchers that foot patrol was more "egalitarian." It may also help explain why foot patrol appears to be far more effective at changing citizens' feelings about their safety and about police services than in actually changing risks of being victimized. If a larger proportion of foot patrol contacts are at the *officer's* discretion, the officer will seek out people of higher social and economic status in the community—or at least those people likely to offer a pleasant interchange. Stated another way, given more personal freedom to choose, police officers on foot will spend less time with troublemakers. This situation may make potential victims contacted by the police *feel* safer without actually *being* safer.

Oakland.   A final NIJ-sponsored foot patrol study was conducted in Oakland, California.[5] As part of a field study of Oakland's efforts to improve policing in its central district, foot officers were observed and interviewed, and two-week activity statistics were obtained. Oakland's interviews and observations provide a somewhat different dimension than the other studies, which were based solely on activity statistics.

The Oakland observers noted great diversity in the tactics foot patrol officers employed: keeping drunks moving, rounding up truants, checking buses for fare cheaters and disorderly persons, tailing people who harass others, chasing disorderly people out of the area (in lieu of arrest), surveilling prostitutes, and having abandoned autos disposed of. Sometimes a foot officer restored order to a troubled corner merely by standing there, making his or her presence felt. Although foot officers did respond to assigned calls, their activities were predominately self-selected. The distinctly different impression one gets from these observations is that Oakland foot officers, unlike Edmonton constables, used their discretion to concentrate their attentions on the "troublemakers" of their beat.

BEYOND FOOT PATROL

Of course, foot patrol is only one of many ways police departments can strengthen their links with the community. Others include permanent beat assignments, door-to-door surveys of residents and businesses, park-and-walk patrol, neighborhood substations, and police involvement with citizen groups in crime prevention, problem-solving, and policy guidance. As with foot patrol, there has been little systematic monitoring of how these strategies have been put into effect.

Yet the need for such monitoring and evaluation is particularly strong where problem-oriented policing strategies are undertaken. How much time officers devote to problem-solving, how they do it, with whom, and for whom all remain to be determined.

NIJ TO USE DIRECT OBSERVATION
IN UPCOMING STUDY

NIJ's upcoming research study will use direct observation techniques to get answers to these questions. An observational study of the impact of community policing at the street level will build on already-developed field observation methods.[6] Such methods have provided many insights into what police do and why. For instance, one systematic observation in England[7] suggests that officers with community policing responsibilities deal with incidents differently from other officers.

Accompanying officers for eight-hour shifts, the British researchers observed more than 1200 police encounters with the public. From a statistical analysis of a subset of these encounters, they found that "community constables" dealt with incidents differently from traditionally oriented constables. They were less inclined to seek legalistic solutions in disputes and more likely to serve as impartial referees. They defined their success in terms of what the citizens wanted and tried to establish sustained relationships with members of the public.

NIJ's study will adopt a similar observational methodology to obtain detailed data on the cognitive aspects of police work—those aspects that distinguish good and bad policing. They will observe officers in the course of their work, and debrief them shortly thereafter, to learn what decisions they make and why.

For example, if greater familiarity with the residents and regulars of an officer's beat is a product of community policing, then that should be reflected in the things an officer weighs in deciding how to deal with problems during encounters. If officers are in fact assuming problem-oriented perspective, their decision making should draw on a broad range of concerns extending beyond the immediate circumstances of the situation.

That is, problem-oriented officers would presumably be more in-clined to see how the situation fitted into larger patterns of similar situ-ations. Officers would consider a broader range of alternative responses, would be interested in following up on their chosen responses to see how well they worked, and would incorporate that knowledge into sub-sequent decisions in similar situations.

Single Study Site

The NIJ study will focus on a single municipal police department, one that for at least a year will have been engaged in two aspects of commu-nity policing—community outreach and problem-solving. The depart-ment will have taken a "generalist" approach to community policing rather than focusing on a small specialist unit. Patrol officers will be ob-served throughout the city for approximately 100 full work shifts. In ad-dition, ride-along observations of patrol supervisors will be conducted for approximately ten full shifts.

This study will differ from previous observational studies in two major ways. First, in addition to officer encounters with the public, all other police "activities" will be noted as well. This includes roll call, time enroute to dispatched assignments, general patrol, traffic patrol, crime-focused strategies, information gathering, meeting with the public and other government officials, administrative matters, and personal business.

Notes will be made about which of these activities involve problem-oriented policing. Thus, between "activities" and "encounters," all of the observed patrol officer's work time on a given shift will be accounted for.

The second departure from most previous studies is the systematic debriefing of observed officers about their decision making in the ob-served encounters. This will take place soon after the encounters, usually when the officers begin to complete paperwork on the encounter or re-sume general patrol. The observers will ask the officers to describe what they were thinking as the encounter unfolded and what things affected

 A COMMUNITY POLICE OFFICER'S DAY

In addition to traditional law en-forcement activities, such as patrol and responding to calls for service, the day might include:

- Operating neighborhood substations
- Meeting with community groups
- Analyzing and solving neighborhood problems

- Working with citizens on crime prevention programs
- Conducting door-to-door surveys of residents
- Talking with students in school
- Meeting with local merchants
- Making security checks of businesses
- Dealing with disorderly people

WHAT FOOT PATROL STUDIES SHOW

Although foot patrol studies have offered some insight into what police do when they do community policing, they have many limitations. First, nearly all rely on officers' own reports of their activities, which suffer from the usual problems of diligence in recording and reaction to being monitored. Problems with data reliability were acknowledged by the Flint researchers and suggested as a consideration in Oakland.

Second, department records leave out a great deal that would be useful to know about their activity. They rarely cover brief (but hypothetically important) order-maintenance interventions, such as "move alongs" and inquiries into suspicious situations. And even events that are officially recorded are seldom described in sufficient detail to know the context of the situation, what police actions were taken (aside from arrest), and in what manner.

Third, with few exceptions, department records provide virtually no insight into the decision making that produced a given police response. If, as its advocates suggest, foot patrol really does alter what officers know about the public they serve, and if it changes their beliefs about the means and ends of police work, these changes should be reflected in what information is obtained in public encounters, how it is analyzed, and how it is applied. For example:

- Does foot patrol expand the range of police familiarity with citizens in the assigned beat, or does it limit it to particular segments of the population?
- Do contacts with citizens generate useful information for the police regarding suspects, crimes, and other neighborhood problems?
- Do citizens' personal characteristics (race, sex, age, residency) influence the foot patrol officer's decisions?
- How does a patrol officer's increased knowledge of a citizen's reputation affect the officer's interpretation of the citizen's actions?
- Are the complainant's wishes given greater weight under foot patrol?
- Are foot patrol officers more or less likely to use coercive tactics to control disorderly conduct situations?

their decisions about what to do. While in the field, observers will take only brief field notes. But within twelve hours of the completion of a ride-along session, the observers will record their observations through a systematic process designed to capture all key information.

CONCLUSION

Effecting change is not easy. Police have long valued decisiveness in handling encounters with the public, even when they had sparse information to act on. But now they must be able to make more systematic inquiries into problems. Under community policing, the work of the street-level officer approaches that of the researcher and planner. Giving officers greater leeway to identify and analyze problems, implement solutions, and evaluate these efforts means that differences in work style among officers are likely to increase.

Reshaping the way America is policed is particularly challenging if we review the history of police reform in America. Ideas that look promising on paper may turn out to be quite different when implemented on the beat. It is not too early to pay close attention to what community policing looks like when viewed at the street level—where policing is actually done.

This case study of one police department will take a preliminary step in that direction. It will give police leaders, researchers, and policy makers a better idea of what this reform means to the everyday work of police.

NOTES

1. Police Foundation, *The Newark Foot Patrol Experiment* (Washington, D.C.: Police Foundation, 1981).
2. A. M. Pate and W. G. Skogan, "Reducing the Signs of Crime: The Newark Experience," Technical Report (Washington, D.C.: Police Foundation, 1985).
3. R. C. Trojanowicz, *An Evaluation of the Neighborhood Foot Patrol in Flint, Michigan* (East Lansing: Michigan State University, 1982).
4. J. P. Hronick, B. A. Burrows, I. Tjosvold, and D. M. Phillips, *An Evaluation of the Neighborhood Foot Patrol Program of the Edmonton Police Service* (Canadian Research Institute for Law and the Family, 1989).
5. A. J. Reiss Jr., *Policing a City's Central District: The Oakland Story* (Washington, D.C.: National Institute of Justice, 1985).
6. S. D. Mastrofski and R. B. Parks, "Improving Observational Studies of Police," *Criminology* 28, no. 3 (1990): 475–496.
7. N. Fielding, C. Kemp, and C. Norris, "Constraints on the Practice of Community Policing," in *Coming to Terms With Policing: Perspectives on Policy,* R. Morgan and D. J. Smith, eds. (London: Routledge, 1989), pp. 49–63.

PART 6

CAVEATS

Although community policing receives a vast amount of attention and seems to be the alternative in policing to address all of a police department's past problems, it cannot unburden a department of political baggage, it does not instantaneously improve police-community relations, nor does it promise to solve all of a community's problems. There has been an enormous amount of time spent detailing the history of policing, describing it as ineffective, and juxtaposing community policing against it as the panacea. There are also a number of underlying assumptions to the philosophy of community policing that may or may not be accurate assumptions. Many often refer to community policing by using the childhood fable of "The Emperor's New Clothes" when describing the substantive content of change under community policing. As with any new concept or method of change, we must question at all times the assumptions we are making to ensure we are making good choices. These two articles have become the "classical" articles that have demanded we raise these questions.

The first article is by Samuel Walker. It was written in response to the article "Broken Windows" by James Q. Wilson and George L. Kelling (see part 1, article 1) and challenges many of the historical assumptions those authors make. Specifically, Walker focuses on the relationship between the police and the public before the advent of motorized patrols (i.e. the old days of foot patrol) and challenges the interpretation of how technology has had an impact upon this relationship.

The second article is by Lisa M. Riechers and Roy R. Roberg. This article appeared in 1990 and provided an excellent review of community policing's development during the 1980s. Riechers and Roberg then set out to collect and categorize all of the various theories and assumptions of community policing and presented them in a table format. From there they proceeded to challenge each of the underlying assumptions of Community Policing to make the determination as to whether or not they were accurate assumptions.

325

ARTICLE 20

"BROKEN WINDOWS" AND FRACTURED HISTORY: THE USE AND MISUSE OF HISTORY IN RECENT POLICE PATROL ANALYSIS[1]

Samuel Walker

A fresh burst of creativity marks current thinking about police patrol in the United States. This revival follows a period of doubt and disorientation in the late 1970s when recent research shattered traditional assumptions about patrol strategy. The most notable proposal for a reorientation of police patrol is set forth in "Broken Windows" by James Q. Wilson and George L. Kelling. Drawing partly on recent patrol experiments and on a re-thinking of police history, Wilson and Kelling propose a return to what they see as an older "watchman" style of policing (Wilson and Kelling 1982).

This paper examines the use of history by Wilson and Kelling in their proposal for reorienting police patrol. Because the historical analysis is central to their argument, its viability may well depend upon how well they have interpreted police history. Kelling develops his view of police history even more explicitly in a subsequent article co-authored with Mark H. Moore (Moore and Kelling 1983).

We shall argue here that Wilson, Kelling and Moore have misinterpreted police history in several important respects. Their proposal calls for a restoration—a return to a former tradition of police patrol. Joe McNamara, Chief of the San Jose police, has already responded to the "broken windows" thesis by arguing that the good old days weren't all that good (McNamara 1982). This paper elaborates upon that point and argues that the tradition of policing cited by Wilson, Kelling, and Moore never existed. This does not necessarily mean that the broken windows thesis is completely invalid. But if there is merit in the style of police patrol Wilson and Kelling propose, that style will have to be created anew.

Samuel Walker, "'Broken Windows' and Fractured History: The Use and Misuse of History in Recent Police Patrol Analysis," *Justice Quarterly* 1, no. 1 (1984): 75–90. Reprinted with permission of the Academy of Criminal Justice Sciences.

There is no viable older tradition to restore. Obviously, this is a far more difficult and challenging proposition than they have suggested.

POLICING AND BROKEN WINDOWS

Broken windows are a metaphor for the deterioration of neighborhoods. A broken window that goes unrepaired is a statement that no one cares enough about the quality of life in the neighborhood to bother fixing the little things that are wrong. While a broken window might be a small thing in and of itself, left unrepaired it becomes an invitation to further neglect. The result is a progressive deterioration of the entire neighborhood. Wilson and Kelling cite research in social psychology where abandoned cars were rapidly vandalized when some sign of prior vandalism invited further destructive acts (Zimbardo 1969).

Policing in America has failed, Wilson, Kelling and Moore argue, because it has neglected "the little things," the law enforcement equivalents of broken windows. This neglect is the product of the development of an efficiency-oriented, crime control–focused style of policing over the past fifty years. Eric Monkkonen argues that the shift toward crime control began even earlier and was substantially complete by 1920 (Monkkonen 1981).

Two developments in the 1930s launched a radical reorientation of police patrol. The first was greatly increased use of patrol cars, which took the patrol officer off the street and isolated him from the public. The second was the development of the Uniform Crime Reports [UCR] system, which then became the basic measure of police "success."

By themselves, these two developments might not have exerted such a profound effect on policing. The crucial difference was the influence of O.W. Wilson, who forged a coherent theory of police management in the late 1930s. Wilsonian theory emphasized the suppression of crime as the primary mission of policing. Fulfillment of this mission depended upon maximizing the efficiency of patrol coverage. The automobile allowed a patrol officer to cover his beat in a more unpredictable fashion than foot patrol.

Wilson became the leading proponent of one-officer cars, claiming that two single officer patrol cars were twice as efficient as one two-officer car. He recommended that patrol beats should be organized according to a workload formula that concluded that rapid response time would increase apprehensions and generally enhance public satisfaction with police service (Walker 1977; Fogelson 1977).

Wilson tirelessly propounded his gospel of efficiency from the late 1930s onward. His text "Police Administration" became "the bible" of police management and instructed an entire generation of police executives (Wilson and McLaren 1977). Police departments converted almost entirely from foot to automobile patrol, invested enormous sums of money in sophisticated communications equipment, and encouraged members of the public to avail themselves of their service.

Lost in this process were the personal aspects of routine policing. The car isolated officers from the people in the neighborhoods, which became nothing more than a series of "beat assignments" to the officers. The most professionalized departments, in fact, took extra measures to de-personalize policing. Frequent rotation of beat assignments was adopted as a strategy to combat corruption.

The crime control orientation meanwhile caused the police to concentrate on more serious crimes—primarily, the seven felonies that comprised the Crime Index. Significantly, the police actively adopted the UCR system as the measure of their performance. It was not something imposed on them (Manning 1977). The police lost interest in lesser violations of the law and routine nuisances because they just did not count. These nuisances included drunks, loud and intimidating groups of teenagers, public drug dealing, and the like.[2]

According to Wilson, Kelling and Moore, these nuisances are the "broken windows," the little things that convey the message that no one cares about the quality of life in this neighborhood. Wilson, Kelling and Moore base much of their argument on the recent Newark Foot Patrol Experiment (The Police Foundation 1981). The presence of officers on foot patrol did not reduce crime, but did make people feel safer. Officers were able to establish and enforce informal rules of behavior for the neighborhood. It was alright to be intoxicated in public but not to pass out in the gutter, for example. Wilson and Kelling also cite with apparent approval the technique used by some Chicago police officers to maintain order in public housing projects: if groups of teenagers were troublesome, the officers would simply chase them away. "We kick ass," one officer explained (Wilson and Kelling 1982:35).

The "Broken Windows" article argues that policing should be neighborhood-oriented. More officers should be deployed on foot, and those officers should concentrate less on catching criminals and more on enforcing informal neighborhood norms of behavior. To a certain extent, it advocates a form of team policing, although with some important differences.

Team policing experiments in the 1970s did not emphasize foot patrol, gave insufficient attention to street-level patrol tactics, and maintained the traditional crime control focus. Indeed, the incompatibility of some elements of team policing with the prevailing organizational structure and management philosophy was one of the factors in the failure of early team policing experiments (Sherman 1973; U.S. Department of Justice 1977; Schwartz and Clarren 1977).

"Broken Windows" offers an alternative model precisely because it focuses on what officers would actually do. It characterizes the recommended style of policing as a return to an earlier (pre-1930s) style of "watchman" or "constabulary" policing. At this point, we turn our attention to the historical analysis that underpins this argument.

THE HISTORICAL FRAMEWORK

The historical framework presented by Wilson, Kelling, and Moore consists of three components: the near-term, which embraces the last fifteen years; the middle-term, which includes the last fifty years; and the long-term, which involves all of police history before the last fifty years.

Their reading of near-term history is excellent. One of the most important developments of the past fifteen years has unquestionably been the enormous expansion of our knowledge about all aspects of policing. We can now discuss in an informed fashion issues that were "terra incognita" to the staff of the President's Crime Commission (Walker 1983). The most important findings constitute a systematic demolition of the assumptions underlying O.W. Wilson's approach to police management. We have learned that adding more police or intensifying patrol coverage will not reduce crime and that neither faster response time nor additional detectives will improve clearance rates. Few authorities on policing today could endorse the basic Wilsonian idea that improved management in the deployment of patrol officers or detectives is likely to reduce the crime rate.

Wilson's, Kelling's, and Moore's reading of the last fifty years of police history is mixed. They recognize the most significant developments in the period but misinterpret them in important respects. There are substantial implications of this misinterpretation for their proposed style of policing.

The development of American policing from the 1930s through the 1960s was a far more complex process than historians have lead us to believe. Wilson, Kelling, and Moore can be excused in large part because they have simply drawn upon the available historical scholarship. We will focus here on two aspects of police history since the 1930s, which have not received sufficient attention. The first involves the impact of the patrol car and the second concerns the crime control orientation of policing.

THE TECHNOLOGICAL REVOLUTION

It is indeed true that American police departments largely converted from foot to automobile patrol between the 1930s and the present. We should, of course, be cognizant of the enormous variations that exist even today. Some departments are almost wholly motorized, while others, primarily Eastern cities, still make heavy use of foot patrol (Police Executive Research Forum 1981). And it is also true that car patrols remove officers from the sidewalks, isolate them from casual contacts with ordinary citizens, and damage police-community relations. This analysis is part of the conventional wisdom about policing.

The impact of technology was paradoxical, however. The mid-century revolution in American policing involved not just the patrol car, but the car in conjunction with the telephone and the two-way radio. These served to bring police officers into far more intimate contact with people than ever before. While the patrol car isolated police officers in some respects, the telephone simultaneously increased the degree of contact in other respects. Let us examine this paradox in detail.

In the days of foot patrol, officers had extensive casual contacts with people. But they occurred primarily on the streets or in other public places. The police did not often obtain entry to private residences. The reason for this is obvious: there was no mechanism whereby the ordinary citizen could effectively summon the police. The telephone radically altered that situation with profound ramifications for both policing and public expectations about the quality of life. Stinchcombe (1963) has discussed the impact of privacy considerations on routine police work.

The telephone made it possible for the ordinary citizen to summon the police, and the combination of the two-way radio and the patrol car allowed the police to respond quickly. As we know, the more professional departments acquired a fetish for responding as quickly as possible to all calls. The development of the 911 telephone number was simply the logical conclusion of this effort to advertise and encourage people to use police service. People have in fact availed themselves of this service. The number of calls for service has escalated to the point where serious attention has been given to the idea of restricting or otherwise managing those requests in the last few years (Gay 1977).

Technology radically alters the nature of police-citizen contacts. Most of those contacts now occur in private residences. Albert Reiss reports that 70 percent of all police-citizen contacts occur in private places, 12 percent in semi-public, and 18 percent in open public places (Reiss 1971:16). The police not only gain access to private places, but observe the most intimate aspects of peoples' lives, and are asked to handle their most personal problems.

Research has confirmed that the bulk of police work involves domestic disputes and other problems arising from alcohol, drugs, mental illness, and poverty. Officers refer to all this as "bullshit" or "social work" because it is unrelated to what they believe to be their crime control mission.

Police-citizen contacts became increasingly skewed. The police lost contact with "ordinary" people and gained a great deal of contact with "problem" people, who included not just criminal offenders but those with multiple social problems. David Bayley and Harold Mendelsohn once observed that police officers had more direct knowledge about minorities than did the members of any other occupation. This knowledge was a direct product of the heavy demands upon police service placed by low-income and racial minorities (Bayley and Mendelsohn 1969:156).

Our understanding of the full impact of the telephone on policing remains problematic. Not all experts on policing accept the argument advanced here. Some argue that the police were indeed intimately involved in people's lives prior to the advent of the telephone.[3] Unfortunately, there is no empirical evidence that would permit the resolution of this question. Prior to the late 1950s, there were no observational studies of police patrol activities and thus we have no reliable evidence on what American police officers did on patrol in the pre-telephone era.[4]

THE REVOLUTION IN PUBLIC EXPECTATIONS

One consequence of the technological revolution in policing has been a parallel revolution in public expectations about the quality of life. The availability of police service created and fed a demand for those services. The establishment of the modern police in the early nineteenth century was an initial phase of this process, which created the expectation that a certain level of public order would, or at least should, prevail (Silver 1967).

The technological revolution of the mid-twentieth century generated a quantum leap in those expectations. Because there was now a mechanism for getting someone (the police) to "do something" about minor disorders and nuisances, people came to expect that they should not have to put up with such minor irritations. Thus, the general level of expectations about the quality of life—the amount of noise, the presence of "strange" or "undesirable" people—has undergone an enormous change. Three generations of Americans have learned or at least have come to believe that they should not have to put up with certain problems.

The police are both the source and the victims of this revolution. They have stimulated higher levels of public expectations by their very presence and their policy of more readily available services. At the same time they are the prisoners of their own creation, swamped with an enormous service call workload. The recent effort to restrict or somehow manage this workload faces the problem of a public that expects rapid police response for any and every problem as a matter of right.

Documenting changes in public expectations concerning the police is difficult given the absence of reliable data about public attitudes or police practices prior to the late 1950s and early 1960s. Several indicators do provide evidence of short-term changes in public expectations. The development of three-digit (911) emergency phone numbers for the police increased the number of service calls. In Omaha, Nebraska, for example, the number of patrol car dispatches increased by 36 percent between 1969 and 1971, presumably as a result of a new 911 phone number (Walker 1983:110). These figures represent the dispatch of a patrol car, not the number of incoming calls. Omaha police officials estimate that about 35 percent of all calls do not result in a dispatch.

Additional evidence is found in data on the number of civilian complaints about police misconduct. In New York City, for example, the number of complaints filed with the Civilian Complaint Review Board (CCRB) increased from about 200 per year in 1960 to 1962 to just over 2000 per year in 1967 to 1968, and to more than 3000 annually in 1971 to 1974. It would be difficult to believe that the conduct of New York City police officers deteriorated by a factor of ten or fifteen during this period. Rather, the increase is probably the result of a lower threshold of tolerance for police misconduct on the part of citizens and the increased availability of an apparent remedy for perceived misconduct.

During the period under discussion, the procedures of the New York CCRB were reorganized several times. Each reorganization facilitated complaint filing and at the same time heightened public awareness of the availability of this particular remedy (Kahn 1975:113). The data on civilian complaints supports the argument made herein concerning police services generally: The availability of a service or remedy stimulates demand for that service, thereby altering basic expectations.

THE MYTHOLOGY OF CRIME CONTROL

The conventional wisdom states that police organize their efforts around the goal of crime control. Wilson, Kelling, and Moore restate this conventional wisdom, but the matter is a bit more complex. There is an important distinction between the self-image of the police and the day-to-day reality of routine policing (Goldstein 1977). The emphasis on crime control is and has been largely a matter of what the police say they are doing. Peter Manning argues persuasively that the police consciously created and manipulated this self-image as a way of establishing greater professional and political autonomy (Manning 1977).

As we have seen, however, the day to day reality of policing contradicted this self-image. The sharp contrast between the crime-fighting imagery of the police and the peacekeeping reality of police activities was one of the first and most important findings of the flood of police research that began in the 1960s. When Wilson, Kelling, and Moore suggest that the police are completely crime control-oriented they seriously misrepresent the nature of contemporary policing.

The discrepancy between crime control imagery and operational reality also becomes evident when we look more closely at how police departments utilize their resources. The most recent Survey of Police Operational and Administrative Practices reveals enormous variations among departments (Police Executive Research Forum 1981). Many still distribute their patrol officers equally among three shifts, ignoring even the most rudimentary workload formulas, which were first developed by O.W. Wilson over forty years ago (Wilson and McLaren 1977: appendix J). Departments typically do not revise the boundaries of their patrol districts on a regular basis. Districts remain unchanged for ten or twenty years, or longer. Meanwhile, the composition of the urban environment changes radically, as older areas are depopulated, new residential areas created, and so on.

THE QUESTION OF LEGITIMACY

The most important long-term development in American policing, according to Wilson, Kelling, and Moore, has been the loss of legitimacy. There can be little doubt that legitimacy, by which we mean acceptance of police authority by the public, is a major problem today.

The interpretation of police history offered by Wilson, Kelling, and Moore, which purports to explain how that legitimacy was lost, is seriously flawed. The evidence completely contradicts the thrust of their argument.

The police in the nineteenth century were not merely the "adjuncts" of the machine, as Robert Fogelson (1977) suggests, but were central cogs in it. Wilson, Kelling, and Moore maintain that this role offered certain benefits for the police, which reformers and historians alike have overlooked.

As cogs in the machine, the police served the immediate needs of the different neighborhoods. Political control was highly decentralized and local city councilmen or ward bosses exercised effective control over the police. Thus, the police carried out a wide range of services. Historians have rediscovered the social welfare role of the police, providing food and lodging for vagrants (Walker 1977; Monkkonen 1981). The police also performed political errands and were the means by which certain groups and individuals were able to corrupt the political process. These errands included open electioneering, rounding up the loyal voters, and harassing the opponents. Police also enforced the narrow prejudices of their constituents, harassing "undesirables" or "discouraging any kind of "unwelcome" behavior.

Wilson, Kelling, and Moore concede that there was a lack of concern for due process, but argue there was an important trade-off. By virtue of serving the immediate needs and narrow prejudices of the neighborhoods, the police gained an important degree of political legitimacy. They were perceived as faithful servants and enjoyed the resulting benefits. All of this was destroyed by the reforms of the twentieth century. The patrol car removed officers from the streets, while the new "professional" style dictated an impersonal type of policing. Legal concerns with due process denied officers the ability to use the tactics of rough justice by which they had enforced neighborhood community norms.

This historical analysis is central to the reorientation of policing presented in the "Broken Windows" article. Wilson, Kelling, and Moore propose that the lost political legitimacy could be re-established by what they view as the older "watchman" style of policing. Unfortunately, this historical analysis is pure fantasy.

Historians are unanimous in their conclusion that the police were at the center of urban political conflict in the nineteenth century. In many instances policing was the paramount issue and in some cases the only issue. Historians disagree only on their interpretation of the exact nature of this political conflict. The many experiments with different forms of administrative control over the police (the last of which survives only in Missouri) were but one part of this long and bitter struggle for political control (Walker 1977; Fogelson 1977).

To say that there was political conflict over the police means that the police lacked political legitimacy. Their authority was not accepted by the citizenry. Wilson, Kelling, and Moore are seriously in error when they suggest that the police enjoyed substantial legitimacy in the pre-technology era.

The lack of legitimacy is further illustrated by the nature of the conflicts surrounding the police. Nonenforcement of the various laws designed to control drinking was the issue that most often roused the so-called "reformers" to action. Alcohol consumption was a political issue with many dimensions. In some respects it was an expression of ethnic conflict, pitting sober-sided Anglo-Saxons against the heavy-drinking Irish and Germans. Drinking was also a class issue. Temperance and, later, prohibition advocates tended either to come from the middle class or at least define themselves in terms of the values of hard work, sobriety, thrift, and upward mobility (Gusfield 1963). When nineteenth century Americans fought over the police and the enforcement of the drinking laws, that battle expressed the deepest social conflicts in American society.

In one of the finest pieces of historical scholarship on the American police, Wilbur Miller explores the question of legitimacy from an entirely different angle (Miller 1977). The great difference between the London and New York City police was precisely the extent to which officers in New York were denied the grant of legitimacy enjoyed by their counterparts in London. Miller further argues that the problem of legitimacy was individualized in New York City. Each officer faced challenges to his personal authority and had to assert his authority on a situational level.

Miller does not argue that challenges to police legitimacy were patterned according to class, ethnicity, or race. Thus, an Irish-American cop was just as likely to be challenged by a fellow countryman as he was by someone of a different ethnic background. To be sure, the poor, political radicals, blacks, and other people deemed "undesirable" were victimized more often by the police than were other groups, but it does not follow that the police enjoyed unquestioned authority in the eyes of those people who were members of the same class and ethnic groups as police officers.

THE MYTH OF THE WATCHMAN

With their argument that the nineteenth century police enjoyed political legitimacy, Wilson, Kelling, and Moore have resurrected in slightly different garb the old myth of the friendly cop on the beat. They offer this older "watchman" style of policing as a viable model for contemporary policing. Quite apart from the broader question of political legitimacy, their argument turns on the issue of on-the-street police behavior.

Historians have not yet reconstructed a full picture of police behavior in the nineteenth century. At best, historians can make inferences about this behavior from surviving records. None of the historical accounts published to date presents a picture of policing that could be regarded as a viable model for the present.

What do we know about routine policing in the days before the patrol car? There is general agreement that officers did not necessarily do much work at all. Given the primitive state of communications technology, patrol officers were almost completely on their own and able to avoid effective supervision (Rubinstein 1974). Evidence suggests that corruption was possibly the primary objective of all of municipal government, not just the police department.

Wilbur Miller (1977), meanwhile, places the matter of police brutality in a new and convincing light. His argument that brutality was a response to the refusal of citizens to grant the police legitimacy speaks directly to the point raised by Wilson, Kelling, and Moore.

Recently, some historians have attempted to draw a more systematic picture of police law enforcement activities. The most convincing picture is drawn by Lawrence Friedman and Robert Percival (1981) in their study of the Oakland police between 1870 and 1910. They characterize police arrest patterns as a giant trawling operation. The typical arrestee was a white, working-class adult male who was drunk and was arrested for intoxication, disturbing the peace, or some related offense. But there was nothing systematic about police operations. The people swept up into their net were simply unlucky—there was no reason why they should have been arrested rather than others whose behavior was essentially the same. Nor was it apparent, in Friedman's and Percival's view, that the police singled out any particular categories of people for especially systematic harassment.

The argument offered by Wilson, Kelling, and Moore turns in part on the question of purpose: what the police saw themselves doing. Historians have established that police officers had a few purposes. The first was to get and hold the job. The second was to exploit the possibilities for graft that the job offered. A third was to do as little actual patrol work as possible. A fourth involved surviving on the street, which meant establishing and maintaining authority in the face of hostility and overt challenges to that authority. Finally, officers apparently felt obliged to go through the motions of "real" police work by arresting occasional miscreants.

We do not find in this picture any conscious purpose of fighting crime or serving neighborhood needs. That is precisely the point made by Progressive era reformers when they indicted the police for inefficiency. Wilson, Kelling, and Moore have no grounds for offering this as a viable model for contemporary policing. Chief McNamara is right: the good old days were not that good.

The watchman style of policing described by Wilson, Kelling, and Moore can also be challenged from a completely different perspective. The idea that the police served the needs of local neighborhoods and thereby enjoyed political legitimacy is based on a highly romanticized view of nineteenth century neighborhood life. Urban neighborhoods were not stable and homogeneous little villages nestled in the city. They were heterogeneous, and the rate of geographic mobility was even higher than contemporary rates. Albert Reiss (1971:209–210) in "Police and the Public" critiques recent "community control" proposals on these very grounds: They are based on the erroneous impression that neighborhoods are stable, homogeneous, and relatively well-defined.

SUMMARY AND CONCLUSION

In "Broken Windows," James Q. Wilson and George Kelling offer a provocative proposal for reorienting police patrol. Their argument is based primarily on an historical analysis of American policing. They propose a return to a watchman style of policing, which they claim existed before the advent of crime control–oriented policing in the 1930s. This historical analysis is further developed in a subsequent article by Kelling and Moore (1983).

In this article, we have examined the historical analysis used by these three authors. We find it flawed on several fundamental points.

First, the depersonalization of American policing from the 1930s onward has been greatly exaggerated. While the patrol car did isolate the police in some respects, the telephone brought about a more intimate form of contact between police and citizen by allowing police officers to enter private residences and involving them in private disputes and problems.

Second, the crime control orientation of the police has been greatly exaggerated. Crime control is largely a matter of police rhetoric and self-image. Day-to-day policing is, on the other hand, primarily a matter of peacekeeping.

Third, there is no historical evidence to support the contention that the police formerly enjoyed substantial political legitimacy. To the contrary, all the evidence suggests that the legitimacy of the police was one of the major political controversies throughout the nineteenth century and well into the twentieth.

Fourth, the watchman style of policing referred to by Wilson, Kelling, and Moore is just as inefficient and corrupt as the reformers accuse it of being. It does not involve any conscious purpose to serve neighborhood needs and hardly serves as a model for revitalized contemporary policing.

Where does this leave us? We should not throw the proverbial baby out with the bath water. The fact that Wilson and Kelling construct their "Broken Windows" thesis on a false and heavily romanticized view of the past does not by itself invalidate their concept of a revitalized police research. They correctly interpret the lessons of recent police research. Suppression of crime is a will-o'-the-wisp, which the police should no longer pursue. Enhancement of public feelings of safety, however, does appear to be within the grasp of the police. A new form of policing based on the apparent lessons of the Newark Foot Patrol Experiment, the failures of team policing experiments, and the irrelevance of most official police-community relations programs seems to be a goal that is both worth pursuing and feasible.

Our main point here is simply that such a revitalized form of policing would represent something entirely new in the history of the American police. There is no older tradition worthy of restoration. A revitalized, community-oriented policing would have to be developed slowly and painfully.

There should be no mistake about the difficulty of such a task. Among other things, recent research on the police clearly demonstrates the enormous difficulty in changing either police officer behavior or the structure and process of police organization. Yet at the same time, the history reviewed here does suggest that fundamental long-term changes in policing are indeed possible. Change is a constant; shaping that change in a positive way is the challenge.

NOTES

1. Department of Criminal Justice, University of Nebraska at Omaha. The author would like to thank Lawrence W. Sherman and James Fyfe for their comments on an earlier draft of this article. A revised version was presented at the annual meeting of the American Society of Criminology, Denver, Colorado, November, 1983.
2. James Fyfe argues that prosecutorial and judicial indifference to minor "quality of life" offenses is also responsible for neighborhood deterioration and that the police should not be singled out as the major culprits. By implication, he suggests that reorienting the police role would be futile without simultaneously reorienting the priorities of prosecutors and judges. Personal correspondence, James Fyfe to Walker.
3. Lawrence W. Sherman accepts this view and dissents from the argument advanced in this article. Personal correspondence, Lawrence W. Sherman to Walker.
4. The debate is conducted largely on the basis of circumstantial evidence. Sherman, for example, believes that literary evidence is a reliable guide to past police practices and cites *A Tree Grows in Brooklyn* as one useful example. Personal correspondence, Sherman to Walker.

REFERENCES

Bayley, D., and Mendelsohn, H. 1969. *Minorities and the police.* New York: The Free Press.

Fogelson, R. 1977. *Big City Police.* Cambridge: Harvard University Press.

Friedman, L. M., and Percival, R. V. 1981. *The roots of justice.* Chapel Hill: University of North Carolina Press.

Gay, W. 1977. *Improving patrol productivity.* Vol. 1, *Routine patrol.* Washington: Govt. Printing Office.

Goldstein, H. 1977. *Policing a free society.* Cambridge: Ballinger.

Gusfield, J. 1963. *Symbolic crusade: Status politics and the American temperance movement.* Urbana: University of Illinois Press.

Haller, M. 1976. "Historical roots of police behavior: Chicago, 1890–1925. *Law and Society Review* 10 (winter): 303–324.

Kahn, R. 1975. Urban reform and police accountability in New York City, 1950–1974. In *Urban problems and public policy.* Eds. R. L. Lineberry and L. H. Masotti. Lexington: Lexington Books.

McNamara, J. D. 1982. Dangerous nostalgia for the cop on the beat. *San Jose Mercury-News,* May 2.

Manning, P. K. 1977. *Police work.* Cambridge: MIT Press.

Miller, W. 1977. *Cops and bobbies.* Chicago: University of Chicago Press.

Monkkonen, E. 1981. *Police in urban America, 1860–1920.* Cambridge: Cambridge University Press.

Moore, M. H. and Kelling, G. L. 1983. To serve and protect: Learning from police history. *The Public Interest* 70: 49–65.

Police Executive Research Forum. 1981. *Survey of police operational and administrative practices—1981.* Washington: Police Executive Research Forum.

Police Foundation. 1981. *The Newark foot patrol experiment.* Washington: The Police Foundation.

Reiss, A. 1971. *The police and the public.* New Haven: Yale University Press.

Rubenstein, J. 1974. *City police.* New York: Ballantine Books.

Schwartz, A. I., and Clarren, S. N. 1977. *The Cincinnati team policing experiment.* Washington: The Police Foundation.

Sherman, L. W. 1973. *Team policing: Seven case studies.* Washington: The Police Foundation.

Silver, A. 1967. The demand for order in civil society." In *The police: Six sociological essays.* Ed. David J. Bordua. New York: John Wiley.

Stinchcombe, A. 1963. Institutions of privacy in the determination of police administrative practice. *American Journal of Sociology* 69 (September): 150–160.

U.S. Department of Justice. 1977. *Neighborhood team policing.* Washington: Govt. Printing Office.

Walker, S. 1983. *The police in America: An introduction.* New York: McGraw-Hill.

———. 1977. *A critical history of police reform: The emergence of professionalization.* Lexington: Lexington Books.

Wilson, J. Q., and Kelling, G. L. 1982. Broken windows: Police and neighborhood safety. *Atlantic Monthly* 249 (March): 29–38.

Wilson, O. W., and McLaren, R. C. 1977. *Police administration.* 4th ed. New York: McGraw-Hill.

Zimbardo, P. G. 1969. The human choice: Individuation, reason, and order versus deindividuation, impulse, and chaos." In *Nebraska Symposium on Motivation,* eds. W. J. Arnold and D. Levine. Lincoln: University of Nebraska Press.

Article 21

Community Policing: A Critical Review of Underlying Assumptions

Lisa M. Riechers and Roy R. Roberg

A new "movement" is currently developing in the philosophy of policing, known as community policing. In this paper, the historical development and changes in policing will be discussed to better understand the meaning of this present trend. The major emphasis will be on identifying and analyzing the most prominent assumptions of community policing in an attempt to realistically assess the viability and future directions of this new approach.

The concept of community policing culminated with the community relations programs of the 1950s and 1960s, which developed in order to increase interaction between the community, especially the minority community, and the police, and continued through the 1970s with the team policing concept (Greene 1987). Despite the failure of the team policing concept in some agencies, the idea of a "community context of policing" has remained, due to increasing evidence that the bureaucratic model and conventional police practices have not been effective (for example, Greene 1987; Skolnick and Bayley 1986). Therefore, movements which focus on specific problems faced by communities and overall fear reduction have begun (Brown and Wycoff 1987; Cordner 1986; Eck and Spelman 1987; Goldstein 1987; Greene 1987; Skolnick and Bayley 1986).

THE DEVELOPMENT OF COMMUNITY POLICING

In order to understand the current trend toward community policing, one must view the police within the context of the past twenty-five

Reprinted from *Journal of Police Science and Administration* 17, no. 2 (1990) 105–114. Copyright held by the International Association of Chiefs of Police, 515 N. Washington Street, Alexandria, Virginia 22314. Further reproduction without express written permission from IACP is strictly prohibited.

years. The crises of the 1960s brought the problems of police profession-alism to the fore. As a result of race riots, during which the police were often targets or culprits, and general social upheaval, the adequacy of the goals of professional policing were challenged (Germann 1969; Walker 1983). The President's Crime Commission (1967) and the National Advisory Commission on Civil Disorders (1967) recommended higher personnel standards, improved management, and greater use of science and technology to solve existing problems. The President's Crime Commission also called for an elimination of the single level of entry into the police force, pointing to the need to establish several levels of entry, providing more opportunities for those with higher levels of education and special skills, as well as increased community involvement in planning and executing changes. After these national reports were published, proposals for change to improve police community interactions and to raise personnel standards came forth. Germann (1969), for instance, wrote of the need to broaden the public's perception of the police function and the need for officers to have college degrees and be allowed lateral movement. He also suggested a new type of training, where the police officers consider themselves a part of the community and learn sociological and psychological concepts of deviance, prejudice, and attitude change. Angell (1971, p. 185), on the other hand, suggested radically changing the bureaucratic model of policing and proposed a "democratic" model be adopted. The democratic model, although it had many appealing features, was often "dismissed out of hand because of a single feature: the abolition of middle management" (Sherman 1975, p. 363).

The concept of team policing, though adopted by only a small number of agencies, became the byword of the 1970s. In general, team policing plans involved decentralization and personalized police service from patrol officers assigned to a beat area (Fink and Searl 1974). The assumptions of team policing were that familiarity with a neighborhood would give the police officer a sense of personal responsibility and, in turn, the community's familiarity with the officers would breed trust and cooperation, and would enhance the community's sense of responsibility for crime and social problems. While team policing showed some success, it was not enough to overcome the problems faced by team policing programs. Sherman (1975) points out that the problem with most team policing programs was that middle management functioned only in terms of control, and not in terms of support for team policing officers. In essence, team policing failed because it "required a rethinking of the social and formal organization of policing on a massive scale" (Greene 1987, p.3).

Police managers and researchers are still making attempts to implement the types of changes recommended by the President's Commission in 1967. Some of these changes have been encompassed in the current trend in policing, known as "community policing." The question remains, however, whether community policing will be successful or whether it will fail to be implemented, as have many of the innovative programs that preceded it.

COMMUNITY POLICING: ASSUMPTIONS, GOALS, AND CHARACTERISTICS

While community policing programs vary from city to city, they all share some common assumptions, goals, and characteristics. The concept of community policing is currently being examined by researchers who are questioning whether community policing is merely a rehash of the failed programs of the 1970s (Goldstein 1987) or even a nostalgic attempt to "recapture an imagined past" (Manning 1984, p. 205). There are several assumptions of community policing that have been examined in the literature and several that have yet to be examined. The task of examining the assumptions upon which community policing is based is crucial, since, as Weatheritt (1983) notes, the research on community policing has traded on its philosophical and moral appeal, and not examined closely the assumptions, which may be appealing and universal, but not heuristic. Short (1983) notes all of these criticisms of community policing, but states further that underlying the nostalgia of community policing is an aspiration to create a relationship between the police and the public based on principles of mutual trust, understanding, and respect.

Assumptions

Manning (1984, pp. 212–213) identified several basic assumptions of community policing, questioned their validity, and often found fault with them, including (Assumption 1) the presence of the police through increased visibility reduces the public's fear of crime; (Assumption 2) the public is of one mind, a homogeneous populace whose satisfaction or dissatisfaction with the police can be readily measured; and (Assumption 3) the police should be responsible for actively helping to define and shape community norms.

Both Manning (1984) and Kelling (1987) note that community policing is based in part on the assumption that (Assumption 4) public fear stems more from disorder than crime. Related to this premise is the assumption put forth by Wilson and Kelling (1982) that (Assumption 5) signs of neglect and decay in neighborhoods invite crime. These five assumptions can be gleaned from the literature on order-maintenance policing and foot patrol, and in fact form the basis for many foot patrol programs (Esbensen 1987; Police Foundation 1981; Trojanowicz 1982).

An assumption of community policing put forth by Goldstein (1987) addresses the question of whether the police are relying on nonlegal norms and becoming politically over-involved. Goldstein suggests this is not the case, namely because (Assumption 6) the new programs are starting at the initiative of the police in order to improve service, not simply to give certain groups in the community more control over services than other group members.

Short (1983) questions whether the goals and objectives of community policing can be met without violating the political neutrality of the police. Some researchers, notably Wilson and Kelling (1982) and Sykes (1986) apparently do not view this as a vital consideration; however, if community policing is to work, the mistakes of the past must not be repeated. History shows that a violation of the political neutrality of the police is dangerous, and it certainly threatens the democratic ideals of the constitution upon which this country was founded; therefore, the assumption that (Assumption 7) community policing can be done without violating the political neutrality of the police should be closely examined.

We wish to introduce and examine three additional assumptions of community policing. These assumptions include (Assumption 8) questioning whether the police, given their current mechanistic characteristics, and (Assumption 9) quality of personnel, can be responsive to the demands of community policing, and (Assumption 10) whether the police are the proper agency to attempt to fulfill the goals espoused by community policing.

Goals

The goals of community policing programs include fear reduction among citizens, increased citizen satisfaction with the police, and development of techniques that address the problems of the community (Goldstein 1987; Greene 1987). Another goal of community policing that is being proposed by some researchers, which relates to the goals of reducing fear and improving satisfaction, is the use of the police to help define and reinforce informal norms of the community, in other words as agents of informal social control (Kelling 1985, 1987; Wilson and Kelling 1982). These goals combine to form an often intentionally unstated goal of community policing—that of reducing crime. Many researchers are hesitant to even mention this as the overall goal of community policing, perhaps because it is the "impossible mandate" for the police (Manning 1971, p. 154); and yet, success of the specific programs that attempt to meet the stated goals of community policing is often measured in some way by crime reduction (Esbensen 1987; Trojanowicz 1982).

Characteristics

Some of the characteristics of community policing programs that have developed from these assumptions and goals have been noted in the literature. These characteristics include some type of community involvement in decision making, which focuses on specific priorities and needs of the community; a relatively permanent assignment of police officers to a neighborhood in order to instill mutual feelings of trust and responsibility between the officers and the community and a commitment of resources and personnel to meet the needs of the community (Goldstein 1987). Goldstein points out that it is often an implied characteristic that police officers are given more independence and freedom in decision making, thus creating a more stimulating working environment.

ORDER MAINTENANCE AND
PROBLEM-ORIENTED POLICING

The assumptions and goals of community policing are not always compatible. In fact, there exists what has been termed a "liberal-conservative" dichotomy among researchers in community policing (Greene 1987, p. 3). This polarization can be most readily seen in the debate over order-maintenance policing. While there is no disagreement that an important focus of policing is order maintenance, there is disagreement as to the role of police officers in order maintenance.

Order-maintenance policing refers to the use of the police to control public order crimes, disturbances, and noncrimes, and contributes substantially to the workload of police officers. One component of order-maintenance policing, however, is the use of police discretion to control "problems" (Goldstein 1979, p. 245) that are not within the legal bounds of police power, as advocated by Wilson and Kelling (1982). As Goldstein (1979) points out, there are many social problems, or residual problems of society, that may not be defined as criminal offenses, but nevertheless are and will always be problems for the police. For this reason, those with a "conservative" viewpoint propose that rather than criminalizing annoying or nuisance behaviors so the police will have legal justifications to act on them, a more practical solution is to allow the police to use their discretion to go beyond legal bounds (Kelling 1985, 1987; Sykes 1986; Wilson and Kelling 1982). There are other arguments for the use of police as agents of informal social control as well, such as fear reduction in the citizenry, and the premise that, left unattended, disorder may escalate into crime (Wilson and Kelling 1982).

Manning (1984) rejects this use of the police as agents of informal social control, as do many others (for example, see Klockars 1985; Walker 1984). These researchers worry that reliance on nonlegal norms and community definitions of order can "quickly become extensions of class and racial bias and thereby introduce more injustice into communities than expected" (Greene 1987, p. 4). While the debate on whether police should be agents of informal social control is far from over, at present, the basis of authority that police officers have to deal with community problems is strictly legal in nature (Kelling 1985). And as Klockars (1985, p. 320) points out there is no group in society which is likely to ". . . willingly forgo its belief in the law as the basis for the legitimacy of police action."

One of the most important features of community policing is the attention to substantive community problems, or problem-oriented policing (Goldstein 1979). Problem-oriented policing involves a different way of attempting to make the changes that have been considered necessary since the 1960s. According to Goldstein (1979, p. 238), the failure of team policing was due in large part to a focus on secondary considerations, such as overall organizational change, with a "management-dominated concept of police reform." He proposes a system which focuses on the primary objectives of policing—the end product of quality service to the citizenry. Problem-oriented policing involves a process where problems are systematically defined and researched, then alternative solutions are explored through an interactive process involving both the community and the police. As Eck and Spelman (1986, p. 46) note, problem-oriented policing is ". . . a state of mind, and not a program, technique, or procedure." Part of the mindset of problem-oriented policing involves police officers and communities learning to see the big picture—a global problem rather than a specific incident. This can be difficult, however, since global problems include poverty, homelessness, prejudice, inequality, and so on. These are problems that the police cannot be expected to solve (Goldstein 1987). Therefore, it can be seen that the issues of order-maintenance policing are integral to problem-oriented policing, and both form the basis of what could be good community policing.

COMMUNITY POLICING: UNDERLYING ASSUMPTIONS EXAMINED

We now turn our attention to an examination of what we believe are the most prominent underlying assumptions of community policing, especially as they apply to order maintenance and problem oriented policing. The accompanying table summarizes these underlying assumptions, 1 through 7 as represented in the literature, and 8 through 10 put forth by the authors.

Assumption 1. The presence of the police through increased visibility reduces the public's fear of crime.

Assumption 2. The public is of one mind, a homogeneous populace whose satisfaction or dissatisfaction with the police can be readily measured.

In addressing these assumptions, Manning makes the argument that there are many groups in society who do not want a continued police presence. He points to Mastrofski's (1983) research, which indicated that wealthier households make use of police services at a significantly greater rate than low income households for the categories of less serious crime, less serious order maintenance, and information. On the other hand, lower income households make significantly more use of police services for the categories of violent crime and serious order maintenance. From this, Manning concludes that the nature of the demand for police service "depends on the social class composition, race, and age of the neighborhood" (Manning 1984, p. 214). It should be noted that the class composition of the lower income neighborhoods used in Mastrofski's (1983) study was 75 percent black.

These findings raise questions regarding how the police can define who the community is and determine what the community needs are. Obviously, there is no single community, and thus no single way to conduct "community policing." This assumption is addressed by Alpert and Dunham (1986) as well, in a study conducted in Dade County, Florida, which examined community preferences for, and responses to, different styles of policing. It was found that the degree of importance placed on

UNDERLYING ASSUMPTIONS OF COMMUNITY POLICING

1. The presence of the police through increased visibility reduces the public's fear of crime.
2. The public is of one mind, a homogeneous populace whose satisfaction or dissatisfaction with the police can be readily measured.
3. The police should be responsible for actively helping to define and shape community norms.
4. Public fear stems more from disorder than crime.
5. Signs of neglect and decay in neighborhoods invite crime.
6. Community policing programs are starting at the initiative of the police with the aim of improving service, not to give influential citizens control over police services.
7. Community policing can be done without violating the political neutrality of the police.
8. Police organizations, given their current mechanistic characteristics, can readily adapt to a more organic model required to effectively implement community policing.
9. Police organizations, given their current quality of personnel, can be responsive to the demands of community policing.
10. The police are the proper agency to attempt to fulfill the goals of community policing.

SOURCES: *Assumptions 1, 2, and 3:* taken from Manning's (1984) comments on the assumptions of community policing, especially foot patrol. These assumptions can be seen in the literature on foot patrol (see esp. Police Foundation 1981; Trojanowicz 1982) and order-maintenance policing (see esp. Kelling 1985; and Wilson and Kelling 1982). *Assumption 4:* Kelling (1985; 1987). *Assumption 5:* Wilson and Kelling (1982). *Assumption 6:* Goldstein (1987). *Assumption 7:* Taken from Short's (1983) comments on political neutrality and community policing. *Assumptions 8, 9, and 10:* Current authors.

certain tasks commonly used to evaluate police officers (by police agencies), differed among neighborhoods according to demographic characteristics (for example, race, income, newness of neighborhood). In addition, Brown and Wycoff (1987), in a study of a program aimed at reducing fear of crime in Houston, found that fear of crime was reduced by aspects of the program which increased nonadversarial contact between the police and citizens, but only for certain groups. Blacks and renters did not share in the benefits of the program to the same extent as other racial groups and homeowners.

The above discussion presents research findings that appear contrary to findings on foot patrol programs, which are based, at least in part, on the assumptions now being questioned. Research to date on foot patrol suggests that foot patrol is successful in reducing citizen fear and increasing citizen satisfaction (Esbensen 1987; Police Foundation 1982; Trojanowicz 1982). However, as Manning (1984, p. 214) notes, while the Trojanowicz (1982) study suggests there are people who seem to want nonadversarial contact with the police, "the amount, quality, and character of these contacts is varied, and it is not clear what the activities of the officer were in the opinion of the respondent." In other words, the blanket statement that foot patrol seems to reduce citizen fears and increase citizen satisfaction may be an overgeneralization, and does not take into account the different effects foot patrol may have on various communities. In addition, research on the Citizen Oriented Police Enforcement (COPE) project in Baltimore County showed that only when initial awareness of the presence of the police was low in a neighborhood, did citizens notice increased police presence (Cordner 1986). In neighborhoods where police are often present, then, such as lower class neighborhoods, an increased police presence may not be noticed.

Another important finding of Mastrofski (1983) addresses the measurement of citizen satisfaction or dissatisfaction. Mastrofski (1983) found that citizens are more likely to be pleased with police response to noncrime incidents (order maintenance) and more likely to be displeased with police response to serious crime incidents. Based on Mastrofski's findings regarding the differential demand for police service, an interpolation of this finding would be that wealthier households are more likely to be satisfied with police response than lower income households. Overall, however, the findings of increased satisfaction may not be meaningful, since it has been pointed out that, in general, most people are already satisfied with their police (Esbensen 1987; Manning 1984).

Assumption 3. The police should be responsible for actively helping to define and shape community norms.

This assumption has generated considerable attention as it pertains to order-maintenance policing. As noted earlier, proponents of the more conservative type of order-maintenance policing advocate the role of the police in helping define and shape community norms. This assumption is closely related to the goal, espoused by Wilson and Kelling (1982), Kelling (1985, 1987), and Sykes (1986), of the use of police as agents of informal social control. There are many reasons why this should not occur. One is that it is a violation of the political neutrality of the police (to be discussed later), and it is potentially dangerous to give those with the legal power to enforce laws legal power to enforce norms. While some may argue that the informal norms of the community should be delineated and enforced by the police, several things must be kept in mind. One is that, as Walker (1984) and others have pointed out, in the past, injustices and corruption occurred as a result of police enforcement of nonlegal norms. In addition, as just discussed, there are many different communities with varying expectations and norms, and practically speaking, it would be difficult, if not impossible, to identify and keep track of these diffuse expectations and norms. Furthermore, Manning (1984, p. 217) points out, "there is a certain contentiousness in claiming that the police know the informal control mechanisms found in a community, can accommodate them, and can in some fashion act to enhance them." He further notes that the informal control mechanisms of a community may be overtly illegal and in conflict with the duty of the police to enforce legal norms. Also, the informal control mechanisms can be very subtly illegal and discriminatory. For instance, the tragedy in Howard Beach points to the fact that many people still do not want certain groups in their community at all. Taken to an extreme, it is possible that these citizens could use the police and informal social control to remove "undesirables" from their community.

Assumption 4. Public fear stems more from disorder than crime.

From the above comments, we do not wish to imply that order-maintenance policing is not a vital component of the police role. In fact, research on foot patrol tends to suggest that fear of crime and social disorder can be reduced through the use of order-maintenance techniques (Police Foundation 1981; Trojanowicz 1982). Based on the research of the foot patrol programs discussed previously, this assumption appears correct. However, it is important to remember that fear of crime is a major problem for only a portion of the population. Research has shown that fear of crime is often unrelated to crime rates or probability of victimization (Skogan and Maxfield 1981); therefore, the assumption that public fear stems more from disorder than serious crime can be questioned based on how the "public" is defined. As Mastrofski's research points out, not all members of society want the same police service or visibility. Furthermore, the work of Brown and Wycoff (1987) indicated that blacks and renters were unaffected by attempts to reduce fear of personal victimization and crime. These groups may indeed have realistic fears, which community policing cannot calm.

Assumption 5. Signs of neglect and decay in neighborhoods invite crimes.

In examining whether signs of neglect and decay in neighborhoods can lead to increased crime, a closer look at foot patrol (in other words, closer community contact) and crime may prove beneficial. Research to date on the effects of foot patrol on crime indicates mixed results. While Trojanowicz (1982) found that foot patrol reduced crime in the impact area, this finding was not supported in other studies (Bowers and Hirsch 1987; Police Foundation 1981). Esbensen (1987) found a correlation between foot patrol and a decrease in public order crimes, but noted that in the area immediately surrounding the impact area, public order crimes increased. Thus, even if foot patrol has an impact on crime, perhaps it is merely to displace it. However, simply because foot patrol seems to have no effect on crime does not mean that crime may not escalate without it.

There is some research that indicates that signs of neglect and decay are linked to fear of crime (Taub, Taylor, and Dunham 1984). Perhaps a more realistic assumption would be that signs of neglect and decay in neighborhoods may lead to increased fear of crime. This relationship is somewhat more complex, however, in that fear of crime in deteriorating neighborhoods is increased if the racial composition of the neighborhood is changing (for example, white to black) as well. This creates problems for police that foot patrol alone cannot solve. It would appear then that education about racial matters, prejudice, and discrimination, as well as "mobilization" of a racially diverse neighborhood to address the problems of decline, is necessary. Once again, while this is certainly problem-oriented policing, is it the impossible mandate?

> *Assumption 6.* Community policing programs are starting at the initiative of the police with the aim of improving service, not to give influential citizens control over police services.

> *Assumption 7.* Community policing can be done without violating the political neutrality of the police.

These two assumptions are related to the issue of the role of the police in order maintenance. Goldstein (1987) has suggested that because the changes in policing at present are at the impetus of police officers and departments, the changes are not being made for the purposes of community control. This may well be the case; however, it does not necessarily mean that community control will not occur anyway. Short (1983) succinctly brings the issue of control and political neutrality to the fore in a discussion of her experiences with community policing in Birmingham, England.

She found a basic incompatibility between political neutrality of the police and community policing. While Short felt the use of the police as agents of informal social control was a violation of political neutrality, the objectives of improved community relations, creative problem solving, and crime prevention were seen as the greatest threat to the political neutrality of the police. Her essay includes a discussion of several community policing projects, all of which include a realization that the police must focus not only on the symptoms of crime, but also the causes. As a result, the police have become politically involved in various agencies, even to the point of overseeing the distribution of agency funds. According to Short (1983, p. 72):

> There is, I believe, a danger that community policing will lead more and more policemen to behave—for perfectly good reasons—more and more like politicians. In order to win the trust of the community, they attempt to help members of the community. They develop powers of patronage by advising how grant money should be distributed and by inviting some individuals to sit on committees to represent their community. . . . All of this is entirely well meant, but it leads to a general perception that only groups who keep in with the police will get access to grants for premises and facilities and to power and recognition.

An excellent example of this potential problem is provided by Skolnick and Bayley (1986) in their synopsis of innovative policing in six American cities. One community mini-station police officer in Detroit came up with funds to launch a summer project for youths in his neighborhood by persuading a neighborhood Burger King to donate 10 percent of its profits for three days in exchange for the officer persuading a popular local disc jockey to broadcast from the Burger King one day on behalf of the project. While this may be a creative idea for greater community involvement, it is almost certainly a violation of political neutrality. Furthermore, this appears to be an example where corruption and abuse could become a problem. A further example, possibly less obvious, comes from the research on the COPE project in Baltimore County. The COPE units which were considered to be doing good community and problem oriented policing "became adept at gaining cooperation from other public agencies and from private companies" (Cordner 1986, p. 232). While we do not wish to appear overly cynical with such apparently innovative approaches to policing, neither do we think it wise to be too naive regarding potential abuses.

> *Assumption 8.* Police organizations, given their current mechanistic characteristics, can readily adapt to a more organic model required to effectively implement community policing.
>
> *Assumption 9.* Police organizations, given their current quality of personnel, can be responsive to the demands of community policing.

In the past, Goldstein (1979) warns, a focus on secondary goals, such as management practices and personnel, has been a problem, and the primary goal of quality service should instead be emphasized. While it is true that secondary goals have been given priority, at least in theory, if not in practice, we wonder how quality service can be provided without emphasis on sound management practices and high quality personnel. In fact, it is our contention that community policing can never come to fruition unless secondary goals are taken seriously. Even more importantly, if changes in police organization, management, and personnel are not forthcoming, as the police role continues to become more complex, community policing could turn out not only to be a failure, but actually dangerous to the requirements of policing a democratic society (in other words, through the use of informal control and power).

For instance, in considering whether police personnel are ready to fulfill the demands of such a role, it is necessary to carefully consider the requirements of community policing. In doing community and problem-oriented policing, the line officers are asked to attempt to alleviate specific problems, which they have helped to identify by orienting themselves to the needs of the community, with *creative* and *innovative* solutions in a fair, just, and legal manner. This requires certain skills, including problem conceptualization, synthesis and analysis of information, action plans, program evaluation, and communication of evaluation results and policy implications. Numerous studies have indicated that skills such as these are enhanced by a college education (for example, see Fedman and Newcomb 1969; Meagher 1983; Selznick and Steinberg 1969; Trent and Medsker 1968). While we need not rehash the debate on higher education and policing, suffice it to say that the sensitivity and demands of the role of community policing require an individual with a high degree of intelligence, openmindedness, and nonprejudicial attitudes (for example, see Dalley 1975; Roberg 1978; Smith et al. 1970).

Whether the police organization is equipped to do community policing in terms of its paramilitary organizational structure and autocratic management style is another important consideration. Community policing involves a significant change in the philosophy of policing toward a more flexible, democratic orientation, which requires a concomitant and fundamental change in police organization and management—away from a highly mechanistic, centralized approach, toward more of an organic, decentralized approach (Kuykendall and Roberg 1982). This suggest that there must be input not only from the community in problem definition and decision making, but participation from police employees at all levels as well. Furthermore, the reward structure in most police departments may be an additional hindrance to implementing community policing and will need to be addressed. Undoubtedly, the current emphasis on law enforcement–related activities receiving most, if not all, of the attention will need to be significantly changed toward activities that are community service–oriented. How the majority of police officers will view a change of this magnitude could be problematic. How changes such as these will be accepted by police managers, especially mid-level managers, should also not be overlooked. If the team policing experiments are any indication, and we think they are, the answer is less than favorable. (For example, see Bard and Shellow 1976; Schwartz and Clarren 1977; Sherman 1975). It is likely [that] a new style of mid-level manager is needed to properly implement community policing concepts. Such a leader should possess the same skill levels and characteristics necessary for line officers, as well as participatory leadership abilities.

Again, it would appear that higher education may have a role to play. However, as Fisher, Golden, and Heininger (1985) point out, there is not an abundance of highly educated managers in policing, or for that matter an abundance of highly educated officers or trainees waiting to be promoted.[1] Even though the numbers may not be there, as Scott (1986) notes, it is important to gradually ease higher educated officers into management positions in order that they may act as change agents. Without personnel in mid-level management positions who are willing to facilitate change, change will not occur. We might add this is also true for training personnel, who must be open to new and innovative approaches and methods promoting community policing concepts and ideals. It is not our intent to imply that a college degree is a requirement for effective community policing (the requirements for such a demanding role are yet to be determined); however, we are suggesting that it is necessary to realistically assess whether traditional selection criteria are sufficient.

It is apparent from our discussion of assumptions 8 and 9 that, in general, major structural, managerial, and personnel changes are required in police organizations before community policing (at least as described in the literature), can be implemented. Assuming such changes are possible, they will not happen overnight. Simply adding new training programs, changing a few policies, or putting a new slogan on the door of the patrol car, will not suffice.

Assumption 10. The police are the proper agency to attempt to fulfill the goals of community policing.

In discussing whether the police are the proper agency to fulfill the goals of community policing, it should be remembered that there are many underlying societal problems [that] the police cannot be expected to cure, such as poverty and prejudice. The question to be asked, then, is whether the police should be solving any nonlegal problems or should be relegated strictly to the role of law enforcers. This would result in the removal of the social service and order maintenance roles from the police function. Due to the many problems previously discussed with the use of the police as agents of informal social control and [as] problem solvers, especially [in regard to] the violation of political neutrality, removing from the realm of "police work" any and all nonlegal problems could theoretically be a solution. However, such a "solution" is not feasible, for several reasons. One reason is that there are simply not enough other agencies to handle many of the problems, although certainly new ones could be created. Another is that even if there were, many people would still turn to the police, since they are available twenty-four hours a day, seven days a week.

Practically speaking, it would be impossible to remove nonlegal problems and the roles of social service and order maintenance from the realm of police work. Additionally, it could be unwise to remove these problems from the realm of police work, since many nonlegal problems can escalate into very serious legal problems, requiring a police officer, the only agent with the power and authority to control legal problems, to act. Additionally, to make the police simply law enforcers removes a potentially enriching component of their job.

In the final analysis, there are numerous aspects of community policing that are potentially of value both to society and to the police themselves. However, it should be remembered that community policing is even more sophisticated in approach than team policing, and it too will fail if substantially greater efforts are not devoted to bringing about significant and enduring changes in police organizations as they currently exist. In general, it would appear that the police are not yet equipped to fulfill the goals of community policing. This is not to suggest that relevant changes in police organizations cannot occur, but simply, until they do occur, the goals of community policing are likely to reflect more rhetoric than reality.

SUMMARY AND CONCLUSIONS

The purpose of this paper is to take a realistic look at the concept of community policing and to attempt to determine the viability of such an approach to contemporary policing. While it is difficult to argue with the potential benefits of community policing, it must be given a proper hearing—in which the potential positive and negative consequences are examined—prior to attempts at implementation. At this point in time, a change to community policing by many, if not most, police agencies may be a pipedream—more rhetoric than reality. One thing is certain, however, if such an approach is to have any chance of success—it must be strongly supported by police management. This means that an infusion of creative police chiefs and midlevel managers, supportive of democratic ideals and management practices, must occur in the very near future. In addition, [there must be] the commitment to hiring quality personnel who can handle the increased responsibilities required by community policing, including the ability to identify and analyze problems (both of a legal and nonlegal nature), develop plans for action, and evaluate program effectiveness.

Police leaders should consider as well that community policing has the potential to be enriching and rewarding for patrol officers, as some pilot programs have discovered. Since the success of community policing depends on every officer and manager, the more ego-involved an officer becomes and the more enriching or rewarding the job design, the better the officer's performance will be.

While it may seem as though secondary goals are being overemphasized, that is, organizational structure, management style, and personnel, it is firmly believed that the philosophy of community policing cannot be realized until significant changes are made in these areas. And, assuming such changes do occur, community policing still has a long way to go. The most important issues, accountability of the police, political neutrality, and the use of the police as a form of social control, must be decided. The tone of the interactions between the police and the community, and the police and other agencies, must be set. However, it appears that before community policing can be implemented, some fundamental structural and orientation changes are required to give the police a solid *foundation* upon which to police a democratic society. Only time will tell if such changes are forthcoming.

NOTE

1. This is supported by Sherman (1978) and the National Planning Association (1976). In a 1975 survey done by the NPA, of 2639 agencies, only 5.5 percent required recruits to have some college, and more than one in ten had no educational requirements (National Planning Association 1976; cited in Sherman 1978, p. 174). Sherman notes that this is an improvement over previous requirements, but the trend is "far from rapid" (1978, p. 176). Additionally, Fife (1983) reported a survey of 1087 police departments, which indicated that nearly 80 percent require a high school diploma or GED, while only three percent require a four-year college degree.

REFERENCES

Angell, J. E. 1971. Toward an alternative to the classic police organizational arrangements: A democratic model. *Criminology* 9: 185–206.

Bard, M., and Shellow, R. 1976. Neighborhood police teams. *Issues in law enforcement: Essays and case studies.* Eds. M. Bard and R. Shellow. Reston, Va.: Reston Publishing.

Bowers, W. J., and Hirsch, J. H. 1987. The impact of foot patrol staffing on crime and disorder in Boston: An unmet promise. *American Journal of Police* 6, no. 1: 17–44.

Brown, L. P., and Wycoff, M. A. 1987. Policing Houston: Reducing fear and improving service. *Crime and Delinquency* 33, no. 1: 71–89.

Cordner, G. W. 1986. Fear of crime and the police: An evaluation of a fear-reduction strategy. *J Pol Sci and Admin* 14: 223–233.

Dalley, A. F. 1975. University vs. non-university graduated policeman: A study of police attitudes. *J Pol Sci and Admin* 3: 458–468.

Eck, J. E., and Spelman, W. 1987. Who ya gonna call? The police as problem-busters. *Crime and Delinquency* 33, no. 1: 31–52.

Esbensen, F. A. 1987. Foot patrols: Of what value? *American Journal of Police* 6, no. 1: 45–65.

Feldman, K. A., and Newcomb, T. M. 1969. *The impact of college on students.* San Francisco: Jossey Bass.

Fife, J. F. 1983. Police personnel practices, baseline data reports. Vol. no. 15, 1. Washington, D.C.: International City Management Association.

Fink, J., and Sealy, L. G. 1974. *The community and the police: Conflict or cooperation?* New York: Wiley and Sons.

Finnegan, J. 1976. A study of the relationship between college education and police performance in Baltimore, Md. *Police Chief* (August): 60–62.

Fischer, R. J., Golden, K. M., and Heininger, B. L. 1985. Issues in higher education for law enforcement officers: An Illinois Study. *J Crim Justice* 13, no. 4: 329–338.

Germann, A. C. 1969. Community policing: An assessment. *J Crim Law, Criminology and Pol Sci* 60, no. 1: 89–96.

Goldstein, H. 1979. Improving policing: A problem oriented approach. *Crime and Delinquency* 25, no. 2: 236–258.

———. 1987. Toward community-oriented policing: Potential, basic requirements, and threshold questions. *Crime and Delinquency* 33, no. 1: 6–30.

Greene, J. R. 1987. Foot patrol and community policing: Past practices and future prospects. *American Journal of Police* 6, no. 1: 1–15.

Hayeslip Jr., P. W., and Cordner, G. W. 1987. The effects of community-oriented patrol on police officer attitudes. *American Journal of Police* 6, no. 1: 95–119.

Johnson, D. R. 1981. *American law enforcement: A history.* St. Louis, Missouri: Forum Press.

Kelling, G. L. 1985. Order maintenance, the quality of urban life, and police: A line of argument. In *Police leadership in America,* ed. W. A. Geller, pp. 296–308. New York: Praeger.

———. 1987. Acquiring a taste for order: The community and police. *Crime and Delinquency* 33, no. 1: 90–102.

Klockars, C. B. 1985. Order maintenance, the quality of urban life, and police: A different line of argument. In *Police leadership in America,* ed. W. A. Geller, pp. 296–308. New York: Praeger.

Kuykendall, J., and Roberg, R. R. 1981. Mapping police organizational change: From a mechanistic toward an organic model. *Criminology* 20: 241–256.

Manning, P. K. 1971. The police: Mandate, strategies, and appearances. In *Policing: A view from the street,* eds. P. Manning and J. Van Maanen (New York: Random House, 1978), 273–291.

———. 1984. Community policing. *American Journal of Police* 3, no. 2: 205–227.

Mastrofski, S. 1983. The police and noncrime services. In *Evaluating performance of criminal justice agencies,* eds. G. P. Whitaker and C. D. Phillips (Beverly Hills: Sage), 33–61.

Meagher, M. S. 1983. Perception of the police patrol function: Does officer education make a difference? Paper presented at the annual meeting of the Academy of Criminal Justice Sciences at San Antonio, Texas, March 22–26.

National Advisory Commission on Civil Disorders. 1967. *Task force report.* Washington, D.C.: Govt. Printing Office.

National Planning Association. 1976. A nationwide survey of law enforcement, criminal justice personnel needs, and resources: final report. Unpublished manuscript, pp. 11–170. Washington, D.C.: LEAA.

Police Foundation. 1981. *The Newark foot patrol experiment.* Washington, D.C.: Author.

President's Commission on Law Enforcement and Administration of Justice. 1967. *Task force report: The police.* Washington, D.C.: Govt. Printing Office.

Roberg, R. 1978. An analysis of the relationship among higher education, belief systems, and job performance of patrol officers. *J Pol Sci and Adm* 6: 344–366.

Scott, W. R. 1986. College education requirements for police entry level and promotion: A study. *J Pol and Criminal Psych* 2, no. 1: 10–28.

Selznick, G. J., and Steinberg, S. 1969. *The tenacity of prejudice antisemitism in contemporary America.* New York: Harper and Row.

Sherman, L. W. 1975. Middle management and democratization: A reply to John E. Angell. *Criminology* 12, no. 4: 363–377.

Sherman, L. W., and the National Advisory Commission on Higher Education of Police Officers. 1978. *The quality of police education.* San Francisco: Jossey Bass.

Skogan, W. G., and Maxfield, M. G. 1981. *Coping with crime: Victimization, fear, and reactions to crime.* Beverly Hills: Sage.

Skolnick, J. H., and Bayley, D. H. 1986. *The new blue line.* New York: Free Press.

Smith, A. B., Locke, B., and Fenster, A. 1976. Authoritarianism in policemen who are college graduates and noncollege police. *J Crim Law Criminology and Pol Sci* 6: 313–315.

Sykes, G. W. 1968. Street justice: A moral defense of order maintenance policing. *Justice Quarterly* 3, no. 4: 497–512.

Taub, R. P., Taylor, D. G., and Dunham, J. D. 1984. *Paths of neighborhood change.* Chicago: Chicago Press.

Trent, J. W. and Medsker, L. L. 1968. *Beyond high school.* San Francisco: Jossey Bass.

Trojanowicz, R. C. et al. 1982. *An evaluation of the neighborhood foot patrol program in Flint, Michigan.* Lansing, Michigan: Michigan State University.

Trojanowicz, R. C., and Nicholson, T. 1976. A comparison of behavioral styles of college graduate police officers v. non–college going police officers. *Police Chief* (August) 56–59.

Walker, S. 1977. *A critical history of police reform.* Lexington, Mass.: D.C. Heath and Co.

———. 1983. *The police in America.* New York: McGraw-Hill.

———. 1984. Broken windows and fractured history: The use and misuse of history in recent police patrol analysis. *Justice Quarterly* 1, no. 1: 75–90.

Weatheritt, M. 1983. Community policing: Does it work and how do we know? In *The future of policing,* ed. T. Bennet (Cambridge, England: Institute of Criminology), 127–143.

Wilson, J. Q., and Kelling, G. L. 1982. Broken windows. *The Atlantic Monthly* 249: 29–38.

INDEX

Felson, M., 295
Field support units, 311–312
Field training officers, 309
Figgie Report, 84, 93
Flint, Mich., 66, 68–69, 90, 92, 109, 111, 113, 115, 124, 154, 233, 319
Fogelson, R., 98, 116, 262, 268, 327, 332, 333, 337
Foot patrol, 3–4, 9, 14, 53, 110, 115, 319, 323
Fort Lauderdale, Fla., 113
Fosdick, R. B., 18
Fresno, Calif., 69
Friedman, L., 335
Friedman, M. A., 164
Friedmann, R. R., 164
Fuld, L. F., 18
Fyfe, J., 337

G

Gallup Poll, 84, 94
Garofalo, J., 94
Gates, D., 68
Gay, W. G., 208, 337
Ghostbusters, 82
Glazer, N., 7, 295
Goldstein, H., 1–2, 16, 22, 39, 61, 64, 71, 82, 110, 117, 124, 159, 162, 164, 194, 197–198, 207–208, 255, 260, 262, 267–268, 304, 309, 337, 341–345, 348–349, 353
Greene, J., 165, 339, 342–343, 353
Greenwood, P. W., 59, 209
Grindle, R., 32
Gruber, C., 165
Guardian Angels, 13, 53
Guggenheim Foundation, 68
Gusfield, J., 337
Guyot, D., 316

H

Haller, M., 337
Harrington, M., 159
Harris, L., 93–94
Harris Poll, 84
Hartmann, F. X., 68
Harvard Business School, 238
Harvard University, 41

Harvard University Law School, 7
Hayeslip, P. W., 353
Hayward, Calif., PD, 165
Heroin, 48
Hierarchy, 301
Higher education, 19, 37, 305–306, 350
Hobbes, T., 94
Homes, R. T., 13–14
Hoover, J. E., 101–102, 105, 261
Houston, Texas, PD, 91–92, 110–113, 150, 216–217, 226–229, 231–234, 266, 273
Human resources, 145
Hunt, P., 295

I

Implementation, 138–140
Inchoate crimes, 243
Independent Commission on the Los Angeles PD, 165
Indiana University, 12
Information systems, 146
Integrated Criminal Apprehension Programs, 50
Internal changes, 143, 148
International Association of Chiefs of Police, 122
International City/County Management Association, 26, 165
Internation Union of Police Associations, 65

J

Jacobs, J., 295
Jamieson, K., 255
Jordan, K. E., 116
Journal of Police Science and Administration, 239
Journal of Research in Crime & Delinquency, 21
Justice Quarterly, 326

K

Kahn, R., 337
Kansas City, Kans., PD, 18, 159, 266, 278